Upton Sinclair
An Annotated Checklist

Upton Sinclair

An Annotated Checklist

By Ronald Gottesman
The University of Wisconsin-Parkside

The Kent State University Press

The Serif Series: Number 24
Bibliographies and Checklists
William White, General Editor
Wayne State University

ISBN 0-87338-114-9
Library of Congress Catalog Card Number 72-634010
Manufactured in the United States of America
at the press of The Oberlin Printing Company
Design by Merald E. Wrolstad
First Edition

To my mother and the memory of my father
and to Val, Lann, and Grant.

Contents

Introduction

One offers a bibliographical tool of this nature with mixed feelings. It is satisfying to make available for the first time a reasonably complete record of the publications of a significant and prolific author together with a rough guide to the most important secondary material dealing with the man and his work. At the same time, one must acknowledge inevitable incompleteness and even inaccuracy. Sinclair wrote several hours each day, every day, for more than seven decades. During that time he had dozens of book publishers, appeared in an enormous range of popular and obscure newspapers and periodicals, and became one of the most widely translated American authors of all time. In spite of its scope, then, the present checklist (which does not pretend to be a bibliography) should be understood as a foundation, not as a monument.

Part I of the checklist records annalistically all of Sinclair's publications. The intention here (and in Part II) was to record the development of a career. For the most part, the entries follow standard bibliographic entry style, but a few special features may require explanation. A single asterisk indicates that the item was, at the time of publication, catalogued in the Lilly Library of Indiana University, the major repository of Upton and Mary Craig Sinclair's papers.* For articles in

* For an outline of these holdings see the compiler's *A Catalogue of Books, Manuscripts, and Other Materials from the Upton Sinclair Archives* (Lilly Library,

magazines and journals the title or supplied title comes first, then the periodical name followed by volume number, date in parentheses, and inclusive page numbers. Letters to the editor usually received no titles and supplied titles are printed here without quotation marks. Brief descriptive annotations are supplied especially for early, rare, or unrevealingly titled items; if the article is known to have been reprinted either separately or as part of a book, this information is indicated with an appropriate cross reference. Except that no volume number is supplied, newspaper contributions are treated in parallel fashion. In a few instances certain elements of the entry could not be determined and some of the items, regrettably, are incomplete. Most of the items have been examined directly, but some have been listed on the authority of others; when the latter is the case I have tried to indicate it.

Separately printed items are treated like books. Titles appear in italics even if they are supplied, as in the case of some of the broadsides and most of the circular letters. For circular letters, though often printed without place and publisher, I have supplied easily inferable information without resorting to pedantic and unsightly brackets. For books, the place of publication, followed by the short form of the publisher's name and date of publication are supplied as exactly as they could be determined. The page number signifies the last page of text, including appendices and index material, but excluding advertisements or blank pages. Though not noted each time, many of Sinclair's books of 1918-1950 were published or reprinted in cloth and paper. Information on reprinting is given in a separate paragraph headed *Reprinted*; for reprints, place, publisher, and date are supplied in order of date of publication.

Bloomington, Indiana, 1963), pp. 4–10; "Upton Sinclair and the Sinclair Archives," *Manuscripts*, XVII (1965), 11–21; and *The Literary Manuscripts of Upton Sinclair* (Ohio State University Press), with C. Loring Silet. Of course, items are being added by the Lilly Library all the time.

For the most part reprints are not given the status of separate entries, though a retitling, revision, or special format sometimes convinced me of the need for such treatment. Cross-references to earlier and later forms of publication and to associated items are given by item number. In another paragraph, under the rubric *Foreign Editions*, translations and foreign editions of the book are listed in alphabetical order by country. (Unless a newspaper or periodical article was first published outside of the United States, it is not usually listed in translation or foreign appearance.)

I have made two exceptions to the strict annalistic arrangement: the material contained in the scrapbook of juvenilia assembled by Sinclair's mother and Sinclair's pseudonymous "half-dime novels" are listed as separate continuous units (but roughly in the appropriate place chronologically). In addition, a separate section is devoted to the considerable quantity of tape and disc recordings and films Sinclair was involved in over the years.

The second major part of the checklist, Sinclair's works in foreign editions and translations, was begun with misgivings and is printed with some reluctance. Anyone experienced in the inadequacies, uncertainties, and complexities of international bibliography will not be surprised to hear that the compiler is confident only that this section is incomplete and inaccurate in details of form and content. The main sources of information were the holdings of the Lilly Library, the *Index Translationum* Sinclair's own Bibliographies (see A1277 and A1907), and the librarians of some two-score national libraries. Transliterations of the several non-Roman alphabets were made in accord with Library of Congress procedures, though some idiosyncratic variations doubtlessly appear. With all its faults, however, Part II is an important attempt to show, at least quantitatively, what happens once a writer's words have left his native shores. It simply should be used with slightly more than common scepticism. Along with the mutilations, there are doubtless many ghosts.

The languages involved are listed alphabetically; when the same language is used in more than one country (German or Spanish, for example), the countries are arranged alphabetically within the language heading. The arrangement of items in this section was designed to suggest the nature of Sinclair's foreign reception. Thus these publications are entered chronologically according to the earliest date of publication in the United States. The order of publication of Sinclair's works within the country can be easily reconstructed, though the publication date of some titles was unknown and not easy to infer. The foreign title (sometimes translated with great freedom—e.g., *The Jungle* becomes *Los envenanadores de Chicago*, *The Poisoners of Chicago*, in a Spanish-language edition) is entered under the original American title. The title is followed by the place of publication, the publisher in shortened form, the date and the number of pages and volumes when known. This basic information is followed by the name of the translator, editor, introduction writer, etc., as far as this information was available. When only the date of publication differs for the same title, the "edition" was assumed to be only an impression, and dates of the impressions follow one another separated by commas. When title, publisher, format, or translator differ for the same book, full information is provided for each edition under the same American title according to the date of publication. Collected editions ordinarily appear at the end of the lists.

Part III, publications about Sinclair and his work, carries out the essentially chronological plan of the first two parts by listing secondary material in order of publication date. The section devoted to bibliographical sources is self-explanatory.

In choosing reviews I have been arbitrary as well as selective.* I have listed a number of generally available newspaper and magazine reviews—more, typically, for the more important books—and have tried to represent a variety of critical and socio-political perspectives. Similar criteria inform the choice of articles and books. The section listing unpublished material is as complete for items in English as I could make it. Whereas Parts I and II attempt to suggest the progress of a career, Part III, in spite of its selectivity, may offer some clues as to the impact that career had on Sinclair's contemporaries.

The final section, Supplementary Material, is the first of what will probably be a series of such lists which will correct, fill in, and extend the coverage of the main checklist. Material for these lists will be welcomed by the compiler, who is keenly conscious that there is no end to the making of a checklist.

Many of the problems resulting from the chronological arrangement of the material are answered by the index, which provides a convenient reference, arranged alphabetically, to all names of persons (other than Upton Sinclair) mentioned in the text. This should assist the researcher who wants to know which authors and books Sinclair reviewed, whether he published an article about a particular public figure, or whether he in turn served as a subject for another writer.

Ronald Gottesman

---

*Though incomplete and unreliable, the "Morse Checklist" of reviews in the Belt Collection of Sinclair materials in the Occidental College Library is an important source for reviews of books published before 1933.

Acknowledgments

More so than most scholarly works, a reference tool such as this is the result of elaborate collaboration, and it is a pleasure to acknowledge here the help of many persons and institutions.

I am grateful in the first place to the Research Committee of Indiana University, which provided two generous grants for travel, supplies, and student assistance. Long before these grants were made, however, my interest in bibliography and in the Sinclair Archives had been stimulated by Philip B. Daghlian, and through many sea-changes, he has been both an informed critic and a faithful friend. Another good friend, Edward Allatt, is a nonpareil Sinclair collector and scholar and has urged me on and helped me out by reading the entire manuscript more than once with a devoted and careful eye. Beyond that, he has corrected many errors and added substantially to all portions of the checklist. Yet another good friend, Howell Daniels, checked many items in England for me, promptly and with characteristic thoroughness.

Hensley Woodbridge checked, corrected, and generally improved the penultimate draft of the manuscript. Lawrence Thompson did everything he could to help me improve the section on Sinclair's work in translation and foreign editions; those who know Mr. Thompson know how much that has meant. His daughter, Sarah, was particularly helpful in the struggle to get the Japanese listing correct. Walter Goldwater—the complete bookdealer and bibliographer—supplied information and material with care and patience and with extraordinary disregard for himself. Scott Bennett made several suggestions that improved the format of the checklist. Eugene De Gruson of Kansas State College of Pittsburg answered dozens of inquiries promptly and fully.

David Randall, William Cagle, Katherine Troxell, Elfrieda Lang, and Geneva Warner of the Lilly Library exceeded by far their professional obligations; it is quite literally true that without their cooperation this volume could not have been completed. Sarah Gramentine was my copy editor; it is embarrassing to recall all that she did to improve the format and detail of this work.

The late May Hard Sinclair smiled sunnily on the project when it was in its early stages, and anyone who knew her smile will understand how much encouragement I felt. Upton Sinclair had the strength while he lived to write all that the checklist records, the patience to answer an endless stream of questions about those writings, and the courage to confront several early drafts of the manuscript that has now become a book. His son, David, helped in a variety of ways, as did his wife Jean; one of the happy by-products of these labors is their friendship. Dr. Elmer Belt's interest has been a constant support for a decade.

It is a special pleasure to acknowledge the hard and good work of Loring Silet, who started as a research assistant and ended as a friend and collaborator. Lyle Bachmann and Leslie Clark did a variety of maddening research tasks with good grace and skill. Special thanks are also due Mrs. Connie Loftman and Mrs. Melinda Gurevitz who typed and retyped a most exasperating manuscript. Bea Jagiello assisted greatly with the tedious tasks of proof reading and indexing. Nazaly Bagdasian helped to arrange the non-American names in the index properly.

The following are among those at Indiana University who were kind enough to check details of Part II: Professors Jaako A. Ahokas, Gustav Bayerle, Foster Blaisdell, Gretchen Bueller, Richard Chi, John Dyson, Felix Oinas, and Toyoaki Uehara, along with Dyck Haver Droeze, Seid Keric, A. A. Mutalik-Desae, and Mrs. Linda Raun. Chester Wang of the University of Wisconsin-Madison supplied crucial information for this part. My colleague Sheldon Harsel (and his wife Yoshimi) pointed out many errors among the oriental language translation lists. Other Parksside colleagues helped with other languages.

Librarians by the score supplied much information and corrected a good many errors. The compiler of this checklist and its users are deeply in their debt: Marika Vogli, Directrice, Biblioteka Kombetare, Tirana, Albania; Y. A. Guendet, Biblioteca National, Bueños Aires, Argentina; H. L. White and A. P. Fleming, National Librarians, National Library of Australia, Canberra, Australia; Dr. Friedrick Rennhofer, Leiter d. Katalogabt, Österreichische Nationalbibliothek, Vienna, Austria; J. Lambert, Conservateur, Bibliothèque Royale de Belgique, Bruxelles, Belgium; Margarida Maria Galrão, Librarian, Instituto Brasileiro de Bibliografia e Documentação, Rio de Janeiro, Brazil; K. Kalajdžieva, Director, "Cyril and Methodius" National Library, Sofia, Bulgaria; W. E. Strong, for Ian Wees, Assistant Director Reference Branch, National Library, Ottawa, Canada; T. A. Chow, for Library Adviser, Urban Council Public Libraries, Hong Kong, China; Wan-li Chu, Director, National Central Library, Taipei, Taiwan, China; H. A. Rydings, Librarian, University of Hong Kong Library, Hong Kong, China; Ing. Karel Kozelek, Director, Státní Knihovna, Praha, Czechoslovakia; Dr. Jaroblau Kunc, Director, and Dr. Věra Chválovská, Státní Knihovna

Ceskoslovenskē Socialistickè Republiky, Praha, Czechoslovakia; Rita Ejlersen, Chief Librarian, Danmarks Institut for International Udveksling Af Videnscabelige Publikationer, København, Denmark; Gerda Møller, Dírector, Det kongelige Bibliotek, København, Denmark; Scheffler, Abteilungsdirektorin, Deutsche Bucherei, Leipzig, East Germany; F. Kauba, Director, Eesti NSV Teaduste Akadeemia Teaduslik Raamatukogu, Tallinn, Estonia; V. Lehtiranta, Acting Head of the National Department, Helsinki University Library, Helsinki, Finland; G. Calmette, Conservateur en Chef, Bibliothèque de l 'Université de Paris a la Sorbonne, Paris, France; Roger Pierrot, Conservateur, Bibliothèque Nationale, Paris, France; Dr. L. Nagy, Head of the Section for International Relations, Magyar Tudományos Akadémia, Budapest, Hungary; Gyula Ortutay, Academician Secretary of the Section of Linguistic and Literary Sciences and Dr. Charlotte M. Kretzoi, Magyar Tudományos Akadémia, Budapest, Hungary; Finnbogi Gudmundsson, Chief Librarian, Bibliothèque Nationale d'Islande, Reykjavik, Iceland; S. Balasubramanyam, Assistant Librarian, National Library, Belvedere, India; P. Henchy, Director, Leabharlann Náisiúnta na Héireann, Dublin, Ireland; Kaethe Lewy and Mrs. R. Tronik, Bibliographic Service, The Jewish National and University Library, Jerusalem, Israel; Fr. Ghevont Samoorian, Director, Gulbenkian Library, Jerusalem, Israel; Dott. Luigia Risoldi, Direttore, Biblioteche Nazionali di Roma, Rome, Italy; Y. Sakai, Director, Division for Interlibrary Services, National Diet Library, Tokyo, Japan; E. Aràjs, Director, Latvijas PSR Zinãtnu Akadēmija, Fundamentàlā Biblioteka, Rigā, Latvia; Lietuvos TSR Mokslu Akademija Centrine Biblioteka, Vilnius, Lithuania; Blanca Castañón Morena, Head of Department, Biblioteca Nacional, Mexico City, Mexico; Miss R. Damstra, Union Catalogue Department, Koninblijke Bibliotheek, Amsterdam, Netherlands; Dr. P. M. Morel,

Chief Librarian, Universiteitsbibliotheek, Amsterdam, Netherlands; H. Macaskill, Deputy National Librarian, National Library of New Zealand, Private Bag, New Zealand; Sigmund Skard, Amerikansk Institut, Universitetet I Oslo, Oslo, Norway; Zbigniew Daskowski, Deputy Director, Biblioteka Narodowa, Warsaw, Poland; Manuela Candida Martins, O Chefe da Secretaria, Biblioteca Nacional de Lisboa, Lisbon, Portugal; Director, Academia Republicii Socialiste Romania, Biblioteca, Bucuresti, Romania; Director, Die Staatsbiblioteek, Pretoria, South Africa; J. Almudévar, Biblioteca Nacional, Madrid, Spain; Olof von Feilitzen, Assistant Librarian, Kungliga Biblioteket, Stockholm, Sweden; Director, Schweizerische Landerbibliothek, Bern, Switzerland; Dr. Müjgân Cunbur, Director, Millî Kütüphane, Ankara, Turkey; Dina Abramowicz, Librarian, Yivo Institute for Jewish Research, New York, N. Y.; Mrs. Sylvia M. Gear, Research Library, University of California at Los Angeles; Mrs. Margaret C. Howell, Head, National Collections, Division for the Blind and Physically Handicapped, The Library of Congress; Monte Olenick, Chief, Language and Literature Division, Brooklyn Public Library; Mark Starr, Esperanto Information Center of the Esperanto League for North America, New York, N. Y.; Helen Weekly, Librarian, Braille Institute of America, Los Angeles, California; I. Chernenko, Director, Academy of Science U.S.S.R., Central Scientific Library, Kiev, U.S.S.R.; Charlotte Hoene, Librarian, John F. Kennedy-Institut für Amerikastudien, Freie Universität Berlin, Berlin, West Germany; Peter Kittel, Direktor der Katalogabteilung, Deutsche Staatsbibliothek, Berlin, West Germany; A. L. Seydel, Deutsche Bibliothek, Frankfurt A. M., West Germany; Director, Jugoslovenski Bibliografski Institut, Beograd, Yugoslavia; Mate Baće, Head of the Reference, Univerzitetska Biblioteka, Beograd, Yugoslavia; Jaro Dolar, Director of the National and University Library, Ljubljana, Yugoslavia; and K. Vasić, Information Librarian, Narodna Biblioteka, Beograd, Yugoslavia.

My wife and children have lived with this project for almost as long as they have lived with me. To have done either would deserve a dedication; to have done both demands one. I offer it with thanks and relief commensurate with the size of my debt to them.

I have not thanked many other persons who in countless ways have helped and encouraged me. Neither they nor those whose assistance I have acknowledged are responsible for the errors and omissions that survive their interest and advice.

I. Upton Sinclair's Publications in English

A. Published Writings: A Chronological Checklist

1894

A1 Puzzle, *Harper's Young People*, XIV (6 September), 431.

1895

A2 Puzzle, *Harper's Young People*, XVI (12 February), 110.

A3 Puzzle Answer, *Harper's Young People*, XVI (19 February), 118.

A4 "What's In a Name," *Harper's Young People*, XVI (2 April), 167.

A5 "A Mixed Mickron's 'S.A.,' " *Harper's Round Table*, XVI (4 June), 590.

A6 "Tommy Junior the Second," *Argosy*, XX (July), 357–362.

A7 "When the Redcoats Came to Bennington," *Argosy*, XXI (December), 206–208.

Scrapbook (Numbers A8--A149)

Many of Sinclair's most ephemeral juvenile writings were preserved by his mother in a "Mark Twain" Scrapbook.

Nearly 150 separate items, including cartoon captions, riddles, jokes, and more substantial stories and poems, are mounted. Most of these appear to have been published between 1895 and 1900 and in papers and periodicals such as the *New York Evening Post*, *Life*, *Puck*, *Judge*, *New York Evening Journal*, *Argosy*, *Harper's Young People*, *Harper's Round Table*, and *The Phrenocosmian* (a C.C.N.Y. literary Magazine). A few of these items have been traced to specific sources; most, however, are designated only as clipped from magazines (M.) or newspapers (N.). Several items are repeated in the main body of the *Checklist*; it seemed useful, though, to give a complete and separate account of the contents of this unique collection of Sinclair's earliest publications.

Page 1. [no date]

A8 Upton B. Sinclair, Jr. 1895 [in ink]. "That Bear at Sudbrook."

Eleven hundred word story of false fright given a group of boys and their parents by an escaped tame bear belonging to an Italian; Sudbrook is situated within ten miles of Baltimore, Maryland. N.

A9 Upton B. Sinclair, Jr. "Jingle."

Four lines. N.

A10 Upton B. Sinclair, Jr. "Juvenile Logic."

Four line play on words "June" and "did you know." N.

A11 Upton B. Sinclair, Jr. "What's In A Name?"

Verse: two six line stanzas playing on words ending in "ester" and "eicester." M.

Page 2. [no date]

A12 Upton B. Sinclair, Jr. "The Wise Miller: An Account of How He Acquired His Reputation."

Fourteen hundred word parable of Dutch Miller to point up morals: "First, How little reliance we should put in all rumors. Second: How far the imagination may deceive the senses. Third: How prone we are to jump to conclusions and last: How apt we are to call luck in our neighbors, what in ourselves would be the fruits of honest toil." N.

A13 Unsigned. "Even the Angels."

Eight line joke about swearing angel. N.

Page 3. [no date]

A14 U.B.S. "Love Will Find a Way."

Verse: two four line stanzas in "Irish brogue"; almost certainly from *Phrenocosmian*. M.

A15 Upton B. Sinclair, Jr. "Jingle."

Four line punning verse. N.

A16 Unsigned. "Sally Ann Simple."

Nine line verse. N.

A17 Upton B. Sinclair, Jr. '97. "Ye Olde Tyme Tale of Ye 'Woolf' and Ye (Soph.) Kid."

Verse: three four line stanzas; [*Phrenocosmian*]. M.

A18 Upton B. Sinclair, Jr. "A Mixed Mickron's 'S.A.' "

Twenty-one line letter game in the form of a story, using Greek, German and English Alphabets; *Harper's Round Table*. M.

A19 Upton B. Sinclair, Jr. "Jingle."

Four lines. N.

A20 Upton B. Sinclair, Jr. "Riddle."

Sixteen line verse riddle with solution "CUP" in pencil. N.

A21 U.B.S. '97. "He Knew."

Verse: eight lines poking fun at medicines; *Phrenocosmian*. M.

A22 Upton B. Sinclair, Jr. "How Queer!"

Verse: three four line stanzas. N.

A23 Unsigned. Untitled.

Eight line verse-pun. N.

A24 Upton B. Sinclair, Jr. Untitled.

Verse: four lines. N.

A25 Upton B. Sinclair, Jr. "Jingle."

Four lines. N.

Page 4. [no date]

A26 Upton B. Sinclair, Jun. R.T.F. [Round Table Founder]. "Why ——— is Salty."

Twenty-nine line puzzle requiring seventy-six blanks to be filled with either "sole" or "butter" as the attached printed explanatory note (from a later issue—18 February 1895) indicates; *Harper's Young People.* M.

A27 U.B.S. '97. Untitled.

One five and five four line stanzas of poetry humorously outlining the effects of science study on an "imaginative poet" who had come to C.C.N.Y. "raving of Nature's beauty"; *Phrenocosmian.* M.

A28 U.B.S. '97. "My Belated Valentine."

Three four line stanzas beginning "Desiring to promulgate my erotic cogitations/When Luna's coruscations lit the polyphloesboen sea"; *Phrenocosmian.* M.

A29 O.A.S. '95. Untitled.

Although not by Sinclair, this first recorded printed criticism of Sinclair is here reproduced:

Mr. Sinclair '97 was probably the best of the small sized men who have spoken this year. He was much handicapped by a weak voice. But his earnestness, feeling, spirit, and appreciation of his piece, his freedom from affec[tat]ion, fitting for such an homely piece of oratory as Grady's "The Homes of the People," helped to gain the chapel's attention and a fair sized mark. *Phrenocosmian.* M.

A30 Unsigned. Untitled.
Seventy-five word anecdote. N.

A31 Unsigned. Untitled.
Seventy-five word humorous story about immigrant ignorance. N.

A32 Unsigned. Untitled.
Thirty-five word anecdote. N.

A33 Unsigned. Untitled.
Seven line joke. N.

A34 Unsigned. "He Made Them Ashamed."
Two-hundred word "moral" on the meanness of slander. N.

A35 Unsigned. Untitled.
Two line joke. N.

A36 Unsigned. "A Bad Climate."
Twenty word punning joke. N.

A37 Unsigned. "Concerning Heaven."
Two line joke. N.

Page 5. [no date]

A38 Upton B. Sinclair, Jr. "The Siamese Twins."
Three thousand word story about twins, one of whom is blessed by a fairy. N.

Page 6. [no date]

A39 Unsigned. "A Joke on Jack."
Seven line rhyme. M.

A40 Unsigned. "Bad Management."
Four line joke. N.

A41 Unsigned. "Common Paradoxes."
Illustration and five lines observing that common prayer,

common sense and common wealth are the "most common things in the world." M.

A42 Unsigned. "He Wouldn't Turn Out."

Twenty-five word joke. M.

Page 7. [no date]

A43 Upton B. Sinclair, Jr. "He Met a Wizard."

Eighteen hundred word story of a greedy boy deceived by a vagrant. N.

Page 8. 1896 [in ink]

A44 Upton B. Sinclair, Jr. "A Queer Sign."

One thousand words on ambiguity of sign "This Train Only Stops at New York." N.

A45 Unsigned. "The Fad of Having Fads."

Four hundred word discussion of fin de siècle fads. M.

A46 Unsigned. "Cycling in the Adirondacks."

One thousand word report of a bicycle trip from Brant Lake to Lake Saranac, some seventy-five miles. N.

Page 9. 1896 [in ink]

A47 Upton B. Sinclair, Jr. "All for Eighty Cents."

Eight hundred word discussion of how the complex advantages of civilizations are usually taken for granted. N.

A48 Unsigned. "Good Causes for War."

Forty word joke on "sassiness" of Spain. N.

A49 Upton B. Sinclair '97. "In the Chemistry Room."

Forty word joke; *Phrenocosmian*. M.

A50 Upton B. Sinclair, Jr. "Populists Never Go Crazy."

Letter to the editor of the *New York Sun*, which reads in part: "Sir, the statement that a Populist is capable of going insane is one I did not expect to see in *The Sun*. Will you kindly correct yourself and add that the cause of this phenomenon is simply that people are slowly getting on to 'the Populists.' " *New York Sun*. N.

A51 Unsigned. "Wanted—A Plumber."
Forty word joke. N.

A52 Upton B. Sinclair. "Metaphor a la Manhattan."
Fifty word description of woman in figurative terms drawn from the city. N.

A53 Unsigned. "The Way They Do Now."
Eight line jingle on self-wounding to collect insurance. N.

A54 Unsigned. "Stage Realism."
Forty word joke about truck drivers. N.

A55 Unsigned. "Teaching the Teacher."
Four line joke. M.

Page 10. 1896 [in ink]

A56 Upton Sinclair. "Jack's Burglar."
Four hundred word illustrated story "written for the children's page." N.

A57 Unsigned. "Progress On."
Cartoon. N.

Page 11. 1896 [in ink]

A58 Unsigned. "A Popular Song."
Cartoon. N.

A59 Unsigned. "Political Phrase."
Cartoon. N.

A60 Unsigned. "Have You Tried It?"
Four line joke. N.

A61 Unsigned. "Fulfilling the Prophecy."
Cartoon. N.

A62 Unsigned. Untitled.
Four line verse. N.

A63 Unsigned. "Professors, Old and New."
Three hundred word discussion of "fad" of schoolmasters styling themselves professors. M.

Page 12. 1896 [in ink]

A64 Upton B. Sinclair, Jr. "That Moonlight Fishing Party."
Thirteen hundred word illustrated story in three parts written for the weekly children's page; continued on page 13; part three is missing. N.

Page 13. 1896 [in ink]

A65 Unsigned. "Fun Behind the Scenes."
Cartoon. N.

Page 14. [no date]

A66 Unsigned. "In Old Kentuck."
Four line joke about drinking. M.

A67 Unsigned. "Where Did He Put 'Em?"
Three line joke. M.

A68 Unsigned. "A Relic of the Past."
Seven line joke. M.

A69 Duplicate of A68.

A70 Unsigned. "Fenders."
Seven line joke. M.

A71 Unsigned. "Definitions."
Eight one sentence definitions. M.

A72 Unsigned. "Waste Not, Want Not."
Seven line joke. M.

A73 Unsigned. "Fetching."
Four line punning joke. M.

A74 Unsigned. "Ask and Receive" and "Plenty of Flowers."
Three line joke, eight line joke. M.

A75 Unsigned. "At the Zoo."
Four line joke about missionaries. M.

A76 Unsigned. "He Closed the House."
Twelve line joke about the sandwich at the tavern. M.

A77 Unsigned. "Outdone."
Six line joke. N.

A78 Unsigned. "A Drug on the Market."
Ten line joke. N.

A79 Unsigned. "Choosing the Highest."
Four line joke. N.

A80 Unsigned. "A Riddle."
Ten line joke. N.

A81 Unsigned. "An Acquired Taste."
Seven line punning joke. M.

A82 Unsigned. Untitled.
Six line joke. N.

A83 Unsigned. "A Queer Combination."
Cartoon. N.

A84 Unsigned. "In The Days to Come."
Cartoon. N.

A85 Unsigned. "Corroborative."
Five line punning joke. M.

Page 15. [no date]

A86 Unsigned. "Department Store Marvels."

Four hundred word oblique critique of many leading figures such as Theodore Roosevelt and Anthony Comstock. N.

A87 Unsigned. Untitled.

Two line joke. M.

A88 Unsigned. "A Land of Promise."

Cartoon. M.

A89 Unsigned. "He Never Gave That Up."

Four line joke. N.

A90 Unsigned. "Getting Ready."

Fifteen word joke. N.

A91 Unsigned. "Elucidation."

Four line joke. N.

A92 Unsigned. "A Pretty Experiment."

One hundred word discussion of magnetism. N.

A93 Unsigned. "Come Naturally."

Four line joke. N.

Page 16. [no date]

A94 Unsigned. "The Days of Dingley."

Cartoon. N.

A95 Unsigned. "Diplomatic."

Cartoon. N.

A96 Unsigned. "Etiquette."

Seven line joke about drinking. N.

A97 Unsigned. "Quite a Difference."

Cartoon. N.

A98 Unsigned. "One for Chicago."
Cartoon. N.

Page 17. [no date]

A99 Unsigned. "A Hibernating Belle."
Cartoon. N.

A100 Unsigned. Untitled.
Three line joke. M.

A101 Unsigned. Untitled.
Four line joke. M.

A102 Unsigned. "A Celestial Chesterfield."
Cartoon. N.

A103 Unsigned. "Cause for Alarm."
Seven line joke about joke writers. M.

A104 Unsigned. "An Old Health-Resort Joke."
N.

A105 Unsigned. "The New Cook."
Cartoon. N.

A106 Unsigned. "Oil on the Waters."
Six line joke. M.

Page 18. [no date]

A107 Unsigned. 'Manly Precocity."
Cartoon. N.

A108 Unsigned. "The Ruling Passion."
Cartoon. N.

A109 Unsigned. "Never Learned How."
Cartoon. N.

A110 Unsigned. "An Insinuation Repudiated."
Cartoon. N.

A111 Unsigned. "Careful About His Cooking."
Cartoon. N.

Page 19. [no date]

A112 Unsigned. "Wanted Only the Chance."
Cartoon. N.

A113 Unsigned. "Straight Is the Path That Leadeth."
Cartoon. N.

A114 Unsigned. "Saw It in Time-Fly Time."
Cartoon. N.

A115 Unsigned. Untitled.
Three line joke. N.

A116 Unsigned. "A Reef."
Cartoon. N.

A117 Unsigned. "Ordering Dinner."
Cartoon. N.

A118 Unsigned. "A Full Hand."
Cartoon. N.

Page 20. [no date]

A119 Li Hung Chan [pseud.] "To 'C.A.A.' Editor."
Two hundred word article offering humorous answers to mock questions; letter dated 3 April 1897; probably from *Yellow Kid*. M.

A120 Unsigned. "The Bucolic Idea."
Cartoon. N.

Page 21. [no date]

A121 Unsigned. "Why He Came Back."
Cartoon. N.

A122 Unsigned. "No Cause for Alarm."
Cartoon. N.

A123 Unsigned. "Where It Was Needed."
Cartoon. N.

Page 22. [no date]

A124 Unsigned. "Elucidation."
Four line joke. N.

A125 Unsigned. "A New View."
Eight line joke. M.

A126 Unsigned. "Surprise."
Eight line joke. N.

A127 Unsigned. "The Angler's Art."
Cartoon. N.

Page 23. [no date]

A128 Unsigned. "Four Balls!"
Cartoon. N.

A129 Unsigned. "All Right."
Cartoon. N.

A130 Unsigned. "At a Standstill."
Cartoon. N.

A131 Unsigned. "Suspicious."
Cartoon. N.

Page 24. [no date]

A132 Unsigned. "A Doubtful Promise."
Cartoon. N.

A133 Unsigned. "Vengeance."
Cartoon. N.

A134 Unsigned. "Full of Bumps."
Cartoon. N.

A135 Unsigned. "Just the Size."
Cartoon. N.

A136 Unsigned. "Contents Worthless."
Cartoon. N.

Page 25. [no date]

A137 Upton B. Sinclair, Jr. "A Song of the Summer Season."
Twenty-two lines of humorous verse; probably from *Truth*. M.

A138 Unsigned. "Right This Time."
Three line joke. N.

A139 Unsigned. "Even Among the Lowly."
Cartoon. N.

A140 Unsigned. "Kaleidoscope."
Cartoon. N.

Page 25a. [unnumbered; no date]

A141 Unsigned. "The Bill of Fare Family."
Cartoon. N.

A142 Unsigned. "How He Reckoned."
Cartoon. N.

Page 25b. [unnumbered; no date]

A143 Unsigned. "All Rights So Far As He Knew."
Cartoon. N.

Page 26. [no date]

A144 Unsigned. "The Game of Suburban Burglar."

In feature, Life's Little Pleasantries; two hundred word description of "game." M.

Pages 27–74 blank.

Although exposure to moisture has caused these pages to stick to one another, there seems to be no more clipped material mounted on these remaining pages.

Items found loose in Scrapbook and not listed elsewhere:

A145 Unsigned. Untitled.

Three five line stanzas of verse. N.

A146 Upton B. Sinclair, Jr. "The Man With the Little Green Bag," *The Quaker*, pp. 438–46.

1896

A147 "Latin Question," *Harper's Round Table*, XVII (7 January), 250.

A148 "Verse," *Harper's Round Table*, XVII (21 January), 298.

A149* "The Case of 'Uncle Benjamin,' " *Phrenocosmian*, pp. 4–12.

Story of poor, lazy, drinking Virginia "nigger" who thinks he has gone crazy because he has slept in the moonlight and who is later imprisoned and placed in wife's custody. The story won the *Phrenocosmian* (C.C.N.Y.) prize contest; it may well refer obliquely to the Sinclair family situation.

Half-dime Novels (Numbers A150--A240)

Sinclair initially wrote two series of stories (Mallory and Faraday) under two pseudonyms (Garrison and Fitch) which were originally published under three (probably four) different series titles (*Army and Navy Weekly*, *Half-Holiday*, *True Blue* and, probably, *Starry Flag Weekly*); in addition he wrote under one of these pseudonyms (Fitch) an undetermined number of novelettes for a still different series (*Columbia Library*). With the exception of a part of the *Columbia Library* material, portions of the original material were republished with various changes in at least seven other series: *Medal Library*, *Boys of America*, *Brave and Bold*, *Bound to Win*, *Round the World*, McKay's "Boys' Own Library," and Caldwell's "Famous Books for Boys."

Between 19 June 1897 and 19 November 1898 Sinclair turned out 61 Mark Mallory stories of 10–12 pages and 28 Clif Faraday stories of 30–32 pages. Thus, during an eighteen-month period—most of it coinciding with his full-time graduate study at Columbia University and intensive violin practice—Sinclair produced some 1500 pages of published material for *Army and Navy Weekly*, *Half-Holiday*, and *True Blue*, totalling approximately 1,275,000 words. If not the equivalent of the complete works of Sir Walter Scott, as Sinclair claimed, it is an impressive record for a young man barely out of his teens. A more detailed account of Sinclair's career as a half-dime novelist may be found in my "The Upton Sinclair Dime Novels," *Dime Novel Round-up*, XXXIII (15 March 1964), 20–23.

Most of the *Army and Navy Weekly*, *Half-Holiday*, *True Blue*, and McKay's "Boys' Own Library" titles are available at the Lilly Library; some examples of most of the other series may also be examined there.

Series

ORIGINAL STORIES		Number of Issues Published
Army and Navy Weekly	19 June 1897–29 January 1898	(33)
Half-Holiday	5 February 1898–25 July 1898	(28)
Starry Flag Weekly	7 May 1898–February 1899	(20)
True Blue	14 May 1898–22 April 1899	(50)
Columbia Library	1 September 1898–1 February 1903	(44)
REPRINTS		
Medal Library	23 January 1899–8 May 1917	(858)
Boys of America	5 October 1901–17 October 1903	(107)
Brave and Bold	27 December 1902–11 March 1911	(429)
Bound to Win	7 February 1903–February 1907	(167)
Round the World	January 1925–December 1931	(183)

Clif Faraday Stories (by Ensign Clarke Fitch)

ORIGINAL STORIES		REPRINTS	
True Blue	*Columbia Library*	*Medal Library*	*Round the World*
Nos.	Nos.	Nos.	Nos.
1–3	2	341	
4–6		616	
7–9	4	353	115
10		607	
11–13	6	369	113
14–16	8	384	
17–19	10	525	
20–22	11	541	
23–25	12		
26–28	13	616 (except no. 27)	115 (except no. 27)
	17 (*The Soldier Monk*; original story, not reprint)		

Mark Mallory Stories (by Lieutenant Frederick Garrison)

ORIGINAL STORIES	REPRINTS		
Army and Navy Weekly	*Brave and Bold*	*New Medal Library*	*Boys of America*
Nos. 1–7	195	556, 568, 579?	63–69

Nos. 556, 568 and 579 of *New Medal Library* are believed to contain a reprinting of the Mark Mallory stories from *Army and Navy Weekly* and *Half-Holiday*, but they were not checked. Name changed but the numbering continued from the *Medal Library*.

1897

Army and Navy Weekly

A150 Garrison, Lieut. Frederick. "Mark Mallory at West Point," I (19 June), n.p.

A151 ———. "Mark Mallory's Heroism; or, First Steps Toward West Point," I (26 June), 18–30.

A152 ———. "The Rival Candidates; or, Mark's Fight for a Military Cadetship," I (3 July), 2–13.

A153 ———. "Mark Mallory's Strategem; or, Hazing the Hazers," I (10 July), 18–30.

A154 ———. "In West Point at Last; or, Mark Mallory's Triumph," I (17 July), n.p.

A155 ———. "Mark Mallory's Chum; or, The Trials of a West Point Cadet," I (24 July), 17–31.

A156 ———. "Friends and Foes at West Point; or, Mark Mallory's Alliance," I (31 July), 2–15.

A157 ———. "Mark Mallory's Honor; or, A West Point Mystery," I (7 August), 13–24.

A158 ———. "Fun and Frolic at West Point; or, Mark Mallory's Clever Rescue," I (14 August), 2–11.

A159 ———. "Mark Mallory's Battle; or, Plebe Against Yearling," I (21 August), 445–55.

A160 ———. "A West Point Combine; or, Mark Mallory's New Allies," I (28 August), n.p.

A161 ———. "Mark Mallory's Danger; or, In the Shadow of Dismissal," I (4 September), 578–89.

A162 ———. "Mark Mallory's Feat; or, Making Friends of Enemies," I (11 September), 578–89.

A163 ———. "Mark Mallory in Camp; or, Hazing the Yearlings," I (18 September), 636–48.

A164 ———. "A West Point Comedy; or, Mark Mallory's Practical Joke," I (25 September), 674–86.

A165 ———. "Mark Mallory's Celebration; or, A Fourth of July at West Point," I (2 October), 732–44.

A166 ———. "Mark Mallory on Guard; or, Deviling a West Point Sentry," I (9 October), 779–90.

A167 ———. "Mark Mallory's Peril; or, A Test of Friendship," I (16 October), 818–30.

A168 ———. "A West Point Hop; or, Mark Mallory's Determination," I (23 October), 877–88.

A169 ———. "Mark Mallory's Peril; or, The Plotting of an Enemy," I (30 October), 914–25.

A170 ———. "Mark Mallory's Defiance; or, Fighting a Hundred Foes," I (6 November), 973–84.

A171 ———. "Mark Mallory's Decision; or, Facing a New Danger," I (13 November), 1010–20.

A172 ———. "Mark Mallory's Escape; or, Foiling an Enemy's Plot," I (20 November), 1070–80.

1897 continued

A173 ———. "Mark Mallory's Strange Find; or, The Secret of the Counterfeiter's Cave," I (27 November), 1106–1117.

A174 ———. "Mark Mallory's Treasure; or, A Midnight Hunt for Gold," I (4 December), 1166–77.

A175 ———. "Mark Mallory's Misfortune; or, The Theft of the Counterfeiter's Gold," I (11 December), 1202–12.

A176 ———. "Mark Mallory's Bargain; or, The Story of the Stolen Treasure," I (18 December), 1263–73.

A177 ———. "A Midnight Hazing; or, Mark Mallory's Revenge," I (25 December), n.p.

1898

A178 ———. "Mark Mallory's Arrest; or, A West Point Cadet's Adventures in New York," I (1 January), 1359–73.

A179 ———. "Defending His Honor; or, Mark Mallory's Daring," I (8 January), 1394–1407.

A180 ———. "Mark Mallory's Circus; or, West Point Plebes on a Lark," I (15 January), 1454–66.

A181 ———. "A Midnight Visit; or, Mark Mallory's Escapade," I (22 January), 1490–1503.

A182 ———. "Mark Mallory's Cleverness; or, Turning the Tables on His Enemies," I (29 January), n.p.

Half-Holiday

A183 ———. "Mark Mallory's Defense; or, The Siege of the Devil's Den," I (5 February), n.p.

A184 ———. "Mark Mallory's Hour of Trial; or, The Maniac of the Devil's Den," 1 (12 February), 10–18.

A185 ———. "Mark Mallory's Ruse; or, The Story of an Interrupted Feast," 1 (19 February), 1–9.

A186 ———. "Mark Mallory's Last Chance; or, Saving His Cadetship," 1 (26 February), 10–19.

A187 ———. "Mark Mallory's Surprise; or, The Awakening of Sleepy," 1 (5 March), 1–10.

A188 ———. "A West Point Prank; or, The Misfortune of Parson Stanard," 1 (12 March), 10–18.

A189 ———. "A West Point Hunt; or, 'B'gee' Dewey's Rescue," 1 (19 March), 1–9.

A190 ———. "An Interrupted Hazing; or, The Desperate Perils of Indian," 1 (26 March), 10–17.

A191 ———. "A Perilous Experience; or, The Desperate Plight of Chauncey," 1 (2 April), 3–10.

A192 ———. "The Triumph of 'Texas': An Incident of Camp Life at West Point," 1 (9 April), 11–18.

A193 ———. "Mark Mallory's Hoax; or, Fooling All West Point," 1 (16 April), 3–10.

A194 ———. "Mark Mallory's Rescue; or, To His Enemies Aid," 1 (23 April), 11–18.

A195 ———. "Indian's First Fight; or, Facing an Old Foe," 1 (30 April), 3–10.

A196 ———. "A Comedy of Errors; or, The Mystery of Parson Stanard," 1 (7 May), 12–19.

A197 ———. "Mark Mallory's Pursuit; or, Solving a Mystery," 1 (14 May), 3–10.

1898 continued

A198 ———. "The Return of the Furloughmen; or, Mark Mallory's Last Hazing," 1 (21 May), n.p.

A199 ———. "A West Point Indignation Meeting; or, The Second Awakening of Sleepy," 1 (28 May), 2–9.

A200 ———. "The Mishap of 'Texas'; or, Foiling a Dynamite Plot," 1 (4 June), n.p.

A201 ———. "A Cow-Boy Hero; or, The Strange Outcome of a Practical Joke," 1 (11 June), n.p.

A202 ———. "Mark Mallory's Challenge; or, A Ball Game at West Point," 1 (18 June), 2–9.

A203 ———. "Parson Stanard's Triumph; or, A West Point Oratorical Contest," 1 (25 June), n.p.

A204 ———. "A Runaway Cadet; or, The Misfortune of Sleepy," 1 (2 July), n.p.

A205 ———. "The Young Politician; or, Sleepy's Great Triumph," 1 (9 July), 13–9.

A206 ———. "The Populist Trust Hunters; or, How Sleepy Was Converted," 1 (16 July), 1–8.

A207 ———. "Mark Mallory's Triple Play; or, Holding His Laurels," 1 (23 July), 13–8.

A208 ———. " 'B'gee' Dewey's Joke List; or, The Misfortunes of a Story Teller," 1 (30 July), n.p.

A209 ———. "Mark Mallory's Practical Joke; or, How Dr. Friedburg Fell in Love," 1 (6 August), n.p.

A210 ———. "Saved by His Wit; or, Mark Mallory's Grave Peril," 1 (13 August), n.p.

True Blue

A211 Fitch, Ensign Clarke. "Clif Faraday on the New York; or, A Naval Cadet Under Fire," no. 1 (14 May), pp. 1–31.

A212 ———. "Remember the Maine; or, Clif Faraday's Rallying Cry," no. 2 (21 May), pp. 1–28.

A213 ———. " 'Well Done, Porter'; or, Clif Faraday's Torpedo-Boat Command," no. 3 (28 May), pp. 1–32.

A214 ———. "Clif Faraday Under Havana's Guns; or, The Stroke for a Capture," no. 4 (4 June), pp. 1–32.

A215 ———. "A Traitor on the Flagship; or, Clif Faraday's Strange Clue," no. 5 (11 June), pp. 1–31.

A216 ———. "The Mysterious Prize; or, Clif Faraday's Thrilling Chase," no. 6 (18 June), pp. 1–31.

A217 ———. "In the Enemy's Hands; or Clif Faraday's Eventful Cruise," no. 7 (25 June), pp. 1–31.

A218 ———. "Out of Morro Castle; or, Clif Faraday's Escape," no. 8 (2 July), pp. 1–31.

A219 ———. "Clif Faraday's Test; or, The Mystery of the Unexploded Shell," no. 9 (9 July), pp. 1–31.

A220 ———. "The Shot That Won; or, Clif Faraday's Steady Aim," no. 10 (16 July), pp. 1–31.

A221 ———. "In the Face of Death; or, Clif Faraday's Gallantry," no. 11 (23 July), pp. 1–31.

A222 ———. "Clif Faraday Under Arrest; or, Court-martialed for Patriotism," no. 12 (30 July), pp. 1–31.

A223 ———. "Clif Faraday at Cardenas; or, Hot Shot Where It Did Most Good," no. 13 (6 August), pp. 1–31.

1898 continued

A224 ———. "Caught in a Trap; or, Clif Faraday's Terrible Set-Back," no. 14 (13 August), pp. 1–31.

A225 ———. "Saved by the Enemy; or, Clif Faraday's Desperate Peril," no. 15 (20 August), pp. 1–31.

A226 ———. "Clif Faraday's Hostage; or, To the Aid of A Friend," no. 16 (27 August), pp. 1–31.

A227 ———. "Down With His Ship!; or, Clif Faraday's Double Capture," no. 17 (3 September), pp. 1–31.

A228 ———. "Up to the Cannon's Mouth; or, Clif Faraday's Perilous Ruse," no. 18 (10 September), pp. 1–31.

A229 ———. "Clif Faraday in Desperate Straits; or, Running the Gauntlet of Fire at Santiago," no. 19 (17 September), pp. 1–32.

A230 ———. "The Phantom Cruiser; or, Clif Faraday's Strange Signal," no. 20 (24 September), pp. 1–31.

A231 ———. "Clif Faraday's Plucky Friend; or, The Heroine Nurse of the Navy," no. 21 (1 October), pp. 1–31.

A232 ———. "Holding the Fort; or, Clif Faraday Against a Thousand," no. 22 (8 October), pp. 1–31.

A233 ———. "Through the Enemy's Line; or, Clif Faraday's [Dangerous (on cover)] Perilous Mission," no. 23 (15 October), pp. 1–31.

A234 ———. "Clif Faraday's Honor; or, A Pledge to the Enemy," no. 24 (22 October), pp. 1–31.

A235 ———. "Clif Faraday's Hour of Peril; or, On Board the Admiral's Flagship," no. 25 (29 October), pp. 1–31.

A236 ———. "Wolves of the Navy; or, Clif Faraday's Last Cartridge," no. 27 (12 November), pp. 1–32.

A237 ———. "The Crime of the Trenches; or, Clif Faraday's Last Cartridge," no. 27 (12 November), pp. 1–32.

A238 ———. "Clif Faraday's Telling Blow; or, To Fame and Honor Through Shot and Shell," no. 28 (19 November), pp. 1–32.

Starry Flag Weekly

A239 Garrison, Lieut. Frederick. "Hal Maynard at West Point; or, The New Member of the Seven Devils," 8 December.

1899

A240 ———. " 'Scrap' Powers in Trouble; or, The Seven Devils and the Green Goods Man," 1 February. See Edward T. LeBlanc's note in *Dime Novel Round-up*, XXXIII (15 March 1964), 23.

A241 "Unity and Infinity in Art," *Metaphysical Magazine*, IX (January), 6–17.

A242* "When Melville Woke Up," *Star*, V (April–July).

This story, about two pages per installment, began in the April issue; the July issue—the only one examined—announced that the story was to be continued. The young boy-hero, Ebenezer Briggs, captures an escaped circus buffalo and is rewarded with a mimeograph machine on which he publishes a paper, "The Melville War Whoop." Ebenezer writes the advertising copy himself and arouses the criticism of the community, especially Judge Thompson.

A243* "In the Net of the Visconti," *Argosy*, XXX–XXXI (July–November).

Five part serial. "A tale of the time of the Italian Renaissance. The thrilling experiences of Tito Bentivogli, son to the Duke of Bologna, who is captured while on a hunting trip by Galeazzo, the hereditary enemy of his house. Plot, counterplot, and a

1899 continued

matching of cunning against cunning in a game of which one player's life is the stake."

1900

A244* "A Battle With Misfortune," *Argosy*, XXXII–XXXIV, (January–August).

Seven part serial. "A tale of trials in the great metropolis, wherein is shown that the fight with poverty and illness may have all the exciting features of a contest with life-threatening conditions in the wilder regions of the earth."

Pre-socialist conversion, anticipation of *The Jungle*.

A245 "The Man With the Little Green Bag," *The Quaker*, VII (March), 438–446.

A246* "Chip," *American Boy*, I (April), 161.

This story, which continued in the May issue, tells of an eight-year-old slum urchin, Chip, who runs into a drunk millionaire and takes him home. He then decides to take a train trip to see the country. Interesting parallel to Jurgis's experiences in *The Jungle*.

A247* "The Theft of a God," *Argosy*, XXXIV (August), 1–47.

"The thrilling experiences of two Englishmen in India, consequent on the freak of one of them, who conceives the idea of carrying off a native deity. A night of horror in the temple of Lashmi Gar." The name Howard Bland, a cousin of Sinclair's, is given to one of the characters.

1901

A248 "In the Days of Decatur," *Argosy*, XXXV (January), 185–230.

"The thrilling adventures of a United States navy officer in Tripoli. Sold as a slave, he contrives an escape which precipitates him into fresh disaster, and finally makes him a leading figure in a dramatic episode of the war."

A249* *Springtime and Harvest: A Romance.* New York: The Sinclair Press, January. 281 pp.

Reissued as *King Midas*: A251. In part: A1545, A2049.

A250 St. Clair Beall [pseud.] "The Winning of Sarenne," *Argosy*, XXXV–XXXVI (June–October), about 15 pp. per issue.

As book: A258.

A251* *King Midas: A Romance.* New York and London: Funk & Wagnalls Co., October. 388 pp.

Previously published as *Springtime and Harvest* A249.
Reprinted: New York: Doubleday, Page & Co., 1906.
Foreign Editions: English, Russian.

A252 *Preface to Springtime and Harvest.* New York: The Sinclair Press. 7 pp.

Only known copy at Yale; not examined.

1902

A253 "A Review of Reviews," *Independent*, LIV (6 February), 328–332.

On the difference between the reviews of privately printed *Springtime and Harvest* A249, and those of the Funk & Wagnalls reissue, *King Midas* A 251.

A254* "On the Teaching of Languages," *Independent*, LIV (27 February), 493–497.

". . . the one secret of learning a language—never to pass a word without remembering it, and remembering it forever."

A255* "Language Study: Some Facts," *Independent*, LIV (19 June), 1472–1477.

Results of questionnaire sent to 500 college graduates; language instruction largely futile.

1902 continued

A256* "Cunnylums (An All-True Story)," *Independent*, LIV (31 July), 1827–1830.

How the Sinclairs raised a bird.

A257* "The Confessions of a Young Author," *Independent*, LIV (20 November), 2748–2752.

Tells in anonymous article of his unremunerative career as hackwriter and serious novelist.

A258 St. Clair Beall [pseud.] *The Winning of Sarenne*. New York: The Federal Book Co. 343 pp. With illustrations by Louis F. Grant

Copyright: 1901, by Frank A. Munsey; 1902, by The Federal Book Co.

As serial: A250.

1903

A259* *The Journal of Arthur Stirling*. New York: D. Appleton and Co., February.

Reprinted: New York: Doubleday, Page & Co., 1906; Pasadena: Sinclair, 1923. In part: A469, A1545, A2049.

Foreign Editions: English, Russian.

A260 "My Cause," *Independent*, LV (14 May), 1121–1126.

An extraordinary challenge to the world and vow to himself. "And you who want to know what my cause is—I sum it up for you in this one sentence: That the salvation of American literature depends upon the saving of the young author from the brutalizing slavery of 'What the Public Wants.' "

Reprinted: A1545, A2049.

A261* *Prince Hagen*. Boston: L. C. Page, May. 249 pp.

Reprinted: Chicago: Charles H. Kerr and Co., 1910; House of Gowrie, [n.d.] As play: A360, A412, In part: A469, A1545, A4209.

Foreign Editions: Czech, English, German, Japanese, Russian, Yiddish.

A262* "The Toy and the Man," *Wilshire's Magazine*, VII (December), 52–57.

Reprinted as pamphlet: A272.

1904

A263* "A Country House Built and Furnished for Only $156," *Country Life in America*, VI (June), 178–179.

A264* *Manassas*. New York: Macmillan Co., August. 412 pp.

Reprinted: Pasadena: The Author, 1923; Pasadena; The Author, c. 1933. Revised, as *Theirs Be the Guilt*: New York: Twayne Publishers, 1959; New York: Hillman Books, 1960. In part: A1545, A2049.

Foreign Editions: Chinese, Czech, English, French, German, Hebrew, Hungarian, Japanese, Russian, Swedish.

A265 "You Have Lost the Strike! And Now What Are You Going to do About it?" *Appeal to Reason*, 17 September, p. 1.

Reprinted in *Appeal*, 5 August, as page 1 of a four-page "Extra." Sinclair's first piece of militant Socialism.

A266 "The Spirit That Wins," *Appeal to Reason*, 24 September, p. 3.

A267* "Our Bourgeois Literature: The Reason and the Remedy," *Collier's*, XXXIV (8 October), 22–25.

Response to Gertrude Atherton's essay in May issue of *North American Review*. The reason is the lack of brotherhood; the remedy, Socialist revolution.

Reprinted: A1545, A2049.

A268* "Farmers of America, Unite!" *Appeal to Reason*, 15 October, pp. 2–3.

Urges farmers to join Socialist Party.

A269 "The Socialist Party: Its Aims in the Present Campaign," *Collier's*, XXXIV (29 October), 10, 12.

1904 continued

A270 "Every Man His Own Reviewer," *Independent*, LVII (17 November), 1149–1150.

Manassas reviewed by Upton Sinclair. He describes the book as the first volume of a projected trilogy which will constitute "a try for a national epic."

A271 "To My Comrades Who Read The Appeal," *Appeal to Reason*, 31 December, p. 2.

Urges membership in Socialist Party.

A272 *The Toy and the Man*. Westwood, Mass.; The Ariel Press. 15 pp.

Reprint of A262.

1905

A273 "To My Comrades Who Read Socialist Papers," *The Chicago Socialist*, 7 January, p. 1.

See A271.

A274 *Our Bourgeois Literature*. Chicago: Charles H. Kerr Co., 11 February. 31 pp. (Pocket Library of Socialism, no. 43.)

Reprint of A267.

A275 "Regarding *The Jungle*," *Appeal to Reason*, 11 February, p. 1.

A276 "*The Jungle*," *Appeal to Reason*, 25 February–4 November (except 4 March).

Novel left unfinished in this newspaper serial.
See also 1905, 1906 Jungle entries, especially A280, A286.

A277 Letter regarding *The Jungle*, *Appeal to Reason*, 4 March, p. 3.

A278 St. Clair Beall [pseud.] "The House in the Jungle," *Tom Watson's Magazine*, I (March), 13–31.

A279* "Is Chicago Meat Clean?" *Collier's*, xxxv (22 April), 13–14.

A composite article by Sinclair and Major L. L. Seaman, M.D., with quotations from a series of articles that appeared in the *Lancet* (London). Major Seaman concludes that "there is no tainted meat sold from the stockyards," while Sinclair points up the disgustingly filthy conditions that prevail. Originally titled "New Aspects of the Beef Trust."

A280* "The Jungle: A Story of Chicago," *One Hoss Philosophy*, nos.33–35 (April, July, October).

Ending differs from book version.

See 1905, 1906 *Jungle* entries, especially A276, A286.

A281 "A Letter from Mr. Sinclair," *Collier's*, xxxv (13 May), 30.

A282* "*The Jungle*: A Statement Concerning a Publication Plan," *Appeal to Reason*, 18 November, p. 5.

A283 *Call for an Intercollegiate Socialist Society*. New York: Upton Sinclair. 1 p.

Issued with added text detailing subsequent activities in eight page leaflet dated September 1910.

1906

A284* "A Definite Announcement Concerning Publication of *The Jungle*," *Appeal to Reason*, 27 January, p. 4.

A285 "The Call of the Wild," *New York Times*, 5 February, p. 8.

Protesting distorted reporting of Jack London's speech, "Revolution."

A286* *The Jungle*. New York: Doubleday, Page & Co., and The Jungle Publishing Co., 26 February. 413 pp.

As serial: A276, A280.

Reprinted: Girard, Kansas: Haldeman-Julius (Little Blue Books nos. 583-588), 1920, 1924; Pasadena: Upton Sinclair, 1920;

1906 continued

New York: Vanguard Press, 1926; New York: Upton Sinclair, 1928, 1942; London: Penguin Books, 1936; Modern Classics, 1947, 1965; London: Edwards Brothers, 1945; New York: Viking Press, 1946; New York: Harper and Bros., 1951; New York: New American Library of World Literature, 1960; New York: The Author, [n.d.]; New York: Airmont Publishing Company, c. 1965; New York: Grosset & Dunlap, [n.d.]. In part: A469, A1545, A2049, and in various anthologies; New York: The Heritage Press, 1965 (two formats); New York: Amsco Book Co., 1970 (school edition).

Foreign Editions: Armenian, Bengali, Braille, Bulgarian, Chinese, Czech, Danish, Dutch, English-Australia, English-Canada, English, Finnish, French, German, Hebrew, Hindu, Hungarian, Icelandic, Italian, Latvian, Lithuanian, Marathi, Malayalam, Norwegian, Polish, Portuguese, Romanian, Serbo-Croatian, Slovak, Slovenian, Spanish, Swedish, Tamil, Tatar, Turkish, Ukrainian, Yiddish.

A287 "Stockyards Secrets," *Collier's*, XXXVI (24 March), 24.

Reports of further research into laws governing packing industry, and quotes Theodore Roosevelt's testimony regarding "embalmed beef scandal" following Spanish-American War.

A288 "Sinclair vs. Armour," *Appeal to Reason*, 21 April, p. 1.

Telegram from Sinclair promising "red hot beef trust stuff."

A289 "Significant Illustration of the Growing Tendency to Prejudice the Public Through Systematic Misrepresentation," *Arena*, XXXV (April), 434–435.

Reprint of letter Sinclair sent to *New York Times* to clarify its coverage of Jack London's speech at Yale on behalf of the Intercollegiate Socialist Society. Letter dated 2 February 1906.

A290 "Markets and Misery," *North American Review*, CLXXXII (April), 591–603.

Reprinted as chapter III of *The Industrial Republic*, A328.

A291 "Is *The Jungle* True?" *Independent*, LX (17 May), 1129–1133.

Yes, in every detail and in spirit. Important account of the autobiographical elements in the novel.

A292 "To the Socialists of Chicago: A Letter From Upton Sinclair, Author of *The Jungle*," *The Chicago Socialist*, 26 May, p. 4.

Editorial.

A293 "The Condemned Meat Industry: A Reply to Mr. J. Ogden Armour," *Everybody's Magazine*, XIV (May), 608–616.

Reprinted in Harvey Swados, ed. *Years of Conscience: The Muckrakers*. New York: 1962, pp. 245-257.

A294 "A Home Colony," *Independent*, LX (14 June), 1401–1408.

Reprinted as pamphlet: A316. Solicits replies from people interested in establishing a communal living colony.

A295 "The Meat-Inspection Situation," *Collier's*, XXXVII (16 June), 24, 26.

A296 "Campaign Against the Wholesale Poisoners of the Nation's Food," *Arena*, XXXVI (July), 66–72.

A297 "*Jungle* Vindicated," *Bookman*, XXIII (July), 481–483.

A298 "The Socialist Party in the United States," *World's Work* [London], VIII (July), 140–141.

A299* "The Novel as an Instrument of Reform," *Current Literature*, XLI (August), 163–164.

A300* "In the Days of My Youth: Chapters of Autobiography," *MAP*, CDXXX (8 September), 304–306.

1906 continued

A301 Lieutenant Frederick Garrison, U.S.A. [pseud.] "Mark Mallory's Struggle; or, Friends and Foes at West Point," *Brave & Bold*, no. 195 (15 September), 28 pp.

A302 "Upton Sinclair—The Man of the Hour," *Human Life, the Magazine About People*, III (September), 5–6, 8.

An interview account of Sinclair's hackwriting, marriage, and early writing career. Hugh C. Weir, interviewer.

A303 "A Review of *The Cost of Competition* by Sidney A. Reeve," *International Socialist Review*, VII (2 October), 199–208.

A304 "A Captain of Industry," *Appeal to Reason*, 27 October; 3, 10, 17, 24 November.

As book: A308.

A305* "What Life Means to Me," *Cosmopolitan*, XLI (October), 591–595.

Important early autobiographical statement.

Reprinted: A320, A1199.

A306 "Regarding *The Jungle*," *Appeal to Reason*, 17 November, p. 3.

A307 "The Children of Packingtown," *Success Magazine*, IX (November), 756–757, 797, 798.

A308* *A Captain of Industry*. Girard, Kansas: Appeal to Reason, 1 December. 142 pp.

Reprinted with new preface: Girard, Kansas: Haldeman-Julius (Little Blue Books nos. 634-635), 1924.

See A304.

Foreign Editions: Armenian, Bulgarian, Czech, Danish, Dutch, English, Estonian, Finnish, French, German, Hungarian, Latvian, Lithuanian, Polish, Romanian, Russian, Serbo-Croatian, Spanish, Swedish, Ukrainian, Yiddish.

A309 "The Overman," *Windsor Magazine*, xxv (December), 145–157.

As book: A330.

A310* *Colony Customs*. Englewood, N.J.: Upton Sinclair, *c.* December.

Broadside; lists thirty-one "customs which have been evolved out of the practical experience of the Home Colony."

A311* *Circular Letter*. New York: Jungle Publishing Co. 1 leaf.

"About December 15, 1906, The Jungle Publishing Company will publish a novel by Upton Sinclair, entitled, *A Captain of Industry*."

A312* *Advertisement for* The Jungle *by Upton Sinclair*. Girard, Kansas: Appeal to Reason. 8pp.

A313* *The Books of Upton Sinclair*. New York: Jungle Publishing Co. 8 pp.

Lists *The Jungle*, *Manassas*, *Journal of Arthur Stirling*, *Prince Hagen*, *King Midas*.

A314* *Circular Letter*. New York: Jungle Publishing Co. 1 leaf.

"Circulate *The Jungle* . . . (Published February 15, 1906)." Contains a letter from Jack London, endorsing the book.

A315* *The Helicon Home Colony*. Englewood, N.J.: Constitution.

Broadside; seems to be entirely or largely by Sinclair.

A316 *A Home Colony*: *A Prospectus*. New York: Jungle Publishing Co. 23 pp.

Outlines building plans and living options.

Reprint of A294.

1906 continued

A317* *Circular Letter*. Girard, Kansas: Appeal to Reason. 6 pp.

Order blank, offering the book at a reduced price; letter from Jack London and comments on the book.

A318* *Circular Letter*. New York: Jungle Publishing Co. 4 pp.

Advertising leaflet headed: "*The Jungle*, by Upton Sinclair."

A319* *Circular Letter*. Princeton, N.J.: Jungle Publishing Co. 4 pp.

Headed: "leaflet advertising *The Jungle*."

A320* *What Life Means to Me*. Girard, Kansas: Appeal to Reason. 12 pp.

Reprint of A305; see also A857, A1199.

1907

A321* *The Helicon Home Colony Cottage Plans*. [n.p.], *c.* 15 January.

Broadside; outlines plans, expected costs, and restrictions for the construction of cement block cottages on the grounds of the Helicon Home Colony.

A322* *Helicon Home Colony*. Englewood, N.J.: Upton Sinclair, *c.* January.

An illustrated brochure describing the organization, purposes, costs, requirements for membership, financing, and future plans of the Home Colony Company. Solicits inquiry.

A323 "The Home Colony: Six Months After," *Independent*, LXII (7 February), 306–313.

A324 "The Industrial Republic," *Wilshire's Magazine* [London], XI (February), 5–7.

Serial continued in *Wilshire's*, March-July. As book, see A328.

A325 "The Best Book I Have Been Reading," *Life*, XLIX (7 March), 344.

H. G. Wells' *A Modern Utopia.*

A326 "A Co-operative Home Colony," *World's Work* [London], IX (March), 382–387.

A327 Letter, *Wilshire's Magazine* [London], XI (April), 4.

Reading *Wilshire's Magazine* made Sinclair a Socialist.

A328* *The Industrial Republic.* New York: Doubleday, Page and Co., 1 June. 284 pp.

Chapter III, "Markets and Misery," published as an article in *North American Review* (1906). As serial, A324. In part: A1545, A2049.

Foreign Editions: Danish, English, French, German, Russian, Swedish.

A329 "A Letter from Mr. Upton Sinclair," *American Magazine*, LXIV (July), 329–330.

Sinclair corrects the widespread rumors concerning the cause of the fire that burned down Helicon Hall, and the alleged neglect of precautions. The cause of the fire was never determined.

A330* *The Overman.* New York: Doubleday, Page and Co., *c.* 30 September. 90 pp.

Reprinted: Girard, Kansas: Haldeman-Julius (Little Blue Book no. 594), 1924. As serial: A309. In part: A1545, A2049.

Foreign Edition: Czech.

A331* *Circular Letter.* Jungle Publishing Co. 1 leaf.

"Dear Comrade:—On February 28 next, being one year from the date of publication of *The Jungle. . . .*"

A332* *The Helicon Home Colony. A Confidential Statement.* Englewood, N.Y.: Upton Sinclair. 1 leaf.

A333* Preface to Second Edition: An Interpretation. In *The Journal of Arthur Stirling.* London: William Heinemann, pp. xv–xix.

See English Editions.

1908

A334 "The Metropolis," *American Magazine*, LXV (January–March), 227–236.

Substantial parts of the novel; see A335.

A335* *The Metropolis*. New York: Moffat, Yard and Co., *c.* 14 March. 376 pp.

Reprinted: Pasadena and Long Beach: The Author, 1923.
In part: A1545, A2049.

Foreign Editions: Braille, Bulgarian, Chinese, Czech, English-Canada, English, Estonian, Finnish, French, German, Italian, Japanese, Polish, Romanian, Russian, Serbo-Croatian, Yiddish.

A336 "Metropolis; Fairy Story," *Outlook*, LXXXVIII (25 April), 909–911.

A337 "Upton Sinclair Defends Himself," *New York Times* (*Saturday Review of Books*), 25 April, p. 240.

Concerning *The Jungle* and *The Metropolis*.

A338 "How Sinclair Knows the Smart Set," *Literary Digest*, XXVI (9 May), 687–688.

Extensive quotations by Sinclair in anonymous article.

A339 "Upon A Steamship, A Poem," *Independent*, LXIV (25 June), 1432.

Reprinted in *Current Opinion*, August; *Current Literature*, August. See also A469, A1545.

A340* "The Muckrake Man," *Independent*, LXV (3 September), 517–519.

Explains "psychology" of muckrakers: "He represents the effort of the race to profit by experience; . . . He is the forerunner of a revolution. . . ."

Appeared also in *Current Opinion*, August.

A341* *The Moneychangers*. New York: B. W. Dodge and Co., 19 September. 316 pp.

Reprinted: Pasadena: The Author, 1926 (rev. ed.); Upper Saddle River, N.J.: The Gregg Press, 1968 (introductory notes by Clarence Gohdes and F.C.S.).

Foreign Editions: Chinese, Czech, Dutch, English, Estonian, Finnish, French, German, Hebrew, Hungarian, Polish, Russian, Serbo-Croatian, Slovenian, Swedish, Yiddish.

A342* *A Plan for a Co-operative Group*. New York: Upton Sinclair, September. 8 pp.

Privately printed; outlines plan for a new colony similar to Helicon Hall.

A343* *Upton Sinclair's Report on the Bishop Creek Mines*. n.p., 20 October. 4 pp.

Open letter from Sinclair to H. G. Wilshire expressing confidence in the potentiality of Wilshire's gold mine.

A344 "Advice to a Stranger," *Town Talk*, XVII (19 December), 16.

1909

A345 "A Protest," *Independent*, LXVI (14 January), 84.

Against "slanderous" statements by Mrs. Harris, an *Independent* reviewer. Written from Palo Alto, California.

A346 "Sinclair on Marriage," *San Francisco Examiner*, 30 January, pp. 1–2.

Feature article reprinting an interview with Upton Sinclair. He hates the idea of legal ties: so does his wife of five [eight] years; marriage is merely legalized slavery. Gross misrepresentation of Sinclair's views in what purports to be a verbatim interview.

A347* *The Sinclair Players. Results of Opening Performances*. San Francisco, *c*. 1 February. 1 leaf.

Broadside proposal-letter concerning Sinclair's Socialist drama group.

1909 continued

A348 Upton Sinclair and Michael Williams. *Good Health and How We Won It.* New York: Frederick A. Stokes Co., *c.* 13 February. 302 pp.

Sinclair wrote the preface and revised the text, most of which was written by Williams.

Reprinted as *Health and Strength.* New York: F. A. Stokes Co., 1910.

Foreign Edition: English (as *The Art of Health*)

A349* "Socialism's Triumph in 1913," *Saturday Evening Post,* CLXXXI (8 May), 8–9.

Sinclair's contribution to an article: "Practical Socialism—Is There Any Such Thing?"

A350 "The Warren Defenders," *Appeal to Reason,* 19 June, p. 1.

Concerning Fred D. Warren, editor of the *Appeal.*

A351* "The Red Flag: A Poem," *The Socialist* [Melbourne, Australia], no. 167 (20 August), p. 3.

Reprinted in *Appeal to Reason,* 3 September; *Current Literature,* September. Dedicated to Fred D. Warren, editor of the *Appeal,* who had been sentenced to six months in jail.

A352 "War: A Manifesto Against It," *Clarion* [London], 27 August, pp. 1-2.

Reprinted in *Barrier Daily Truth* [New South Wales], 28 August; *Socialist* [Melbourne, Australia], 3 September; *Wilshire's,* XIII (September). As pamphlet: A361. Also with F47 as pamphlet: *Pass On Pamphlets* no. 27. London: The Clarion Press, 16 pp.

A353* "A New Helicon Hall," *Independent,* LXVII (9 September), 580–583.

Tells of his discovery of fast, "natural" food diet, and solicits replies from people interested in establishing a communal boarding school for boys.

A354* "A Drama With A Socialistic Moral," *Barrier Daily Truth* [New South Wales], 11 September, p. 1.

Also published as *The Second-Story Man* in *Wilshire's*, XIII (October); *New York Call*, 12, 19, 26 March 1911; *Plays of Protest*, New York: Mitchell Kennerley, 1912; and at Girard, Kansas: Haldeman-Julius (Little Blue Book no. 630), 1925.

Foreign Editions: Armenian, Czech, Dutch, German, Japanese, Latvian, Lithuanian, Polish, Russian, White-Russian.

A355* "De Inbreker," *De Notenkraker* [Amsterdam], no. 38 (19 September), pp. 7–8; no. 39 (26 September), pp. 7–8.

Apparently first appearance of *Second Story Man*, A412.

A356* "A Physical Culture School for Boys," *Physical Culture*, XXII (October), 357–360.

Program and prospectus for school for 8 to 10-year-old boys; never established.

A357* "Prince Hagen," *Physical Culture*, XXII (December, January–June 1910).

As novel: A261; as play: A360, A412.

A358* "Read This," *Everybody's Magazine*, XXI (December), 856–857.

Letters refer readers to an article written by Judge Benjamin B. Lindsey.

A359 *A Message of Socialism To Collegians*. Girard, Kansas: Appeal to Reason. 4 pp.

See A377.

A360 *Prince Hagen: A Drama in Four Acts*. Privately printed. 104 pp.

"*Prince Hagen* was tried out at the Valencia Theater, San Francisco, in January 1909. In the light of the experience thus gained, it has been entirely rewritten." See A261, A360, A412.

Reprinted: Girard, Kansas: Haldeman-Julius (Little Blue Book no. 633), 1925.

1909 continued

A361 *War: A Manifesto Against It.* Girard, Kansas: Appeal to Reason. New York: Wilshire Book Co. 8 pp.
Originally published: A352.

1910

A362* "The Indignant Subscriber: A Comedy," *Socialist Review*, IV (January), 398–400.
Reprinted with minor revisions in *Wilshire's Magazine*, August: A379.

A363* " 'John D.' An Adventure," *Wilshire's Magazine* [London], XIV (January), 3–5, 10–11.
A play. Performed by "Sinclair Players." Reprinted in *International Socialist Review*, January/February, pp. 463–480.

A364* "The Raw Food Table," *Physical Culture*, XXIII (January/February), 33–36, 137–140.
Appeared also in *Pacific Graphic*, October.

A365* "Some New Books," *Wilshire's Magazine* [London], XIV (February), 16.
Review of *Ann Veronica* by H. G. Wells, *A Certain Rich Man* by William Allen White, *Toil of Men* by Israel Querido.

A366* *Samuel the Seeker*. New York: B. W. Dodge and Co., 21 March. 315 pp.
Reprinted: Pasadena: Upton Sinclair, 1923; Racine, Wisconsin: Whitman, 1923. In part: A2049.
Foreign Editions: Chinese, Czech, Dutch, English-Australia, English, Finnish, French, Georgian-Caucasian, German, Gujarati, Hebrew, Hungarian, Polish, Romanian, Russian, Slovenian, Spanish, Swedish, Ukrainian, Yiddish.

A367 "Living on Raw Foods," *Collier's*, XLV (16 April), 37–38.

A368 "Starving For Health's Sake," *Contemporary Review*, XCVII (April), 429–440.

Appeared also in *Cosmopolitan*, May; *Hearst's International Magazine*, May.

Reprinted: A401.

A369* "*The Jungle*'s Aftermath, Part I," *Physical Culture*, XXIII (April), 354–358.

Part II, *Physical Culture*, XXIII (May), 503–506.

A370* "The Endowment of Genius," *New Age* [London], 16 June, pp. 157–159.

Reply to Alfred E. Randall's article in the 19 May issue.

A371 "Warren at St. Paul," *Clarion* [London], 24 June, p. 1.

Trial of Fred D. Warren, editor of *Appeal to Reason*.

A372* "The Ideal Diet—How May We Find It?" *Physical Culture*, XXIII (June), 380–382.

A373* Introduction to "*The Jungle*'s Aftermath," *Physical Culture*, XXIII (June), 547–554.

Article by Mrs. Ella Reeve Bloor.

A374 "The Ethics of Jesus," *Outlook*, XCV (23 July), 695–696.

A375* "The Endowment of Young Writers," *Independent*, LXIX (28 July), 170–176.

Reprints text of letter Sinclair sent to "over fifty of the leading writers of the United States and Europe" with the replies from Herbert Quick, H. G. Wells, John Bigelow, William De Morgan, Arnold Bennett, Eden Philpotts, Bliss Carman, Charles Edward Russell, Stewart Edward White, William James, Jack London, Henry Van Dyke, John Galsworthy, Frederick van Eeden, Edwin Markham, Gerald Stanley Lee.

A376* "Mothers: the Old and the New," *Physical Culture*, XXIV (July), 59–63.

1910 continued

A377* "Message of Socialism to Collegians," *Independent*, LXVIII (8 August), 353–358.

First delivered as an address before the Ruskin Club of Oakland, California; see A359.

A378* "The Endowment of Genius," *New Age* [London], 11 August, p. 356.

Prints letters he had received from G. B. Shaw and E. G. Craig concerning his plan to "endow genius."

A379 "The Indignant Subscriber," *Wilshire's Magazine* [London], XIV (August), 10–12.

A380* "The Truth about Fasting," *Physical Culture*, XXIV (August), 135–142.

A381 "Two Notable Books," *New Age* [London], 8 September, pp. 444–445.

Review of *Twentieth Century Socialism* by Edmond Kelley and *Karl Marx: His Life and Work* by John Spargo.

Reprinted in *Wilshire's Magazine,* XIV (15 September).

A382* "On Fasting: A Letter to the Editor," *Contemporary Review*, XCVIII (September 1910), 380–382.

Followed by letters by others about his article, A386.

A383* "Wheat—The King of Foods," *Physical Culture*, XXIV (September), 233–238.

A384* "Experiments with the Exclusive Meat Diet," *Physical Culture*, XXIV (October), 361–367.

Appeared also in *Pacific Graphic,* December.

A385 "The Raw Food Table," *Pacific Graphic*, I (October), 161–163.

A386* "Starving for Health's Sake," *Cosmopolitan*, XLVIII (October), 661–662 and 60, 68 in advertising section.

Follow-up of the reaction to May article; prints letters, including one of his own to the *New York Times* in protest over its treatment of him.

A387* "Diseases and Common Sense," *Physical Culture*, XXIV (November), 497–503.

A388* "The Humours of Fasting," *Contemporary Review* [London], XCVIII (December), 726–732.

A389* "My Golden Rule of Health," *Physical Culture*, XXIV (December), 613–617.

A390 Commander Luther G. Brownell [pseud.] *An Annapolis Adventure*; *or*, *Square Shooting*. New York: Street & Smith.

Allegedly by Sinclair; not seen.

A391 Letter. In *Francisco Ferrer. His Life, Work and Martyrdom*. New York: Ferrer Assoc.; San Francisco: [n.p.].

Not seen.

1911

A392 "Bewilderment," *Wilshire's Magazine*, XV (January), 10–12.

Appreciative essay-review of Robert Herrick's *A Life for a Life*.

A393* "New Year's Resolutions," *Physical Culture*, XXV (January), 49–55.

A394 "Socialist Fiction," *Clarion* [London], 24 February, p. 1.

Review of three "socialist novels": George Cram Cook's *The Chasm*, Charles Tenney Jackson's *My Brother's Keeper*, H. G. Wells' *The New Machiavelli*.

Appeared also in *Wilshire's Magazine*, February.

A395* "Fasting—the Foe of Sickness," *Cosmopolitan*, L (February), 328–336.

1911 continued

A396* "How Shall We Point the Way to Manhood?" *Physical Culture*, xxv (February), 183–188.

A397* "The Machine: A Drama in Three Acts," *New York Call*, 12 March, p. 14; 19 March, pp. 12, 16; 26 March, p. 12.

Reprinted: Girard, Kan.: Haldeman-Julius (Little Blue Book no. 632), 1925; see A412.

A398* *Love's Pilgrimage*. New York and London: Mitchell Kennerley, March. 663 pp.

Reprinted: Pasadena: The Author, 1926, with prefatory note to second edition; New York: Vanguard, 1929 (2 vols.)
In part: A1545, A2049.

Foreign Editions: Chinese, Czech, Danish, English, French, German, Gujarati, Hungarian, Polish, Romanian, Russian, Serbo-Croatian, Spanish, Swedish.

A399 *Four Letters about "Love's Pilgrimage,"* [n.p.]: The Author, *c.* April. 8 pp.

Letter (1) Robert Herrick to Upton Sinclair, pp. 1–4; (2) Upton Sinclair to Robert Herrick, pp. 4–6; (3) Frederick van Eeden to Upton Sinclair, pp. 6–7; (4) Eden Philpotts to Upton Sinclair, pp. 7–8.

A400 "The Controversy Over Fasting," *Current Literature*, L (May), 510–511.

A401* *The Fasting Cure*. New York: Mitchell Kennerley, May. 153 pp.

Most of this book was originally published as articles in 1910. 1911.

Reprinted: New York: Mitchell Kennerley, 1913; Los Angeles and Pasadena: The Author, 1923; [n.p.]: Health Research, 1955.

Foreign Editions: Danish, English, Tamil.

A402* "How, When, and Why to Fast," *Physical Culture*, xxv (May), 543–548.

A403* "The Principles of Scientific Management," *American Magazine*, LXXII (June), 243–244.

Criticism by Upton Sinclair and a reply by Frederick W. Taylor, pp. 244–245.

A404 "Returning to Nature," *Physical Culture*, XXV (June), 623–628.

A405 "The Spread of Fasting," *Physical Culture*, XXVI (August), 168–172.

A406* "Exercise for Brain Workers," *Physical Culture*, XXVI (September), 279–285.

A407 "Marriage and Divorce," *World To-Day*, XXI (October), 1197–1201.

Appeared also in *Hearst's Magazine*, October.

A408* "Daring to be a Daniel," *Physical Culture*, XXVI (November), 461–467.

A409* "Some Comments on Books," *New York Call*, 3 December, p. 13.

Review of Archibald Henderson's *George B. Shaw*, A. M. Simons' *Social Forces in American History*, Hudson Maxim's *The Science of Poetry*, Sir Oliver Lodge's *The Survival of Man*, Theodore Dreiser's *Jennie Gerhardt*, David Graham Phillips's *The Conflict*, Susan Glaspell's *The Visioning*, and Robert Herrick's *The Healer*.

A410* "The Health of Little Algernon, Being the Story of a Twenty Million Dollar Quest for Health," *Physical Culture*, XXVI (December), XXVII (January–June 1912).

A411 "Divorce and Public Health," *Physical Culture*, XXVI (December), 316–320.

1912

A412* *Plays of Protest*. New York: Mitchell Kennerley, 15 January. 226 pp.

See separate entries for: *The Naturewoman*, *The Machine*, *The Second-Story Man*, *Prince Hagen* (A354, A357, A397, A974, A1020).

Reprinted: St. Clair Shores, Mich.: Scholarly Press, 1970 (facsimile).

A413* "How Censorship Actually Works," *Everybody's Magazine*, XXVI (January), 135–136.

Tells of meeting in the Newcastle, Delaware Workhouse a man jailed for several months because he could not provide bail while the Post Office Department's case against him for mailing an "obscene" book was pending.

A414 "F. T. Cook's *Life of Ruskin*," *Milwaukee Leader*, 19 February, p. 8.

A415 "The Syndicalist," *The Coming Nation*, no. 85 n. s. (22 April), p. 11.

A416* *The International League*. Chicago: Charles H. Kerr, *c*. April. 2 pp.

Plus "An International Peace Tribunal of Labor," 1 p., not by Sinclair.

A417* "How Stands Old England's Health?" *Physical Culture*, XXVIII (July), 7–11.

A418* "A Health-Seeker in Italy," *Physical Culture*, XXVIII (August), 134–138.

A419* "A Bold Plan," *New York Call*, 15 September, p. 10.

A420* "What a Physical Culturist Sees in Germany," *Physical Culture*, XXVIII (September), 256–260.

A421* "*The Fasting Cure* in Europe," *Physical Culture*, XXVIII (October), 391–396.

A422* "The Convict," *Labour Leader* [Manchester, England], 7 November 1912–2 January 1913, pp. 715, 716, 733, 751, 765, 780, 796, 812, 834; (1913), p. 11.

This transparently autobiographical weekly serial was published while Sinclair was in England waiting for his divorce.

A423 "The Cost of Living in Europe," *Physical Culture*, XXVIII (November), 491–496.

A424* "The Diet Problem in Europe," *Physical Culture*, XXVIII (December), 631–638.

A425 "Making Real Men of Our Boys," *Physical Culture*, XXVIII (December), 47–53.

1913

A427* "Paris and the Parisites," *Physical Culture*, XXIX (January), 61–66.

How French cheat American tourists.

A428* "The Real Marriage—What It Is," *Physical Culture*, XXIX (February), 129–133.

A429* "Fasting Experiments and Experiences," *Physical Culture*, XXIX (March), 227-232.

A430* "Happy Marriage: How Can It Be Assured?" *Physical Culture*, XXIX (April), 297–302.

Plea to legalize the dissemination of "sex harmony" information.

A431 "On Re-Reading Homer," *The New Statesman*, 10 May, p. 145.

"There is more real passion, more fire and colour, more philosophic depth and absolute human value, in any volume of of Sienkiewicz's *Polish Trilogy* than there is in the Homeric poems." Recommends Veblen's *Theory of the Leisure Class* to college graduates.

1913 continued

A432* *Sylvia*. Philadelphia and Chicago: The John C. Winston Co., 15 May. 413 pp.

Reprinted: Long Beach and Pasadena: The Author, 1913, 1927; St. Clair Shores, Mich.: Scholarly Press, 1970 (facsimile).
In part: A2049.

Foreign Editions: Czech, Dutch, English, Flemish, Hungarian, Polish, Russian.

A433 "Some Light on the Race Suicide Question," *Physical Culture*, XXIX (May), 427–433.

A434* "Damaged Goods," *Physical Culture*, XXIX (June–November).

As book: A438.

A435* "Mr. Upton Sinclair's Speech," *The Citizen* [Letchworth, England], 15 August, p. 2.

At open-air meeting to protest arrest of George Lansbury and others for allegedly seditious speech in Albert Hall.

A436 "Upton Sinclair Against the One-Leg Dance," *Wilshire's Magazine* [London], XVII (August/September), 1.

Letter regarding usefulness of ballet in advancing Socialism; see A439.

A437* "The Sculptor of Revolt," *Independent*, LXXVI (16 October), 128–130.

Essay on exhibition of J. Mowbray-Clarke's work.

A438* *Damaged Goods*. Philadelphia: The John C. Winston Co., 18 October. 194 pp.

As serial: A434.

Reprinted: Pasadena: The Author, 1932; Girard, Kansas: Haldeman-Julius Publications (B-710), 1948.

Foreign Editions: Czech, English, Gujarati, Malayalam, Marathi, Russian.

A439* "A Butterfly Net for a Rhinoceros Hunt: A Continuation of the Upton Sinclair-Wilshire Debate," *Wilshire's Magazine* [London], XVII (October), 1–5.

A440 "Six Authors," *New York Sun*, 23 November.

Replies to charges of frankness when dealing with "matters of sex and questions of sex hygiene." Signed by Jack London, Reginald Wright Kauffman, Upton Sinclair, Daniel Carson Goodman, James Oppenheim, T. Everett Harre.

A441* "Socialist Propaganda on the High Seas," *Appeal to Reason*, 6 December, p. 2.

A442 "Sinclair Challenges Hapgood to 'Make Good,'" *Appeal to Reason*, 13 December, p. 1.

A443* "Mr. Sinclair Protests," *Life*, LXII (25 December), 1162.

Letter to editor protesting magazine's treatment of his private life and review of *Sylvia*.

A444* "Sinclair Appeals to Wilson," *New York Times*, 30 December, p. 3.

Text of telegram sent to President Wilson following the abduction of Charles H. Moyer, President of the Western Federation of Miners, at Calumet, Michigan.

A445* "Why and How We Must Conquer the Social Evil," *Physical Culture*, XXX (December), 583–588.

On prostitution.

1914

A446* "A Christmas Letter," *New York Call*, 3 January, p. 6.

Letter dated 20 December 1913 appealing to Mr. Vincent Astor to help the "dispossessed" with his fabulous wealth. Also published in *Appeal to Reason*, 10 January, and *New York Times*, 12 January, and as separate pamphlet: A461.

1914 continued

A447* "The War of the Sexes," *Physical Culture*, XXI (January), 7–12.

A448* "Vincent Astor's Reply is Shattered to Bits by Upton Sinclair," *Appeal to Reason*, 14 February, p. 5.

A449* "Her Two Ventures," *Physical Culture*, XXXI (February), 117–125.

A450* "To Marry or Not to Marry?" *Physical Culture*, XXXI (March), 223–228.

Against "free-love."

A451* "The Millennium: A Story," *Appeal to Reason*, 19 April–1 August.

Eighteen chapters in sixteen consecutive weekly installments. As book: A976.

A452* "The Laying on of Hands," *Hearst's International Magazine*, XXV (April), 467–476.

On his experiences "curing" Mary Craig Sinclair.

A453* "John D. and Governor of Colorado Lied to President Wilson, and Associated Press Suppressed the Facts," *Appeal to Reason*, 30 May, pp. 1–2.

On Colorado coal strike and the use of federal troops to restore order.

A454 "Press Silent About Lindsey Departure," *Appeal to Reason*, 30 May, p. 1.

On Colorado coal strike.

A455* "Wage Slaves in Colorado," *Business America*, XV (May), 497–502.

A456* "To Frank Tannenbaum in Prison," *International Socialist Review*, XIV (June), 756.

A poem.

A457* *A Collection of the Literature of Socialism.* Croton-on-Hudson, New York, July. 1 leaf.

Broadside requesting help for anthology, *The Cry for Justice*; see A469.

A458* "The Marseillaise in the Tombs," *International Socialist Review*, xv (July), 24.

Poem written while in Tombs prison for "picketing" John D. Rockefeller's office.

A459* *Sylvia's Marriage.* Philadelphia and Chicago: The John C. Winston Co., *c.* 26 September. 348 pp.

Reprinted: Pasadena and Long Beach: The Author, 1928; New York: A. & C. Boni, 1928.

Foreign Editions: Chinese, Czech, Dutch, English Flemish, Polish, Russian.

A460* "*A Circular Letter . . . to Various Recipients.* Croton-on-Hudson: Upton Sinclair, 1 October. 1 leaf.

A461 *The Sinclair-Astor Letters: Famous Correspondence between Socialist and Millionaire.* Girard, Kansas: Appeal to Reason. 32 pp.

Including Edward Bellamy's *The Parable of the Water Tank.*

A462 *The Social Problem As Seen from the Viewpoint of Trade Unionism, Capital and Socialism.* New York: Industrial Economics Dept. of the National Civic Federation. 53 pp.

Pamphlet, with Vincent Astor and others; see A461. Not seen.

1915

A463 *Circular Letter.* Croton-on-Hudson: The Author, January. 1 leaf.

Concerning proposed anthology of social protest.

1915 continued

A464* "Satire That Failed," *Clarion* [London], 19 March, p. 6.

About Mrs. Sinclair's poem, "Challenge," satirizing German "kultur" but printed by the pro-German *Fatherland* which failed to see satirical intent. See also "None So Blind," *Harper's Weekly*, 27 March 1915.

A465 Letter, *The Masses*, VII (April), 24.

Protesting laws prohibiting circulation of birth-control information.

A466* "What Terms of Peace Shall Close Them?" *Clarion* [London], 7 May, p. 3.

Forecasts constructive social revolution in Germany after the war unless the terms of the peace are "so humiliating as to leave a permanent sense of wrong" in the hearts of the Germans and thus make another war inevitable.

A467* *Circular Letter*. Gulfport, Miss.: The Author, 25 May. 1 leaf.

Proposed open-letter to John D. Rockefeller, Jr.

A468* *Circular Letter*. Gulfport, Miss.: The Author, 17 June. 1 leaf.

Open letter to John D. Rockefeller, Jr. (proposed above, A467); from Frank Shay, New York City, and Sinclair, Gulfport, Miss.

A469* *The Cry for Justice*. Philadelphia: The John C. Winston Co., *c*. 26 September. 891 pp.

Reprinted: Pasadena: The Author, 1921, with dedicatory note to Dr. John Haynes; Girard, Kansas: Haldeman-Julius, 1944; New York: Lyle Stuart, 1963 (rev. ed.).

Foreign Edition: Russian.

A470* *A Proposition for the First Serial Rights of a New Novel* King Coal *by Upton Sinclair*. *c*. 15 October. 1 leaf.

See A472, A491.

A471* "After the War: A Forecast," *American Socialist*, II (30 October), 2.

A472* "*King Coal*," Gulfport, Miss.: Jungle Publishing Co., *c.* 27 November. 4 pp.

Portion of *King Coal* plus synopsis of remainder.

A473* "I Met Them, Will," *New York Call*, 19 December, p. 5, Mag. Sect.

In poem dedicated to Will Dyson, cartoonist of the *London Herald*, Sinclair claims to have met the real-life counterparts of a fat capitalist and his wife drawn in caricature.

A474* "His Five Wives," *Physical Culture*, XXXIV–XXXV (December and January–May 1916).

1916

A475* "*Wilshire Bishop Creek Mine*," [n.p.], 28 July. 4 pp.

Subtitled: "A Report by the Upton Sinclair Committee on the Audit made by the Audit Company of Los Angeles." Includes letter from Sinclair to Gaylord Wilshire.

A476 "[Jack] London's Work 'Bugle Call' to the Soul," *San Francisco Bulletin*, 23 November, p. 7. (See A477.)

A477 "A Sad Loss to American Literature," *Oakland Tribune*, 23 November, p. 13.

On Jack London's death; appeared also in California's Writer's Club *Quarterly Bulletin*, no. 4, pp. 3–4.

A478* "Vers Libertinism, A Challenge by Upton Sinclair," *The Masses*, IX (November), 19–20.

Attack on "free verse" and "poly-rhythmics."

A479 "The Interesting Career of Jack London," *Oakland World*, 1 December, p. 3.

A480 "Truth," *New Age*, XX (7 December), 127–128.

Address delivered before a dinner of Southern California Women's Press Club, Los Angeles, 24 October 1916.

1916 continued

A481 "The Socialist's Speech." In *The Socialist Appeal; Prose Passages Which Voice the Call for a New Social Order.* Appeal Socialist Classic, no. 11. Girard, Kansas: Appeal to Reason, pp. 18–19.

Reprinted from *The Jungle*, pp. 358–360.
Second edition: 1918, published by *The New Appeal.*

1917

A482 "Reflections of a Strong Man," *The Masses*, IX (January), 39.

A483 "Jack London," *New Age*, XX (1 March), 421–423.

A484* "Democratic Defense: A Practical Program for Socialism," *New Republic*, X (31 March), 262–263.

Statement from group of prominent American Socialists; signed by W. J. Ghent, Charmian London, Charles Edward Russell, Mary Craig Sinclair, Upton Sinclair, George Sterling, J. G. Phelps Stokes, and William English Walling.

A485* "The Price I Paid," *Pearson's Magazine*, XXXVIII (April), 320–321.

Letter to A. Maurice Low, Esq. Reprinted: A493, A1947.

A486* "A Society Doctor," *Physical Culture*, XXXVII–XXXVIII (May–August).

A487* "Letter of Resignation," *Chicago Sunday Tribune*, 22 July, p. 5.

Sinclair's resignation from Socialist Party; Sinclair believed America should enter the war and defeat German militarism. Also printed in *New York Call.*

A488* "A Socialist Peace," *Pearsons' Magazine*, XXXVIII (August), 81-83, 86–87.

As offprint. Pasadena: The Author, 6 pp.

A489* *King Coal*. New York: Macmillan Co., September. 396 pp.

With an introduction by Dr. Georg Brandes. Reprinted: Condensed, 1918; Pasadena: Upton Sinclair, 1921 and 1930.

Foreign Editions: Azerbaijani, Bulgarian, Chinese, Czech, Danish, Dutch, English-France, English, Finnish, French, Georgian-Caucasian, German, Hebrew, Hungarian, Icelandic, Japanese, Lithuanian, Norwegian, Polish, Russian, Serbo-Croatian, Spanish, Swedish, Turkman, Ukrainian, Uzbek, Yiddish.

A490 "About Jack London," *The Masses*, x (November/December), 17–20.

A491* "A Socialist and Sinclair," *Pearson's Magazine*, XXXVIII (November), 219-221.

A letter from a poor Socialist who was upset by Sinclair's resignation from the Socialist Party; Sinclair's reply; and editorial comment on Sinclair's reply and attitude.

A492* *Letter to J. F. Kerensky, Minister of Justice, Petrograd, Russia*. [n.p.] 1 leaf.

From unidentified newspaper. Sinclair urges that Catalina island be made a refuge for the deposed crowned heads of European countries. "Colony of ex-rulers off L.A. Coast urged."

A493 "*The Price I Paid*." Pasadena: The Author.

Offprint; see A485, A494.

A494* "*Upton Sinclair; Biographical and Critical Opinions*." Pasadena: The Author. 32 pp.

Includes "The Price I Paid;" see A485, A493.

1918

A495 "King Coal," *Hearst's International Magazine*, XXXIII (January), 44, 70–71.

As book: A489.

1918 continued

A496* "Two Socialist Poets," *Pearson's Magazine*, XXXVIII (January), 314-315.

Discusses poetry of Gerald Lively and Robert P. Scripps.

A497* "Peace and Its Meaning," *Western Comrade*, V (March/April), 20, 37.

Text of address to Commercial Board of Los Angeles, 4 February, 1918.

A498 Editorial, *Upton Sinclair's*, I (April), 1.

A499* "A Credential," *Upton Sinclair's*, I (April), 2.

A500* "A Clean Peace," *Upton Sinclair's*, I (April), 3–5.

A501* "The Internation," *Upton Sinclair's*, I (April), 5.

A502* "Socialism and War," *Upton Sinclair's*, I (April), 5–7.

Reprints most of "War: A Manifesto Against It" and explains why he now believes Germany must be fought and defeated. See A352.

A503* "A California Crime-Factory," *Upton Sinclair's*, I (April), 7–8.

A504* "The Profits of Religion," *Upton Sinclair's*, I (April–September).

As book: A543.

A505* "The Business Side," *Upton Sinclair's*, I (April), 16.

Sinclair explains desire to be his own publisher and how he hopes to support the enterprise.

A506* Editorial, *Upton Sinclair's*, I (May/June), 2.

A507* "Our Smiles to the Censor," *Upton Sinclair's*, I (May–June), 2.

Explains difficulties encountered in getting magazine approved for mailing by the Post Office Department.

A508* "Teaching by Force," *Upton Sinclair's*, I (May/June), 2.

A509* "The Emergence of Labor," *Upton Sinclair's*, I (May/June), 3–6.

"I happen to be one of those who believe that the salvation of humanity depends on thinking."

A510* "The Battle of France," *Upton Sinclair's*, I (May/June), 7.

A511* "Mrs. Gertrude Atherton," *Upton Sinclair's*, I (May/June), 7.

A512* "How Sharper Than a Serpent's Tooth," *Upton Sinclair's*, I (May/June), 7.

About ungrateful and "envenomed" Michael Williams, co-author of *Good Health and How We Won It*; see A348.

A513* "The Palma Case," *Upton Sinclair's*, I (May/June), 7.

A514* Letters and Notes, *Upton Sinclair's*, I (May/June), 8.

A515* "Concerning Advertisements," *Upton Sinclair's*, I (May/June), 16.

A516* "Farmers of America," *Upton Sinclair's*, I (May/June), 16.

Urges support of the non-partisan *Leader* [St. Paul, Minnesota].

A517* "Supplement," to *Upton Sinclair's*, I (May).

Enclosed as a four page "Supplement" to the May/June issue: three pages of letters pro and con on the first issue and on page four a reprint of the front page editorial of first (April) issue.

A519* *Circular Letter*. Pasadena: The Author, 9 July. 1 leaf.

Concerning President Wilson's treatment of conscientious objectors.

A520 "[Frank] Harris's Life of Oscar Wilde," *Pearson's Magazine*, XXXIX (July), 167–169.

1918 continued

A521* Editorial, *Upton Sinclair's*, I (July), 1.

Calls for conscription of wealth. Government should take eighty per cent of incomes over five thousand dollars, one hundred per cent of incomes over ten thousand dollars.

A522* "A Letter from H. G. Wells," *Upton Sinclair's*, I (July), 2.

Wells describes Lenin as "just a Russian Sidney Webb." Sinclair tells of his long acquaintanceship with Wells.

A523* "The Alberich Line," *Upton Sinclair's*, I (July), 3–4.

A524* "Money-Land and No-Money Land," *Upton Sinclair's*, I (July), 6–7.

A525* "The High Romance," *Upton Sinclair's*, I (July), 7.

About Michael Williams, co-author of *Good Health and How We Won It* (1910); see A348, A512.

A526* "Gertrude Atherton," *Upton Sinclair's*, I (July), 7.

A527* "To President Wilson," *Upton Sinclair's*, I (July), 16.

A528* "Gentlemen of America," *Upton Sinclair's*, I (August), 1.

A529* Editorial, *Upton Sinclair's*, I (August), 1.

A530* "Dividing Up," *Upton Sinclair's*, I (August), 2.

A531* "Sherlock Holmes at War," *Upton Sinclair's*, I (August), 3–5.

A532* "A Telegram for Russia," *Upton Sinclair's*, I (August), 5.

To President Woodrow Wilson.

A533* "An Attack of Appendicitis," *Upton Sinclair's*, I (August), 6–8.

Sinclair reports on books he has read while convalescing from appendectomy: from Russia (Dostoevsky "has no vision, either political or social"), Austria, South America, France, Holland, England.

A534* "John Reed vs. Maxim Gorky," *Upton Sinclair's*, I (August), 8.

Chiefly letter from Reed explaining Gorky's recent statements concerning the Russian Revolution.

A535* "Our Letter Box,"*Upton Sinclair's*, I (August), 16.

A536* Editorial, *Upton Sinclair's*, I (September), 1 .

A537* "*Jimmie Higgins*: An Announcement," *Upton Sinclair's*, I (September), 2.

Announces that he has been working on *Jimmie Higgins* between putting out issues of the magazine and that it will be published serially beginning with the next issue.

A538* "Capitalist vs. Socialist Peace," *Upton Sinclair's*, I (September), 3–5.

A539* "An Appeal to President Wilson," *Upton Sinclair's*, I (September), 5.

For special treatment of "political prisoners."

A540* "Notes," *Upton Sinclair's*, I (September), 6.

A541* "Economic Peace," *Upton Sinclair's*, I (September), 7.

A542* "Mr. Mencken and the Hen," *Upton Sinclair's*, I

Concerning H. L. Mencken's cynicism.

A543* *The Profits of Religion*. Pasadena: The Author, *c*. 15 October. 315 pp.

Sinclair's review, A598.

As serial: A504. Reprinted: Pasadena: The Author, 1926; New York: Vanguard, 1927, 1931, 1938; Girard, Kansas: Haldeman-Julius Publications, 1947; St. Clair Shores, Mich.: Scholarly Press, 1970 (facsimile). In part: A1545, A2049.

Foreign Editions: Chinese, Dutch, English, German, Japanese, Russian, Serbo-Croatian, Swedish.

1918 continued

A544* Editorial, *Upton Sinclair's*, I (October), 1.

A545* "To Our Readers," *Upton Sinclair's*, I (October), 2.

A546* "Premiums," *Upton Sinclair's*, I (October), 2.
Profits of Religion ready first week in September or at least by 1 October; see A543.

A547* "Remaking the World," *Upton Sinclair's*, I (October), 3–5.

A548* "Conscription of Wealth," *Upton Sinclair's*, I (October), 6.

A549* "Concerning 'Political Prisoners,' " *Upton Sinclair's*, I (October), 6–7.

A550* "Jimmie Higgins Goes to War," *Upton Sinclair's*, I (October–December, January–February, 1919).
Serial continued in *Appeal to Reason*: final installment published 9 August 1919. As book: A624.

A551* "A Riot in the Editorial Sanctum," *Upton Sinclairs'*, I (October), 16.

A552* Editorial, *Upton Sinclair's*, I (November), 1.

A553* "More About Political Prisoners," *Upton Sinclair's*, I (November), 2.

A554* "Free Speech in Wartime," *Upton Sinclair's*, I (November), 3–4.

A555* "The Peace Offer," *Upton Sinclair's*, I (November), 4.

A556* "The Problem of Russia," *Upton Sinclair's*, I (November), 5.

A557* "American Journalism," *Upton Sinclair's*, I (November), 6.

A558* "Henry Dubb at School," *Upton Sinclair's*, I (November), 7.

A559* "Sherlock Holmes Again," *Upton Sinclair's*, I (November), 7.

A560* "A Visit From an Angel," *Upton Sinclair's*, I (November), 16.

A561* "A German for World-President," *Upton Sinclair's*, I (November), 1–2.

A562* "An Effort at Prophecy," *Upton Sinclair's*, I (November), 2–4.

A563* "When Is a Subscription Blank?" *Upton Sinclair's*, I (November), 3.

A564* "A Friend in Need," *Upton Sinclair's*, I (November), 4.

A565* "*The Profits of Religion.*" Pasadena: Upton Sinclair, *c.* November.

Twenty page pamphlet (pp. 92–109 of book) printed at the request of Eugene V. Debs. Variant copy bears letter from John Haynes Holmes on front cover. One with a comment from Eugene Debs. See A543.

A566 "All About Love," *Pearson's Magazine*, XL (November), 42.

Frank Harris and Mrs. Champ Clark also contribute.

A567* Editorial, *Upton Sinclair's*, I (December), 1.

A568* "The Lion's Den," *Upton Sinclair's*, I (December), 2.

A569* "John Reed on the Bolsheviki," *Upton Sinclair's*, I (December), 3–4.

A570* "Christian Science," *Upton Sinclair's*, I (December), 4.

1918 continued

A571* "Social Insurance," *Upton Sinclair's*, I (December), 4–5.

A572* "Prince Hopkins and Free Speech," *Upton Sinclair's*, I (December), 6.

A573* "The Blind Who Will Not See," *Upton Sinclair's*, I (December), 16.

A574* "Sacred Egoism," *Upton Sinclair's*, I (December), 16.

1919

A575* Editorial, *Upton Sinclair's*, I (January), 1.

A576* "A Change of Policy," *Upton Sinclair's*, I (January), 2.

A577* "To Our Readers," *Upton Sinclair's*, I (January), 2.

A578* "What About Bolshevism?" *Upton Sinclair's*, I (January), 3–4.

A579* "Watchful Waiting," *Upton Sinclair's*, I (January), 5.

A580* "An Appeal for Amnesty," *Upton Sinclair's*, I (January), 5.

A581* "Taxes for the Rich," *Upton Sinclair's*, I (January), 5–6.

A582* "New Books," *Upton Sinclair's*, I (January), 6.
Brief comments on Ibañez's *The Four Horsemen of the Apocalypse*, H. G. Wells' *Joan and Peter: The Story of an Education*, Louise Bryant's *My Six Months in Russia*, Bessie Beatty's *The Red Heart of Russia*, Alice S. Blackwell's *The Little Grandmother of the Russian Revolution*.

A583* "A Telegram that Succeeded," *Upton Sinclair's*, I (January), 7.
To California's Governor Stephens concerning Tom Mooney.

A584* "The Bolshevik at the Country Club," *Upton Sinclair's*, I (January), 16.

A585* "Supplement," *Upton Sinclair's*, I (January), unpaged.

A586* "Amnesty for Political Prisoners," *Upton Sinclair's*, I (January), 1–3.

Letters from prisoners describing horrible treatment and jail conditions.

A587* "The Clean Slate League," *Upton Sinclair's*, I (January), 3.

A588* "An Appeal to the President," *Upton Sinclair's*, I (January), 4.

A589* Editorial, *Upton Sinclair's*, I (February), 1.

A590* "Concerning *The Profits of Religion*," *Upton Sinclair's*, I (February), 2.

A591* "What Is Coming in Germany?" *Upton Sinclair's*, I (February), 3–4.

A592* "Abolish the Censorship!" *Upton Sinclair's*, I (February), 5.

A593* "The Conscience-Striken Millionaire," *Upton Sinclair's*, I (February), 6.

A594* "The Red Flag," *Upton Sinclair's*, I (February), 7.
First published: A351.

A595* "Christian Science Again," *Upton Sinclair's*, I (February), 7.

A596* "Our Office," *Upton Sinclair's*, I (February), 16.

Tells how five houses were bought and pieced together to make enough room to publish the magazine. Final issue of *Upton Sinclair's*.

1919 continued

A597* "Upton Sinclair's," *New Appeal*, 8 February, p. 3.

a. "Goodbye, Teddy Roosevelt"

b. "Plea for Unity" [Among liberal factions against "Capitalist reactionaries."]

c. "Sinclairograms"

A598* "*The Profits of Religion*," *Chicago Daily News*, 12 February. 1 leaf.

Broadside reprint of Sinclair's review of his own book; see A543.

A599* "Upton Sinclair's," *New Appeal*, 15 February, p. 4.

a. "Selling Climate" [On business in Pasadena during the influenza epidemic.]

b. "A Rebel in Jail" [Letter and poem from Ralph Chaplin, then serving a twenty year jail sentence as an IWW conspirator.]

c. "The Revolution" [Relates Sinclair's argument with Mary Craig Sinclair over Socialism and human nature.]

d. Miscellaneous

A600 Upton Sinclair's," *New Appeal*, 22 February, p. 4.

a. "The Russian Debt" [On Bolsheviks' refusal to pay fifteen billion dollar debt of Tsars.]

b. "Labor's Crimes" [On migrant laborers.]

c. "Rail Men Awake" [On Railroad Brotherhood's plans to share railroad profits with government.]

d. "Dollar Worship"

A601* "Good News" [from an unidentified periodical dated February 1919, p. 13].

A602* "Upton Sinclair's Page," *Appeal to Reason*, 1 March, p. 6.

a. "Let Us Have Peace" [Plea for release of "political prisoners," etc.]

b. "The Single Tax" [Land tax not sufficient.]

A603 "Upton Sinclair's Page," *Appeal to Reason*, 8 March, p. 4.

a. "A Catholic Miracle" [On program for social betterment proposed by several Catholic Bishops.]

b. "Unemployment"

c. "Mental Foot-binding" [Promises to write a book on education with this title.]

A604 "Upton Sinclair's Page," *Appeal to Reason*, 15 March, p. 4.

Long account of his interview-walk with Henry Ford.

A605 "Upton Sinclair Protest Against Persecution of Bible Students," *Appeal to Reason*, 22 March, p. 1.

Bible students were conscientious objectors.

A606 "Upton Sinclair's Page," *Appeal to Reason*, 29 March, p. 4.

a. "What the Soviets Are"

b. "Our Heroes at Home"

A607* *Circular Letter*. Pasadena: The Author, *c.* March. 1 leaf.

Announcing publication of *Jimmie Higgins*, A624.

A608 "Russia: A Challenge," *Appeal to Reason*, 5 April, p. 1.

As pamphlet: A612.

A609 "Upton Sinclair's Page," *Appeal to Reason*, 12 April, p. 2.

"Censorship and Secret Treaties"

A610 "Upton Sinclair's Page," *Appeal to Reason*, 19 April, pp. 2, 4.

a. "The League of Old Men," pp. 2, 4

b. "Picket the Prison," p. 4

A611 "Spirit of Debs Cannot Be Shut Up Behind Walls of Steel or Stone," *Appeal to Reason*, 26 April, p. 1.

1919 continued

A612* *Russia: A Challenge*. Girard, Kansas: *Appeal to Reason*, 26 April, 24 pp.

See A608.

Reprinted: *New Justice*, I (1 May), 12–15.

A613* "Strangling the News," *New Justice*, I (1 May), 3–6.

A614 "A Series of Communications," *New Justice*, I (1 May), 11.

Exchange of letters between Upton Sinclair and Dr. Albert Shiels, Supt. of Los Angeles schools, in which latter refuses to debate on Russia with either Upton Sinclair or Louise Bryant.

A615 "Upton Sinclair's Page," *Appeal to Reason*, 3 May, p. 4.

"Strangling the Truth" [Sinclair uses the press coverage of Louise Bryant's talk on Russia as evidence for a book he is writing on American journalism, tentatively titled: "A Glimpse of Journalism Through an Editor's Eyes"; see A676.]

A616 "Upton Sinclair's Page," *Appeal to Reason*, 10 May, p. 4.

a. "Hell Holes in America" [Sedgwick County Jail, Witchita, Kansas.]

b. "Our Friends in Jail"

c. "New Books" [Emile Vanderveld's *Socialism Versus the State*; Samuel Hopkins Adams's *Common Cause*; W. A. White's *In the Heart of a Fool.*]

d. "Nationalized Women" [Scoffs at allegations that Russian women are nationalized.]

A617 "Upton Sinclair's Page," *Appeal to Reason*, 17 May, p. 4.

a. "A New 'Preaching Order' " [On Socialist scheme to alleviate poverty.]

b. "Reminiscences" [Sinclair's of Crown Prince Frederick Wilhelm Hohenzollern and Walter Rathenau.]

c. Miscellaneous.

A618 "Socialism and Prohibition," *Appeal to Reason*, 24 May, p. 2.

Goes on record as opposing "No Beer, No Work" movement.

A619 "Upton Sinclair's Page," *Appeal to Reason*, 24 May, p. 2.

a. "Kings and Kinks"

b. "Concerning Violence"

c. "Revolutionary Philosophers" [Review of Morrison I. Swift's *Can Mankind Survive?*]

d. "Reply to a Critic" [Of *Profits of Religion*]

e. "Killing Rabbits and Men" [On *The Life of Frederick S. Courtenay.*]

A620 "Upton Sinclair's Page," *Appeal to Reason*, 31 May, p. 4.

a. "Commercialism and 'War' "

b. "The Peace Terms"

c. "Jabbergrab"

A621* "Henry Ford Tells How Happy His Great Fortune has Made Him—And Why," *Reconstruction: A Herald of the New Time*, I (May) 129–132.

A622 "Censorship and Secret Treaties," [Viereck's] *American Monthly*, X (May), 69–70.

A623* Introduction to *Hellaloo Pete O'Reno*, by Jim Seymour. Pasadena: Upton Sinclair, *c*. May. 17 pp.

Introduction, pp. [1–2].

A624* *Jimmie Higgins*. New York: Boni and Liveright; Pasadena: Upton Sinclair, c. May. 282 pp.

As serial: A550.

Reprinted: New York: A & C. Boni, 1929; Pasadena and Los Angeles: Upton Sinclair, 1933; Lexington: The Universities Press of Kentucky, 1970. In part: A2049.

Foreign Editions: Azerbaijani, Bulgarian, Chinese, Czech, Dutch, English, Esperanto, Finnish, French, German, Hungarian, Icelandic, Italian, Japanese, Latvian, Lettish, Macedonian, Norwegian, Polish, Portuguese, Romanian, Russian, Serbo-Croatian, Slovenian, Spanish, Swedish, Tatar, Ukrainian, Yiddish.

1919 continued

A625 "Upton Sinclair's Page," *Appeal to Reason*, 7 June. p. 4.

a. "How Shall We Get Peace?"

b. Miscellaneous

A626 "Upton Sinclair's Page," *Appeal to Reason*, 14 June, p. 4.

a. "Our Contemporaries" [Praise of *The New Republic, Reconstruction, Pearson's Magazine*.]

b. "High-Life and High-Ball"

c. "Democracy and Lumber"

d. "Widows and Orphans"

e. "Our Stolen Senate"

A627 "Upton Sinclair's Page," *Appeal to Reason*, 21 June, p. 4.

a. "The New Holy Alliance"

b. "Art Under Bolsheviks"

c. "Wanted: A Land Tax Bill"

d. "Strangling Russia"

e. "The Chorus of the Critics"

A628 "Upton Sinclair's Page," *Appeal to Reason*, 28 June, p. 4.

a. "Criminal Capitalism"

b. "What Is Fame"

c. "The Kept Press"

d. "New Books" [Clement Wood's *The Earth Turns South*; John Niehardt's *The Song of Three Friends*; Albert Mordell's *The Erotic Motive in Literature*; J. D. Beresford's *The Jervaise Comedy*; W. L. George's *Blind Alley*; J. C. Smith's *The Undefeated*; Henri Barbusse's *Clarte*; Johan Bojer's *The Great Hunger*.]

A629* "Desmond's Democracy," *Chicago Daily News*, 2 July, p. 12.

Review of Shaw Desmond's book. Offprint: *Chicago Daily News*, 1919, 1 leaf.

A630 "And Meantime Debs Stays in Jail," *Appeal to Reason*, 5 July, p. 3.

A631 "Upton Sinclair's Page," *Appeal to Reason*, 12 July, p. 3.
  a. "The Revolt in Europe and Capitalist Lies About It"
  b. "The War on Russia"

A632 "Upton Sinclair's Page," *Appeal to Reason*, 19 July, p. 4.
  a. "Russia and Democracy"

A633 "Upton Sinclair's Page," *Appeal to Reason*, 26 July, p. 4.
  a. "Don't Let Them Fool You" [Bolshevik "scare" is nothing but propaganda by capitalists to keep workingmen down.]
  b. "Gompers on Prohibition"
  c. Miscellaneous

A634 "Upton Sinclair vs. George Sylvester Viereck," [Viereck's] *American Monthly*, x (July), 149.

A635 "Upton Sinclair's Page," *Appeal to Reason*, 2 August, p. 4.
  a. "Being Bourgeois" [On Dr. Frank Crane.]
  b. "Concerning Kolchak"
  c. "Not Fit To Print" [On *New York Times*'s refusal to print Sinclair's letter objecting to and answering its review of *Jimmie Higgins*.]
  d. "Socialists and the Land" [On single tax.]

A636 "Upton Sinclair's Page," *Appeal to Reason*, 9 August, p. 4.
  a. "What Americans Don't Know"
  b. "Bread and Circuses"
  c. "The Right of Asylum" [On deportation of Hindu revolutionaries.]

A637 "Newspaper Faking," *Appeal to Reason*, 16 August, p. 3.

1919 continued

A638 "Upton Sinclair's Page," *Appeal to Reason*, 16 August, p. 4.

a. "Russia: Pro and Con" [Prints letters from J. G. Phelps Stokes.]

A639 "Upton Sinclair's Page," *Appeal to Reason*, 23 August, p. 4.

a. "The Cost of Competition"

b. "A Message from Denmark" [Prints letter from Georg Brandes.]

A640 "Upton Sinclair's Page," *Appeal to Reason*, 30 August, p. 4.

a. "Explaining President Wilson"

b. "Democracy for Railroads."

A641* *Circular Letter*. Pasadena: Upton Sinclair, August. 4 pp. Announcing completion of *Brass Check* and soliciting pre-publication orders.

A642 "Upton Sinclair's Page," *Appeal to Reason*, 6 September, p. 4.

a. "Soldiers and Strikers"

b. "*Russia in 1919* by Arthur Ransome, is a Great Book"

c. "Diplomatic Lying"

A643 "Upton Sinclair's Page," *Appeal to Reason*, 13 September, p. 4.

a. "Strangling Strikes"

b. "The Post Office Gag"

c. "A Parlor Bolshevik"

A644 "Upton Sinclair's Page," *Appeal to Reason*, 20 September, p. 4.

a. "What They Are Doing To Debs"

b. "New Books" [Blasco Ibañez's *Blood and Sand*; Julian Hawthorne's *The Subterranean Brotherhood*.]

c. "Nationalizing Women"

d. "Napoleon and Lenin"

A645 "A Letter to Kate R. O'Hare from Upton Sinclair," *Appeal to Reason*, 27 September, p. 1.

Dated 12 September 1919.

A646 "Upton Sinclair's Page," *Appeal to Reason*, 27 September, p. 4.

a. "To the Plain Everyday American"

b. " 'We Heard Kate O'Hare and She Was Innocent' "

A647* "Lincoln Libelled," *Pearson's Magazine*, XL (September), 522–523.

Answer to letter of Frank Harris charging that Sinclair libelled Lincoln, together with Harris's further comments.

A648 "Sinclair Reviews Efforts to Crush Soviet Russia," *Appeal to Reason*, 4 October, p. 3.

A649 "Upton Sinclair's Page," *Appeal to Reason*, 11 October, p. 4.

a. "The President Comes to Town"

b. "Cruelty to Prisoners"

A650 "Upton Sinclair's Page," *Appeal to Reason*, 18 October, p. 3.

"The President Speaks"

A651 "Upton Sinclair's Page," *Appeal to Reason*, 25 October, p. 3.

a. "The Lie Industry" [On magazines.]

b. "Feeding Our Children"

A652 "*High Cost of Living Due to Profit System*, Says Upton Sinclair in Los Angeles Speech," *Appeal to Reason*, 1 November, pp. 1, 3–4.

Text of Sinclair's speech to Los Angeles City Club.

Reprinted: A653.

1919 continued

A653 *The High Cost of Living*. Girard, Kansas: People's Press, *c*. 1 November. 41 pp.

With H. G. Wells's *This Misery of Boots*, pp. 42–63; see A652.

A654* "Inside Facts About Moral Lynching of Herron and Gorky by the Capitalist Newspapers are Exposed by Upton Sinclair," *Appeal to Reason*, 8 November, pp. 1–2.

Brass Check, chapters x and xx; large portions of *Brass Check* were published in the *Appeal* during the latter part of 1919 and early part of 1920. As book: A676.

A655* "Wanton Wreck in Raid on Radical Soldiers' Magazine," *Appeal to Reason*, 8 February, p. 1.

On wrecking of office of *The Dugout*.

A656 "Upton Sinclair's Page," *Appeal to Reason*, 8 November, p. 4.

a. "Governments and Their Lies"
b. "Working Class Suicide"
c. "No Apologies"

A657* "How the Capitalist Press Shot Its Poisoned Arrows at the Cooperative Colony Established by Upton Sinclair," *Appeal to Reason*, 15 November, pp. 1–2.

Brass Check, chapters XI–XII; A676.

A658* "Upton Sinclair's Page," *Appeal to Reason*, 15 November, p. 4.

a. "Hoatzins at Home" [Sinclair thinks that Hoatzin—a bird from British Guiana—is good name for reactionaries since it is fat, stinks, and reverts to early stages of its development.]
b. "The Coal Strike"
c. "Forgot Banker's Bail"

A659* "An Adventure With Yellow Journalism, in Which There Was a Story Stolen and a Helpless Woman Was Robbed," *Appeal to Reason*, 22 November, p. 1.

Brass Check, chapter XXIII; A676.

A660* "Upton Sinclair's Page," *Appeal to Reason,*" 22 November, p. 4.

a. "Two Views of Russia"

b. "Lying 'Officially' "

c. "The Price of White Paper"

d. "Justice and the Poor"

e. "The Truth About Russia"

A661* "How Kept Press Poisoned the People's Mind to Shield the Packers Who Poisoned the People's Meat Supply," *Appeal to Reason*, 29 November, p. 1.

Brass Check, chapters IV–V; A676.

A662* "Upton Sinclair's Page," *Appeal to Reason*, 29 November, p. 5.

"Violence Retards Socialism"

A663 "Lincoln and Freedom," *Pearson's Magazine*, XL (November), 659–661.

A664* *The National News*. Pasadena: The Author, 1 December. 12 pp.

"A practical plan for an honest newspaper."

A665* "Further Glimpses behind Newspaper Scenes in *Jungle* Fight," *Appeal to Reason*, 6 December, p. 1.

Brass Check, chapter VI; A676.

A666* "Upton Sinclair's Page," *Appeal to Reason*, 6 December, p. 4.

a. "Real News From Russia"

b. 'Nationalization of Women" [False *Los Angeles Times* report regarding Russia.]

c. 'The Supreme Court"

A667 "How Associated Press Became a Concrete Wall Blocking News of Great Colorado Coal Strike," *Appeal to Reason*, 13 December, p. 1.

Brass Check, chapter XXX; A676.

1919 continued

A668 "Upton Sinclair's Page," *Appeal to Reason*, 13 December, p. 3.

a. "The White Terror" [On violence against I.W.W.]
b. "More About Centralia"

A669 "How Coal Barons Were Protected by Press and Politicians in Crushing Colorado Workers," *Appeal to Reason*, 20 December, p. 2.

A670 "Upton Sinclair's Page," *Appeal to Reason*, 20 December, p. 3.

a. "The Clouds Are Breaking"
b. "Justice in Los Angeles"
c. "The Truth About Mexico"

A671* *Offering for Sale "The Profits of Religion."* Pasadena: The Author, *c*. December. 1 leaf.

1920

A672* "How Capitalist News Channels Pour Forth Petty and Abusive Tirades Upon Radicals," *Appeal to Reason*, 3 January, pp. 1, 3.

Brass Check, chapter LI; A676.

A673* Upton Sinclair's Page," *Appeal to Reason*, 3 January, p. 4.

a. "Extremes and Reaction"
b. "Rounding the Profiteers"

A674* "Profits and Propaganda: How Capitalist Press Serves Business," *Appeal to Reason*, 10 January, p. 1.

Brass Check, chapter XXXVIII; A676.

A675* "The Brass Check: A Study of American Journalism," *Appeal to Reason*, 10 January, p. 1.

Announcing thesis and content of *The Brass Check* and its availability through *Appeal* book department at 55 cents paper, $1.10 cloth, 448 pp.

A676* *The Brass Check*. Pasadena: The Author, 10 January. 440 pp.

First offered for sale in the *Appeal to Reason* for 10 January. Verso of title page gives February as publication date. Large portions of the book appeared serially in the *Appeal* from late 1919 through early 1920.

Reprinted: Pasadena: The Author, 1926, paper. New York: A. & C. Boni, 1936. Girard, Kansas: Haldeman-Julius (Big Blue Book no. B-411), paper, 2 vols. In part: A678, A736, A2049.

Foreign Editions: Braille, Chinese, Czech, English, German, Hungarian, Italian, Japanese, Norwegian, Russian, Spanish.

A677* "Upton Sinclair's Page," *Appeal to Reason*, 17 January, p. 4.

Speech delivered by Upton Sinclair 12 December, 1919 at Church of All Nations in Los Angeles, California.

A678* *Press-titution*. Girard, Kansas: Appeal to Reason (People's Pocket Series no. 47), 17 January. 188 pp.

On 17 January 1920, the *Appeal to Reason* offered for sale *Press-titution*, a pamphlet made up of Sinclair's weekly articles on Press which had appeared during the preceding 10 weeks; see A676.

A679* "Hand of Greed and Self-Interest Controls Powerful Daily Press of the United States," *Appeal to Reason*, 17 January, p. 2.

A680* "Upton Sinclair's Page," *Appeal to Reason*, 17 January, p. 4.

a. "A Logical Fool"

b. "*The Profits of Religion*"

c. "A Fooler Fooled"

d. "The *Clarion* On Russia"

e. "*Collier's* on Russia"

1920 continued

A681* "Upton Sinclair's Page," *Appeal to Reason*, 24 January, pp. 3–4.

a. "The Story of a Frame-up," p. 3
b. "Prohibition and the Workers," p. 4

A682* "Upton Sinclair's Page," *Appeal to Reason*, 31 January, p. 3.

a. "As Others See Us"
b. "Our Shame in Siberia"

A683* "Upton Sinclair's Page," *Appeal to Reason*, 7 February, p. 4.

a. "Renegades and Spies"
b. "Russia Saved"
c. "Poverty for Poets"
d. "The Revolution Finished"
e. "Isahia: Criminal Syndicalist!"
g. "The Sparticist"
g. "Advertising Socialism"
h. "Democracy in Russia"

A684 "Building an Honest Newspaper," *Nation*, CX (7 February), 168–170.
Summary of *Brass Check* and proposal for *National News*.

A685 "Upton Sinclair's Page," *Appeal to Reason*, 14 February, p. 4.

a. "Blasco Ibañez" [Sinclair's recent meetings with him.]
b. "Reaction in Hungary"
c. "Concerning *Jimmie Higgins*"
d. "Lying by Picture"
e. "Caught Red-Handed!"

A686 "Upton Sinclair's Page," *Appeal to Reason*, 21 February, p. 4.

a. "A Visit from the Enemy" [Tells of four "plants" who came to buy one copy of *Brass Check* for 50 cents (*Appeal* advertised it for 55 cents) and thus suppress the book on false advertising. "I would sell a book to the devil; for that matter, I would give him one if he would promise to read it!" But Sinclair wasn't fooled by these men.]

b. "Militarism and Lies"

c. "The Art of Controversy"

d. "The I.W.W. and the Ballot"

A687 "Upton Sinclair's Page," *Appeal to Reason*, 28 February, p. 4.

a. "Reflections on Tennis"

b. "A Test for Your Editor"

c. "A Lesson for a Lord"

d. "Crooks in Office"

A688 "Upton Sinclair's Page," *Appeal to Reason*, 6 March, p. 4.

a. "World Fears and Greeds"

b. "The Poison Press Again"

c. "Prostitutes, Male and Female"

d. "Watch Your Step!"

A689 "Save My Book!" *Appeal to Reason*, 13 March, p. 4.

Full details on printing of *Brass Check* and attempts to cut off paper supply.

A690 "Upton Sinclair's Page," *Appeal to Reason*, 20 March, p. 4.

a. "Choosing a President"

b. "Assessing Land"

c. "Making Bolshevists"

A691* "Upton Sinclair's Page," *Appeal to Reason*, 27 March, p. 4.

a. "The Poison Squad"

b. "Deporting a 'White' "

1920 continued

A692* "Upton Sinclair's Page," *Appeal to Reason*, 3 April, p. 3.

a. "The Fourteen Points in Hungary"
b. "Justice for the I.W.W.
c. "A Little Story for *Collier's*"
d. "An English Editor on American Journalism" [Reprint of Robert Blatchford's review of *Brass Check* in *Clarion* (London).]

A693* "Upton Sinclair's Page," *Appeal to Reason*, 10 April, p. 3.

a. "Wilson the Morning After"
b. " 'It Pays to Advertise' "
c. "For An Honest Newspaper"
d. "Justice in Montesano"

A694* "Comment on *Nation's* Article for a Free Press," *Appeal to Reason*, 10 April, p. 4.

A695* "Europe and Me," *Appeal to Reason*, 17 April, p. 1.

A696* "Upton Sinclair's Page," *Appeal to Reason*, 17 April, p. 2.

a. "Our Attorney General"
b. "Life in Atlanta"
c. "An Anti-Red May Day"
d. "New Books" [H. G. Wells's *The Undying Fire*; Sir Henry Johnson's *The Gay-Dombeys*.]
e. "Public Ownership"

A697* "Upton Sinclair's Page," *Appeal to Reason*, 24 April, p. 2.

a. "The Twilight of Capitalism"
b. "Reviewers on the *Brass Check*"[H. L. Mencken and Heywood Broun.]

A698* "Upton Sinclair's Page," *Appeal to Reason*, 5 June, pp. 2–3.

a. "Wanted—an Honest Newspaper"

b. Miscellaneous

A699* "Upton Sinclair's Page," *Appeal to Reason*, 12 June, p. 3.

"E. W. Howe to the Bat" [Prints correspondence with Atchison, Kansas "Philosopher-humorist" on *Brass Check*.]

A700* "Upton Sinclair's Page," *Appeal to Reason*, 19 June, pp. 3–4.

a. "Concerning Human Nature"

b. "The Flowers Case," pp. 3–4.

c. "Bonuses for Us All," p. 4 [Reprinted in *World Tomorrow*, June 1920.]

A701* "Upton Sinclair's Page," *Appeal to Reason*, 26 June, p. 3.

a. "Are Socialist Papers Honest?"

b. "Critics of *The Brass Check*" [Answers Heywood Broun and *New York Tribune*.]

c. "The Railroad Strike"

d. "Where the Profits Go"

e. "Concerning Prostitutes"

A702* "Upton Sinclair's Page," *Appeal to Reason*, 3 July, pp. 3–4.

a. "Sympathizing With Government"

b. "Lady Astor" [Several letters on *Brass Check*.]

A703* *Circular Letter*. Pasadena: Upton Sinclair, 6 July. 1 p.

Announcing the publication on 15 September 1920 of *100%*.

A704 "Upton Sinclair's Page," *Appeal to Reason*, 10 July, p. 3.

"The Next War" [Surveys world situation and some "thirty wars going on at present."]

1920 continued

A705* *Circular Letter*. Pasadena, *c*. April.
Broadside explaining delays in publishing *The Brass Check*.

A706 "Shylocracy: American Journalism," *Pearson's Magazine*, XXXXV (April), 827–832.

A707 "Upton Sinclair's Page," *Appeal to Reason*, 1 May, p. 4.
"Making Life Over"

A708* "Upton Sinclair's Page," *Appeal to Reason*, 8 May, p. 3.
a. "Who Is the Notoriety Seeker?"
b. "The Japs in Siberia"
c. "The Railway Strike"

A709* "Upton Sinclair's Page," *Appeal to Reason*, 15 May, p. 3.
a. "Politics for Socialists"
b. "Books in Bed" [In mid-April, Sinclair spent several days in bed recovering from a hernia operation. Books discussed: Christopher Morley's *Parnassus on Wheels*; Henry Marks's *Peter Middleton*; A. P. Herbert's *The Secret Battle*; Blasco Ibañez's *La Bodega*; J. B. Cabell's *Jurgen*.]
c. "The Flowers Case"

A710* "Imprisonment of Debs Is Part of Conspiracy Against Your Liberty," *Appeal to Reason*, 22 May, pp. 1, 3.

A711* "Upton Sinclair's Page," *Appeal to Reason*, 29 May, p. 2.
a. "Trial for Opinion" [On Sinclair's court testimony in Flowers case.]
b. "Straw Ballots"
c. "Honest Newspapers"
d. "Paying Germany Back"
e. "The Perfect Letter-Writer"
f. "The Badge of Sacrifice"

A712* "Interviewing Upton Sinclair on Free Love," *Current Opinion*, LXVIII (May), 669–671.

A713* "Upton Sinclair's Page," *Appeal to Reason*, 17 July, p. 3.

a. "A Letter to the Socialist Party" [Asks for readmission into Party, giving reasons for his previous break; see A487.]

b. "Emma Goldman on Russia"

A714* "Upton Sinclair's Page," *Appeal to Reason*, 24 July, p. 3.

"Honesty of the Capitalist Mind" [Concerns violent attack by Mrs. Gertrude Atherton.]

A715* "Upton Sinclair's Page," *Appeal to Reason*, 31 July, p. 3.

a. "Freedom in Advertising"

b. "The Farmer-Labor Party"

c. "Criminal Statesmen"

d. "An Industrial Republic" [On *The Industrial Republic* by Paul V. Litchfield.]

A716* "Upton Sinclair's Page," *Appeal to Reason*, 7 August, pp. 3–4.

a. "The Fall of Poland," p. 3

b. "What Is Insanity?" pp. 3–4

A717* "Upton Sinclair's Page," *Appeal to Reason*, 14 August, p. 3.

a. "*The Rip-Saw*" [On a monthly publication edited by Kate Richards O'Hare.]

b. "The Class War Spreads"

c. "Fooling America"

A718* "Sinclair Accepts . . . ," *Voice of Labor*, I (18 August), 1–3.

Text of speech accepting the nomination of the Socialist Party for Congressman from California's Tenth District.

Reprinted as broadside: Los Angeles, [n.d.] 1 leaf.

1920 continued

A719* "Upton Sinclair's Page," *Appeal to Reason*, 21 August, p. 3.

a. "The Issues of this Campaign"
b. "Optimism of Bunk"
c. "On Calling Names"

A720* "Los Angeles Press Boycotts Sinclair . . . ," *Appeal to Reason*, 28 August, p. 1.

Telegram from Upton Sinclair concerning alleged boycott of his name during campaign for Congressman from 10th District as Socialist.

A721* "Upton Sinclair's Page," *Appeal to Reason*, 28 August, p. 2.

a. "The Crisis in Europe"
b. "The Brass Check Weekly" [Quotes from article in *New Republic* by Walter Lippmann and Charles Merz on *New York Times* coverage of Russian Revolution.]

A722* "Upton Sinclair's Page," *Appeal to Reason*, 4 September, p. 2.

a. "The League of Nations"
b. "The *Los Angeles Times*"
c. "A Socialist Novel" [Clement Wood's *Mountain*.]
d. "Esperanto"

A723* "Upton Sinclair, Socialist Candidate for Congress, Denounces the Profiteers and Prostitute Press," *Appeal to Reason*, 11 September, pp. 1, 3.

Speech delivered at Socialist Party Picnic at Los Angeles, 22 August 1920.

A724* "Upton Sinclair's Page," *Appeal to Reason*, 18 September, p. 3.

a. "The Author's Soviet"
b. "The Churches and the Steel Trust"

c. "Boycotting a Candidate!" [Letter to *New Republic* concerning *Los Angeles Times.*]

d. "From a Labor Chautauqua"

e. "Concerning Prohibition"

A725* "Upton Sinclair's Page," *Appeal to Reason*, 25 September, p. 2.

"What Keeps Debs in Jail?"

A726* "Upton Sinclair's Page," *Appeal to Reason*, 2 October, p. 3.

a. "The Organized Liars"

b. "The Plumb Plan"

c. "Women's Suffrage"

d. "The *New York World* to the Bat" [Letter concerning *Brass Check.*]

A727* "Upton Sinclair's Page," *Appeal to Reason*, 9 October, pp. 3–4.

a. "The News from Italy," p. 3

b. "Bolshevik Gold," p. 3

c. "The Wall Street 'Bomb,' " p. 4

d. "Letters on *Brass Check*, p. 4

A728* "Letter to Soviet Business Agent in United States," *Appeal to Reason*, 9 October, p. 4.

A729* *100%: The Story of a Patriot*. Pasadena: The Author, 15 October. 329 pp.

No reprints identified. In part: A1545, A2049.

Foreign Editions: Azerbaijani, Bulgarian, Chinese, Czech, Dutch, English (*The Spy*), Estonian, Finnish, French, German, Hebrew, Hungarian, Italian, Japanese, Lithuanian, Polish, Russian, Serbo-Croatian, Spanish, Swedish, Taijk, Tatar, Turkish, Ukrainian, Yiddish.

1920 continued

A730* "Upton Sinclair's Page," *Appeal to Reason*, 16 October, p. 3.

a. "The Wall Street 'Bomb' Again"

b. "The Socialists at Albany"

c. "Concerning Fasting"

A731* "Upton Sinclair's Page," *Appeal to Reason*, 23 October, p. 6.

a. "Concerning Baseball"

b. "Concerning MacSwiney"

c. "A Book About Debs" [Explains how Sinclair came to publish *Debs and the Poets*, A740.]

d. "Our Friends in Poland"

A732* "Solution of Minorities Problem . . . ," *Natal Advertiser* [Durban, South Africa], 25 October.

A733* "Sinclair Offers $1,000 in Challenge to *Los Angeles Times* to Prove Slanders," *Appeal to Reason*, 20 October, pp. 1–2.

A734* "Printing Press More Potent Than Cannon in Destroying Capitalism, Says Sinclair," *Appeal to Reason*, 30 October, p. 2.

Speech by Sinclair at Eagle Rock Park, Los Angeles, 10 October 1920.

A735 *Circular Letter*. Pasadena: The Author, *c.* October. 4 pp.

Concerning the publishing history of *The Brass Check*.

A736* *The Associated Press and Labor*. Pasadena: The Author, *c.* 1 November. 64 pp.

Seven chapters from *The Brass Check* (A676): pp. 150–175, 271–281, 353–376.

A737* "Upton Sinclair's Page," *Appeal to Reason*, 6 November, p. 3.

"Election Day—and After" [Address of Sinclair's at Clune's

Auditorium, Los Angeles on 17 October to protest expulsion of elected Socialists from New York State Assembly.]

A738* "Upton Sinclair's Page," *Appeal to Reason*, 6 November, p. 2.

Praise of novel, *Mountain*, by St. John Ervine.

A739* "On Talking Backwards!" *Appeal to Reason*, 6 November, p. 4.

A740* Introduction to *Debs and the Poets*, ed. Ruth Le Prade. Pasadena: Upton Sinclair, *c.* 6 November, pp. 5–6.

See also Sinclair's contribution to this collection, "From Upton Sinclair," p. 47.

A741* "Upton Sinclair's Page," *Appeal to Reason*, 13 November, pp. 2–3.

a. "The 'Bomb' Again," p. 2
b. "Single Tax," p. 2
c. "*The Liberator* Again," p. 2
d. "Our Liberties," p. 3
e. "Our New President," p. 3

A742* "The *Christian Science Monitor*," *Appeal to Reason*, 13 November, p. 3.

A743* *Circular Letter*. Pasadena: The Author, 15 November. 4 pp.

Concerning his publishing business.

A744* *Circular Letter*. Pasadena: The Author, 15 November. 4 pp.

From Upton Sinclair: a statement to the readers of his books.

A745* "Police Officer Who Helped Frame Tom Mooney Confesses and *Appeal*'s Charges Against Conspirators Are Vindicated," *Appeal to Reason*, 20 November, p. 1.

Followed by telegram from Sinclair pointing out that he had guessed truth in *100%*.

1920 continued

A746* "Upton Sinclair's Page," *Appeal to Reason*, 20 November, pp. 2–3.

a. "Socialism and How It Is Coming," p. 2 [Text of address delivered by Sinclair at Labor Temple, Los Angeles, Sunday 31 October 1920.]

b. "Sydney Flowers Disappears," p. 3

c. "Me and W. J. Ghent!" p. 3 [On Ghent's review of *Brass Check*.]

A747* "Upton Sinclair's Page," *Appeal to Reason*, 27 November, p. 4.

a. "The Grand Duke of Los Angeles"

b. "H. G. Wells and the Liars"

c. "The Birth of a New Day"

d. "A Mandate for Mexico"

A748 "Frank Harris: Ad Memoriam" *Pearson's Magazine*, XLVI (November), 158–160.

A749* "*The Brass Check*," *Freeman*, II (1 December), 281. Letter to the editor.

A750* "Upton Sinclair's Page," *Appeal to Reason*, 4 December, p. 4.

a. "Letting a Bear Alone"

b. "Some More Wall Street 'Bomb' "

c. "More About Ghent"

A751* "Upton Sinclair's Page," *Appeal to Reason*, 11 December, p. 4.

a. "The Shaving of Karl Marx"

b. "German Spies"

c. "The Communists Underground"

d. "The *Saturday Evening Post*"

A752* "Upton Sinclair's Page," *Appeal to Reason*, 18 December, p. 4.

a. "The Third International"

b. "The Japanese Question"

c. "Filling Our Prisons"

A753 "The Book of Life," *Appeal to Reason*, 18–25 December; 1 January–16 April 1921.

As book: A814.

A754* "More About W. J. Ghent," *Appeal to Reason*, 25 December, p. 3.

Long letter to *Weekly Review*.

A755* *Books by Upton Sinclair*. Pasadena: The Author. 4 pp.

Lists 8 books with descriptions.

A756* *Books by Upton Sinclair*. Pasadena: The Author, 4 pp.

Lists 12 books with descriptions.

A757* *From Upton Sinclair: A Statement to the Readers of His Books*. Pasadena: The Author. 4 pp.

A758* "*The Jungle*": *What English Reviewers Think of It*. New York: Jungle Publishing Company, 2 pp.

Twenty-one opinions of *The Jungle* by English reviewers.

A759* *A New Edition of "The Jungle."* Pasadena: Upton Sinclair. 4 pp.

Jack London letter, p. 4

A760* *A New Edition of "The Jungle."* Pasadena: The Author. 4 pp.

Advertising brochure promoting the sale of the 1920 edition of *The Jungle*.

A761* *A New Novel by Upton Sinclair—100%: A Story of a Patriot*. Pasadena: Upton Sinclair. 4 pp.

Advertising brochure, see A729, A764.

1920 continued

A762* *Order Blank*. Pasadena: The Author. 1 leaf.

Offering for sale a selected list of his books beginning with *The Brass Check*.

A763* *A Proposition from Upton Sinclair*. Pasadena: The Author. 1 leaf.

Proposes series of pamphlets made up of parts of *The Brass Check*.

A764* *To Be Published October 1st, A New Novel by Upton Sinclair*. Pasadena: Upton Sinclair. 1 leaf.

A765* *Who Owns the Press and Why? . . . "The Brass Check."* Pasadena: Upton Sinclair. 4 pp.

1921

A766* "Statement to *Appeal* by Upton Sinclair," *Appeal to Reason*, 1 January, p. 4.

Appeal for support of Sinclair's publishing venture.

A767* "Concerning Sydney Flowers," *Appeal to Reason*, 15 January, p. 3.

He jumped bail and went to England.

A768* "The Packers at the Bar," *Appeal to Reason*, 15 January, p. 3.

A769* "A Correspondence Between Upton Sinclair and the Young Man Who Refused a Million," *Appeal to Reason*, 15 January, p. 4.

Mr. Charles Garland.

A770* "Is Capital Necessary?" *Appeal to Reason*, 29 January, p. 3.

A771* "Me and the Printer," *Appeal to Reason*, 29 January, p. 4.

On mistakes in setting up 1 January advertisement about Sinclair's publishing business.

A772* "Les Maîtres de la Press," *Lumière*, II (January), 1–3.

Chapter of *The Brass Check*. "Owning the Press."

A773* "The Rich and the Poor," *Appeal to Reason*, 5 February, p. 4.

A774* "The Greatest American," *Appeal to Reason*, 5 February, p. 4.

Abraham Lincoln greatest in wise kindness.

A775 "Truth and Upton Sinclair," *Weekly Review*, IV (9 February), 128–129.

A776* "Doctoring the News," *Appeal to Reason*, 19 February, p. 4.

A777* "A Few Words With Spargo," *Appeal to Reason*, 12 March, p. 4.

Socialist John Spargo.

A778* "The White Terror at Work," *Appeal to Reason*, 12 March, p. 4.

A779 "The *Brass Check* Weekly!" *Nation*, CXII (16 March), 418.

Full page advertisement putting forward case that newspapers ignored.

A780* "Comrades to the Front," *Appeal to Reason*, 26 March, p. 3.

In praise of *Dust*, a novel by Mr. and Mrs. Emanuel Haldeman-Julius.

A781* "Sinclair Answers Mr. Woods," *Appeal to Reason*, 2 April, p. 4.

Editor of *Literary Digest*.

1921 continued

A782* *The Crimes of the "Times": A Test of Newspaper Decency*. Pasadena: The Author, *c*. 15 April. 31 pp.

On *New York Times*.

Reprinted: Long Beach and Pasadena: The Author, 1929.

A783* "Upton Sinclair's Page," *Appeal to Reason*, 30 April, p. 3.

"Marriage Plus Prostitution"

A784* "The New Administration and Its New Row of Faces at the Counter," *Appeal to Reason*, 30 April, p. 1.

A785* "Upton Sinclair's Page," *Appeal to Reason*, 30 April, p. 3.

a. "Sex and Young America"

b. "Adding Insult to Injury"

A786* "The 'White Terror' in Journalism," *Appeal to Reason*, 7 May, pp. 1,4.

On W. J. Ghent.

A787* "Upton Sinclair's Page," *Appeal to Reason*, 7 May, p. 3.

"Depravities in Capitalist Society" [Especially concerns sexual depravities.]

A788* "Upton Sinclair's Page," *Appeal to Reason*, 14 May, p. 3.

"A Letter to Frank Harris" [On Harris's editorial in May *Pearson's*.]

A789 Letter, *New Republic*, XXVI (18 May), 354–355.

On Ghent and *Weekly Review*.

A790* "Upton Sinclair's Page," *Appeal to Reason*, 21 May, p. 3.

a. "Explanatory Note" [On suspension of serial publication of *Book of Life*, A814.]

b. "A Number of Things"

c. "Breaking the Money Trust" [On H. C. Cutting's *The Strangle Hold.*]

A791* *Circular Letter.* Pasadena: The Author, 28 May. 2pp.

Letter to Frederick Roy Martin of the Associated Press concerning his attack on the *Brass Check.*

A792 Letter on *The Autobiography of Andrew Carnegie, Nation,* CXII (1 June), 793.

A793* "A Funny Incident," *Appeal to Reason,* 4 June, p. 3.

On his appearance in curious "dress suit" at party.

A794* "Sinclair's Challenge to the Associated Press!" *Appeal to Reason,* 11 June, p. 1.

A795* "The Case of Gale," *Appeal to Reason,* 18 June, p. 3.

A. E. Gale deported from Mexico and jailed because of his political opinions.

A796* "The Land of the Free," *Appeal to Reason,* 18 June, p. 3.

A797* "Riga: A Lie Factory," *Appeal to Reason,* 25 June, p. 3.

A798* "Lying About the Miners," *Appeal to Reason,* 25 June, p. 3.

A799* "The *Brass Check* Weekly," *Appeal to Reason,* 25 June, p. 3.

A800* "Now Collect Your Money!" *Appeal to Reason,* 2 July, p. 3.

A801* "More Press Lying," *Appeal to Reason,* 9 July, p. 3.

A802* "How the Movies Are Made," *Appeal to Reason,* 9 July, p. 3.

On movie adaptation of Sinclair's *Moneychangers,* which was radically transformed and then released under Sinclair's name.

1921 continued

A803* "My Indictment of the Associated Press Stands!" *Appeal to Reason*, 16 July, pp. 1–2.
James Melvin Lee vs. Upton Sinclair regarding accuracy of *The Brass Check*; see A807, A871.

A804* "The Brass Check Weekly," *Appeal to Reason*, 16 July, p. 3.

A805* "A.P. against A.P.," *Appeal to Reason*, 23 July, p. 3.
Conflicting reports on food being burned to keep prices up.

A806* "They Still Lie," *Appeal to Reason*, 23 July, p. 3.

A807* "Sinclair Again Replies to Professor Who Defends the Associated Press," *Appeal to Reason*, 6 August, pp. 1–2.
Professor James Melvin Lee; see A871.

A808* "*The Saturday Evening Post* Lies Again," *Appeal to Reason*, 13 August, p. 3.
Letter from Sinclair to *Saturday Evening Post*, and one from Karl Kautsky.

A809* "Morley to the Bat," *Appeal to Reason*, 20 August, p. 4.
Exchange of opinions between Christopher Morley and Sinclair.

A810* "A Debate with T. A. McNeal," *Appeal to Reason*, 3 September, p. 4.
As pamphlet: A816.

A811* "The Book of Life," *Appeal to Reason*, 10 September, p. 3.
Discusses social revolution.

A812* "McNeal Misunderstands Socialism, Says Sinclair in His First Reply," *Appeal to Reason*, 10 September, p. 6.
To Thomas Allen McNeal's opening statement in *Appeal*, 3 September; see A810, A816.

A813* "Socialism is a Definitely Established Proposition, Says Sinclair," *Appeal to Reason*, 24 September, pp. 1, 4.

Second reply to McNeal in debate; see A812, A816.

A814* *The Book of Life: Mind and Body*. Vol. I. New York: MacMillan; Pasadena: Sinclair-Economy, *c.* 24 September. 202 pp.

Originally published in *Appeal to Reason*, 18 and 25 December 1920; 1 January–16 April, 1921; see A753.

Reprinted: Pasadena: Sinclair, 1922; Girard, Kansas: Haldeman-Julius, 1922; Pasadena: Sinclair, 1926; rev. ed. Girard, Kansas: Haldeman-Julius Publications (Big Blue Books nos. B451–454), 4, 11, 18, 23 December 1950. 4 vols., paper. All save last as vol. I of 2 vols. in one.

See also A854.

A815* "American Prisoners in Russia," *Appeal to Reason*, 24 September, p. 3.

A816* *McNeal–Sinclair Debate on Socialism*. Girard, Kansas: Haldeman-Julius (Little Blue Book no. 234), *c.* 24 September. 94 pp.

Originally published in *Appeal to Reason*, 3, 10, 17, 24 September.

A817 "The Breakdown of the Profit System," *Pearson's Magazine*, XVII (September), 113–115.

A818* "What Marx Taught," *Appeal to Reason*, 8 October, p. 3.

A819* "The Associated Press and Its Champion," *Appeal to Reason*, 5 November, p. 3.

Prints long letter to John Haynes Holmes on Sinclair's running battle with J. M. Lee over *Brass Check*; see A807.

A820* "The Disarmament Conference," *Appeal to Reason*, 12 November, p. 3.

1921 continued

A821* "The Powers of Production," *Appeal to Reason*, 19 November, p. 3.

A822* "Saving Money on Useless Battleships to Spend on Airplanes," *Appeal to Reason*, 3 December, p. 1.

A823* "Upton Sinclair's Page," *Appeal to Reason*, 17 December, p. 3.

a. "Shall We Have War or Peace?"

b. "Socialist Prayers"

A824* "The Facts about Amnesty," *Appeal to Reason*, 24 December, p. 2.

A825* *The Associated Press and Labor, Being Several Chapters from "The Brass Check," A Study of American Journalism*. Pasadena: Upton Sinclair. 59 pp.

A826 Letter. In *The Future of the Novel*, by Merideth Starr, p. 73.

Series of interviews with renowned authors.

1922

A827* "Latest Tale of Wall Street Bomb Explosion is Greatest World Plot Against Radicals, Says Sinclair," *Appeal to Reason*, 7 January, pp. 3–4.

A828* "Catholics and Birth Control," *Appeal to Reason*, 14 January, p. 3.

A829* "The Roots of War," *Appeal to Reason*, 14 January, p. 3.

A830* "A Book on Russia," *Appeal to Reason*, 28 January, p. 3.

A831* "Our Political Prisoners," *Appeal to Reason*, 28 January, p. 3.

A832* "Suppressing Thought," *Appeal to Reason*, 11 February, p. 4.

A833* *Circular Letter*. Pasadena: The Author, *c*. February, 1 leaf.

Raising questions concerning his proposed book on American education.

A834* "Upton Sinclair's Page," *Appeal to Reason*, 11 March, p. 3.

"Breaking the Money Trust"

A835* "What Shall Be Our Attitude Towards Next War? Asks Sinclair," *Appeal to Reason*, 18 March, p. 1.

A836* "Lying About Debs," *Appeal to Reason*, 18 March, p. 3.

A837* "Golden Words," *Appeal to Reason*, 18 March, p. 3.

A838* "A Labor Colony," *Appeal to Reason*, 25 March, p. 3.

A839* "The Product of Our Labor," *Appeal to Reason*, 25 March, p. 3.

A840* "Upton Sinclair's Page," *Appeal to Reason*, 1 April, p. 2.

a. "On Being Charlie Chaplin"
b. "A Story from Arden"
c. "Two Unusual Books"

A841* "Three Novels of Marriage," *Appeal to Reason*, 8 April, p. 2.

Hergesheimer's *Cytherea*, Ben Hecht's *Eric Dorn*, and Floyd Dell's *The Briary Bush*.

A842* "Russia and the Allies," *Appeal to Reason*, 8 April, p. 2.

A843* "A Challenge to [the] Associated Press," *Appeal to Reason*, 15 April, p. 1.

1922 continued

A844* "Upton Sinclair's Page," *Appeal to Reason*, 15 April, p. 3.
"Propaganda"

A845* "A Letter from Sinclair," *Appeal to Reason*, 15 April, p. 4.

A846* "Upton Sinclair's Page," *Appeal to Reason*, 22 April, p. 2.
"Stick Around Kid!"

A847 "Mr. Sinclair's 'The Spy,' *New Age*, xxx (27 April), 347.
Letter to editor regarding *100%*, A729.

A848* "Sinclair Asks McAdoo About Amnesty After Free Speech Address But Finds Democratic Politician Dodging Issue," *Appeal to Reason*, 29 April, p. 1.

A849* "The Associated Press and the Catholics," *Appeal to Reason*, 29 April, p. 3.

A850 "Sinclair to Birge," *The Capital Times*, 29 April, pp. 1, 8.
University of Wisconsin President, E. A. Birge, does not allow Sinclair to speak to Social Science Club.

A851* "Big Business and Its Movies," *Screenland*, XXIII (April), pp. 91–92.
On control of movie industry by big business and banning of movie version of *The Jungle*.

A852* "Upton Sinclair's Page," *Appeal to Reason*, 6 May,
a. "Concerning Emma Goldman"
b. "The Brass Check Weekly"
c. "A School for Scandal"
d. "Moral New Zealand"
e. "Concerning Anarchists"
f. "The Dying Children are Silent"

A853* "Upton Sinclair's Page," *Appeal to Reason*, 13 May, p. 3.

"On Being a Jew" [Ludwig Lewisohn's *Up Stream* discussed.]

A854 *The Book of Life: Love and Society*. Vol. II; and as composite, 2 vols. in one. Pasadena: Sinclair-Paine, *c.* 15 May. Vol. II, 224 pp.

Originally appeared in *Appeal to Reason*, 23–30 April; 7, 28 May–10 December; 24–31 December; 7 January–25 February 1922.

Reprinted: Girard, Kansas: Haldeman-Julius, 1922; Pasadena: Sinclair, 1926; rev. Girard, Kansas: Haldeman-Julius, [n.d.], 4 vols., paper. All save last as Vol. II of 2 vols. in one. See A814.

Foreign Editions: Bulgarian, Chinese, Czech, English, German, Japanese, Polish, Russian, Spanish, Yiddish.

A855* "Despite Opposition, Sinclair Delivers Speech at University of Wisconsin," *Appeal to Reason*, 20 May, p. 1.

While on fact-finding trip for *The Goose-step*.

A856* "Upton Sinclair's Page," *Appeal to Reason*, 20 May, p. 3.

a. "On Making Money"

b. "Christians and Christianity"

A857* "What Life Means to Me," *Appeal to Reason*, 27 May, p. 3.

See A305, A320.

A858* "The College Student and the Modern Critics," *Appeal to Reason*, 27 May, p. 2.

Address given at University of Wisconsin Gymnasium, 3 May.

A859* "How Associated Press Newspapers Dodged Upton Sinclair's Challenge," *Appeal to Reason*, 3 June, p. 1.

A860* "Upton Sinclair's Page," *Appeal to Reason*, 3 June, p. 3.

a. "Hard Times"

b. "A Warning to Socialists" [About man posing as friend of Sinclair's.]

1922 continued

A861* "Upton Sinclair's Page," *Appeal to Reason*, 10 June, p. 3.

"An Appeal to the Colleges" [Address to University of Chicago Student Liberals' Club; to be continued 24 June].

A862* "Vanzetti—A Tribute and an Appeal," *Appeal to Reason*, 17 June, p. 1.

A863* "Communism in China," *Appeal to Reason*, 24 June, p. 1.

A864* "Our Secret Service Criminals," *Appeal to Reason*, 24 June, p. 1.

A865* "Me and Main Street," *Appeal to Reason*, 24 June, p. 1.

A866* "The Individual in Society," *Appeal to Reason*, 24 June, p. 2.

A867 "The House of Wonder: An Account of the Revolutionary Discovery of Dr. Albert Abrams, the Diagnosis of Disease from the Radio Activity of the Blood," *Pearson's Magazine*, XLVIII (June), 9–17.

Reprinted in *Era*, Section 2 of a supplement to *Pearson's Magazine*, September; see A882.

A868* "Shall We Save America? And Do You Want a Fighting Paper for the Job?" *Appeal to Reason*, 1 July, pp. 1, 4.

Sinclair invites W. J. Bryan to debate E. A. Birge, President of University of Wisconsin.

A869* "Publishing Filth," *Appeal to Reason*, 8 July, p. 1.

On George H. Doran Co., which had rejected Sinclair's work.

A870* "Upton Sinclair's Page," *Appeal to Reason*, 8 July, p. 2.

a. "Lobster Palace 'Independent' "

b. "Credit Reform"
c. "A Great American Play" [Susan Glaspell's *Inheritors.*]
d. "New Suppression"

A871* "The Reward of Labor," *Appeal to Reason*, 8 July, p. 3.

A872* "Upton Sinclair's Page," *Appeal to Reason*, 22 July, pp. 2–3.

a. "The Money Problem," p. 2
b. "Busting a Boycott," p. 3 [Explains background of his experience with *Book of Life* and reaction of reviewers, several of whom are quoted.]

A873* "Upton Sinclair's Page," *Appeal to Reason*, 29 July, p. 2.

"Home Again" [After trip to gather information for *The Goose-Step.*]

A874 "They Call Me Carpenter," *Hearst's International Magazine*, XLVII (July–October).

As book: A880.

A875* "Upton Sinclair's Page," *Appeal to Reason*, 5 August, p. 3.

a. "Newspaper Lynchings"
b. "Trotsky and His Parents"
c. "Communism in China"
d. "Poison by Radio"
e. "*The Book of Life* Again" [On reviews.]
f. "Me and the Jews" [Letter to editor of *Jewish Tribune* answering criticism of Sinclair's characterization of a man in *They Call Me Carpenter.*]

A876* "The Goose-step," *Appeal to Reason*, 12 August–24 March 1923.

As book: A894.

1922 continued

A877* "Upton Sinclair's Page," *Appeal to Reason*, 12 August, p. 2.

"A Lawyer Who Got Fooled"

A878* "Sinclair Favors Soldiers' Bonus," *Appeal to Reason*, 19 August, p. 4.

A879* *Circular Letter*. Pasadena: The Author, 10 September. 1 leaf.

Offering *They Call Me Carpenter*, at special rates.

A880* *They Call Me Carpenter*. Pasadena: Sinclair; New York: Boni and Liveright, 15 September. 225 pp.

As serial: A874; in part: A1545, A2049.

Foreign Editions: Bulgarian, Czech, Danish, Dutch, English, Finnish, French, German, Hungarian, Icelandic, Japanese, Norwegian, Polish, Romanian, Russian, Serbo-Croatian, Slovene, Spanish, Swedish, Ukranian, Yiddish.

A881* "Sinclair's Letter of Acceptance," *Appeal to Reason*, 30 September, p. 4.

As Socialist candidate for United States Senate from California, dated 31 August.

A882* Letter to the *Journal of the American Medical Association*, *Pearson's Magazine*, XLVIII (September), 28.

See A867.

A883* "The House of Wonder," *Era* (Section 2), *Pearson's Magazine*, XLVIII (September), 6–14.

Electronic Reaction of Abrams as method for diagnosing illness; see A867.

A884* *Circular Letter*. Pasadena: The Author, 25 October. 4 pp.

Announcing a book on American education.

A885* "*They Call Me Carpenter*," *Appeal to Reason*, 28 October, p. 2.

Reprints Heywood Broun's review and Sinclair's letter in reply.

A886 "Standardized America," *Life and Letters*, I (November), 12.

A887* "The Black Hand at Work," *Appeal to Reason*, 23 December, pp. 3–4.

On action taken against editor for printing in *Laughing Horse* (University of California at Berkeley) a letter by D. H. Lawrence and a fragment of *The Goose-step* dealing with the University of California.

A888* "The Black Hand at Work," *Appeal to Reason*, 30 December, pp. 3–4.

On expulsion from the University of California of Roy Chanslor, editor of *Laughing Horse*; see A887.

A889* Letter to the Editor, *New Pearson's Magazine*, XLIX (December), 57.

Sinclair denies that he was paid for supporting Dr. Adams.

A890* *A Book on American Education*. Pasadena: Upton Sinclair, Winter, 1922. 1 p.

Announces that he is writing a book on the problems of American education.

A891* Afterword by Upton Sinclair. In *100% ní vlastenec*. New York: Cesko-Americká.

See Czech edition, C123.

1923

A892 "Scientist or Charlatan?" *Nation*, CXVI (3 January), 16.

On Coué.

A893* Letter: "On Abrams' Cure," *New Pearson's Magazine*, XLIX (January).

1923 continued

A894* *The Goose-step: A Study of American Education.* Pasadena: The Author, c. 10 February. 488 pp.

Reprinted: Girard, Kansas: Haldeman-Julius, 1923; Pasadena: The Author, 1924; rev. ed. Pasadena and Los Angeles: The Author, [n.d.]; Pasadena: The Author, 4 vols., paper; St. Clair Shores, Mich.: Scholarly Press, 1970 (facsimile). In part: A929.

Foreign Editions: Chinese, English, German, Japanese, Russian.

A895 *Circular Letter.* Pasadena: The Author, 13 February.

Broadside offering to allow profit to students who take advance orders for *The Goose-Step.*

A896 *The Goose-Step: A Study of American Education.* Pasadena: The Author, 2 pp. *c.* 15 February.

Advertising brochure prepared by the Author, including a few comments on the book, and a list of other books for sale by the Author.

A897 "Carpenter and Coué," *Haldeman-Julius Weekly*, 17 February, pp. 3–4.

A898 *Circular Letter.* Pasadena: The Author, 20 February.

Broadside proposing a simple experiment to determine scientific validity of Dr. Abrams's E.R.A. methods equipment.

A899 "The Story of My Education," *Haldeman-Julius Weekly*, 24 February, p. 3; 3 March, p. 4.

A900 "In Defense of Albert Abrams," *Survey*, XLIX (15 March), 809.

A901 "A Prize for *The Goose-Step*," *Haldeman-Julius Weekly*, 24 March, p. 6.

Sinclair offers set of his books for best review by high school or college students.

A902 "*The Goose-Step: A Study of American Education*," *Haldeman-Julius Weekly*, 24 March, pp. 2–3.

Portion of Sinclair's book; see A894.

A903 "Sick Novels of a Sick World," *Haldeman-Julius Weekly*, 31 March, p. 4.

Review of Mrs. Gertrude Atherton's *Black Oxen* and Sherwood Anderson's *Many Marriages*.

A904* "Social Art," *Modern Quarterly*, I (March), 51–52.

A905* *Circular Letter*. Pasadena: The Author, 18 April. 4 pp.

Reporting on sale of *Goose-Step* and other books.

A906 "On Writing for Hearst," *Nation*, CXVI (25 April), 494.

A907 "Sinclair Answers McLaughlin," *Haldeman-Julius Weekly*, 5 May, p. 2.

A908 "My Friends Write Books," *Haldeman-Julius Weekly*, 5 May, p. 2.

A909 "Hell in West Virginia," *Haldeman-Julius Weekly*, 5 May, p. 2.

A910 "Sinclair Wins Judgement of 500,000 Crowns in Libel Suit Brought against Dr. Max Hussarck, Former Premier of Austria," *Haldeman-Julius Weekly*, 5 May, p. 3.

A911 "Upton Sinclair's Page," *Haldeman-Julius Weekly*, 12 May, p. 2.

a. "Dr. William J. Robinson and Upton Sinclair Debate"

b. "Dr. Abrams's Theory" [Exchange of long letters.]

A912 "Russia Today," *Haldeman-Julius Weekly*, 12 May, pp. 2–3.

A913 "The United Front," *The Worker*, 12 May, p. 4.

John Pepper's reply on p. 1.

A914* *Circular Letter*. Pasadena: The Author, 17 May. Broadside.

Letter to Louis D. Oaks, Chief of Police, Los Angeles.

Reprinted: A950. See A916.

1923 continued

A915 "Upton Sinclair's Page," *Haldeman-Julius Weekly*, 19 May, p. 2.

a. "The Future of Russia"

b. "Concerning *The Goose-step*" [Letter to Literary Editor of *Springfield Republican*.]

c. "Concerning *The Book of Life*" [Exchange of letters with Ernest Thompson Seton.]

A916 "Upton Sinclair Braves Prison in Fight to Uphold People's Constitutional Rights," *Haldeman-Julius Weekly*, 26 May, p. 1.

On Sinclair's arrest by Los Angeles police for reading Constitution.

A917 "Upton Sinclair's Page," *Haldeman-Julius Weekly*, 26 May, pp. 2–3.

"Who Said Burns?"

A918 "Upton Sinclair's Page," *Haldeman-Julius Weekly*, 2 June, p. 2.

a. "God Versus the Devil"

b. "A Modern Morality Play"

c. "The Associated Press Again"

d. "A *Brass Check* Editor"

A919 "Upton Sinclair Defends the Law," *Nation*, CXVI (6 June), 647.

A920 "Labor and the Motion Pictures," *Soviet Russia Pictorial*, VIII (June), 124.

A921 "Protecting Our Liberties," *Nation*, CXVII (4 July), 9–10.

A922 "Upton Sinclair's Arrest," *New Republic*, XXXV (11 July), 180.

Free speech in California.

A923 "We Get Arrested a Little," *Liberator*, July, pp. 16–17, 120–122.

A924 "Why Are Our College Students Young Barbarians and Their Professors Tired and Discouraged?" *New York American*, 5 August, LII, p. 2.
Review of *Town and Gown* by Lynn Montross and Lois Syster Montross.

A925 "The Great Problem the American People Have to Solve Is Getting Big Hog's Feet Out of the National Trough," *New York American*, 12 August LII, p. 3.
Review of *Capitol Hill* by Harvey Fergusson.

A926 "Epic Struggles of Norway's Vikings No More Terrible Than Those of Laborers on Modern 'Hell Fleets' Off Alaska." *New York American*, 19 August, LII, p. 3.
Review of *The Lust of the Vikings* by Johan Bojer.

A927 "Modern Economic Forces Break All Barriers of Nationality," *New York American*, 26 August, LII, p. 4.
Review of *Nacha Regules* by Manuel Galvez.

A928* "Civil Liberties in Los Angeles," *Industrial Pioneer*, I (August), 27–29.

A929 "*The Goose-step*—Condensed," *Hearst's International Magazine*, XLIV (August), 103–104, 128–129.
See A894.

A930* "We Get Arrested a Little," *Râssegna Internationale—Cahiers Internationaux*, V (August–September), 828–841.

A931 "Novelist of New Russia Shows Pity for Oppressed," *New York American*, 2 September, LII, p. 4.
Review of *A Week* by Iruy Libedensky.

A932 "A Soldier Reports on Mental Things about War and Moral Fog of War," *New York American*, 9 September, LII, p. 2.
Review of *Through the Wheat* by Thomas Boyd.

1923 continued

A933 "Now As in the Days of Henry D. Thoreau, Massachusetts Has Its Greatest Soul in Jail," *New York American*, 16 September, LII, p. 3.

Review of *The Story of a Proletarian Life* by Bartolemeo Vanzetti.

A934 "West of the Water Tower," *New York American*, 23 September.

Review. Not seen.

A935 "What Women Put in Their Heads Will Do Them More Good Than What They Put on Top," *New York American*, 30 September, LII, p. 3.

Review of *Bread* by Charles Norris.

A936 *Circular Letter*. Pasadena: The Author, 5 October, 4 pp.

Reports on availability of six reprints and sale of *The Goslings* and reception of *Hell*; also mentions winning half million crowns in libel suit against former Austrian premier.

A937 "The Shoe-Worker's Children Must Go Barefooted to School Because He Has Produced Too Many Shoes," *New York American*, 7 October, LII, p. 3.

Review of *Mr. Podd* by Freeman Tilden.

A938 "Farmers Who Made the World Safe for Democracy Have Forgotten to Make It Safe for Themselves," *New York American*, 21 October, LII, p. 2.

Review of *Weeds* by Edith Summers Kelly.

A939 "White Slave Law Merely Provides a Harvest for Blackmailers; Some Courageous Legislator Ought to Propose Its Modification," *New York American*, 28 October, LII, p. 3.

Review of *Cytherea* by Joseph Hergesheimer.

A940 "All Over America a Poor Man Is Guilty Until He Has Been Proved Innocent," *New York American*, 4 November, LII, p. 3.
Review of *Crucibles of Crime* by Joseph Fishman.

A941 "Parents Do Not Want to Know the Truth about Young People," *New York American*, 11 November, LII, p. 5.
Review of *Janet March* by Floyd Dell.

A942 Letter: A Protest from Mr. Sinclair, *New Republic*, XXXVI (14 November), 310.

A943 "If We Only Could Reorganize Our Industries Sanely, We Could All Be Rich on 3 or 4 Hour's Work a Day," *New York American*, 18 November, LII, p. 2.
Review of *The Challenge of Waste* by Stuart Chase.

A944 "Secret Diplomacy Is the Greatest Peril to Modern Civilization; Let Congress Force Full Publicity for All Our Foreign Dealings," *New York American*, 25 November, LII, p. 3.
Review of *The Secret History of a Great Betrayal* by E. D. Morel.

A945 "The United-Front-in-Spite-of-Yourself," *Haldeman-Julius Weekly*, 15 December, p. 2.

A946 "Upton Sinclair, in a Delightful Letter, Exposes Another Case of Journalistic Harlotry," *Haldeman-Julius Weekly*, 15 December, p. 2.

A947 "The League of the Old Men," *Haldeman-Julius Weekly*, 22 December, p. 3.

A948 *Biographical Letter and Critical Opinions*. Pasadena: The Author. 32 pp.
See A1360.

1923 continued

A949* *The Charter of the "Appeal to Reason."* Minneapolis: Murray E. King. 1 p.

See A1015.

A950 *To the Chief of Police of Los Angeles*, Pasadena: The Author. 4 pp.

See A914.

A951* *The Goose-Step, A Study of American Education.* Pasadena: The Author, 4 pp.

Advertising brochure prepared by the Author, with manuscript corrections and deletions.

A952* *The Goose-Step, A Study of American Education.* Pasadena: The Author. 2 pp.

List of other books on back.

A953* *Hell: A Verse Drama and Photo-Play.* Pasadena: The Author. 128 pp.

Reprinted: Girard, Kansas: Haldeman-Julius, [n.d.]

Foreign Editions: Chinese, French, German, Japanese, Russian, White-Russian.

A954* *Circular Letter.* Pasadena: The Author. 1 leaf.

Order blank, beginning with *The Goose Step*, paper, and ending with *Debs and the Poets.*

A955* *Circular Letter.* Pasadena: The Author. 1 leaf.

Printed blank form for ordering a selected list of Sinclair's books. List headed by *The Goose-Step* and concluded by *Samuel the Seeker.*

1924

A956 "Here Is Detailed and Positive Proof That Fasting Is a Cause of Rejuvenation to the Human Organism," *New York American*, 6 January, LII, p. 3.

Discussion of *The Fasting Cure* and article in *Journal of Metabolic Research.*

A957 "Marriage Used to Be a Sacrament; Now It Is a Lottery; I Look Forward to the Time When It May Become a Science," *New York American*, 13 January, LII, p. 2.

Review of *Upstream* by Ludwig Lewisohn.

A958* *Circular Letter*. Pasadena: Upton Sinclair, 15 January. 1 leaf.

Announcing that *The Goslings* will be ready the first week in February.

A959 "Would You Like to Be De-Bunked?" *Halderman-Julius Weekly*, 26 January, p. 3.

Discussion of *Bunk* by W. E. Woodward.

A960* "Money Is Like Gunpowder or Oil Flung on Love's Fire Causing It to Leap into Fierce, Consuming Flame," *New York American*, 27 January, LII, p. 2.

Review of *The Nuptial Flight* by Edgar Lee Masters. Used as foreword to later edition.

A961 "Pocket Series Has Solved Problems of Culture . . . ," *Life and Letters*, II (January), 8.

A962* "Since Leaving Home," *Pearson's Magazine*, L (January), 55–56.

Review of *Since Leaving Home* by Albert Wehde.

A963 "Radio Is Giving Immediate Impulse to an International Language That in a Generation Will Make Us Tire of Our Mother Tongue," *New York American*, 10 February, LII, p. 2.

Review of *A Short History of the International Language Movement* by Albert Leon Guerard.

A964* *The Goslings*. Pasadena: Upton Sinclair, 15 February. 454 pp.

As serial, in part: *Appeal to Reason*, 19 January–9 February. Reprinted: St. Clair Shores, Mich.: Scholarly Press, 1970

1924 continued

(facsimile). *The Schools of Los Angeles*, a pamphlet contains the first 64 pages; see A981.

Foreign Editions: Czech, English, German, Japanese, Russian.

A965 "Ancient Workers Were Slaves, But the British Workers Are Free Men, Educating Themselves and Training Leaders," *New York American*, 24 February, LII, p. 6.

Review of *Tom Mann's Memoirs* by Tom Mann. Also in *Washington Herald*, 9 March.

A966 "You Can Hear Through the Bones of Your Skull, Even Though Deaf . . . ," *New York American*, 2 March, LII, p. 6.

About Riverbank Laboratories, Geneva, Illinois. Also in *Washington Herald*, 16 March; see A970.

A967 "The Unions See That Information Reaches the Public," *Los Angeles Examiner*, 9 March.

A968 "Prison Conditions Will Not Be Changed Until Grafting Politicians Are Ousted from Control," *New York American*, 9 March, LII, p. 5.

Review of *In Prison* by Kate Richards O'Hare. Also in *Washington Herald*, 23 March.

A969 "World's Vital Raw Materials Must Not Serve as Playthings for Wealthy Gentlemen . . . ," *New York American*, 16 March, LII, p. 4.

Review of *The Challenge of War: An Economic Interpretation* by Norman Thomas. Also in *Washington Herald*, 30 March.

A970 "Cures for Deafness and Laws of Sound Found in Dungeon-like Cell," *New York American*, 16 March, LII, p. 4.

See A966.

A971 "Multi-Millionaire Proposes Merging Chief U. S. Industries . . . ," *New York American*, 23 March, LII, p. 4.
Review of *The People's Corporation* by King C. Gillette. Also in *Washington Herald*, 6 April. Sinclair was involved in rewriting and revising this book. MS. at the Lilly Library.

A972 "To Help People, Especially Children, Read Worthwhile Books . . . ," *New York American*, 30 March, LII, p. 5.
Review of *The Beginning and the End of the Best Library Service in the World* by Mrs. Laura Steffens Sugget. Also in *Washington Herald*, 13 April.

A973 Letter: Concerning Sale of Muscle Shoals, *Nation*, CXVIII (16 April), 424.

A974* *The Second-Story Man*. Girard, Kansas: Haldeman-Julius (Little Blue Book no. 630), *c.* 9 May. 32 pp.
See A412.

A975 "Upton Sinclair Advises Vanderlip to Start Paper Devoted to Bringing Truth to the People," *Haldeman-Julius Weekly*, 17 May, p. 2.

A976* *The Millennium*. Girard, Kansas: Haldeman-Julius (Little Blue Books nos. 590–592), *c.* 28 May.
Reprinted: Pasadena: Upton Sinclair, 1929. As serial: A451; see also A1002.
Foreign Editions: Bulgarian, Chinese, Czech, Danish, Dutch, English, Estonian, Finnish, German, Gujarati, Hungarian, Icelandic, Lithuanian, Norwegian, Polish, Romanian, Serbo-Croatian, Slovak, Slovenian, Swedish, Tamil, Ukrainian, Yiddish.

A977 "Behold This Writer!" *Liberator*, V (May), 29.
See A1298.

A978* *Circular Letter*. Pasadena: The Author, May. 4 pp.
Announcing the completion of *Singing Jailbirds*.

A979* *Circular Letter*. Pasadena: The Author, 25 June. 1 leaf.
Offering *The Brass Check* and *100%* at bargain prices.

1924 continued

A980* "Screen Misrepresentations," *Authors' League Bulletin*, XII (June), 5–6.

Letters about changes in movie version of Sir Hall Caine's *Eternal City* which alter the motive and the spirit of the novel. Hall Caine's letter and Upton Sinclair's introduction.

A981* *The Schools of Los Angeles*. Pasadena: The Author, *c.* June. 62 pp.

See A964.

A982* "Why Condemn Abrams' Method?" *Physical Culture*, LII (July), 29–30, 104–105.

A983 "Mammonart," *Haldeman-Julius Weekly*, 9 August–21 February, 1925.

As book: A1012.

A984 Sinclair's Endorsement of La Follette, *New Leader* [London], I (13 September), 1, 9.

A985 "Campaign for La Follette for President," *Open Forum*, I (6 October).

A986* "Upton Sinclair Writes to La Follette," *Justice*, VI (17 October), 5.

A987 "Upton Sinclair Makes Political Speech at La Follette Mass Meeting," *Haldeman-Julius Weekly*, 25 October, p. 4.

Stenographic report of an address delivered by Sinclair in Pasadena High School, 3 October.

A988* *Circular Letter*. Pasadena: The Author, 4 November. 1 leaf.

Calling for pledges to support proposed liberal newspaper.

A989 Letter: On Anti-La Follette Arguments in California, *Nation*, CXIX (5 November), 496–497.

A990* *Circular Letter*. Pasadena: The Author, November. 4 pp.
Announcing serial publication of *Mammonart* in *Haldeman-Julius Weekly*.

A991* "My Life and Diet," *Physical Culture*, LII (November), 37–38, 82, 84, 86.
Reprinted: A1003.

A992 "Let in the Light," *Open Forum*, I (6 December), 1.

A993 *The Naturewoman*. Girard, Kansas: Haldeman-Julius (Little Blue Book no. 631), *c.* 8 December. 85 pp.
See A412.

A994 Letter, *Haldeman-Julius Weekly*, 20 December, p. 2.
Long letter to E. Haldeman-Julius complaining of his failure to understand historical Jesus.

A995 "The California Empire," *Open Forum*, I (20 December), 1.

A996* "Gandhi's Colossal Experiment," *Swarjya* [India], December, pp. 1–3.
Annual supplement.

A997 "Toleration," *Haldeman-Julius Monthly*, I (December), back wrapper.

A998* Preface to *A Captain of Industry*. 2 vols. Girard, Kansas: Haldeman-Julius, *c.* December, vol. I, p. 5.
This preface suggests that Sinclair had forgotten that the book had been published before; see A308. Preface dated July 1924.

A999* *Books by Upton Sinclair*. Pasadena: Upton Sinclair. 1 leaf.
With an order blank at the bottom.

A1000* *The Goslings, A Study of the American Schools*. Pasadena: Upton Sinclair. 1 leaf.
Advertising brochure prepared by the Author.

1924 continued

A1001* *The Goslings, A Study of the American Schools.* Pasadena: Upton Sinclair. 1 leaf.

Copy 1: Order from The Baker and Taylor Co., N. Y.
Copy 2: For sale by Upton Sinclair, Pasadena.

A1002* *The Millennium: A Comedy of the Year 2000.* Pasadena: Upton Sinclair. 246 pp.

Apparently published about same time as Haldeman-Julius edition; see A976.

Foreign Editions: See A976.

A1003* *My Life and Diet.* Pasadena: The Author. 4 pp.

"I have been my own guinea pig, on which I have done a lot of experimenting; . . ." See A991.

A1004* *Circular Letter.* Pasadena: The Author. 1 leaf.

Order blank offering for sale a selected list of his books, beginning with *The Goslings.*

A1005* *The Pot Boiler, Comedy in Four Parts.* Girard, Kansas: Haldeman-Julius (Little Blue Book no. 589). 119 pp.

Foreign Edition: Russian.

A1006* *Singing Jailbirds. A Drama In Four Acts.* Pasadena: Upton Sinclair. 95 pp.

Reprinted: Long Beach: The Author, [n.d.]. In part: A1545, A2049.

Foreign Editions: Armenian, Chinese, Czech, English, German, Japanese, Russian, Swedish.

A1007* *Circular Letter.* Pasadena: Upton Sinclair. 1 leaf.

"This Is to Notify You that . . . Has Paid for a Copy of *Mammonart* by Upton Sinclair.

A1008 "Pocket Series Has Solved Problem of Culture," *Life and Letters,* II (1924), 8.

1925

A1009 "Sinclair as Governor," *Open Forum*, II (10 January), 1.

A1010 Letter, *Haldeman-Julius Weekly*, 7 February, p. 1.
On *Mammonart*, especially concerning Balzac.

A1011* Letter: "What About It, Harvard?" *Nation*, CXX (11 February), 143.

A1012* *Mammonart*. Pasadena: The Author, *c.* 15 February. 390 pp.
As serial: A983; in part: A1545, A2049.
Foreign Editions: Bulgarian, Chinese, Czech, English, Finnish, German, Hungarian, Japanese, Russian, Serbo-Croatian, Swedish, Turkish, Yiddish.

A1013 Preface to *Sonnets*, by M. [ary] C. [raig] S. [inclair]. Pasadena: The Author, *c.* 15 February. 39 pp.; preface, pp. 3–6.

A1014 Letter, *Haldeman-Julius Weekly*, 28 February, p. 2.
On *Mammonart*.

A1015 "Why I Must Print the Books I Write," *Authors' League Bulletin*, XII (February), 7.
Reprinted: A 1069.

A1016 *The Charter of the "Appeal to Reason."* Pasadena: The Author, *c.* February.
Broadside; supports revival of *Appeal to Reason*; see A949.

A1017* "Jack London's Books Inspiration of Youth Movement the World Over," *Rochester Sunday American*, 22 March, p. 3.

A1018 "Memories of Jack London," *Houston Chronicle*, 22 March, p. 48.

A1019* "Two Letters from Upton Sinclair," *Nation*, CXX (25 March), 326.

1925 continued

A1020 "The Laborer and His Hire," *New Leader* [London], II (28 March), 5.

A1021 *The Machine*. Girard, Kansas: Haldeman-Julius (Little Blue Book no. 632), 31 March. 91 pp.
See A412.

A1022 "Mother Eddy's *Science and Wealth*," *Haldeman-Julius Monthly*, I (March), 225–227.

A1023 "Memorial to Jack London Suggested by Sinclair," *San Francisco News*, 3 April.

A1024 "Artificial Childhood," *New Leader* [London], II (11 April), 11.

A1025 "Floyd Dell Looks at Life," *Haldeman-Julius Weekly*, 11 April, p. 3.

A1026* *Circular Letter*. Pasadena: The Author, 23 April. 1 leaf.
Announcement is made that the American Fund for Public Service, generally known as the Garland Fund. . . ." See A1027.

A1027* *Circular Letter*. Pasadena: The Author, 25 April. 2 pp.
Requesting suggestions for forthcoming series of "Radical Classics."

A1028* *Circular Letter*. Pasadena: The Author, 25 April. 1 leaf.
To friends of the radical and labor movements concerning series of "Radical Classics."

A1029* "Memories of Jack London, the Bitter Rebel," *Sunday Advocate* [Bombay], 26 April, p. 5.
"Specially contributed"; also appeared in *Hindustan Advocate* [Bombay], 1 May; *New Empire* [Calcutta], 4 May; *The Bengalee* [Calcutta], 24 April.

A1030 "Bunk-Hungry America," *Haldeman-Julius Monthly*, I (April), 293.

A1031 "The Church and Slavery," *Haldeman-Julius Monthly*, I (April), 282–283.

A1032 "Memories of Jack London," *The Labor World*, 1 May. pp. 10–11.

Supplement to *The Labor World*, 21st Annual Issue; see A1018.

A1033 Letter: To Friends of the Radical and Labor Movement, *Milwaukee Leader*, 8 May, p. 24.

A1034* *Circular Letter*. Pasadena: The Author, 15 May. 1 leaf.

Explaining inability to fill orders for *The Jungle* and *King Coal*.

A1035 "A Thought for Today," *Daily Standard* [Brisbane, Australia], 18 May.

A1036* *Circular Letters*. Pasadena: The Author, 20 May. 4 pp.

Proposing a co-operative organization for the publishing of his books.

A1037 "A Letter from Sinclair," *Haldeman-Julius Weekly*, 30 May, p. 4.

Announcing his co-operative publishing plan.

A1038 "From Upton Sinclair," *Open Forum*, II (30 May), 3.

A1039 "Educators Deny That College Education is a Shame," *American Monthly Magazine*, XVII (May), 86.

A1040 "The Sabbath Taboo," *Haldeman-Julius Monthly*, I (May), 336–337.

A1041 Letter: Classics for Workers, *New Republic*, XLIII (10 June), 77.

Reprints circular letter concerning "Radical Classics," A1027.

A1042* *Circular Letter*. Pasadena: The Author, *c*. June. 1 leaf.

"Letter to acknowledge receipts of your communication regarding my proposed co-operative. . . ."

1925 continued

A1043 "Editorial: Upton Sinclair's Pen," *Nation*, CXXI (8 July), 57.

Reprint of letter addressed to the *Los Angeles Examiner*.

A1044* A Circular Letter, *New Republic*, XLIII (8 July), 182–183.

See A1036.

A1045 "Treatment of Political Prisoners in Russia and California," *Open Forum*, II (11 July), 3.

A1046 Letter: On Psychic Phenomena, *New Republic*, XLIII (22 July), 239.

Complains of Edmund Wilson's failure to do justice to Houdini's "Margary" phenomena.

A1047* *Circular Letter*. Pasadena: The Author, 25 July. 4 pp.

Concerning "People's Classics" with list of three hundred titles from which the reader is asked to select two hundred for publication.

A1048* *Circular Letter*. Pasadena: The Author, 28 July. 4 pp.

Announcing change from "Co-operative" to "Loan" Plan.

A1049 "Holy Rollers," *Haldeman-Julius Monthly*, II (July), 142–143.

A1050 "The Truth About Russia," *Haldeman-Julius Monthly*, II (July), 136–140.

A1051 "Radical Classics," *World Tomorrow*, VIII (July), 215.

A1052 Letter, *Open Forum*, II (8 August), 3.

On the treatment of political prisoners in Russia.

A1053 "Bill Porter: A Drama of the Prison Life of O. Henry," *Haldeman-Julius Monthly*, II (August), 195–246.

As book: A1054.

A1054* *Bill Porter*. Pasadena: The Author, 1 September. 58 pp.
As serial: A1053.
Foreign Editions: Japanese, Russian.

A1055* *Circular Letter*. Pasadena: The Author, 12 September. 1 leaf.
Reminding reader of pledges in connection with Sinclair's publishing enterprise.

A1056* *Circular Letter*. Pasadena: The Author, *c*. 15 September. 1 leaf.
Announcing the publication of *Bill Porter*.

A1057 *Circular Letter*. Pasadena: The Author, 20 September. 4 pp.
Announcing further news about "Sinclair Loan Plan."

A1058 "The Flapper," *Open Forum*, II (26 September) 3.

A1059 Letter: About Bruce Bliven on Flappers, *New Republic*, XLIV (7 October), 179.

A1060 "Upton Sinclair Protests," *Open Forum*, II (24 October), 1.

A1061* "Upton Asks Leave to Print," *Public Relations*, I (October), 22–25.
Article refutes charges in letter from Sinclair that business corrupts politics.

A1062* "Sinclair to Governor Richardson," *Open Forum*, II (14 November), 3.
On jailing of Charlotte Anita Whitney.

A1063 Letter to Editor of *New Republic*, *Open Forum*, II (21 November) 3. See A1059.

1925 continued

A1064* "The Governor and Sinclair," *Open Forum*, II (28 November), 1

Exchange of letters between Sinclair and Governor F. W. Richardson.

A1065 "The Martyr," *Open Forum*, II (5 December), 1.

Verse, "addressed to the Worthy Government."

A1066 Letter: "Not the Wisdom of Solomon," *Nation*, CXXI (9 December), 652.

Corrects quotation.

A1067 Letter: "The Peasant in Russia and America," *New Republic*, XLV (9 December), 89.

Critical of J. M. Keynes's account of economic conditions in Russia.

A1068* "Memories of Edward MacDowell," *The Sackbut*, December. pp. 127-132.

See A1079.

A1069* *Why I Must Print the Books I Write*. Pasadena: The Author. 8 pp.

See A1015.

A1070* *Circular Letter*. Pasadena: The Author. 1 leaf.

I acknowledge with thanks. . . .

A1071* *Circular Letter*. Pasadena: Upton Sinclair. 2 pp.

Sinclair offers a list of his books for sale.

A1072* "*Mammonart*," *Pro and Con*. Pasadena: Upton Sinclair. 2 pp.

Opinions of *Mammonart* precede list of books.

A1073* *Circular Letter*. Pasadena: The Author. 1 leaf.

Order blank beginning: "If you organize the Sinclair Co-operative, and if the terms and conditions are satisfactory to me, you may count upon me for the sum of . . . dollars; I enodrse the sum of . . . as a personal loan"; a list of books offered for sale, headed by *Mammonart*.

A1074* *Circular Letter*. Pasadena: The Author. 1 leaf.
Order blank; list of books offered for sale beginning with *Moneychangers*: (a New Edition), *Mammonart*; ending with *Parlor Provocateur*.

A1075 *Circular Letter*. Pasadena: The Author. 1 p.
Order blank beginning with *Mammonart* and ending with either *The Goose-Step* or *The Goslings*.

A1076* *Circular Letter*. Pasadena: The Author. 1 leaf.
Order blank offering for sale a selected list of his books.

A1077 Introduction to *Sonnets to Craig*, by George Sterling. Long Beach: Upton Sinclair. 120 pp.; preface, pp. 3–8.
See A1078.

A1078* Foreword to *Der Sonnettenkranz*, trans. W. L. Rosenberg. Introduction by Dr. Ernst Jockers. Cleveland: Siebenbürgerisch-Amerikanisches Volksblatt, pp. 15–18.
See A1077.

1926

A1079 "The Sins of [Harry] Sinclair," *Nation*, CXXII (27 January), 86–87.
Letter on Tarbell's *History of Standard Oil*.

A1080* "MacDowell," *American Mercury*, VII (January), 50–54.
Sinclair's reminiscences about the composer Edward A. MacDowell; see A1068, A1739, A2057.

A1081 "In Lincoln's Land," *Open Forum*, III (13 February), 1.

A1082 "Will Problems Solve Themselves?" *Open Forum*, III (20 February), 3.

A1083 "American Counter Reformation," *Open Forum*, III (20 February), 3.

1926 continued

A1084 "Unwanted Children in China," *New Republic*, XLVI (24 February), 21.

A1058* *Upton Sinclair, Candidate for Governor*. Pasadena: The Author, 28 February. 1 leaf.

Circular letter accepting the nomination of the Socialist Party.

A1086* "For Romain Rolland," *Europe: Révue Mensuelle*, no. 38 (February), p. 199.

Sinclair's contribution to this special Rolland number.

A1087 "Governor Upton Sinclair," *Open Forum*, III (13 March), 1.

A1088* *Circular Letter*. Pasadena: The Author, 15 March. 4 pp.

Discussing the publication of *Letters to Judd*.

A1089 "Sinclair on Dictatorship," *Open Forum*; III (27 March), 4.

A1090* *Letters to Judd*. Pasadena: Upton Sinclair, 1 April. 64 pp.

Reprinted: Pasadena: Upton Sinclair, 1932, 1934, rev., paper; Girard, Kansas: Haldeman-Julius, 1934, 1949. See *This World of 1949 and What to Do about It*, A2071. In part: A1545, A2049.

Foreign Editions: Finnish, German, Icelandic, Japanese, Norwegian, Russian, Spanish, Swedish, Yiddish.

A1091 "Sinclair on Atheism," *Open Forum*, III (17 April), 4.

A1092 "Ornithological Note," *Nation*, CXII (21 April), 450.

A1093 "Word Picture of Edward MacDowell," *Musician*, XXXI (April), 34.

See A1068, A1080, A1739, A2057.

A1094 "Oil!" *The Daily Worker*, 1 June–4 September.

The book in part; see A1128.

A1095* "Upton Sinclair Defends His Attitude," *Jewish Tribune*, 11 June, pp. 3, 18.

Includes editorial comment and the full text of the statement Sinclair contributed to *Judenhass*, an anti-Semitic anthology published in Vienna, Austria; see A1101, A1122.

A1096* "A Letter to an American Capitalist," *Open Forum*, III (26 June), 1.

Also in *The New Magazine*, supplement to *The Daily Worker*, 26 June, p. 2. Letter dated 5 June; to Mr. Charles Carpenter.

A1097* "An Evangelist Drowns," *New Republic*, XLVII (30 June), 171 .

On Aimee Semple McPherson.

A1098* "Government and Business," *Open Forum*, III (3 July), 3.

A1099* "More Letters to a Capitalist," *Open Forum*, III (3 July), 3.

A1100* "*The Story of a Proletarian Life*," *Open Forum*, III (3 July), 3.

Review of Bartlomeo Vanzetti's autobiography. See A933.

A1101 "Upton Sinclair Again," *Jewish Tribune*, 9 July, p. 7.

A letter to the editor plus a comment on his June 11 discussion of his contribution to *Judenhass*; see A1095, A1122.

A1102* *Circular Letter*. Pasadena: The Author, 15 July. 4 pp.

Announcing the publication of *The Spokesman's Secretary*.

A1103 "More Letters to a Capitalist," *Open Forum*, III (24 July), 3.

A1104* *The Spokesman's Secretary*. Pasadena: The Author, *c.* August. 94 pp.

Foreign Editions: German, Russian.

1926 continued

A1105* *What's the Use of Books?* New York: Vanguard Press, *c.* 1 September. 11 pp.

A1106 "Sinclair to Mencken," *Open Forum*, III (18 September), 3.

A1107 "Hey, Mr. Priestley!" *Open Forum*, III (18 September), 3.

A1108 "Campaign Speech by Sinclair," *Open Forum*, III (9 October), 3.

A1109* *Circular Letter*. Pasadena: The Author, 10 October. 4 pp.

Letter discussing the reception of *Love's Pilgrimage*.

A1110 "Education à la Legion," *Nation*, CXXIII (13 October), 348.

A1111 "Political Address," *Open Forum*, III (23 October).

A1112 "Sinclair's Tribute to Debs," *Open Forum*, III (30 October), 1.

A1113 *Circular Letter*. Pasadena: The Author. 2 pp.

Announcing 1 November as publication date for new edition of *Love's Pilgrimage*.

A1114 "Labor Should See 'Processional,'" *Open Forum*, III (20 November), 3.

A1115 "Chicago Stockyard Reverts to *The Jungle*," *Open Forum*, III (4 December), 3.

A1116 "Sinclair Prods Mencken's Memory," *Open Forum*, III (11 December), 3.

A1117 "Sinclair On George Sterling," *Open Forum*, III (25 December), 3.

A1118 "Killers of Thought: Shall We Abolish Intercollegiate Football?" *Forum*, LXXVI (December), 838–843.
A debate: No, Dr. Morton Prince; Yes, Upton Sinclair.

A1119 "A Fighting Magazine," *New Masses*, II (December), 13.

A1120* *Circular Letter*. Pasadena: The Author. 1 leaf.
Order blank beginning with: "I Enclose the Sum of . . . Dollars, According to Your Loan Plan Proposition"; and a list of books offered for sale, beginning with *The Spokesman's Secretary*, and ending with *The Goslings*.

A1121* *Circular Letter. Sinclair's New Novel in Sweden.* Long Beach: The Author. 1 leaf.
Refers to *Oil!*. Various critical comments from Swedish papers.

A1122 In *Judenhaas*: *Eine Anthologie*. (Herausgegeben von der Arbeitsgemeinschaft fur kulterelle Propoganda "Prometheus") Vienna: Selbstverlag, pp. 90–91.
Sinclair's contribution without title—translated from English; see A1095, A1101 for responses.

1927

A1123 "Ike is Set Right on Debs," *Open Forum*, IV (1 January), 3.

A1124 "Critics Disagree," *Open Forum*, IV (29 January), 3.

A1125* "Sinclair Calls Wedge's Bluff," *Open Forum*, IV (12 February), 3.
Letter to F. R. Wedge.

A1126 "The Best Thing for America," *Open Forum*, IV (26 February), 2.

A1127* *Circular Letter*. Long Beach: The Author, 12 March. 1 leaf.
Announcing that *Oil!* is to be published by A. & C. Boni.

1927 continued

A1128* *Oil*! New York: A. & C. Boni; Long Beach: The Author, 25 March. 527 pp.

As serial in part: A1094.

Reprinted: Fig Leaf Edition: Long Beach: The Author, 1927; New York: Grosset & Dunlap, 1927; Girard, Kansas: Haldeman-Julius, [n.d.], 4 vols.; New York: Washington Square Press, 1966, paper. In part: A1545; as play: A1235.

Foreign Editions: Arabic, Braille, Bulgarian, Chinese, Czech, Danish, Dutch, English, Esperanto, Estonian, Finnish, French, German, Hebrew, Hindi, Hungarian, Japanese, Latvian, Lithuanian, Norwegian, Polish, Portuguese, Romanian, Serbo-Croatian, Slovak, Slovenian, Spanish, Swedish, Yiddish.

A1129* "Letter to a Red Army Soldier," *Open Forum*, IV (26 March), 3.

A1130* *Circular Letter*. Long Beach: The Author, March. 4 pp.

Announcing the publication of *Oil!*.

A1131* "Revolution—Not Sex," *New Masses*, II (March), 11.

A1132 "Go To It,—Sinclair," *Open Forum*, IV (16 April), 3.

A1133 "Brains in Religion," *Open Forum*, IV (23 April), 3.

A1134 "Russia, Avoid War At All Hazards," *Open Forum*, IV (7 May), 3.

A1135 *Circular Letter*. Long Beach: The Author, *c*. 1 June.

Broadside requesting privacy for the sake of his wife's health and so that he can write *Money Writes*!

A1136 "Send Miss Whitney to Jail—Upton Sinclair," *Open Forum*, IV (4 June), 2.

A1137 "Poor Me and Pure Boston," *Nation*, CXXIV (29 June), 713–714.

On banning of *Oil!*

A1138* *Circular Letter.* Long Beach: The Author, 1 July. 4 pp.

Reporting on his experiences in Boston with the sale of *Oil!*.

A1139 "How to be Obscene," *New Yorker*, III (2 July), 25–26.

Concerns *Oil!*

A1140 "The Class War," *Saturday Review of Literature*, III (16 July), 980.

Reply to Professor Tugwell's review of *Oil!*

A1141* "Money Writes!" *Haldeman-Julius Quarterly*, I and II (July/August/September, October/November/December 1927 and January/February/March 1928.).

As book: A1154.

A1142 "On Teaching Religion," *Open Forum*, IV (6 August), 3.

A1143 "Try It on Rabelais," *Open Forum*, IV (6 August), 3.

A1144* "Die Zensur von Boston," *Die Weltbuhne* [Berlin], XXIII (16 August), 257–259.

On *Oil!*

A1145 "Would Indict Massachusetts," *Nation*, CXXV (24 August), 175.

For "murder" of Sacco and Vanzetti. Telegram.

A1146* "Sinclair on George Sterling," *New York World*, 27 August.

A1147 "Censor: Fool or Knave," *New Masses*, III (August), 16.

A1148* "Upton Sinclair Voices His Objections to the Editorial Article in *The News*," *Denver Evening News*, 9 September, p. 6.

Sinclair later brought suit for libel, but lost the case; see A1216.

1927 continued

A1149 "Kept Press Retaliates," *Open Forum*, IV (10 September), 3.

A1150 "Sinclair's Appreciation," *Open Forum*, IV (24 September), 1.

A1151* "My Friend, George Sterling," *Bookman*, LXVI (September), 30–32.

A1152 "Russia Congratulated on Tenth Anniversary," *Open Forum*, IV (29 October), 2.

A1153* *Circular Letter*. Long Beach: The Author, 1 November. 4 pp.

Announcing the publication of *Money Writes*!.

A1154* *Money Writes*! New York: A. & C. Boni; Long Beach: The Author, *c*. 1 November. 227 pp.

As serial: A1141.

Foreign Editions: Chinese, Czech, Dutch, English, German, Japanese, Russian, Serbo-Croatian.

A1155 "Book Urchins," *Forum*, LXXVIII (November), 739.

A1156 "Mr. Mencken Calls on Me," *Bookman*, LXVI (November), 254–256.

A1157 "Mind and Face," *New Masses*, III (November), 28–29.

Review of René Fulop-Miller's *The Mind and Face of Bolshevism*.

A1158 "What of Tom Mooney?" *Open Forum*, IV (10 December), 3.

A1159 "My Friend George Sterling," *Overland Monthly*, LXXXV (December), 365.

A1160* *Books of Upton Sinclair*. Long Beach: The Author. 4 pp.

Advertising list: *Money Writes*! to be published October 1927. Variant 2nd copy: note by Gertrude Atherton at end.

A1161* *Is This Book Obscene?* Long Beach: Upton Sinclair. 1 leaf.

Opinion of *Oil*!

A1162* *Circular Letter*. Long Beach: The Author. 1 leaf.

Order blank beginning with *Money Writes*! and ending with a combination offer.

A1163* *Circular Letter*. Long Beach: The Author. 1 leaf.

Order blank for a selected list of his books, beginning with *Oil!*

A1164 Preface to *Jimmie Higgins*, trans H. Maidako. Tokyo: [n.p.], p. [iii].

See Japanese editions. Photoprint of a letter from Upton Sinclair to H. Maidako dated 27 July 1926.

A1165 Introduction to *Mammonart*, trans. Shoji Kimura. Tokyo: [n.p.], p. [iii].

See Japanese editions. Photoprint of a letter from Upton Sinclair dated 23 December 1925. Additional note on p. 3.

1928

A1166 "Gerald Lively's Poems," *Nation*, CXXVI (11 January), 44.

Letter urging production of a book of Lively's poems.

A1167 "*Money Writes*!" *New Republic*, LIII (8 February), 325.

A1168 "Letters That Fly," *Nation*, CXXVI (22 February), 212.

Letter complaining about air mail service.

1928 continued

A1169* "Boston, a Contemporary Historical Novel," *Bookman*, LXVI–LXVIII (February–November).

The final installment (November) was issued as a separate supplement. As book: A1195.

A1170 "About Russia," *Open Forum*, V (3 March), 3.

A1171 "As to Russia," *Open Forum*, V (31 March), 3.

A1172 "What Should Be Translated," *Nation*, CXXVI (4 April), 380.

A1173 "At Odds: A Reply to Walter Lippmann," *Saturday Review of Literature*, IV (7 April), 744.

Reprinted: *Saturday Review of Literature*, 5 August 1944.

A1174 "A Slogan for Hoover," *Nation*, CXXVI (11 April), 408.

"He sat in the Harding cabinet and he never peeped."

A1175 "Helpful Herb Can't Live Down Harding's Cabinet," *Open Forum*, V (21 April), 3.

A1176 "Upton Sinclair and Lawrence Morris," *New Republic*, LIV (9 May), 352–353.

Rejoinder to Morris's article on Sinclair, "The Way of a Reformer," which appeared in *New Republic*, LIV (7 March), 90–93.

A1177 "Henry James Defended by His Near-Countrymen," *Open Forum*, V (12 May), 3.

A1178 "The Facts about Russia," *Open Forum*, V (19 May), 3.

A1179* Preface to *Sonnets to Craig*. New York: A. & C. Boni; Long Beach: Upton Sinclair, 28 May.

A selection of these sonnets appeared originally in *Bookman*, January. Sinclair's preface, pp. 3–8.

A1180 "The Rights of a Columnist," *Nation*, CXXVI (30 May), 609.

Comments by several authors regarding Heywood Broun's "dismissal" from *New York World* over Sacco-Vanzetti affair.

A1181 "A Prohibition Plank for Al Smith," *New Republic*, LV (6 June), 73.

A1182* "Speaking of Russia," *Open Forum*, V (16 June), 3.

A1183 Sane Station WEVD!" *Open Forum*, V (30 June), 3.

A1184 Letters: Upton Sinclair to H. L. Mencken, *Forum*, LXXVIII (June), 952.

A1185 "My Private Utopia," *Nation*, CXXVII (11 July), 39–40.

A1186* "*Money Writes!*" *Author, Playwright, and Composer*, July, p. 153.

Letter to the editor in answer to H. M. Walbrooke's review of *Money Writes*! in April issue.

A1187* "George Sterling's Sonnets," *New York Herald Tribune Book Section*, 12 August, p. 14.

Letter defending his preface to *Sonnets to Craig*.

A1188* "Jim Tully—A Story of Ingratitude," *Haldeman-Julius Monthly*, VIII (August), 7–14.

A1189* "Justice, Bought and Paid For," *Forum*, LXXIX (August), 653–657.

Sinclair's side of a debate with Arthur C. Train on the subject "Can a Rich Man Be Convicted?"

A1190* "Allegation Confirmed," *Forum*, LXXX (August), 311.

A1191 "How Upton Sinclair Votes," *Nation*, CXXVII (12 September), 247.

1928 continued

A1192* *Circular Letter.* Long Beach: The Author, *c.* October.

Broadside soliciting support of new Playwrights' production of *Singing Jailbirds.*

A1193* *Circular Letter.* Long Beach: The Author, October. 4 pp.

Announcing forthcoming publication of *Boston.*

A1194 "Statements of Belief II," *Bookman*, LXVII (October), 207.

Brief "Credos" of fourteen authors. Sinclair's statement: "It is my idea that a writer, to be of any consequence, should have something to say which is likely to be of use to other men in understanding how to live."

A1195* *Boston.* New York: A. & C. Boni; Pasadena and Long Beach: Upton Sinclair, 11 November. 2 vol. Vol. I, 374 pp.; Vol. II, 755 pp. (numbered continuously).

As serial: A1169.

Reprinted: New York: Grosset & Dunlap, 1930. Girard, Kansas. Haldeman-Julius (Big Blue Book no. B-409), 1946, 4 vols., paper; Condensation: *August 22nd*, New York: Universial Publishing and Distributing (Award Books), 1965. In part: A1545, A2049.

Foreign Editions: Bulgarian, Chinese, Czech, Danish, Dutch, English, French, German, Hindi, Japanese, Polish, Russian, Spanish, Swedish, Tamil, Yiddish.

A1196* A Letter from Upton Sinclair, *New Masses*, LV (November), 14.

Part of "Upton Sinclair's 50th year: Anniversary Number." Includes tributes from Floyd Dell, Art Young, Scott Nearing, Roger Baldwin, and Robert Wolf.

A1197 Letter. *New York Times*, 23 December, sect. VIII, p. 4.

About performance of *Singing Jailbirds.*

A1198* "*Singing Jailbirds*," *New Republic*, LVII (26 December), 167.

Letter to editor requesting funds to move play to larger theater.

A1199 "What Life Means to Me, Parts I, II," *Open Forum*, V (29 December), 1; (5 January 1929), 2.

See A305.

A1200 "Artless Art," *New Masses*, IV (December), 14.

On Art Young.

A1201* *Circular Letter*. Long Beach: The Author. 4 pp.

Brochure advertising *Boston*. Letter from John Haynes Holmes.

A1202* *Circular Letter*. Long Beach: The Author. 1 leaf.

Order blank offering for sale his books, beginning with *Boston*.

A1203* Preface to *Oil!* Moscow: Gosizdat, 1928, pp. 5–12.

See Russian editions.

1929

A1204* Introductory statement in *Poems of the Chinese Revolution*, ed. H. T. Tsiang. New York: Hsi-Tseng Tsiang, Box 465, T. C. Columbia University, *c*. January, p. 3. In English.

A1205 "Prohibition Prohibits, Says Upton Sinclair," *Open Forum*, VI (2 February), 2.

A1206 "Boston Paper Shows Signs of Imagination," *Open Forum*, VI (23 February), 3.

A1207 "*Singing Jailbirds*," *New Republic*, LVIII (13 March), 200.

Letter to the editor; Sinclair on Stark Young.

A1208 "The Centralia Horror," *Nation*, CXXVIII (27 March), 373.

1929 continued

A1209* *Circular Letter.* Long Beach: The Author, 27 March. 1 leaf.

A poet in need: ill health and poverty interfere with James Larkin Pearson's work. Printed in the *New York Times* on 4 April.

A1210* "To Set the People Free," *Daily Standard* [Brisbane, Australia], 8 April.

Poem.

A1211 "Bring Sacco, Vanzetti Back to Life in Boston," *Open Forum*, VI (4 May), 3.

A1212* *Circular Letter.* Long Beach: The Author, May. 4 pp.

Concerning *Boston* and the Pulitzer Prize.

A1213 Letters: What Is the Basis of the Pulitzer Prize Award? *Authors' League Bulletin*, XVII (May), 18–20.

A1214 "Upton Sinclair Suggests," *Nation*, CXXVIII (12 June), 700.

A1215 "Sinclair Loses Suit," *Open Forum*, VI (29 June), 3.

A1216 "High Treason," *Nation*, CXXIX (24 July), 91.

A1217* *Circular Letter.* Pasadena: The Author, 1 August. 1 leaf.

Reporting on amount of money received for sending *Boston* to public libraries.

A1218* *Circular Letter.* Pasadena: The Author, 1 August. 1 leaf.

Asking if library will accept gift of *Boston.*

A1219* "Fiat Justitia! A Socialist Seeks Justice in Denver," *New Leader*, VIII (3 August), 4.

On Sinclair's unsuccessful libel suit against the *Rocky Mountain News* [Denver].

As offprint: New York: The Author, 1929. 4 p.

A1220 Review of Idwall Jones's *Steel Chips*, *New Masses*, V (August), 17.

A1221* "The Story of Upton Sinclair, As Told by Upton Sinclair to a *Record* Reporter," *Los Angeles Record*, 11–21 September.

Autobiography in eleven installments.

A1222* "Sinclair's *Boston*," *The Equitist* [Phoenix, Ariz.], no. 579 (11 October), pp. 3–4; no. 580 (18 October), p. 4; no. 581 (25 October), pp. 3–4.

Extensive quotations. See A1195.

A1223 "Fascism in America," *Open Forum*, VI (26 October), 3.

A1224 "Man, the Rebel," *Birth Control Review*, XIII (October), 282.

Excerpt from *The Book of Life*, A854.

A1225 "He Won't Be So Polite," *Open Forum*, VI (16 November), 3.

A1226 "Communist 'Criminals' in California," *Nation*, CXXIX (20 November), 582–584.

See A1229, A1238.

A1227 "Sinclair Should Answer," *Open Forum*, VI (23 November), 3.

A1228 "As to the Red Cross," *Open Forum*, VI (23 November), 3.

A1229* "Land of Orange Groves and Jails," *Open Forum*, VI (23 November), 1–2.

See A1226, A1238.

A1230 "Nobody Sees the Joke," *Open Forum*, VI (30 November), 3.

1929 continued

A1231 Letter, *New Masses*, V (November), 22.
Asserts college men have been strike-breakers. See A1237.

A1232 "A Plea for the United States of Europe," *Clarion* [London], I (November), 6.

A1233* "Upton Sinclair on Workers' Art," *New Masses*, V (November), 20.

A1234* *Oil!* [Drama]. Pasadena: The Author, *c.* November or December. 30 pp.
See A1128.

A1235 Letter: to Arthur Conan Doyle, *The American Freeman*, 21 December, p. 1.

A1236 "Faith Betrayed," *Open Forum*, VI (28 December), 1.

A1237 Letter: Sinclair on College Men, *New Masses*, V (December), 22.

A1238* *Land of Orange Groves and Jails*. Pasadena: The Author. 1 leaf.
See A1226, A1229.

A1239 Contribution to *On Parade*, by Eva Herrman, ed. Erich Posselt. New York: Coward-McCann, p. 134.

A1240* *The Pulitzer Prize and "Special Pleading."* Pasadena: The Author. 4 pp.

A1241* Preface to *The Brass Check*, trans. Jirow Hayasaka. Tokyo: [n.p., n.d.], p. [v].
See Japanese edition. Photoprint of a letter from Upton Sinclair to Jirow Hayasaka dated 12 September 1929.

1930

A1242 Letter on the First Edition of *The Jungle*: Facsimile, *Publisher's Weekly*, CXVII (18 January), 342.

A1243 "Free Speech and No Foolishness, Mr. Sinclair," *Open Forum*, VII (25 January), 3.

A1244 "Socialist Asks Cardinal to Explain Discrepancy," *Open Forum*, VII (25 January), 3.

A1245* "The Radio Mind," *Ghost Stories*, VIII (January–February).

Portions of *Mental Radio*: A1254.

A1246* *The Scrubwomen—Fragment of a Chorus*. Pasadena: The Author, *c*. January. 1 leaf.

Poem attacking Harvard University for having fired twenty scrubwomen.

A1247 "How to End Famine, War," *Open Forum*, VII (1 February), 3.

A1248 Letter to Cardinal O'Connell, *New Republic*, LXI (12 February), 330–331.

Reprinted: A1302.

A1299 "Upton Sinclair and Pity," *Survey*, LXIII (15 February), 600.

An open letter to Leon Whipple who had criticized Sinclair as "lacking in pity. . . ."

A1250* *Mountain City*. New York: A. & C. Boni; Long Beach: Upton Sinclair, 21 February. 399 pp.

Foreign Editions: Bulgarian, Chinese, Czech, Danish, English-Germany, English, Finnish, French, German, Hungarian, Japanese, Polish, Romanian, Russian, Serbo-Croatian, Slovenian, Spanish, Swedish.

A1251 "The Newer Education in Plush-lined Pasadena," *Open Forum*, VII (22 February), 3.

A1252* *Circular Letter*. Pasadena: The Author, February. 4 pp.

Announcing the publication of *Mountain City*.

1930 continued

A1253* "It Depends on How You Look at Soviet Russia," *Open Forum*, VII (1 March), 3.

Letter to George S. Viereck refuting charge that Russians are starving and Americans are not.

A1254* *Mental Radio*. New York: A. & C. Boni; Pasadena: Upton Sinclair, 2 March. 239 pp.

Portions previously published: A1245. Rev. 2nd ed.: Springfield, Ill.: C. C. Thomas, 1962. In part: A1545, A1955, A2049, A2203. Foreign Editions: English, German, Spanish, Swedish.

A1255 "Soviet Figures Reliable," *Open Forum*, VII (15 March), 3.

A1256 "For Freedom of Speech," *Open Forum*, VII (29 March), 2.

A1257 "The Hindus and Pan-Europa," *Open Forum*, VII (29 March), 3.

A1258 "Fascism Active in Yugoslavia," *Open Forum*, VII (5 April), 3.

A1259 "Propaganda Not Allowed," *Open Forum*, VII (19 April), 3.

A1260 "Upton Sinclair Answers Tory," *Open Forum*, VII (26 April), 1.

A1261* *Circular Letter*. Pasadena: The Author, 29 April. 1 leaf.

Letter to editors announcing that *Mental Radio* has just been published and informing them that review copies are available upon request.

A1262 Letter: On "Booze" Fighters, *New Masses*, V (April), 22.

A1263 *An Educational Radio. Some Notes by Upton Sinclair.* Pasadena: The Author, April. 2 pp.

A1264 "Excellent Book on Banking," *Open Forum*, VII (10 May), 3.

A1265 "Non-Understandable School," *Open Forum*, VII (24 May), 3.

A1266* "Success and the Movies," *Screenland*, XXXVIII (May), 103.
See A1271.

A1267 "In Defense of Pacifists," *Open Forum*, VII (7 June), 7.

A1268 "Letter to a Lady Novelist," *Open Forum*, VII (7 June), 3.

A1269 "For Vital Point of View," *Open Forum*, VII (28 June), 3.

A1270 "Wanted—a Martyr," *Survey*, LXIV (1 June), 238–239.
Review of *A History of a Crime Against the Food Law* by Harvey W. Wiley, M. D.

A1271* "Money and the Movies," *Screenland*, XXXVIII (June), 93.

A1272 "The Associated Press," *Nation*, CXXXI (2 July), 17.
On *The Brass Check.*

A1273 Letter, *Living Age*, CCCXXXVIII (15 July), 626.

A1274 Letter: How Accurate Was the *Digest* Poll? *New Republic*, LXIII (13 August), 373–374.
On attitudes towards Prohibition.

A1275 "Sinclair Praises Contest [for] Best Jimmie Higgins," *New Leader* [London], XI (16 August), 1.

1930 continued

A1276 "Soviet Rule is Discussed by Famous Socialist Writer," *Open Forum*, VII (30 August), 3.

A1277* *Books of Upton Sinclair in Translations and Foreign Editions*. Pasadena: The Author, August. 34 pp.
Pamphlet lists 525 titles in 34 countries. Reissued and revised, A1907.

A1278 "Sinclair Sees Suppression of Arrogant, Illegal Booze," *Open Forum*, VII (6 September), 3.

A1279 "*Money Writes*! Goes Over Big in Sunrise Kingdom," *Open Forum*, VII (6 September), 3.

A1280 "More Centralia Case Letters," *New Republic*, LXIV (17 September), 128–129.
With two enclosures: an exchange of letters between Kate Crane-Gartz and Roland C. Hartley.

A1281 "A Letter about Russia," *Open Forum*, VII (20 September), 3.

A1282 Letter: As Candidate for Governor, *Sierra Educational News*, XXVI (September), 11–23.

A1283 "Not Without Laughter," *Open Forum*, VII (4 October), 3.

A1284* "Upton Sinclair Speaks on Campaign Issues at State Wide Picnic," *Labor World* [San Francisco], 10 October, pp. 1–4.
Text of address delivered in Los Angeles.
Reprinted in *The American Freeman*, 18 and 25 October.

A1285 "Mr. Rolph Declines Debate," *Open Forum*, VII (18 October), 3.

A1286* "Cooperation vs. Competition," *Open Forum*, VII (1 November), 3.

A1287 Letter: The *Digest* Poll Again, *New Republic*, LXIV (5 November), 326.
Regarding Prohibition.

A1288 "What Do You Mean—Liberal?" *Open Forum*, VII (8 November), 3.

A1289 "Sinclair Congratulates Rolph," *Open Forum*, VII (15 November), 1.

A1290 "Soviet Dumping," *Forum*, LXXXIV (November), 37–40.

A1291* "Upton Sinclair Exposes 'Red' Commission Tricky Tactics," *The American Freeman*, 6 December, p. 2.

A1292 "Too Rational View of Life," *Open Forum*, VII (6 December), 2.

A1293 "If This Be Authoritarianism—," *Open Forum*, VII (27 December), 3.

A1294 Letter: Sinclair Protests, *New Masses*, VI (December), 23.

A1295 "There Is No Excuse for Poverty in America," *National Magazine*, LIX (December), [119].
In Christmas Supplement.

A1296 "Upton Sinclair Backs Struggle for Class-War Prisoners," *Labor Defenders*, V (December), 251.

A1297* "Is This Jack London?" *Occult Review*, LII (December), 394–400; LIII (January 1931), 10–14.

A1298* "Behold This Writer!" in *Fulton Oursler: A Critical Study*, by several hands, p. 13.
Originally in A977.

A1299* *Books of Upton Sinclair*. Pasadena: The Author. 4 pp.

1930 continued

A1300* *Circular Letter*. Long Beach: The Author. 1 leaf.

Letter beginning: "To my California readers: Being candidate for Governor has its disadvantages. Of the forty-six thousand persons who voted for me, it appears that forty-six thousand want to come and tell me about it. . . ."

A1301* *Circular Letter*. Pasadena: The Author. 1 leaf.

Order blank offering for sale a selected list of his books, beginning with *Mountain City*.

A1302 *To a Cardinal*. Pasadena: The Author. 1 leaf.

See A1248.

A1303* Preface to *Hell*!, trans. Goshuen Chien. Shanghai, China: [n.p.], p. iv.

See Chinese editions. Photoprint of a letter from Upton Sinclair to G. Chien, dated 18 May 1929, giving permission to translate the book into Chinese.

A1304* Preface to *Mountain City*, trans. Ge Kin-Ling. Shanghai, China: [n.p.], p. vii.

See Chinese editions. Printed letter from Upton Sinclair to translator Ling, dated 3 June 1930, in English.

A1305 *Peter Gudge Becomes a Secret Agent*. Moscow: State Publishing House. 35 pp.

Pamphlet from *100%*. See A729.

1931

A1306 *Roman Holiday*. New York: Farrar and Rinehart; Pasadena: The Author, *c*. 3 January. 288 pp.

Reprinted: New York: Grosset & Dunlap, 1932. In part: A1545, A2049. As serial: A1789.

Foreign Editions: Bulgarian, Chinese, Czech, Dutch, English-Germany, English, French, German, Hungarian, Norwegian, Portuguese, Russian, Serbo-Croatian.

A1307* *Circular Letter.* Pasadena: The Author, 8 January. 1 leaf.

Letter to Willi Munzenberg, Secretary, International Defense Committee, protesting unauthorized use of his name.

A1308 "I'll Be Popular in America," *Open Forum*, VIII (17 January), 3.

A1309 "No Argument Necessary," *Open Forum*, VIII (17 January), 3.

A1310* *Circular Letter.* Pasadena: The Author, January (date corrected by Author to 1931). 4 pp.

Announcing forthcoming publication of *Roman Holiday.*

A1311* "Suppressing Einstein," *Open Forum*, VIII (14 February), 1.

United Press releases had "cut" certain of Albert Einstein's statements on militarism and unemployment.

A1312 "Remedy for Unemployment," *Open Forum*, VIII (21 February), 3.

A1313* *Circular Letter.* Pasadena: The Author, February. 1 leaf.

Soliciting support for a special anniversary edition of *The Jungle* to be illustrated by Diego Rivera. Edition never published.

A1314* Letter, *The Whitman College Blue Moon*, VI (February), 4,25.

Letter precedes "What the Public Wants," from *Money Writes!.*

A1315* Letter: Is It Fair Play? *Equitist* [Del Rosa, Calif.], 13 March, p. 3.

To W. E. Brokaw, editor.

A1316* "Einstein Needs No Guardian," *Open Forum*, VIII (14 March), 3.

1931 continued

A1317 "Private Ownership of Women," *Open Forum*, VIII (14 March), 3.

A1318* "Liberty in USA and USSR," *Open Forum*, VIII (21 March), 2.
Exchange of letters with Sherwood Eddy.

A1319* "La Tragédie de Mark Twain," *Nouvel Age*, no. 3, (March), pp. 197–199.
Translated by Henry Muller.

A1320 "Progress in New Russia," *Open Forum*, VIII (4 April), 3.

A1321 "Sinclair's Stand Explained," *Open Forum*, VIII (18 April), 3.

A1322* "Unemployed in Los Angeles Organize to Assert Social Rights," *The American Freeman*, 2 May, p. 2.

A1323 "Russia's Great Achievement," *Open Forum*, VIII (23 May), 3.

A1324 "Three Years Are Too Much," *Open Forum*, VIII (30 May), 3.

A1325 *Books of Upton Sinclair in Russia: Proceedings of Literary Groups and Workers' Clubs of the Metal Workers of Leningrad*. Pasadena: The Author, May. 35 pp.

A1326* "Prohibition-Minded America," *Open Forum*, VIII (6 June), 3.
Letter to editor.

A1327 "Socialism and Culture," *The American Freeman*, 6 June, p. 2; 13 June, p. 2.
Reprinted: A1330.

A1328 Letter: Wets Want the Saloon Back, *Unity*, CVII (15 June), 255.

A1329* "Two Per Cent Buttons," *Nation*, CXXXII (17 June), 659.
Letter to editor.
Reprinted in *New Leader*, 10 July.

A1330* *Socialism and Culture*. Girard, Kansas: Haldeman-Julius (Little Blue Book no. 690), *c*. June. 32 pp.
Originally: A1327.

A1331 "Can Capitalism Work a Planned Economy?" *Open Forum*, VIII (11 July), 1.

A1332* " 'Spirits' or Telepathy?" *Occult Review*, LIV (July), 11–18.
Part I; Part II in August, pp. 82–87. See A1254.

A1333* "Mr. Upton Sinclair and *Money Writes*!" *Public Opinion* [England], 7 August, p. 134.

A1334 "Comrade Kautsky and the Dromedary," *International Press Correspondence*, XI (13 August), 789–791.
Critical of Kautsky's *Bolshevism at a Deadlock*; see A1343, A1369.

A1335* "Karl Kautsky and the Russian Dromedary," *New Leader* [London], XIII (15 August), 4.
Continued in 4 September, p. 6; 18 September, p. 9; 25 September, p. 9; see A1334.

A1336 "Left Column Doesn't Know What Right Column's Saying," *Open Forum*, VIII (22 August), 3.

A1337 "The Vilarino Deportation," *Open Forum*, VIII (22 August), 3.

A1338* *Circular Letter*. Pasadena: The Author, 1 September. 4 pp.
Outlining establishment of Sinclair Foundation.

1931 continued

A1339 "Paging Mr. Chambless," *New Republic*, LXVIII (2 September), 76.

On Edgar Chambless' *Roadtown*.

A1340* *The Sinclair Foundation: A Declaration of Trust.* Pasadena: Upton Sinclair, 2 September. 12 pp.

A1341* "Sinclair Congratulates British Labor in Stand Against MacDonald," *New Leader*, XIII (5 September), 6.

A1342* "Sinclair Replies to Communists," *Open Forum*, VIII (5 September), 1–2.

In response to an open letter from Somerset Logan.

A1343* "Socialism, Red or White," *Nation*, CXXXIII (9 September), 261–262.

Review of Karl Kautsky's *Bolshevism at a Deadlock*; see A1334.

A1344* "Wheelbarrows and Monkey-Wrenches," *Open Forum*, VIII (12 September), 2–3.

Answers letter from T. H. Bell.

A1345* *The Wet Parade.* New York: Farrar and Rinehart; Pasadena: The Author, *c.* 12 September. 431 pp.

Reprinted in part: A1545, A2049. As play: A1388.

Foreign Editions: Czech, Dutch, English, German, Hungarian, Norwegian, Polish, Portuguese, Romanian, Russian, Slovenian, Spanish, Swedish, Tamil.

A1346 "Yes, We Have Small Tools," *Open Forum*, VIII (19 September), 3.

A1347 "The Wayward Press," *New Republic*, LXVIII (23 September), 156.

A1348* *Circular Letter.* Pasadena: The Author, September. 4 pp.

Letter outlining the plot of *The Wet Parade*. There is a variant of this letter with slightly more text.

A1349* *Circular Letter.* Pasadena: The Author, 12 and 16 October. 2 pp.

Letter to the City Manager of Glendale, California, asking removal of Glendale's Chief of Police. On verso letter to *The Glendale News.*

A1350 "Glendale, City of Homes, Now Known As City of Rowdyism," *Open Forum*, VIII (24 October), 1.

A1351* "Sinclair Flays Pasadenans," *Open Forum*, VIII (7 November), 1, 3.

A1352* "For Free Speech," *World Wide* [Montreal], 7 November, p. 1778.

A1353 "From Upton Sinclair," *New Leader* [London], XII (14 November), 5.

Letter to editor on Sinclair's Kautsky article.

A1354 "Sinclair Reveals Note From Shaw," *Los Angeles Examiner*, 3 December, p. 6.

A1355 "When American Went Crazy," *Pasadena Post*, 5 December, p. 23.

Reprinted: *Middle-West Review*, December.

A1356 "Shaw Might Be Safe Here," *Open Forum*, VIII (12 December), 1.

A1357 "Lost: An Open Letter," *New Republic*, LXIX (12 December), 1.

To Lincoln Steffens.

A1358* "On a Steamship," *The Indian Education* [Madras], VII (December), 559.

A1359* "The Permanent Crisis," *The Thinker*, IV (December), 22–28.

Reprinted: *Canadian Forum* (December), pp. 87–90.

1931 continued

A1360* *Biographical and Critical Opinions.* Pasadena: The Author. 32 pp.

See A948.

A1361* *Books of Upton Sinclair.* Pasadena: The Author, 4 pp.

The Wet Parade heads list with quotes from famous people under each title.

A1362* *Books of Upton Sinclair.* Pasadena: The Author. 4 pp.

Roman Holiday heads list.

A1363* *Circular Letter.* Pasadena: The Author, *c.* 1931. 1 leaf.

Explaining his inability to meet all demands on his time.

A1364* *Circular Letter.* Pasadena: The Author. 1 leaf.

Announcing *Oil!* has just been published in Germany.

A1365 "The Settin' Down Job," *Writers' Year Book and Market Guide* (Annual).

A1366* *Circular Letter.* Pasadena: The Author. 1 leaf.

Order blank offering for sale a selected list of his books, beginning with *The Wet Parade.*

A1367* *The Pulitzer Prize and "Special Pleading."* Pasadena: The Author. 4 pp.

Argument against Dr. Richard (University of Minnesota), Head of Pulitzer Prize Commission.

A1368* *Circular Letter.* Pasadena: The Author. 1 leaf.

Opinions of *The Wet Parade.*

A1369 *Upton Sinclair on 'Comrade' Kautsky.* Moscow: Co-operative Publishing Society of Foreign Workers in the USSR. 15 pp.

Foreign Edition: Russian

1932

A1370 "How to Lie in Headlines," *Open Forum*, IX (2 January), 3.

A1371 "A Case of Spiritual Values," *Open Forum*, IX (23 January), 3.

A1372 *The Candidacy of Upton Sinclair for the Nobel Prize For Literature.* Pasadena: Published by the Committee, *c.* January. 39 pp.

A1373 "Prohibition Primer," *Open Forum*, IX (20 February), 3.

A1374 "Save the Five Year Plan," *International Literature*, nos. 2–3. (February–March), p. 8.

A1375* "Not Really Pacifistic," *Nation*, CXXXIV (16 March), 313.

Letter to editor concerning mass meeting of students at the University of Southern California.

A1376 "Why, Comrade Sinclair!" *Open Forum*, IX (9 April), 3.

A1377* *American Outpost.* New York: Farrar and Rinehart; Pasadena: The Author, 14 April. 280 pp.

Reprinted: Girard, Kansas: Haldeman-Julius (Big Blue Book no. B-706), 19 March 1948. In part: A1545, A2049. See A1378.

Foreign Editions: Chinese, English-Germany, English, French, German, Hungarian, Portuguese, Russian, Serbo-Croatian.

A1378* "From the *American Outpost*," *Contempo*, I (15 April), pp. [1], 2.

See A1377.

A1379 "Is City Ruled by Red Squad?" *Open Forum*, IX (16 April), 3.

A1380* "Einstein and Spiritualism," *New Republic*, LXX (27 April), 301–302.

1932 continued

A1381 "Artists, Slaves, and Men," *The Modern Thinker and Author's Review*, I (April), 152–154.
Review of his *Money Writes!*

A1382* *Circular Letter.* Pasadena: The Author, April. 4 pp.
Announcing forthcoming publication of *American Outpost.*

A1383 "Martyrdom Only Weapon," *Open Forum*, IX (28 May), 3.

A1384 "Sinclair Appeals to Porter," *Open Forum*, IX (2 July), 3.

A1385 "Einstein and *Mental Radio*," *New Republic*, LXXI (13 July), 237.
Comments on C. Hartley Grattan's opinions of Einstein's attitude toward spiritualism and telepathy.

A1386 "A Lesson in Grammar for Mayor Porter," *Open Forum*, IX (16 July), 3.

A1387* Letter: On the Conditions of the Times, *Nation*, CXXXV (27 July), 84.

A1388 Foreword to *The Wet Parade* (Dramatization by Mina Maxfield and Lena Eggleston). Washington, D.C.: Board of Temperance, Prohibition, and Public Morals, M. E. Church, *c.* August, pp. iii–iv. See A1345.

A1389* "Say It with Fountain Pens," *New Republic*, LXXXI (3 August), 318–319.
Two letters on his complaint against the Waterman Pen Company's contest.

A1309* "A Most Significant Change," *New Masses*, VIII (September), 10.

A1391* "The Menagerie (Night in County Workhouse)," *The Orient*, II (September/October), 7.
Verse.

A1392 "Technocracy: The New Hope," *Rob Wagner's Script*, VIII (24 December), 1–2.

A1398 "Demon Rum," *New Republic*, LXXIII (28 December), 192.

A1394* *Books of Upton Sinclair.* Pasadena: Upton Sinclair. 4 pp.

American Outpost heads list.

A1395 "Graft in America." In *America as Americans See It*, ed. Fred J. Ringel. New York: Harcourt Brace, pp. 177–180.

A1396 "The Literary Radical," *Writer's 1932 Year Book and Market Guide*, III, 18–19, 22.

1933

A1397* "The Machine Menace: Civilization Awakes To It," *New Leader* [London], 6 January, p. 3.

Reprinted: A1947.

A1398* "The Only Hope of Peace, Part I," *Open Forum*, X (28 January), 1.

Address of Upton Sinclair before the Student Conference Against War, University of California at Los Angeles. Part II, 4 February.

A1399* "Upton Sinclair and Will Durant," *The American Freeman*, 1 February, p. 1.

A letter to the editor replying to Durant's article in the 17 December 1932 issue of the *Saturday Evening Post.*

A1400* "Sinclair is Hopeful," *World Wide*, 11 February, p. 160.

A1401* *Circular Letter.* Los Angeles The: Author, 12 February. 1 leaf.

Beginning: "I am taking the liberty of sending you by prepaid express an approval copy of a new book (*Upton Sinclair Presents William Fox*) which I am publishing."

1933 continued

A1402* *Circular Letter.* Los Angeles :The Author, February. 4 pp.

Announcing the forthcoming publication of *Upton Sinclair Presents William Fox.*

A1403* "Upton Sinclair on War—And How It's Made," *New Clarion* [London], 11 March, p. 268.

A1404 "Smash the Strangle Hold of Finance!" *Common Sense,* I (March), 14–15.

A1405 "Mr. Sinclair's Attitude," *Saturday Review of Literature,* IX (1 April), 518.

A1406* "Making People Discontented," *Open Forum,* X (8 April), 3.

An open letter to Mother St. Jerome, Rosemont College, Rosemont, Pennsylvania.

A1407* *Circular Letter.* Los Angeles: The Author, April. 1 leaf.

Beginning: "I am taking the liberty of sending you by express, all charges prepaid, a copy of my new book, *Upton Sinclair Presents William Fox.*"

A1408* *Circular Letter.* Los Angeles: The Author, May. 4 pp.

Announcing: *The Way Out, What Lies Ahead for America.*

A1409* "Nearest To My Heart," *Writer's Digest,* XIII (May), 13–15.

Criticism of capitalism. Mentions William Fox. Reprinted: A1947.

A1410 "An Open Letter to the American People," *Liberty,* X (10 June), 36–38.

A1411 "How To Restore Prosperity, Part 2," *Open Forum,* X (17 June), 2–4.

Part 1 probably published in May.

A1412* "What Rights Has an Author?" *Writer's Digest*, XIII (June), 13–14.

A1413 "Thunder Over Eisenstein," *New Republic*, LXXV (5 July), 210.

See discussions in *New Republic*, LXXV (9 August), 344–345; LXXVI (23 August), 49; LXXVI (6 September), 104. See also extensive bibliography in Harry M. Geduld and Ronald Gottesman, *Sergei Eisenstein and Upton Sinclair: The Making and Unmaking of* Que Viva Mexico*!* (F352).

A1414 "In Defense of Bernard Shaw," *Real America*, I (July), 59, 81–82.

A1415* "Upton Sinclair Presents William Fox," *Socialist Review*, V (July–February 1934).

As book: A1434.

A1416* *Circular Letter.* Los Angeles: The Author, 21 August. 1 leaf.

Beginning: "After twenty-three months the chariot-wheels of Sergei Eisenstein have rolled on . . ."; see A1413, A1417, A1419, A1425.

A1417* Letter: on Eisenstein picture *Thunder Over Mexico*, *New York Post*, 26 August.

A1418 "Mad," *Nation*, CXXXVII (30 August), 243.

A1419* "Upton Sinclair Replies," *New Clarion* [London], 9 September, p. 232.

Reply to Ivor Montagu's criticism of *Thunder Over Mexico* in August 5 issue.

A1420* *Circular Letter.* Los Angeles: The Author, 20 September. 1 leaf.

Beginning: "After thirty-three months the chariot-wheels of Sergei Eisenstein have rolled on"; see A1416.

1933 continued

A1421 "Sinclair Explains," *New York Sun*, 22 September, p. 30.

A1422* *Circular Letter*. Los Angeles: The Author, 18 October. 4 pp.

Announcing: the forthcoming publication of *I, Governor of California, and How I Ended Poverty*.

A1423* "Answering the Call of the N.R.A.," *Independent Woman*, XII (October), 333.

A1424* "Converting the Rich to Socialism," *Call of Youth* [New York], October, pp. 3, 7.

A1425* "*Thunder Over Mexico*," *Modern Monthly*, VII (October), 575–576.

Letter to the editor justifying his position vis-a-vis Eisenstein.

A1426* "Poverty, Surplus Profits Must End, Sinclair Declares; Farms Owned by State are Author's Plan," *Southern California Daily Trojan* [Los Angeles], 24 November, pp. 1, 2.

A resumé by Ernest Foster of a speech made by Sinclair at a Graduate School luncheon at UCLA.

A1427* "Noted Author Renews Battle for Humanity," *Upton Sinclair's Paper End Poverty*, I (26 December/2 January 1934), 1.

A1428* "It's Up to You," *Upton Sinclair's Paper End Poverty*, I (26 December/2 January 1934), 1.

A1429* "*I, Governor of California, and How I Ended Poverty*," *Upton Sinclair's Paper End Poverty*, I (26 December/2 January 1934), 4–7.

As book: A1432.

A1430* *Books of Upton Sinclair.* Los Angeles: Upton Sinclair and End Poverty League; New York: Farrar and Rinehart; Los Angeles: The Author. 4 pp.

Beginning with *I, Governor of California, and How I Ended Poverty.*

A1431* *Books of Upton Sinclair.* Los Angeles: Upton Sinclair and End Poverty League; New York: Farrar and Rinehart; Los Angeles: The Author. 4 pp.

Beginning with *Upton Sinclair Presents William Fox.*

A1432* *I, Governor of California, and How I Ended Poverty.* Los Angeles: Upton Sinclair and End Poverty League; New York: Farrar and Rinehart.

As serial: A1429. In part: A1545, A2049. See A1537.

Foreign Edition: English.

A1433* *Thunder over Mexico.* Los Angeles: The Author. 1 leaf.

A1431* *Upton Sinclair Presents William Fox.* Los Angeles: The Author. 377 pp.

Reprinted: New York: Arno Publications, 1970. As serial: A1415. In part: A1545, A2049.

Foreign Editions: Bulgarian, English, Hungarian, Russian, Swedish.

A1435* *The Book Sensation of Our Time; "Upton Sinclair Presents William Fox."* Los Angeles: The Author. 1 leaf.

Advertising circular.

A1436* *The Way Out—What Lies Ahead for America?* New York: Farrar and Rinehart; Los Angeles and Pasadena: The Author.

Reprinted with postscript to the second edition: 1933. Serial reprint: A1528. In part: A1545, A2049.

Foreign Editions: Dutch, English, Polish, Spanish.

1934

A1437* "And Henry VIII Was the First Pope of the Church of England," *Rob Wagner's Script*, X (20 January), 22.

A1438* "Upton Sinclair Prescribes," *Modern Living*, IV (January), 8, 9, 26–27.

A1439* "Film Censorship," *New English Weekly*, IV (1 February), 382.

Letter to the editor protesting British Censorship Board's cutting *Thunder Over Mexico*.

A1440* "Put Unemployed at Productive Labor," *Upton Sinclair's Paper End Poverty*, I (February), 3.

A1441* "*Thunder Over Mexico*," *The New Statesman and Nation*, VII (10 March), 339–340.

Letter to the editor concerning Ivor Montagu.

A1442* "Building the New Society," *Upton Sinclair's Paper End Poverty*, I (March), 3.

A1443* "Editor's Challenge Answered," *Upton Sinclair's Paper End Poverty*, I (March), 10.

A1445* "No Room in EPIC for Fascism," *Upton Sinclair's Paper End Poverty*, I (March), 6.

A1446* "Stock Gambling Levy to Replace Sales Tax," *Upton Sinclair's Paper End Poverty*, I (March), 6.

A1448* "Socialist Army," *Time*, XXIII (23 April), 2.

A1449* "No Excuse for Poverty in California," *The Overland Monthly*, XCII (April), 81.

A1450* "Taxing Stock Transfers," *Upton Sinclair's Paper End Poverty*, I (April), 10.

A1451* "What This Campaign Means," *End Poverty News*, II (April), 1–2.

A1452* "Will Democracy Work or Perish?" *Upton Sinclair's Paper End Poverty*, I (April), 3.

A1453* "Letter: *Thunder Over Mexico*," *The New Statesman and Nation* [London], VII (5 May), 673.

A1454* "Sinclair on Upton Sinclair," *The World Tomorrow*, XVII (10 May), 260–261.

Letter to editor concerning Norman Thomas and EPIC.

A1455 "Room for All in EPIC Movement," *Upton Sinclair's EPIC News*, I (28 May), 3.

A1456* "Democracy Takes the Offensive in California," *The Outrider, A Journal For the Civilized Minority*, I (May), 1–2.

A1457* "Ending Poverty is the Only Issue," *Upton Sinclair's Paper End Poverty*, I (May), 3.

A1458 "The EPIC Plan: Can Poverty Be Ended?" *Common Sense*, III (May), 6–8.

A1459* "The EPIC Plan for America," *The Fraternity Monthly*, I (May), 11, 62.

A1460* "Explain EPIC to the People!" *Upton Sinclair's Paper End Poverty*, I (May), 3.

A1461* "Expected Attacks on EPIC Begin," *Upton Sinclair's EPIC News*, I (4 June), 3.

A1462* "Concerning Registration," *Upton Sinclair's EPIC News*, I (4 June), 6.

A1463* "EPIC is Workingmen's Way Out," *Upton Sinclair's EPIC News*, I (11 June), 3.

1934 continued

A1464* "Sinclair Writes Home," *Upton Sinclair's EPIC News*, I (11 June), 4.

A1465* "Enemy, Scared, Calls Bad Names," *Upton Sinclair's EPIC News*, I (18 June), 3.

A1466* Printed Telegram to Manchester Boddy from U. S., *Illustrated Daily News* [Los Angeles], 19 June, p. 8.

A1467* "Sinclair Commands EPIC Ticket," *Upton Sinclair's EPIC News*, I (25 June), 3.

A1468* *Circular Letter.* Pasadena: The Author, June. 4 pp.
Giving news of the sales of his books, as well as the progress of his campaign for the democratic nomination for Governor of California.

A1469* "EPIC Plan Draws Civic Leaders," *Upton Sinclair's EPIC News*, I (2 July), 3.

A1470* " 'Kept' Rivals Start Slander," *Upton Sinclair's EPIC News*, I (9 July), 3.

A1471* "Real Issues Fogged by Rivals," *Upton Sinclair's EPIC News*, I (16 July), 3.

A1472* "Boost Special News Editions Says Sinclair," *Upton Sinclair's EPIC News*, I (16 July), 4.

A1473* "Sacramento Editor Told Witnesses, Jury, Judge Admit Mooney Framed," *Upton Sinclair's EPIC News*, I (23 July), 3.

A1474* "The Lie Factory Starts," *Upton Sinclair's EPIC News* (Special Section), I (23 July), 1–3.
See A1541.

A1475* Letter: "I Oppose Communism, Mr. Wardell," *Upton Sinclair's EPIC News* (Special Section), I (23 July), 4.

A1476* "Sinclair Answers Critics," *The Independent-Review* [Los Angeles], I (26 July), 1, 20.

A1477* "Have the People Had Enough?" *Upton Sinclair's EPIC News*, I (30 July), 3.

A1478* "Vote for the Entire EPIC Ticket," *Upton Sinclair's EPIC News*, I (6 August), 3.

A1479* "Immediate EPIC Starts Here," *Upton Sinclair's EPIC News*, I (6 August), 3.
As pamphlet: A1539.

A1480* "EPIC Will Redeem Pre-War Promises Made to Veterans, Sinclair Declares," *Upton Sinclair's EPIC News*, I (6 August), 4.

A1481* "He's Heard Lots of Liars in Life but Justus Tops Them All, Says Sinclair," *Upton Sinclair's EPIC News*, I (6 August), 6.

A1482* "We Shall Operate for Use, Not Profit," *Upton Sinclair's EPIC News*, I (13 August), 3.

A1483* "Sinclair Invites Rivals into EPIC," *Upton Sinclair's EPIC News*, I (25 August), 1, 2.

A1484* "The Funny *Fresno Bee*! U. S. Plan Isn't Sinclair Plan, It's Only EPIC Plan!" *Upton Sinclair's EPIC News*, I (25 August), 5.

A1485* "Take This Ballot to the Polls—Letter from Sinclair," *Upton Sinclair's EPIC News* (Special Primary Edition), I (28 August), 1.

A1486* "EPIC Means Food for the Hungry," *Upton Sinclair's EPIC News* (Special Primary Edition), I (28 August), 3.

A1487* "Sinclair on Lindsey," *Upton Sinclair's EPIC News*, V (28 August), 2.

1934 continued

A1488* "Pledges Adoption of New Deal Principles," *Upton Sinclair's EPIC News*, I (29 August), 1–2.

A1489* "Here's Sinclair's Own Victory Statement," *Upton Sinclair's EPIC News* (Victory Edition), I (29 August) 1–8.

A1490* "Ex-Comrade Sinclair Voices a Protest," *Call of Youth* [New York], II (August), 6.
Letter to the editor on the campaign in California.

A1491* "Sinclair Explains EPIC Platform Planks," *MacFadden's Weekly*, 3 September, pp. 1, 21.

A1492* "Sinclair Regards Nomination as Extraordinary Victory of the People," *Upton Sinclair's EPIC News*, I (3 September), 1, 4, 5.

A1493* "The Method of Free Co-operation," *Upton Sinclair's EPIC News*, I (3 September), 3.

A1494 Telegram printed in Arthur Brisbane's Column "Today," *Examiner* [Los Angeles], 6 September, pp. 1, 2.

A1495* "Upton Sinclair's Position," *New Republic*, LXXX (12 September), 132–133.
Letter to the editor correcting some errors in Carey McWilliams's report of his EPIC plan and political position in California.

A1496* "Sinclair Diary Records Trip East," *Upton Sinclair's EPIC News*, I (17 September), 3.

A1497* "Emergency Tax Needed for State," *Upton Sinclair's EPIC News*, I (24 September), 7.

A1498* "Sinclair Decries Presidency Talk," *Upton Sinclair's EPIC News*, I (24 September), 7.

A1499* "Sinclair Discusses His Proposed First Measures, If Elected," [Los Angeles] *Evening Post Record*, 25 September, pp. 1, 5.

A1500 "End Poverty in Civilization," *Nation*, CXXXIX (26 September), 351.

A1501* "Making Democracy Work: My Campaign for Governor . . . ," *Common Sense*, III (September), 25–26.

A1502 "World As I Want It," *Forum*, XCII (September), 157.

A1503* "Don't Joke With the *Times*!" *Upton Sinclair's EPIC News*, I (1 October), 1.

A1504* "EPIC Tax Fair and Just Levy," *Upton Sinclair's EPIC News*, I (1 October), 1.

A1505* "Résponse à Eisenstein," *Le Petit Bara*, III (5 October), 3.

A1506* "Merriam Won't Aid Aged, Says Sinclair," *Upton Sinclair's EPIC News*, I (8 October), 1.

A1507* "EPIC 'Not Back to Nature,'" *Upton Sinclair's EPIC News*, I (8 October), 2.

A1508* *Open Letter to the Christian Science Board of Directors*. Pasadena: Upton Sinclair, 9 October. 1 leaf.
To assure them that he would allow religious freedom if elected Governor.

A1509* "Meaning of Movement to End Poverty in California," *Literary Digest*, CXVIII (13 October), 8, 38.

A1510* "End of Poverty 'Up to You,' Says Sinclair in 'Immediate EPIC,'" *Upton Sinclair's EPIC News*, I (15 October), 3.

1934 continued

A1511* "What I Am Really Going to do . . . ," *Liberty*, II (20 October), 6–7.

Explains his EPIC plan to the nation.

A1512* "G.O.P. Lies Build 'Bogey Man,' " *Upton Sinclair's EPIC News*, I (22 October), 8.

A1513* " 'I Back Old Age Relief!' " *Upton Sinclair's EPIC News*, I (22 October), 8.

A1514* "Is EPIC Reactionary?" *Today*, III (27 October), 16.

A1515* "Can They Fool You?" *Upton Sinclair's EPIC News*, I (29 October), 1, 3.

A1516 "Planning the Model State," *The Modern Thinker*, V (October), 23–25.

A1517 "Sinclairiana," *Time*, XXIV (5 November), 2.

A1518* "Use Your Ballot," *Upton Sinclair's EPIC News*, I (5 November), 1.

A1519 "A Political Prayer," *New Republic*, LXXX (7 November), 350.

A1520* *Upton Sinclair's Story: I, Candidate for Governor, and How I Got Licked*." Pasadena: The Author, 9 November. 1 leaf.

On serialized story of EPIC campaign.

A1521* "EPIC Victory Sure, Election Only Skirmish, Says Sinclair," *Upton Sinclair's EPIC News*, I (12 November), 1, 5.

A1522 "What I Shall Do If I Win and What I Shall Do If I Lose," *Liberty*, XI (17 November), 34–35.

A1523* "To Members and Friends of the End Poverty League," *Upton Sinclair's EPIC News*, I (19 November), 1.

A1524* "Hold the Fort, EPICS!" *Upton Sinclair's EPIC News*, I (19 November), 1.

A1525 "I, Candidate for Governor, and How I Got Licked," *Illustrated News*, 21–24 November.
As book: A1644.

A1526* "A Call to Work," *Upton Sinclair's EPIC News*, I (26 November), 1, 2.

A1527* "Future of EPIC," *Nation*, CXXXIX (28 November), 616–617.
Comments on the EPIC campaign and the mud-slinging.

A1528* "The Way Out: What Lies Ahead for America," *Upton Sinclair's EPIC News*, I (3 December–8 April 1935).
As book, A1436.

A1529* "EPICS and Democrats," *Upton Sinclair's EPIC News*, I (3 December), 7.

A1530* "To All Friends of EPIC," *Upton Sinclair's EPIC News*, I (17 December), 5.

A1531* "Merry Christmas to EPIC," *Upton Sinclair's EPIC News*, I (24 December), 4.

A1532 "Remark by Sinclair Hurls Movie Power Against Candidacy," *The Valley Daily News* [Tarentum, Pennsylvania], 24 December, p. 8.

A1533* "What is Fascism?" *Upton Sinclair's EPIC News*, I (31 December), 5.

A1534* *Books by Upton Sinclair.* Pasadena: The Author. 4 pp.
At head of list is *An Upton Sinclair Anthology*, collected by I. O. Evans and published in London, 1934; see C299, also A1545.

1934 continued

A1535* *Circular Letter.* Pasadena: Upton Sinclair. 1 leaf.
Beginning: "Dear Friend: I print this statement to avoid hurting the feelings. . . ."

A1536* "The Coming New Day," *Writer's 1934 Year Book and Market Guide*, pp. 15–18, 64.

A1537* *EPIC Plan for California.* New York: Farrar and Rinehart.
Includes: *I, Governor of California, and How I Ended Poverty, EPIC Answers, The Lie Factory Starts*, and *Immediate EPIC*; with a foreword by Sinclair. See A1432, A1538, A1539, A1541.

A1538* *EPIC Answers: How to End Poverty in California.* Los Angeles: End Poverty League. 32 pp. See A1537.

A1539* *Immediate EPIC.* Los Angeles: End Poverty League. 38 pp.
As serial: A1479. See A1537.

A1540* *Circular Letter.* Pasadena: The Author, 4 pp.
Concerning the author's publication and activities; dated June 1934.

A1541* *The Lie Factory Starts.* Los Angeles: End Poverty League, 64 pp.
Pamphlet written to explain some of the slander and the misconceptions leveled at him in EPIC campaign. As serial: A1474. See A1537.

A1542* *Reply to Eisenstein.* Pasadena: The Author, 4 pp.
Offprint of letter to the *New Leader* [London], 26 March.

A1543* *The Social Worker and the Depression in Relation to the EPIC Plan.* Long Beach: Moyle Print. 2 pp.

A1544* *"Thunder Over Mexico," Speech by Upton Sinclair Made May 10 to Press and Writers at Preview at the Carthay Circle.* Hollywood: Sol Lesser. 4 pp.

A1545* *An Upton Sinclair Anthology*; preface by Upton Sinclair. Compiled by I. O. Evans. New York: Farrar and Rinehart; Los Angeles: The Author. 328 pp.

Reprinted with additions: A2049. Foreign Edition: English.

"Genius" (*American Outpost* [*Candid Reminiscences*], 1932) pp. 31–34.

"Creation" (*The Journal of Arthur Stirling*, 1903), pp. 34–37.

"Thyrsis Studies Music" (*Love's Pilgrimage*, 1911), pp. 38–41.

"Kip's Proposal" (*The Wet Parade*, 1931), pp. 42–48.

"The Purpose of Love" (*Love's Pilgrimage*, 1911), pp. 49–52.

"Psychic Research" (*Mental Radio*, 1930), pp. 53–68.

"Experiments in Health" (*American Outpost* [*Candid Reminiscences*], 1932), pp. 68–73.

"Science and Life" (*The Profits of Religion*, 1918), pp. 73–80.

"The Stockyards" (*The Jungle*, 1906), pp. 81–91.

"The Burning Oil Well" (*Oil*! 1927), pp. 91–96.

"In the Backwoods" (*Love's Pilgrimage*, 1911), pp. 97–105.

"Puritan's Progress" (*American Outpost* [*Candid Reminiscences*], 1932), pp. 106–111.

"Christ and Nietzsche" (*The Journal of Arthur Stirling*, 1903), pp. 111–116.

"The Glory That Was Greece" (*Mammonart*, 1925), pp. 117–124.

"The Grandeur That Was Rome" (*Roman Holiday*, 1931), pp. 124–128.

"John Brown" (*Manassas*, 1904), pp. 128–135.

"Early Difficulties of the Kinema" (*Upton Sinclair Presents William Fox*, 1933), pp. 136–146.

"The Cordage Factory" (*Boston*, 1928), pp. 149–152.

"The Fertilizer Man" (*The Jungle*, 1906), pp. 152–157.

"The Banquet" (*The Metropolis*, 1908), pp. 158–160.

"To a Rich Young Man" Mary Craig Sinclair (*Sonnets*, 1925), p. 160.

"The Decay in the Souls of the Rich" (*Letters to Judd*, 1926), pp. 161–162.

1934 continued

"The Menagerie" (*The Cry for Justice*, 1915), pp. 163–164.
"Winter in the Jungle" (*The Jungle*, 1906), pp. 164–169.
"Sisterhood," Mary Craig Sinclair (*Sonnets*, 1925), pp. 169–170.
"Christmas in Prison" (*The Jungle*, 1906), pp. 171–174.
"Russia: 1918," Mary Craig Sinclair (*Sonnets*, 1925), pp. 174–75.
"The Case for the Anarchist" (*Boston*, 1928), pp. 175–181.
"The Execution" (*Boston*, 1928), pp. 182–198.
"Red Adams" (*Singing Jailbirds*, 1924), p. 199.
"Christ Visits Western City" (*They Call Me Carpenter*, 1922), pp. 200–206.
"Dominie of the Wobblies" (*Singing Jailbirds*, 1924), pp. 206–211.
"Prince Hagen" (*Prince Hagen*, 1903), pp. 211–214.
"The Graft of Grace" (*The Profits of Religion*, 1918), pp. 214–217.
"The Legacy of Israel" (*The Profits of Religion*, 1918), pp. 218–222.
"Friends, Romans, Countrymen" (*Roman Holiday*, 1931), pp. 222–227.
"Renaissance Realities" (*Mammonart*, 1925), pp. 227–233.
"The Nation's Food Supply" (*The Jungle*, 1906), pp. 233–239.
"A Prophecy of War" (*The Industrial Republic*, 1907), pp. 240–244.
"War," Mary Craig Sinclair (*Sonnets*, 1925), p. 244.
"America—The Past" (*The Journal of Arthur Stirling*, 1903), pp. 245–248.
"America—The Present" (*The Journal of Arthur Stirling*, 1903), pp. 248–249.
"America—The Future" (*The Journal of Arthur Stirling*, 1903), pp. 249–251.
"The Old America" (*The Way Out*, 1933), pp. 251–255.
"Children in the Jungle" (*The Jungle*, 1906), pp. 251–259.
"We're Real Bums" (*100%* [*The Spy*], 1920), pp. 260–262.
"Arthur Stirling" (*The Journal of Arthur Stirling*, 1903), pp. 263–268.

"Springtime and Harvest" (*Springtime and Harvest*, 1901), pp. 268–272.

"My Cause" (*The Independent*, 14 May, 1903), pp. 272–285.

"Our Bourgeois Literature" (*Collier's Weekly*, 8 October, 1904), pp. 285–296.

"Socialism" (*Love's Pilgrimage*, 1911), pp. 297–306.

"Jurgis Hears a Socialist Speech" (*The Jungle*, 1906), pp. 306–309.

"On a Steamship" (*Independent*, 25 June, 1908), p. 309.

"The Twelve Principles of EPIC" (*I, Governor of California*, 1933), p. 310.

"Art and the Future" (*Mammonart*, 1925), pp. 311–314.

"The Overman" (*The Overman*, 1907), pp. 314–316.

A1546* *Upton Sinclair's Last Will and Testament.* Los Angeles: End Poverty League. 12 pp.

A1547* *Upton Sinclair Refuses to Accept Dictation from Democratic Machine.* Los Angeles: Upton Sinclair Headquarters. 4 pp.

Letter dated 12 May: "Upton Sinclair appeals to President Roosevelt for Tom Mooney."

A1548* *We, People of America, and How We Ended Poverty; A True Story of the Future.* Pasadena: National EPIC League. 64 pp.

Foreign Edition: Dutch.

A1549* "What Rights Has an Author?" *Writer's Digest Year Book.*

1935

A1550* "Upton Sinclair on End Poverty League," *Upton Sinclair's EPIC News*, I (7 January), 2.

A1551* "Our EPIC Legislators," *Upton Sinclair's EPIC News*, I (7 January), 5.

1935 continued

A1552* "Sinclair's Message Is Broadcast to State," *Upton Sinclair's EPIC News*, I (14 January), 1, 3.

A1553* "End Poverty Movies," *Upton Sinclair's EPIC News*, I (21 January), 5.

A1554* "Merriam's Budget," *Upton Sinclair's EPIC News*, I (28 January), 5.

A1555* "EPIC's Next Task," *Upton Sinclair's EPIC News*, I (4 February,) 1, 14.

A1556* "Work vs. Dole: Roosevelt May Adopt PFU Yet," *Upton Sinclair's EPIC News*, I (18 February), 1, 10.

A1557* "Sinclair Would Eradicate Evils Breeding Crime," *Upton Sinclair's EPIC News*, I (18 February), 1, 10.

A1558* "Wanted—An EPIC Drama," *Upton Sinclair's EPIC News*, I (25 February), 9.

A1559* "Today's Outlook: A Warning to Young People," *Upton Sinclair's EPIC News*, I (4 March), 1, 11.

A1560* "Today's Outlook: A Call to the Times," *Upton Sinclair's EPIC News*, I (11 March), 1, 11.

A1561* "Today's Outlook," *Upton Sinclair's EPIC News*, I (18 March), 1, 10.

A1562* "Today's Outlook: Speech at Olympic Auditorium, Los Angeles, California, 28 March, 1935," *Upton Sinclair's EPIC News*, I (1 April), 1, 5, 10.

A1563* *Circular Letter*. Pasadena: The Author, 7 April. 2 pp.

A1564* "Sinclair Sees Good in New Townsend Film," *Upton Sinclair's EPIC News*, I (8 April), 1.

A1565* "Sinclair Protests to *EPIC News*, But Receives No Reply," *Upton Sinclair's EPIC News*, I (8 April), 2.

A1566* "Today's Outlook," *Upton Sinclair's EPIC News*, I (15 April), 3.

A1567* "End Poverty League to Be Reorganized Democratically for Tremendous Jobs Ahead," *Upton Sinclair's EPIC News*, I (15 April), 1, 2.

A1568* "Today's Outlook," *Upton Sinclair's EPIC News*, I (15 April), 3.

A1569* "Today's Outlook: Talk United States," *Upton Sinclair's EPIC News*, I (22 April), 1, 8.

A1570* "A Statement," *Upton Sinclair's EPIC News*, I (22 April), 12.

A1571* "Today's Outlook: A New Birth for EPIC," *Upton Sinclair's EPIC News*, I (29 April), 1, 4.

A1572* "EPIC Marchs On," *Real America*, V (April), 34, 59–60.

A1573* "Today's Outlook," *Upton Sinclair's EPIC News*, I (6 May), 1, 7.

Excerpts from stenographic notes of speech at conference of District Secretaries, 27 April.

A1574* "Upton Sinclair Protests Against A.B. 106A," *Upton Sinclair's EPIC News*, I (6 May), 11.

A1575* "Today's Outlook," *Upton Sinclair's EPIC News*, I (13 May), 1, 8.

Letter to convention of the National Farmers Holiday Association.

A1576* "The Election Results," *Upton Sinclair's EPIC News*, I (13 May), 12.

1935 continued

A1577* "Today's Outlook: Greetings to the Convention," *Upton Sinclair's EPIC News*, I (20 May), 1.

A1578* "Today's Outlook: *The Brass Check* in Los Angeles," *Upton Sinclair's EPIC News*, II (27 May), 1, 3.

A1579* "Announcement: The National EPIC News," *Upton Sinclair's EPIC News*, II (27 May), 12.

A1580* "Here's Your New Baby!" *Upton Sinclair's National EPIC News*, II (3 June), 1, 3.

A1581* "From the Speech of Upton Sinclair at the EPIC Convention, Los Angeles Labor Temple, 19 May," *Upton Sinclair's National EPIC News*, II (3 June), 12.

A1582* "Supreme Court for EPIC," *Upton Sinclair's National EPIC News*, II (10 June), 1, 2.

A1583* "Here's the Text of Sinclair's Letter to President Roosevelt," *Upton Sinclair's National EPIC News*, II (17 June), 1, 2, 3.

A1584* "Choosing the New Board of Directors," *Upton Sinclair's National EPIC News*, II (17 June), 5.

A1585* "Upton Sinclair to President Roosevelt," *New Republic*, LXXXIII (19 June), 168.

A1586* "In the Enemy's Camp," *Upton Sinclair's National EPIC News*, II (24 June), 1, 2.

A1587* "Production for Use Congress," *Upton Sinclair's National EPIC News*, II (24 June), 4.

A1588* "Sinclair-Fish Debate: A Statement by Upton Sinclair," *Upton Sinclair's National EPIC News*, II (1 July), 3.
Congressman Hamilton Fish.

A1589* "Mrs. Bauning Replies to Upton Sinclair's Editorial: Upton Sinclair's Reply," *Upton Sinclair's National EPIC News*, II (1 July), 11.

A1590* "Text of Sinclair Note," *Evening Post-Record* [Los Angeles], 1 July, pp. 1, 6.

A1591* "Ending Poverty Without Pain," *Upton Sinclair's National EPIC News*, II (8 July), 1, 2.

A1592* " 'Soak-the-Rich' Taxes No Aid to Production," *Upton Sinclair's National EPIC News*, II (8 July), 10.

A1593* "EPIC in the Northwest," *Upton Sinclair's National EPIC News*, II (15 July), 1, 2.

A1594* "An Open Letter from Upton Sinclair to James A. Farley," *Upton Sinclair's National EPIC News*, II (22 July), 1, 2.

A1595* "To the New Board of Directors," *Upton Sinclair's National EPIC News*, II (22 July), 5.

A1596* "EPIC is Spreading," *Upton Sinclair's National EPIC News*, II (29 July), 1.

A1597* "A Letter to the Chicago Conference," *Upton Sinclair's National EPIC News*, II (29 July), 2, 6.

A1598* "Report on a Tour," *Upton Sinclair's National EPIC News*, II (5 August), 1, 2.

A1599* "The Ohio Plan Fails," *Upton Sinclair's National EPIC News*, II (5 August), 2.

A1600* "Communists and EPIC," *Upton Sinclair's National EPIC News*, II (12 August), 1, 2.

A1601* "Statement About Organization," *Upton Sinclair's National EPIC News*, II (12 August), 5.

1935 continued

A1602* "Mobilizing the Movies," *Upton Sinclair's National EPIC News*, II (19 August), 1, 2.

A1603* "Comments on the Debate," *Upton Sinclair's National EPIC News*, II (26 August), 1, 2.

A1604* "Complete Text of Debate: Upton Sinclair Speaks First; First Sinclair Rebuttal; Sinclair Closes Argument," *Upton Sinclair's National EPIC News*, II (26 August), 3, 4, 8.

A1605* "Statement by Upton Sinclair," *Upton Sinclair's National EPIC News*, II (26 August), 7.

A1606* "Upton Sinclair Answers L.A. *Times* Columnist," *Upton Sinclair's National EPIC News*, II (26 August), 11.

A1607* "Open Letter: Program of Production for Use for the Unemployment," *New Republic*, LXXXIV (28 August), 76.

A1608* "National Epic," *Common Sense*, IV (August), 9–10.

A1609* "We Choose Our Future. Thesis: Capitalism Has Used Up All Markets and Must Turn to War, Fascism, or Collectivism," *Esquire*, IV (August), 20, 167–168.

A1610* " 'Old Harry' Again," *Upton Sinclair's National EPIC News*, II (2 September), 4, 6–7.

A1611* "Help Wanted," *Upton Sinclair's National EPIC News*, II (9 September), 1, 2.

A1612* "An Open Letter From Upton Sinclair to the Editor of *The New Republic*; Upton Sinclair's Reply," *Upton Sinclair's National EPIC News*, II (9 September), 2, 9.
See A1635.

A1613* "What is Coming?" *Upton Sinclair's National EPIC News*, II (16 September), 1, 2.

A1614* "*The National EPIC News* Prints News About EPIC!" *Upton Sinclair's National EPIC News*, II (16 September), 6.

A1615* "The Permanent Unemployed," *Upton Sinclair's National EPIC News*, II (23 September), 1, 2.

A1616* "Sinclair on the Ethiopian War," *Upton Sinclair's National EPIC News*, II (23 September), 2.

A1617* "Depression Island," *Upton Sinclair's National EPIC News*, II (23 September–23 December).

As book: A1643.

A1618* "To President Roosevelt," *Upton Sinclair's National EPIC News, II* (30 September), 1, 2.

A1619* "*The Brass Check*, As Ever," *Upton Sinclair's National EPIC News*, II (7 October), 1, 2, 11.

A1620* "Double the Townsend Offer," *Upton Sinclair's National EPIC News*, II (14 October), 1, 2.

A1621* "Keep Our Paper—Help *National EPIC*," *Upton Sinclair's National EPIC News*, II (14 October), 3.

A1622* "Amputation in Installments," *Upton Sinclair's National EPIC News*, II (14 October), 3.

A1623* "Profits Plus Speed-Up Means Crisis Foreseen by Sinclair in 1911," *Upton Sinclair's National EPIC News*, II (21 October), 1, 3.

Reprints letter in June, 1911, issue of *American Magazine*; see A403.

A1624* "Travel Report," *Upton Sinclair's National EPIC News*, II (28 October), 1, 2.

1935 continued

A1625* "My Plans for 1936," *Real America*, VI (October), 27, 59.

Exclusive article obtained by Max Knepper.

A1626* "More Travel Report," *Upton Sinclair's National EPIC News*, II (4 November), 1, 2.

A1627* "Upton Sinclair Sends Message to Tugwell," *Upton Sinclair's National EPIC News*, II (4 November), 3.

A1628* "Correspondence: EPIC Plan," *Nation*, CXLI (6 November), 535–536.

A1629* "Still More Travel," *Upton Sinclairs' National EPIC News*, II (11 November), 1, 2.

A1630* "7000 Miles for EPIC," *Upton Sinclair's National EPIC News*, II (18 November), 1, 2.

A1631* "A Rag-Tag Economy," *Upton Sinclair's National EPIC News*, II (18 November), 4.

A1632* "EPIC in the East," *Upton Sinclair's National EPIC News*, II (25 November), 1.

A1633* "In a Skyscraper," *Upton Sinclair's National EPIC News*, II (2 December), 1, 2.

A1634* "EPIC in Forida," *Upton Sinclair's National EPIC News*, II (9 December), 1, 2.

A1635* "Open Letter: Program of Production for Use for the Unemployment," *New Republic*, LXXXV (11 December), 131.

A1636* "The Crime of Charity," *Upton Sinclair's National EPIC News*, II (16 December), 1, 2.

A1637* "News and Comment," *Upton Sinclair's National EPIC News*, II (23 December), 1, 2, 10.

A1638* "Spread the EPIC Word," *Upton Sinclair's National EPIC News*, II (30 December), 1, 2.

A1639* "What God Means to Me," *Woman's Home Companion*, LXII (December), 18, 85.
Continued in January and February, 1936.
As book: A1751.

A1640* *The Beginning of National EPIC! We the People of America, and How We Ended Poverty.* Pasadena: The Author. 1 leaf.

A1641* *Books by Upton Sinclair.* Pasadena: The Author. 4 pp.
List beginning with *We the People of America. . . .*

A1642 *Dear Friend: Through the Kindness of Providence, I Am Once Again a Writer. . . .* Pasadena: The Author. 1 leaf.

A1643 *Depression Island.* Pasadena: The Author. 124 pp.
As serial: A1617.
Foreign Editions: English, German.

A1644 *I, Candidate for Governor, and How I Got Licked.* Pasadena: The Author: New York: Farrar and Rinehart; Los Angeles: End Poverty League. 215 plus ix pp.
See A1520.
Foreign Editions: German, Polish.

A1645 *Circular Letter.* Pasadena: The Author. 1 leaf.
Beginning: " 'I, Candidate for Governor, and How I Got Licked' ran serially in 60 newspapers, and now our mail is full of letters saying that this is the best inside view of American politics ever given to the people . . ."; see A1644.

A1646 *Preface to "Sodom and Gomorrah,"* by Max Knepper. Los Angeles: End Poverty League. 3 pp., unnumbered.

1935 continued

A1647 *We, People of America, and How We Ended Poverty: A True Story of the Future.* Pasadena: National EPIC League; Los Angeles: End Poverty League. 64 pp.

1936

A1648* "Portrait of Fascism," *Upton Sinclair's National EPIC News*, II (6 January), 1, 2.

A1649* "Upton Sinclair's Letter to the Board of Directors," *Upton Sinclair's National EPIC News*, II (6 January), 6.

A1650* "The Supreme Court Speaks," *Upton Sinclair's National EPIC News*, II (13 January), 1, 2.

A1651* "A Statement to the EPICs," *Upton Sinclair's National EPIC News*, II (13 January), 1, 2.

A1652* "Sinclair Replies to *New Republic*," *Upton Sinclair's National EPIC News*, II (13 January), 2.

A1653* "To the EPIC Convention," *Upton Sinclair's National EPIC News*, II (20 January), 1.

A1654* "Townsend Plan Prospects," *Upton Sinclair's National EPIC News*, II (20 January), 1, 2.

A1655* "A Reply to Harold King," *Upton Sinclair's National EPIC News*, II (20 January), 4.
Also in *Pacific Weekly*, IV (20 January), 28–29.

A1656* "The Dole, and Other Things," *EPIC News*, II (27 January), 1, 2.

A1657* "Sinclair's Real Message Sent to EPIC Convention, *EPIC News*, II (27 January), 4.

A1658* "Production-for-Use Must Come," *American Guardian*, XVIII (31 January), 3.

A1659* "Forward EPIC!" *EPIC News*, II (17 February), 1.

A1660* "Sinclair Reaffirms His Support of EPIC," *EPIC News*, II (17 February), 1, 5.

A1661* "Welcome to Convention," *EPIC News*, II (24 February), 1.

A1662* "Unfair Harvard," *EPIC News*, II (24 February), 5.
Also in *Common Sense*, V (February), 14, 16–17.

A1663* "The Strange Case of Carey McWilliams," *Pacific Weekly*, IV (24 February), 88–89.

A1664* "Upton Sinclair's Address Before the EPIC Convention," *EPIC News*, II (2 March), 1, 2, 5.

A1665* "The Campaign Opens," *EPIC News*, II (9 March), 1, 2.

A1666* "Delegates-at-Large Chosen," *EPIC News*, II (9 March), 1, 6.

A1667 "One Old Socialist to Another, the Way Out for Fascism: How I Interviewed Mussolini," *Forward*, XXX (14 March), 4.

A1668* "A Campaign of Education," *EPIC News*, II (16 March), 1, 2.

A1669* Letter to the Editor, *New York Times Book Review*, 22 March p, 27.
Exchange of letters with Alfred Kazin concerning his adverse review of Sinclair's *What God Means to Me*, A1751.

A1670* "Build EPIC Press," *EPIC News*, II (23 March), 1,2.

A1671* "Sinclair Comments on War Rumors," *EPIC News*, II (30 March), 1.

1936 continued

A1672* "What This Campaign Means," *EPIC News*, II (30 March), 1, 2.

A1673* "EPIC Education is Needed," *National EPIC Magazine*, I (March) 1.

A1674* "*Love in Arms*," *Westways*, XXVII (March), 37.
Letter to the editor about Carey McWilliams's unkind reviews about his play *Love in Arms*.

A1675* "Third EPIC Funeral," *EPIC News*, II (6 April), 1, 7.

A1676* "A Letter From Upton Sinclair to the Board of Directors," *EPIC News*, II (6 April), 2.

A1677* "Why Believe New York Newspaper Headlines?" *EPIC News*, II (6 April), 3.

A1678* "EPIC and the Townsend Plan," *EPIC News*, II (13 April), 1, 7.

A1679* "A Statement to EPICs," *EPIC News*, II (13 April), 2.

A1680* "Sinclair's Radio Address," *EPIC News*, II (13 April), 3, 4.

A1681* "Orders from America; Being a Reply to Anna Louise Strong," *Pacific Weekly*, IV (13 April), 196.

A1682* "Three Questions for Upton Sinclair," *Pacific Weekly*, IV (13 April), 198–199.

A1683* "Can We Civilize Machines?" *EPIC News*, II (20 April), 1, 2.

A1684* "How to Kill the Tiger?" *EPIC News*, II (27 April), 1, 2.

A1685* "One Thousand Percent Dividends," *EPIC News*, II (4 May), 1, 2.

A1686* "What Next for EPIC?" *EPIC News*, II (18 May), 1, 2.

A1687* "Upton Sinclair's Statement to the Press on 6 May," *EPIC News*, II (18 May), 2.

A1688* "God for Capitalism," *EPIC News*, II (25 May), 1, 2.

A1689* "Mr. Sinclair Replies," *Pacific Weekly*, IV (25 May), 303.

Reply to Mr. King about EPIC.

A1690* "Concerning Race Prejudice," *EPIC News*, III (1 June), 1, 2.

A1691* "Slush for the Women," *EPIC News*, III (8 June), 1, 2.

A1692* "Who Will Steal EPIC?" *EPIC News*, III (15 June), 1, 2.

A1693* "Black Legion Politics," *EPIC News*, III (22 June), 1, 2.

A1694* "Conservative America," *EPIC News*, III (29 June), 1, 2.

A1695* "Upton Sinclair vs. H. L. Mencken," *American Mercury*, XXXVIII (June), iv–v.

Mencken replies, vi–vii.

A1696* "The Inventor's Reward," *EPIC News*, III (6 July), 1, 2.

1936 continued

A1697* "Sinclair Asks Stitt Wilson to Keep Pledge: Sinclair Wins Wager to Include PFU Plank," *EPIC News*, III (6 July), 1, 2.

A1698* "Sinclair Corrects N.Y. Minister's Mis-statement," *EPIC News*, III (13 July), 1.

A1699* "Lying to the People," *EPIC News*, III (13 July), 1, 2.

A1700* "Co-op," *EPIC News*, III (13 July–14 June 1937). As book: A1747.

A1701* "Blind Leaders," *EPIC News*, III (20 July), 1, 2.

A1702* "Europe and America," *EPIC News*, III (27 July), 1, 2.

A1703* "Upton Sinclair vs. H. L. Mencken," *American Mercury*, XXXVIII (July), 4–5.

A1704* "Experiments in Mind Reading," *Lilliput*, I (July), 65–67.

A1705* "Alf Landon Put on Spot," *EPIC News*, III (3 August), 1.

A1706* "A Problem of Tactics," *EPIC News*, III (3 August), 1, 2, 12.

A1707* "Stand by Democracy," *EPIC News*, III (10 August), 1, 2, 12.

A1708* "Explaining Our Politics," *EPIC News*, III (17 August), 1, 2.

A1709* "In Sympathy," *EPIC News*, III (17 August), 12.

A1710* "Earl Browder Calls," *EPIC News*, III (24 August), 1, 2, 12.

A1711* "My Question Box," *EPIC News*, III (31 August), 1, 2.

A1712* "Why Not Tory-Baiting?" *Common Sense*, V (August), 12–15.

A1713* "Answering Critics," *EPIC News*, III (7 September), 1, 2, 12.

A1714* "*Literary Digest* Poll," *EPIC News*, III (14 September), 1, 2.

A1715* "The War in Spain," *EPIC News*, III (21 September), 1,2.

A1716* "A Word to the Convention," *EPIC News*, III (21 September), 3.

A1717* "Swap Your Vote," *EPIC News*, III (28 September), 1, 2, 3.

A1718* *Circular Letter.* Pasadena: The Author, September. 4 pp.

Announcing the publication of *Co-op: a Novel of Living Together*; see A1725.

A1719* "Questions Unanswered," *EPIC News*, III (5 October), 1–2.

A1720* "Upton Sinclair on Third Party," *EPIC News*, III (5 October), 3.

A1721* "The Haves and Have Nots," *EPIC News*, III (12 October), 1, 2, 3.

See A1759.

A1722* "Coasting Down Hill," *EPIC News*, III (19 October), 1, 2.

A1723* Letter to Editor, *Time*, XXVIII (19 October), 4.

1936 continued

A1724* "Election Prospects," *EPIC News*, III (26 October), 1, 2.

A1725* *Circular Letter*. Pasadena: The Author, October. 4 pp.
Announcing the publication of *Co-op: A Novel of Living Together*. Same as A1718 except note at top of page 1: "Cash discount to co-operatives." See A1747.

A1726* "One Policy Only . . . ," *The Wharton Review*, X (October), 11.
A letter to the editor about relief money.

A1727* "Looking Forward," *EPIC News*, III (2 November), 1, 2.

A1728* "The Future of EPIC," *EPIC News*, III (9 November), 1, 2.

A1729* "Songs Before Sixty," *Pacific Weekly*, V (9 November), 1, 2.
Four poems: "War News," "Lament," "For Children," "Real Estate Note; (February in Pasadena)."

A1730* "Mrs. Dilling Entertains," *EPIC News*, III (16 November), 1, 2, 8.
Mrs. Elizabeth Dilling, author of anti-Communist books; reprinted in *Common Sense*, V (November), 13–15.

A1731* "Walter Lippmann Clears His Mind," *EPIC News*, III (23 November), 1, 2, 8.

A1732* "Hired Yes-man," *EPIC News*, III (30 November), 1, 2, 8.

A1733* "Address of Upton Sinclair at the Western Writers' Congress," *EPIC News*, III (7 December), 1, 2, 4.
Reprinted: A1947.

A1734* Let Us Educate and Explain," *New Masses*, XXI (8 December), 15–17.
Autobiographical reminiscences.

A1735* "A Civil-Liberty Case in Poland," *New Republic*, LXXXIX (9 December), 177.
Letter to editor.

A1736* "A Democratic Ring vs. Hypocrisy," *Los Angeles Examiner*, 10 December, pp. 3, 4, 6.
On the abdication of Edward VIII.

A1737* "A King and a Rebel," *EPIC News*, III (14 December), 1, 2, 8.

A1738* "Capitalism Has Made It Plain: Pointing Out That Events are Moving Fast, the Founder of EPIC Cautions on Tactics," *New Masses*, XXI (15 December), 26.

A1739* "Mac Dowell," *Boston Symphony Orchestra, Inc. Fifty-sixth Season 1936–37*, 18 and 19 December, pp. 442–451.
An excerpt from an article originally in *American Mercury*, January 1926; see also A2057.

A1740* "What I Expect of Roosevelt," *EPIC News*, III (21 December), 1.

A1741* "Use American Technique Advises Upton Sinclair," *EPIC News*, III (21 December), 2.

A1742* "Wanted: An Opinion from Biologists," *New Republic*, LXXXIX (23 December), 248.
Letter to the editor.

A1743* "Who Won the Election?" *EPIC News*, III (28 December), 1, 2.

1936 continued

A1744* *Circular Letter*. Inglewood:*National EPIC Magazine*. 4 pp.

Announces he has written *Co-op*, A1747.

A1745* *Books of Upton Sinclair*. Pasadena: The Author. 4 pp.

Begins with *What God Means to Me*.

A1746* *Cinderella from Baltimore*. Pasadena: The Author. 1 leaf.

Offering for sale to editors of periodicals his three short articles on the abdication of Edward VIII.

A1747* *Co-op: A Novel of Living Together*. New York: Farrar and Rinehart; Pasadena: The Author. 426 pp.

Reprinted in part: A2049. As serial: A1700. See also A1725.

Foreign Editions: Bulgarian, Czech, Dutch, English, German, Hungarian, Japanese, Polish, Swedish.

A1748* *The Gnomobile: A Gnice Gnew Gnarrative with Gnonsense but Gnothing Gnaughty*. New York: Farrar and Rinehart. 181pp.

Reprinted: Indianapolis: Bobbs-Merrill, 1962; New York: Grossett and Dunlap, 1966 (paper; with accompanying disc recording). Walt Disney Feature Film: 1966.

Foreign Editions: Czech, English, French, German, Portuguese, Spanish, Swedish.

A1749* *Circular Letter*. Pasadena: The Author. 4 pp.

Announcing "that his forthcoming novel *No Pasaran*! is about one-third written, will be finished about the middle of March, and be ready for shipping about two weeks later." On last page is an advertisement for *Co-op*.

A1750* *Wally for Queen! The Private Life of Royalty*. Pasadena: Upton Sinclair. 16 pp.

A1751* *What God Means to Me: An Attempt at a Working Religion*. New York: Farrar and Rinehart; Pasadena: The Author. 140 pp.

Reprinted in part: A2049. As serial: A1639.

Foreign Editions: English, French, Italian, Portuguese.

A1752 "The Movies and Political Propaganda." In *The Movies on Trial*, ed. and comp. William J. Perlman. New York: Macmillan, pp. 189–195.

1937

A1753* "Sinclair Refuses Plea of Former Foe to Run for Political Office," *EPIC News*, III (4 January), 1, 2.

A1754* "Sinclair Calls 'March of Time' to Account," *EPIC News*, III (4 January), 6.

A1755* "The Writer in a Changing World," *EPIC News*, III (4 January), 1, 2, 3.

A1756* "What Price Prosperity?" *EPIC News*, III (11 January), 1, 2.

A1757* "War and Prosperity," *EPIC News*, III (18 January), 1, 2.

A1758* "Neutrality for Fascism," *EPIC News*, III (25 January), 1, 2.

A1759* "The Haves and Have Nots," *New Outlook*, I (January), 9–11.

Comment on the capitalist system and the Spanish Civil War; see A1721.

A1760* "*No Pasaran*! (*They Shall Not Pass*)," *EPIC News*, III (1 February), 1, 2.

As book: A1853.

1937 continued

A1761* "The Case of Jerome Davis," *Unity*, CXVIII (1 February), 217.

Comment on Jerome Davis's latest book, *Capitalism and Culture*.

A1762* "Here's to Crime," *EPIC News*, III (8 February), 1, 2.

A1763* "Business and Ballots," *EPIC News*, III (15 February), 1, 2.

A1764* "The Answer," *EPIC News*, III (15 February), 8.

A1765* "The Supreme Court," *EPIC News*, III (22 February), 1, 2.

A1766* "Instead of an Editorial," *EPIC News*, III (1 March), 1.

A1767* "To Hell with Capital?" *EPIC News*, III (8 March), 1, 2.

A1768* "Big Business Neutrality," *EPIC News*, III (15 March), 1, 2.

A1769* "Pirates and Bankers," *EPIC News*, III (22 March), 1, 2.

A1770* "The People at Bay," *EPIC News*, III (29 March), 1, 2.

A1771* "Mental Underworld," *Forum*, XCVII (March), 153–158.

A1772* "The Sit Down Strikes," *EPIC News*, III (5 April), 1, 2.

A1773* "Trial for Plagiarism," *EPIC News*, III (12 April), 1, 2.

A1774* "Magazine Propaganda," *EPIC News*, III (19 April), 1, 2.

A1775* "Burning Books in Boston," *EPIC News*, III (26 April), 1, 2.

A1776* "The Russian Trial," *New Republic*, XC (28 April), 360.

Letter to the editor on Malcolm Cowley's study of the text of the Russian Trial.

A1777* "The Writer in a Changing World," *New Outlook*, III (April), 173–175.

"An address delivered . . . at the Western Writers' Congress held in San Francisco."

A1778* "What Price Liberty?" *EPIC News*, III (3 May), 1, 2.

A1779* "PFU Not Forgotten," *EPIC News*, III (10 May), 1, 2.

A1780* "Sinclair Outlines Methods for Ending Unemployment," *EPIC News*, III (17 May), 1, 2.

A1781* Letter, *EPIC News*, III (17 May), 5.

A1782* "Start the Idle Factories," *EPIC News*, III (24 May), 1, 2.

A1783* "*No Pasaran*!" *Deutsches Volkescho* [New York], I (29 May), 6.

See A1853.

A1784* "Exchanging for Use," *EPIC News*, IV (31 May), 1, 2.

A1785* "Truth Wanted," *EPIC News*, IV (7 June), 1, 2.

A1786* "Safety of Freedom Concerns Sinclair," *EPIC News*, IV (14 June), 3.

Message to National Writers' Conference.

A1787* "Socialism and Liberty," *EPIC News*, IV (14 June), 1, 2.

1937 continued

A1788* "Security Plus Liberty," *EPIC News*, IV (21 June), 1, 2.

A1789* "Roman Holiday," *EPIC News*, IV (21 June–14 February, 1938).
As book: A1306.

A1790* "Freedom for Workers," *EPIC News*, IV (28 June), 1, 2.

A1791* "Intellectual Freedom," *EPIC News*, IV (5 July), 1, 2.

A1792* "Change Without Disorder," *EPIC News*, IV (12 July), 1, 2.

A1793* "Help for Spain," *EPIC News*, IV (19 July), 1, 2.

A1794* "The Reds Arrive," *EPIC News*, IV (26 July), 1, 2.

A1795* "Mother Bloor in *The Jungle*," *Mother Bloor 75th Birthday Souvenir Book*, July, p. 8.

A1796* "Our Unbalanced Magazine Diet," *Call of Youth* [New York], V (July), 5–6.

A1797* "Freedom for Judges," *EPIC News*, IV (2 August), 1, 2.

A1798* "An Open Letter to President Roosevelt," *EPIC News*, IV (9 August), 1, 2.
Reprinted: A1800, A1808.

A1799* "Fascist Invaders Show Brutality," *EPIC News*, IV (9 August), 3.
Letter from *Rob Wagner's Script*.

A1800* "An Open Letter to President Roosevelt," *Liberty*, XVI (14 August), 10–11.
See A1798, A1808.

A1801* "Collectivism Coming," *EPIC News*, IV (16 August), 1, 2.

A1802* "Sinclair Sends Sympathy," *EPIC News*, IV (16 August), 7.

A1803* "The Problem of Land," *The Progressive*, I (21 August), 3.

A1804* "What is the Answer?" *EPIC News*, IV (23 August), 1, 2.

A1805* "Food for the People," *The Voice* [Durban], 25 August, pp. 11, 13.

A1806* "Eine Frau aus Iowa," *Die Neue Weltbünne* [Zürich], XXXIII (26 August), 1095–1099.

A1807* "Notes on Collectivism," *The Progressive*, I (28 August), 3.

A1808* "An Open Letter to President Roosevelt," *EPIC News*, IV (30 August), 1, 2.
See A1798, A1800.

A1809* "Greetings from Upton Sinclair," *EPIC News*, IV (30 August), 6.

A1810* "Wages and Profits," *New Republic*, XCII, (1 September), 106.
Letter to the editor on business reports in various magazines.

A1811* "What's the Answer?" *The Progressive*, I (4 September), 3.

A1812* "Poverty the Issue," *EPIC News*, IV (6 September), 1, 2.

A1813* "Sinclair Asks for the Truth," *EPIC News*, IV (13 September), 1, 5.
First half of a letter to John L. Lewis; see A1815.

1937 continued

A1814* "Congress's Betrayal?" *The Progressive*, I (18 September), 3.

A1815* "Wanted: the Truth," *EPIC News*, IV (20 September), 1, 5.

Second half of letter to John L. Lewis; see A1813.

A1816* "On Another's Washing," *The Progressive*, I (25 September), 3.

Reprinted: A1817.

A1817* "Stealing One Another's Washing," *EPIC News*, IV (27 September), 1, 5.

See A1816.

A1818* "Writing Books for Labor," *United Automobile Worker* [*Detroit*], 2 October, p. 10.

A1819 "A Letter to John L. Lewis," *The Progressive*, I (2 October), 3; I (9 October), 3.

See A1813, A1815.

A1820 "EPIC Problems Discussed," *EPIC News*, IV (4 October), 1, 5.

A1821* "EPIC Transformations," *EPIC News*, IV (11 October), 1, 5.

A1822 "I'm Out of Politics!" *The Progressive*, I (16 October), 3.

A1823* "Letting Them Starve," *EPIC News*, IV (18 October), 3.

Also in *The Progressive*, I (30 October), 3.

A1824* "To the Board of Directors, Women's Civic League of Pasadena," *EPIC News*, IV (18 October), 5.

A1825 "My 'EPIC' Idea Spreads," *The Progressive*, I (23 October), 3.

A1826* "Organize the World," *EPIC News*, IV (25 October), 1, 5.

A1827* "Sinclair on Haight," *California Progressive*, I (October), 2.

Excerpt from *I, Candidate for Governor*, A1644.

A1828* "Greetings to U.S.S.R.," *EPIC News*, IV (1 November), 1, 5.

A1829* "International Bandits," *The Progressive*, I (6 November), 3.

A1830* "200,000 Men Bite Dog," *EPIC News*, IV (8 November), 1, 5.

A1831* "Demand Civilized Treatment," *EPIC News*, IV (8 November), 1, 5.

A1832* "Biographical Note," *Saturday Review of Literature*, XVII (13 November), 21.

A1833 "Soviet Anniversary," *The Progressive*, I (13 November), 3.

See A1828.

A1834* "*The Brass Check* Certified!" *EPIC News*, IV (15 November), 1, 5.

Also in *The Progressive*, I (27 November), 3.

A1835* "And the Press Is Silent," *The Progressive*, I (19 November), 3.

A1836* "The Unemployed Still With Us," *EPIC News*, IV (22 November), 1, 5.

1937 continued

A1837* "The New Depression," *EPIC News,* IV (29 November), 1, 5.

A1838* "Sinclair Protests Against Outrage," *EPIC News,* IV (29 November), 8.

A1839* "Hollywood and Detroit," *EPIC News,* IV (6 December), 1, 2.

A1840 "When Is a Book Not a Book?" *New York Herald-Tribune,* 10 December.

Letter to the editor; see A1856.

A1841* "First Principles," *EPIC News,* IV (13 December), 1, 2.

A1842* "Use Versus Profit," *EPIC News,* IV (20 December), 1, 2, 3.

A1843* "Christmas Thoughts," *EPIC News,* IV (27 December), 1, 2.

A1844* "My Long Love Affair," *Personal Romances,* I (December), 12–16, 66, 68.

A1845* *Announcing the "Flivver King."* Pasadena: The Author. 1 leaf.

Beginning: "The booklet is sent to you in hope that after you have read it, you may be moved to work out a method of making it accessible to your group.

A1846* *Announcing "No Pasaran!"* Pasadena: The Author. 1 leaf.

Circular advertising *The Flivver King* and *No Parasan!*

A1847* *Broadside Proposal.* Pasadena: The Author. 1 leaf.

To the editors, exploring the possibility of his selling a syndicated column. At end of article: "Stealing One Another's Washing," by Sinclair; see A1817.

A1848* *Broadside.* Pasadena: The Author. 1 leaf.

"*The Moscow News* of November 7th . . . gives interesting figures regarding the sales of books. . . . It would appear that Upton Sinclair constitutes 19.3% of World's Classics in the opinion of present day Russian readers. . . ."

A1849* *Broadside.* Pasadena: The Author. 1 leaf.

"10,000 copies of *No Pasaran*! sold in first two weeks: 40,000 waiting. . . ."

A1850* *Broadside.* Pasadena: The Author. 1 leaf.

Upton Sinclair offers for sale a list of his books, beginning with *The Flivver King*; see A1851.

A1851* *The Flivver King.* Pasadena: The Author; Girard, Kansas: Haldeman-Julius. 119 pp.

Reprinted: Girard, Kansas: Haldeman-Julius, n.d. Special edition presented to the UAW Social Justice Awards banquet, 6 May 1962; New York: Phaedra Press, 1970.

Foreign Editions: Bulgarian, Czech, Dutch, English, French, German, Hebrew, Hungarian, Latvian, Lettish, Lithuanian, Norwegian, Portuguese, Russian, Serbo-Croatian, Slovak, Swedish, White-Russian.

A1852* Letter to the Editor, *International Literature*, no. 12 (December), pp. 106–107.

On the 20th anniversary of Russian Revolution Soviet Union stands alone against world run by gangsters.

A1853* *No Pasaran*! (*They Shall Not Pass*). Pasadena: The Author; New York: The Labor Press. 96 pp.

As serial: A1760.

Foreign Editions: Bulgarian, Czech, Danish, Dutch, English, Finnish, French, German, Hebrew, Icelandic, Italian, Lithuanian, Marathi, Norwegian, Spanish, Swedish, White-Russian.

A1854* *No Pasaran*! (*They Shall Not Pass*): *A Story of the Battle of Madrid.* Pasadena: The Author. 1 leaf.

Circular prepared by Sinclair to advertise his book; see A1853.

1937 continued

A1855* *Outline Sketch of 3 Act Drama: "Our Lady."* Pasadena: The Author. 4 pp.

A1856* *"When Is a Book Not a Book?" Pasadena: The* Author. 4 pp.

A letter to the editor of *New York Herald-Tribune Book Review* protesting refusal to review several of Sinclair's books; see A1840.

A1857* Preface to *Irodalom torténete*, trans. Benamy Sandor. Budapest: Epocha Konyvkiado, p. 5.

See Hungarian edition of *Mammonart*. Prefatory note dated 4 January 1937.

1938

A1858* "A Letter to Henry Ford," *EPIC News*, IV (3 January), 1.

A1859* "The Two-Headed Calf," *EPIC News*, IV (10 January), 1, 2.

A1860* "No Boycott," *New York Herald-Tribune*, 12 January, 1, 2.

Letter on the boycott in the press of *The Flivver King.*

A1861* "Wars and Rumors of Wars," *Upton Sinclair's Circular Letter*, I (15 January), 1.

A1862* "The Insatiable Author," *New York Herald-Tribune*, 16 January, p. 11.

Another letter on *The Flivver King.*

A1863* "Rumors of War," *EPIC News*, IV (17 January), 1, 6.

A1864* "The Problems of Russia," *EPIC News*, IV (24 January), 1, 6.

A1865* "Groping in a Fog," *EPIC News*, IV (31 January), 1, 2.

Reprinted in *The Progressive*, II (12 February), 3.

A1866* "Your Universe and You," *Psychology Magazine*, XXIII (January), 17–18, 55.

A1867* "The Problem of Russia," *The Progressive*, II (5 February), 3.

One of the articles in the correspondence with Eugene Lyons that led to *Terror in Russia: Two Views*, A1916.

A1868* "A Triumph for P.F.U.," *EPIC News*, IV (7 February), 1, 6.

A1869* "Another Victory for P.F.U.," *EPIC News*, IV (14 February), 1, 6.

Reprinted in *The Progressive*, II (19 February), 3. One of the articles in the correspondence with Eugene Lyons; see A1867.

A1870* "Russia in Controversy," *EPIC News*, IV (21 February), 1, 2.

Continued in *EPIC News*, IV (28 February), 1,2,8.

A1871* Letter to the Editor, *New Republic*, XCIV (23 February), 76.

Making a plea for funds to film *The Flivver King*.

A1872* "Sinclair Denounces Traitors: Treason at Home," *EPIC News*, IV (7 March), 1, 4.

A1873* "A Lost Leader," *EPIC News*, IV (14 March), 1, 2, 7.

A1874* "The New Deal Sleeps," *EPIC News*, IV (21 March), 1, 2.

A1875* "International Treason," *Steelworker*, 26 March, pp. 5, 12–13.

1938 continued

A1876* "The World's Crisis," *EPIC News*, IV (28 March), 1, 2.

Concluded in *EPIC News*, IV (4 April), 1,2. Reprinted: A1947.

A1877* "A Review of *The Prodigal Parents*, by Sinclair Lewis," *Common Sense*, VII (March), 22–23.

Says Lewis has gone over to Chamber of Commerce in new novel about "Reds" in America.

A1878* "How to Keep Out of War," *Nation*, CXLVI (2 April), 377.

Various writers answer this question.

A1879* "History Repeats Itself," *EPIC News*, IV (11 April), 1, 2.

A1880* "Upton Sinclair's Message to EPIC's Birthday," *EPIC News*, IV (11 April), 8.

A1881* "Depression Continues," *EPIC News*, IV (18 April), 1, 2.

A1882* "Pump-Priming Again," *EPIC News*, IV (25 April), 1, 2.

A1883* "Blank Check Politics," *EPIC News*, IV (2 May), 1, 2.

A1884* "A Couple of Telegrams Which Speak for Themselves," *EPIC News*, IV (9 May), 2.

A1885* "Former EPIC Director Succumbs," *EPIC News*, IV (9 May), 5.

A1886* "Out of the Frying Pan," *EPIC News*, IV (9 May), 1, 2.

A1887* "I Will Not Let the People Down," *EPIC News*, IV (16 May), 1, 2.

A1888* "Suicide Bridge," *EPIC News*, IV (23 May), 1, 2.
Note: *EPIC News* stopped publication with the 30 May issue, vol. V, no. 1.

A1889* "American-Soviet Friendship," *Soviet Russia Today*, VII (May), 24.

A1890* "America's False Democracy," *American Mercury*, XLIV (June), 208–210.

A1891* "This Brave New Party," *The Progressive*, II (16 July), 1, 3.
Also contains an article by Mary Craig Sinclair supporting Raymond Haight for Governor of California.

A1892* "To My Readers," *New Masses*, XXVIII (19 July), 10–11.

A1893* *To the People of South Africa.* Pasadena: The Author, 2 August. 4 pp.
Letter about the South African Government barring *No Pasaran*!

A1894* "About Pension Plans," *The Progressive*, II (27 August), 3.

A1895* "Upton Sinclair Says," *The Progressive*, II (10 September), 3.

A1896* *Circular Letter.* New York: The Author, 20 September. 4 pp.
Announcing that on this day, his sixtieth birthday, his sixtieth book, *Little Steel*, is being published; see A1911.

A1897* "Changes I Have Seen," *Writer's Digest*, XVIII (September), 17–19.
Reprinted: A1947.

1938 continued

A1898* *Circular Letter.* Pasadena: The Author, 1 October. 1 leaf.

To editors, announcing a series of sixteen short articles, setting forth the breakdown which lies ahead for the New Deal.

A1899 "Communal Collaboration," *Living Age*, CCCLV (November), 276.

A1900* "Your Million Dollars; Letters to Joe, Letter V," *Progressive*, II–III (3 December–11 March, 1939).

As pamphlet: A1949.

A1901 "An Open Letter to William Allen White," *New Republic*, XCVII (7 December), 131–132.

A1902* "Technicians Awake!" *New English Weekly*, XIV (15 December), 153–154.

Reprinted: A1947.

A1903 "Message to Soviet Russia," *American Mercury*, XLV (December), 464–469.

A1904* "The Soviet Union and the Fascist Menace to the World," *International Literature*, no. 12 (December), p. 52.

A letter.

A1905* "Upton Sinclair Offers His Aid," *China Today*, V (December), 11.

Letter to the editor. Will provide Chinese with copies of his books to be translated.

A1906* "What I Believe," *Common Sense*, VII (December), 12–15.

A1907* *Books of Upton Sinclair in Translation and Foreign Editions.* Pasadena: The Author. 48 pp.

A bibliography of 772 titles in 47 languages, 39 countries. Second edition, August 1938; see A1277.

A1908* *Books by Upton Sinclair.* New York: Upton Sinclair. 4 pp.

Selected list of his books offered for sale, beginning with *Little Steel.*

A1909* *Circular Letter.* New York: The Author. 1 leaf.

Begins: "Dear friend: I have a new short novel. It is called *Our Lady.*"

A1910* *A Letter to My Readers.* Pasadena: The Author. 1 leaf.

To the editor: Publication requested. Release date, 20 June 1938.

A1911* *Little Steel.* New York: Farrar and Rinehart; Pasadena: The Author. 308 pp.

Foreign Editions: Bulgarian, English, Hungarian, Russian, Spanish.

A1912* *Order Blank.* New York: Upton Sinclair. 1 leaf.

For a selected list of books beginning with *Little Steel,* A1911.

A1913* *Our Lady.* Emmaus, Pa.: Rodale Press; Pasadena and New York: The Author. 162 pp.

Reprinted: Girard, Kansas: Haldeman-Julius (B17), 1948. In part: A2049.

Foreign Editions: Dutch, English, French, German, Romanian, Spanish.

A1914* *A Parable for Moderns*; *Four Opinions of "Our Lady."* Pasadena: The Author. 1 leaf.

Reprinted from the *Brooklyn Eagle,* 11 July.

A1915* *St. Louis Post-Dispatch Symposium on Freedom of the Press.* St. Louis. 62 pp.

Expressions by 120 representative Americans.

Reprinted from 13–25 December issues of St. Louis *Post-Dispatch.*

A1916* *Terror in Russia? Two Views.* New York: Richard R. Smith. 63 pp.

As serial: A1867.

Reprinted: New York: Rand School Press, 1938. Series of five essays, two by Eugene Lyons, with an introduction by Eugene Lyons.

1938 continued

A1917* "Une Lettre d'Upton Sinclair aux Écrivains Soviétiques," *La Litterature Internationale* [Moscow], VIII (1938), 102–104.

Preceded by a letter from the editors: "60 ème anniversaire de Upton Sinclair."

A1918* *Upton Sinclair on the Soviet Union.* New York: Weekly Masses Co. 15 pp.

Upton Sinclair's letter reprinted from *New Masses*, 8 March.

1939

A1919* "The Encyclicals and the EPIC," *Commonweal*, XXIX (6 January), 296–297.

Letter to the editor.

A1920* "Forward Pass to Mr. White," *New Republic*, XCVII (11 January), 289.

Letter to the editor, William Allen White.

A1921* "Technicians Turn to Life, Review and Comment," *New Masses*, XXX (17 January), 23–24.

A letter agreeing with their program.

A1922* *American Challenges Anti-Semitism and Race Hatred.* New York: Jewish People's Committee for United Action against Fascism and Anti-Semitism.

Sinclair's contribution, p. 28.

A1928* "The American Rich," *Progressive Weekly* (*The Sunday Worker*), 19 February, pp. 1, 2.

Reprinted: A1947.

A1924* "Whom Did She Mean," *Rob Wagner's Script*, XXI (25 February), 32.

Letter to the editor.

A1925* "Praise for John Longo," *New Republic*, XCVIII (29 March), 224.

Letter to the editor concerning recent *New Republic* article by Dewey H. Palmer on auto mileage testing, "Automobiles in 1939." Palmer's answer follows.

A1926* "The American Press," *Pravda*, 22 April.

Reprinted: A 1947.

A1927* "An Open Letter to George Bernard Shaw about Lady Astor," *Liberty*, XVI (22 April), 11–12.

Critical of Lady Astor and Clivedon Set.

Reprinted: A1947.

A1928* "Upton Sinclair Writes . . . ," *The Arbitrator*, XXI (April), 3.

Letter to the editor, concerning Fritz Kuhn and the "surrender" of New York.

A1929* "Life is Not All Entertainment," *Hollywood Tribune*, 5 May, p. 3.

Comment on question whether film maturity will come from social, political involvement of industry.

A1930* "Sinclair Salutes Steinbeck," *Common Sense*, VIII (May), 22–23.

Review of *Grapes of Wrath*.
Reprinted: A1947.

A1931* "America and the Next War," *New Republic*, XCIX (21 June), 178.

Comments by various prominent people.

A1932* "Can Democracy Survive?" *Modern Quarterly*, XI (Summer), 68–80.

Sinclair's response, p. 78.

1939 continued

A1933* "Peter's Poem," *New Republic*, C (23 August), 77.
A letter to the editor containing a poem by a refugee from the Sudetenland.

A1934* *Upton Sinclair Speaks: Radio Address.* Los Angeles, 20 October. 4 pp.
Committee opposed to "Ham and Egg Plan." Complete text of talk by Upton Sinclair.

A1935* "Sinclair vs. Hook," *New York Call*, 11 November, p. 4.

A1936* "What Will America Do?" *New Masses*, XXXIII (14 November), 7–8.
Upton Sinclair's prophecy concerning the role of the United States in Europe.

A1937* "Hook Can't Rule Me Out!" *New York Call*, 18 November, p. 4.
Defends himself as a Socialist and anti-Communist. "Sinclair evades the question!" by Prof. Sidney Hook appears with the Sinclair article, under the headline, "Upton Sinclair vs. Sidney Hook." See A1935, A1952.

A1938* *Circular Letter.* New York: The Author, November. 4 pp.
Offering for sale his pamphlet "What Can Be Done about America's Economic Troubles?" See A1948.

A1939* *Circular Letter.* New York: The Author, November. 4 pp.
Reporting his progress on the writing of *World's End.*

A1940* "Upton Sinclair Has a Dream," *Nation*, CXLIX (9 December), 659.
A full page about his publishing career and wishing his readers "Merry Christmas." Appeared in *New Republic*, 20 December.

A1941* "Sinclair Replies to His Son," *New York Call*, 23 December, p. 1.

A1942* *The Case of Rosika Schwimmer vs. Upton Sinclair: A Statement by Upton Sinclair.* Pasadena: The Author. 1 leaf.

A1943* "Comment J'ai Ecrit *La Jungle*, "*La Litterature Internationale*, no. 5, pp. 84–92.

A1944* *Expect No Peace*! Girard, Kansas: Haldeman-Julius; New York and Pasadena: The Author. 57 pp.
Reprinted: A1947.

A1945* *Marie Antoinette.* New York: Vanguard Press; Pasadena and New York: The Author. 200 pp.
Reprinted as *Marie and Her Lover*; see A2061.
Foreign Edition: English.

A1946* *News from Upton Sinclair.* New York: Upton Sinclair. 1 leaf.
Vanguard Press is publishing *Marie Antoinette.*

A1947 *Telling the World.* London: T. Werner Laurie. 205 pp.
"Note by the Author," p. 5.
"Except No Peace" (*New Masses*, 1938), pp. 9–20.
"War—And How It Is Made" (*The New Clarion*, 11 March 1933), pp. 21–25.
"The Machine Menace—Civilization Awakes To It" (*New Leader*, 6 January 1933), pp. 26–30.
"The Stranglehold of Finance" (*Common Sense*, 1939), pp. 31–36.
"The World's Crisis" (an address delivered in 1938, to a mass meeting at Mecca Temple, New York City, over telephone from Pasadena, California), pp. 37–47.
"The American Press" (*Pravda*, 22 April 1939), pp. 48–55.
"The American Rich" (*Forward*), pp. 56–61.

1939 continued

"The American Supreme Court" (*Pravda*), pp. 62–65.

"The Blood Test" (*Isvestia*), pp. 66–68.

"An Open Letter to George Bernard Shaw About Lady Astor" (*Liberty*, 22 April 1939), pp. 69–75.

"The Reds Arrive" (*EPIC News*), pp. 76–80.

"An Interview with Upton Sinclair" (*Federated Press*), pp. 81–84.

"Nearest to My Heart" (*Writer's Digest*, May 1933), pp. 85-89.

"The Price I Paid" (*Pearson's Magazine*, April 1917), pp. 90–99.

"My Long Love-Affair" (no source given), pp. 100–123.

"Changes I Have Seen" (*Writer's Digest*, September 1938), pp. 124–128.

"Let us Educate and Explain!" (an address to the Western Writers' Congress, San Francisco, November 1936), *EPIC News*, 7 December 1936), pp. 129–136.

"A Lost Leader" (*Common Sense*), pp. 137–142.

"The Story of Agnes Smedley" (*Liberty*), pp. 143–149.

"*Grapes of Wrath*" (*Common Sense*, May 1939), pp. 150–153.

"Technicians Awake!" (*New Masses* and *New English Weekly*), pp. 154–158.

"The Unknown Universe: Experiments in Psychic Research" (no source given), pp. 159–186.

"The Lady From Baltimore" (circulated by an American newspaper syndicate), pp. 187–205.

A1948* *What Can Be Done About America's Economic Troubles?* Girard, Kansas: Haldeman-Julius; New York and Pasadena: The Author. 22 pp.

A1949* *Your Million Dollars.* New York and Pasadena: Upton Sinclair. 32 pp.

As serial: A1900.

Foreign Editions: Bulgarian, English (as *Letter to a Millionaire*).

1940

A1950 "Upton Sinclair Has a Dream," *Survey Graphic*, XXIX (1 January), 49.

A1951* "A California View: Foolish Plan, Says Famed Liberal," *Liberty*, XVII (20 January), 48.
Discusses California life retirement plan.

A1952* "Where Does Russia Stand Today?" *The Plebs* [London], XXXII (January), 8–10.
Debate between Upton Sinclair and Sidney Hook in the organ of the National Council of Labor Colleges. Professor Hook's rejoinder, pp. 10–13. See A1935, A1937.

A1953* "Munitions King, a Short Story," *Friday*, I (15 March), 5, 22.
An excerpt from *World's End*; see A1957.

A1954* "Upton Sinclair, Answering Max Eastman, 'Reconsiders' Socialism, Russia and EPIC," *Common Sense*, IX (April), 30–31.
Letter to the editor.

A1955* "The Technique of Telepathy," *Armchair Science*, XII (April), 52–55.
An excerpt from *Mental Radio*, A1254.

A1956* "Correspondence," *The Arbitrator*, XXII (May), 3.
Quote from an Upton Sinclair letter on pacificism.

A1957* *World's End*. New York: Viking Press; New York and Pasadena: The Author, 21 June. 740 pp.
Reprinted in part: A2049; excerpts in *Friday*, I (31 May, 7 and 26 June 1940). Abridged: New York: Pocket Books (Permabook), 1960.
Foreign Editions: Chinese, Czech, Danish, English-Canada, English, French, German, Hungarian, Italian, Japanese, Norwegian, Portuguese, Russian, Spanish, Swedish.

A1958* "Novelist Sinclair Wonders," *Time*, XXXVI (15 July), 4–5.
Letter to the editor on review of *World's End*, A1957.

1940 continued

A1959* "World's End Impending," *Wings*, XIV (July), 4–8.
Note on the writing of *World's End*.
Reprinted: A1964.

A1960* "Where the Gallup Poll Errs," *New Republic*, LIII (18 November), 695–696.
Letter to the editor enclosing a letter written by Sinclair to George Gallup.

A1961* *Circular Letter*. New York: The Author. 1 leaf.
Beginning: "Dear Friend: June 17 Viking Press will publish. . . ."

A1962* "The Epic-urean Dinner." In *Famous Recipes by Famous People*, comp. and ed. Herbert Cerwin. San Francisco: Lane Publishing Co., p. 14.
"My favorite dish is apples."

A1963* *Is the American Form of Capitalism Essential to the American Form of Democracy?* Girard, Kansas: Haldeman-Julius Publications; New York and Pasadena: The Author. 16 pp.
Debate with George Sokolsky, 15 January, Los Angeles. Binding variant on front wrapper: Published by the Author: New York City and Pasadena, California.

A1964* *World's End Impending: Notes on the Writing of "World's End."* New York: Upton Sinclair. 4 pp.
A reprint of the article written for *Wings* (July), with addition of comments on the book by noted authors; see A1959.

A1965* *Favorite Novelists of Australia*. Pasadena: The Author. 1 p.
Tabulations of votes from a Freemantle newspaper poll showing Sinclair as Australia's favorite living author.

A1966* Preface to *Mi se Spune Dulgherul*, trans. Bar S. Bar. Bucharest: "Cultura Romaneasca," p. vii.

See Romanian Edition of *They Called Me Carpenter*, A880. Photoprint of a telegram from Upton Sinclair to the publisher, December 1939, with a translation underneath.

1941

A1967* First Aid to Nazism," *Nation*, CLII (11 January), 56.

Letter sent to the editor concerning a telegram Sinclair sent to Mark O. Prentiss, America First Committee, New York.

A1968* "Tomorrow's World Must Wipe Out Profit System," *Daily Pennsylvanian*, LVII (17 January), 3, 5.

A1969* "Upton Sinclair Sees Long Era of Peace in Allied Victory and World Federation," *New Leader* [London], XXIV (1 February), 4.

A1970* "Jack London Speaks to Upton Sinclair," *Psychic Observer*, no. 58 (10 February), pp. 1–2, 4.

Sinclair talks with Jack London through Arthur Ford's mediumship. Dispels any doubts he had about spiritualism.

A1971* "Spirits or Mind-Reading?" *Psychic Observer*, no. 59 (25 February), pp. 3–4, 6.

Further "proof" after another session with Arthur Ford.

A1972* "Stand Firm! Norwegians!" *News of Norway*, I (13 March), 5.

Highlights of Upton Sinclair's message to Norway via WRUL, Boston. Mimeographed; see A1975.

A1973* *Between Two Worlds*. New York: Viking Press; New York and Pasadena: The Author, March. 859 pp.

Reprinted in part: A2049.

Foreign Editions: Czech, Danish, Dutch, English-Canada, English, German, Hungarian, Italian, Japanese, Norwegian, Russian, Spanish, Swedish.

1941 continued

A1974* "Martin Birnbaum," *City College Alumnus*, XXXVII (March), 24.

Biographical sketch and remarks on Birnbaum's *John Singer Sargent*. Birnbaum aided Sinclair with art and music references in the Lanny Budd series.

A1975* "Stand Firm, Norwegians!" *Norway*, 9 April, pp. 47, 70.

See A1972.

A1976* "To the Conquered Peoples," *Knickerbocker Weekly* [Free Netherlands], I (14 April), 14.

Broadcast from station WRUL, Boston.

A1977* "Open Letter to the President," *Common Sense*, X (April) 124–125.

Encouraging Roosevelt to act against the aggression of the Nazis in Europe. Reprinted widely.

A1978* "Concerning *Between Two Worlds*," *The Publishers' Circular and Booksellers' Record*, CLIV (17 May), 213–214.

Genesis of and comment on the first two volumes of the Lanny Budd series. As offprint: A1985.

A1979* "Upton Sinclair and the Helicon Home Colony," *American Notes and Queries*, I (June), 46.

A1980* "To the Conquered Peoples of Europe," *Central European Observer*, XVIII (8 August), 210.

Reprinted widely.

A1981* "Upton Sinclair Apologizes and Explains His Position," *Open Forum*, XVIII (4 October), 2.

Has no sympathy with those who abuse civil liberties during war time.

A1982* "Letter to an Isolationist," *New Republic*, CV (13 October), 479.

To an isolationist friend urging the United States to fight Hitler with Britain and Russia before he destroys them and fights us alone.

A1983* "To George Viereck," *Nation*, CLII (29 November), 551.

A1984* "The World's Worst Book—a Symposium," *Books Abroad*, XV (Winter), 51.

Sinclair's choice is Gibbon's *Decline and Fall of the Roman Empire*.

A1985* *Concerning "Between Two Worlds."* New York: The Author. 4 pp.

Offprint of an article, A1978.

A1986* Foreword to *I Was Hitler's Doctor*, by Kurt Krueger, M.D. New York: Biltmore Publishing Co., pp. v–vi.

See 1942 edition as *Inside Hitler*, A1999.

A1987* *Peace or War in America?* Girard, Kansas: Haldeman-Julius Publications; New York and Pasadena: The Author. 27 pp.

Binding variant with material from the *Post* [Pasadena] and *Star-News* [Pasadena], 13 March 1941. A debate between Upton Sinclair and Philip F. La Follette.

A1988* *To the Conquered Peoples of Europe*. New York: Upton Sinclair. 4 pp.

See A1976.

A1989* Frederick Garrison [pseud.] *Songs of Our Nation*. New York: Marks Music Corporation. *c.* 1941. 9 pp.

Listed at Library of Congress; not seen.

1942

A1990* *Dragon's Teeth*. New York: Viking Press; New York and Pasadena: The Author, 5 January. 631 pp.

1942 continued

Reprinted: New York: Viking, 1954. Abridged: A2008. In Part: A2049; New York: Pocket Books (Permabook), 1961.

Foreign Editions: Braille, Czech, Danish, Dutch, English-Canada, English, French, German, Hungarian, Italian, Japanese, Norwegian, Russian, Spanish, Swedish.

A1991* "What Can a Writer Do to Aid His Country?" *Author's League Bulletin*, I (January), 13.

Sinclair's contribution to symposium concerns avoiding repetition of mistakes in peacemaking after World War I.

A1992 "The Man Within," *New Republic*, CVI (2 March), 308–309.

Review of Kurt Krueger's *Inside Hitler*; see A1986.

A1993 "Is Socialism Coming?" *World Review* [London], XLIII (March), 51–54.

A1994* "*Dragon's Teeth*," *Omnibook*, IV (April), 3–32.

Abridged version of the novel; see A1990.

A1995* "A Labor Day Message to American Labor," *War Bond Labor News*, 30 August, p. 1.

Importance of winning the war for American labor to avert Axis' suppression of labor.

A1996* "Second Front Next Wednesday," *Tribune* [London], 18 September, p. 8.

Sinclair outlines plans for keeping Russia from collapsing and for invading continental Europe.

A1997* "This Is Ours: This Song of Freedom," *Defender* [Chicago], XXXVIII (26 September), 29.

Contains parts of "To the Conquered Peoples of Europe," and "anti-Nazi" material; see A1976.

A1998* *Books by Upton Sinclair.* New York: Upton Sinclair. 4 pp.

List of books beginning with *Dragon's Teeth*.

A1999* Prelude for the second printing of *Inside Hitler*, by Kurt Krueger, M.D. Introduction by Otto Strasser and Preface by K. Arvid Enlid. New York: Avalon Press, pp. 5–7.

See *I Was Hitler's Doctor*, A1986.

A2000* *Letters Concerning the "World's End" Series*. New York: Upton Sinclair. 4 pp.

Letters concerning *World's End* (A1957), *Between Two Worlds* (A1973), and *Dragon's Teeth* (A1990).

1943

A2001* *Wide Is the Gate*. New York: Viking Press; Monrovia, Calif.: The Author, 4 January. 751 pp.

Reprinted: Abridged, A2005.

Foreign Editions: Czech, Dutch, English-Canada, English, French, German, Hungarian, Italian, Japanese, Norwegian, Portuguese, Spanish, Swedish.

A2002* Letter to the editor, *New York Times Book Review*, 31 January, pp. 23, 27.

About the review of *Wide Is the Gate* by R. L. Duffus.

A2003* "Heavy Take at 'The Gate,'" *Time*, XLI (8 March), 6.

A letter to the editor defending the success of his Lanny Budd series.

A2004* "A Letter by Upton Sinclair," *Letters Issued by the American Russian Institute*, I (April), 3.

Concerning need to crush Nazism.

A2005* "*Wide Is the Gate*," *Omnibook*, V (April), 75–102.

Abridged version of the novel in the author's own words; see A2001.

A2006 *Circular Letter*. Monrovia, Calif.: The Author, 28 July. 2 pp.

Asking the War Production Board for a further allotment of paper for his publishing.

1943 continued

A2007* "To Solve the German Problem, A Free State?" *New York Times Magazine*, 15 August, pp. 6, 34, 36.

See reprint as a pamphlet: A2014.

A2008* "*Dragon's Teeth*," *Liberty*, XX (28 August), 25–32, 45–52.

Condensation of novel; see A1990.

A2009* "Upton Sinclair to the Indians," *New Republic*, CIX (30 August), 287.

Letter to the editor: reprint of his letter to the Bombay Progressive Writers Association and the Upton Sinclair Society.

A2010* Letter to the Editor, *Canadian Forum*, XXIII (December), 211.

About Margot Thompson's review of *Wide Is the Gate*.

A2011* *Books by Upton Sinclair*. Monrovia, Calif: Upton Sinclair. 4 pp.

List beginning with *Wide Is the Gate*.

A2012 *Circular Letter*. New York: Upton Sinclair. 1 leaf.

A Merry Christmas and New Year's greeting from Upton Sinclair.

A2013* *Index to the Lanny Budd Story*. New York: Viking Press. 24 pp.

An index to the first four volumes of the series with commentary by Upton Sinclair and other well known writers.

A2014* *To Solve the German Problem—a Free State?* Monrovia, Calif.: The Author. 16 pp.

Reprint of article, A2007.

1944

A2015* "What Shall Be Done with Hitler?" *Free World*, VII (February), 121–124.

Suggests that war criminals should be put on Catalina Island. Reprinted as offprint: 4 pp.

A2016 "The Other Japan," *New Republic*, cx (8 May), 636.
Review of Taro Yashima's *The New Sun.*

A2017* *Presidential Agent.* New York: Viking Press; New York and Monrovia, Calif.: The Author, 2 June. 655 pp.
Reprinted in part: A2049.
Foreign Editions: Braille, Bulgarian, Czech, Dutch, English-Canada, English, German, Hungarian, Italian, Japanese, Norwegian, Spanish, Swedish.

A2018* "My Plan for Germany," *Picture Post*, xxv (30 September), 24.
Followed by "The Plan Is Not Realistic," a critique by economist Sir Walter Layton.

A2019* "Beware Campaign Dishonesties," *Editors' Bulletin for the Roosevelt-Truman Ticket*, no. 4 (1 November), p. 8.
Radio and newspaper chains behind big business will slander Roosevelt in the campaign.

A2020* A Safe World: How to Make It," *Writer's War Board*, no. 10 (December), p. 14.
Mimeographed.

A2021* *Books by Upton Sinclair.* Monrovia, Calif.: Upton Sinclair. 4 pp.

A2022* *Circular Letter.* Monrovia, Calif.: Upton Sinclair. 1 leaf.
Fifth volume of the Lanny Budd Story now ready. Variant printed on a postcard.

A2023* *Dragon's Teeth.* In *A Treasury of Modern Best Sellers.* New York: Simon and Schuster, pp. 313–380.
An abridgement with an introduction by Orville Prescott; see A1990.

1945

A2024* "Let Us Have Democracy Whole," *New Leader* [London], XXVIII (10 February), 8.

Excerpt from an address given to the 14th anniversary dinner of the League for Industrial Democracy in which Sinclair discusses the Intercollegiate Socialist Society, the League's predecessor; see A2025.

A2025 "Let's Have Democracy Whole," *Rob Wagner's Script*, XXXI (3 March), 3–5.

A2026* "Humanity United," *Call*, XIII (March), 10.

A statement to organized labor.

A2027* "The Shepherd Is Dead," *Rob Wagner's Script*, XXXI (12 May), 10.

Poem on Franklin Delano Roosevelt with an introduction.

A2028* "A Good Start Has Been Made," *Common Sense*, XIV (May), 13.

A symposium: San Francisco—Peace in Our Time? Sinclair's contribution: abolish capitalism, "competitive commercialism."

A2029* *Dragon Harvest.* New York: Viking Press; New York and Monrovia, Calif.: The Author, *c.* 8 June. 703 pp.

Reprinted in part: A2049. Abridged: A2031.

Foreign Editions: Czech, Dutch, English-Canada, English, French, German, Hungarian, Italian, Romanian, Spanish, Swedish.

A2030 "Now, Now, Mr. Jones: A Reply to Howard Mumford Jones," *Saturday Review of Literature*, XXVIII (7 July), 24.

Objects to review of *Dragon Harvest.*

A2031* "*Dragon Harvest,*" *Omnibook*, VII (September), 41–80.

Abridged version of novel; see A2029.

A2032* *Books by Upton Sinclair.* New York: Upton Sinclair. 4 pp.

A2033* *Circular Letter.* Pasadena: Upton Sinclair. 1 leaf.
Letter explaining that he has no money to help European refugees.

A2034* *Opinion Concerning "Dragon Harvest."* Monrovia, Calif.: Upton Sinclair. 4 pp.
Opinions of the other Lanny Budd volumes as well.

1946

A2035* "Theodore Dreiser: In Memoriam," *Book Find News*, II (March), 8.
One of a group of letters.

A2036* Letter to the Editor, *Life*, XX (29 April), 8, 10.
Criticizing Evelyn Waugh.

A2037* *A World to Win.* New York: Viking Press; Monrovia, Calif.: The Author, *c.* 25 May. 581 pp.
Reprinted in part: A2049; Abridged, A2042.
Foreign Editions: Czech, Dutch, English-Canada, English, German, Hungarian, Japanese, Romanian, Spanish, Swedish.

A2038* "Book Readers vs. Critics," *Time*, XLVIII (1 July), 8.
Letter to the editor objecting to review of *A World to Win*, A2037.

A2039* "Sinclair on Sinclair," *New Republic*, CXV (5 August), 143.
Letter to the editor objecting to review of *A World to Win*, A2037.

A2040* *Boston: A Novel.* Girard, Kansas: Haldeman-Julius Publications (Big Blue Book no. B-409, vols. 1, 2, 3, and 4), *c.* 19 August. 756 pp.
Vol. 1 published 19 August; vol. 2, 26 August; vol. 3, 7 September, vol. 4, 14 September. See A1195.

A2041* Concerning Lanny Budd," *Book Find News*, II (August), 1, 5.

1946 continued

A2042* "*A World to Win*," *Omnibook*, VIII (October), 81–120.

An abridgement of the novel; see A2037.

A2043* "Author to Critic," *Atlantic Monthly*, CLXXVIII (October), 29.

Letter to editor objecting to H. M. Jones's article; see A2030.

A2044* "A Utopian Bookshelf," *Saturday Review of Literature*, XXIX (7 December), 20–21.

Sinclair pleads for a collectivist society.

A2045* *Books by Upton Sinclair*. Monrovia, Calif.: Upton Sinclair. 4 pp.

A2046* Introduction to *The Jungle*. New York: Viking Press, 1946, pp. vii-xi.

Reprinted in *The Jungle* (Harper's Modern Classics), 1946.

1947

A2047* "If Writers Had a Magic Wand," *Saturday Review of Literature*, XXX (11 January), 11–12.

Review of *I Wish I'd Written That*, ed. Eugene J. Woods. New York: 1946.

A2048* *Presidential Mission*. New York: Viking Press; Monrovia, Calif.: The Author, *c.* 19 May. 641 pp.

Foreign Editions: Braille, Dutch, English, English-Canada, French, German, Serbo-Croatian, Spanish, Swedish.

A2049* *Upton Sinclair Anthology*. Introduction by Lewis Browne and Irving Stone. Culver City, Calif.: Murray and Gee, 31 May.

Reprints *An Upton Sinclair Anthology*, A1545, with additions and preface by Sinclair.

"Genius" (*American Outpost* [*Candid Reminiscences*], 1932), pp. 21–24.

"Creation" (*The Journal of Arthur Stirling*, 1903), pp. 24–27.
"Thyrsis Studies Music" (*Love's Pilgrimage*, 1911), pp. 27–31.
"Kip's Proposal" (*The Wet Parade*, 1932), pp. 32–38.
"The Purpose of Love" (*Love's Pilgrimage*, 1911), pp. 38–42.
"Sylvia Loves" (*Sylvia*, 1913), pp. 42–45.
"Psychic Research" (*Mental Radio*, 1930), pp. 46–48.
"Experiments in Health" (*American Outpost* [*Candid Reminiscences*], 1932), pp. 49–53.
"Science and Life" (*The Profits of Religion*, 1918), pp. 53–60.
"The Process of Life" (*Samuel The Seeker*, 1910), pp. 61–64.
"Extrasensory Perception" (*Dragon Harvest*, 1945), pp. 64–65.
"The Stockyards" (*The Jungle*, 1906), pp. 66–76.
"The Burning Oil-Well" (*Oil!*, 1927), pp. 76–81.
"A Bear Market" (*Between Two Worlds*, 1941), pp. 82–83.
"News For Sale" (*The Brass Check*, 1920), pp. 83–87.
"Munition Makers" (*World's End*, 1940), pp. 87–90.
"Relief" (*Co-op*, 1936), pp. 90–94.
"In the Backwoods" (*Love's Pilgrimage*, 1911), pp. 95–103.
"Puritan's Progress" (*American Outpost*, [*Candid Reminiscences*], 1932), pp. 104–108.
"Christ and Nietzsche" (*The Journal of Arthur Stirling*, 1903), pp. 109–114.
"Religious Faith" (*What God Means To Me*, 1936), pp. 114–116.
"The Glory That Was Greece" (*Mammonart*, 1925), pp. 117–124.
"The Grandeur That Was Rome" (*Roman Holiday*, 1931), pp. 124–128.
"John Brown" (*Manassas*, 1904), pp. 128–135.
"Early Difficulties of the Cinema" (*Upton Sinclair Presents William Fox*, 1933), pp. 135–146.
"Hell Trembles" (*Presidential Agent*, 1944), pp. 146–148.
"The Voice of the People" (*Dragon's Teeth*, 1942), pp. 148–149.
"The Cordage Factory" (*Boston*, 1928), pp. 153–156.
"The Fertilizer Man" (*The Jungle*, 1906), pp. 156–161.
"The Banquet" (*The Metropolis*, 1908), pp. 162–164.

1947 continued

"To a Rich Young Man," Mary Craig Sinclair (*Sonnets*, 1925), p. 164.

"The Decay in the Souls of the Rich" (*Letters to Judd*, 1926), pp. 164–166.

"The Menagerie" (*The Cry for Justice*, 1915), p. 166.

"Winter in the Jungle" (*The Jungle*, 1906), pp. 167–172.

"Sisterhood," Mary Craig Sinclair (*Sonnets*, 1926), p. 172.

"Christmas in Prison" (*The Jungle*, 1906), pp. 173–176.

"Russia: 1918," Mary Craig Sinclair (*Sonnets*, 1925), pp. 176–177.

"The Case for the Anarchist" (*Boston*, 1928), pp. 177–183.

"Six Transit Gloria" (*Wide Is the Gate*, 1943), pp. 183–185.

"A Social Rebel" (*American Outpost* [*Candid Reminiscences*], 1932), pp. 185–187.

"The Execution" (*Boston*, 1928), pp. 188–204.

"Red Adams" (*Singing Jailbirds*, 1924), p. 205.

"Christ Visits Western City" (*They Call Me Carpenter*, 1922), pp. 206–212.

"Dominie of the Wobblies" (*Singing Jailbirds*, 1924), pp. 212–217.

"Prince Hagen" (*Prince Hagen*, 1903), pp. 217–220.

"The Graft of Grace" (*The Profits of Religion*, 1918), pp. 220–223.

"Marya and Her Son" (*Our Lady*, 1938), pp. 224–228.

"The Legacy of Israel" (*The Profits of Religion*, 1918), pp. 229–233.

"Friends, Romans, Countrymen" (*Roman Holiday*, 1931), pp. 233–238.

"Renaissance Realities" (*Mammonart*, 1925), pp. 238–244.

"The Führer Explains" (*Dragon's Teeth*, 1942), pp. 244–246.

"The Nation's Food Supply" (*The Jungle*, 1906), pp. 247–253.

"Pitiless Storm" (*A World To Win*, 1946), pp. 253–256.

"To the Highest Bidder" (*Wide Is the Gate*, 1943), pp. 256–257.

"Diplomacy and High Finance" (*Between Two Worlds*, 1941), pp. 257–258.

"Prophecy of War" (*The Industrial Republic*, 1907), pp. 259–263.

"War," Mary Craig Sinclair (*Sonnets*, 1925), p. 263.
"World War I" (*World's End*, 1940), pp. 264–266.
"A Ringside Seat" (*Presidential Agent*, 1944), pp. 266–267.
"A Secret Agent Reports" (*Dragon Harvest*, 1945), pp. 267–269.
"War's Horrors" (*Jimmie Higgins*, 1919), pp. 269–273.
"America—The Past" (*The Journal of Arthur Stirling*, 1903), pp. 274–277.
"America—The Present" (*The Journal of Arthur Stirling*, 1903), pp. 277–278.
"America—The Future" (*Letters to Judd*, 1926), pp. 278–279.
"The Old America" (*The Way Out*, 1933), pp. 280–283.
"A Change in Italy" (*Between Two Worlds*, 1941), pp. 284–285.
"Children in the Jungle" (*The Jungle*, 1906), pp. 286–292.
"We're Real Bums" (*100%* [*The Spy*], 1920), pp. 290–292.
"Arthur Stirling" (*The Journal of Arthur Stirling*, 1903), pp. 293–298.
"Springtime and Harvest" (*Springtime and Harvest*, 1901), pp. 298–301.
"My Cause" (*Independent*, 14 May, 1903), pp. 302–313.
"Our Bourgeois Literature" (*Collier's Weekly*, 8 October 1904), pp. 314–325.
"Socialism" (*Love's Pilgrimage*, 1911), pp. 326–335.
"Jurgis Hears a Socialist Speech" (*The Jungle*, 1906), pp. 335–338.
"On a Steamship" (*Independent*, 25 June 1908), p. 338.
"The Twelve Principles of EPIC" (*I, Governor of California*, 1933), p. 339.
"Art and the Future" (*Mammonart*, 1925), pp. 340–343.
"The Overman" (*The Overman*, 1907), pp. 343–345.
"Even the Socialists Waver" (*Dragon Harvest*, 1945), pp. 345–346.

A2050* "Modern Character in a Bygone Milieu," *American Notes and Queries*, VII (May), 29.

1947 continued

A2051 "Upton Sinclair's Standing," *Saturday Review of Literature*, XXX (14 June), 19.

Letter to the editor.

A2052* Preface to *Samuel the Seeker.* Bombay, India: Bharati Sahitya Sangh, pp. 5, 6–8.

See Gujarati edition. Two letters date 23 November 1933, as a Preface.

1948

A2053* "Loose in Limbo," *New Leader* [London], XXXI (January), 8–9; XXXI (10 January), 8–9; XXXI (17 January), 607.

In three installments: "A Midsummer Night's Dream," "The People's Corporation and Razor Blades," "Pain and the Mental Universe." Comment on the atomic threat and a "re-visit" with Lincoln Steffens, Henry Ford, King Gillette and others; see A2060.

A2054* "Sinclair's Side of It, *Nation*, CLXVI (10 January), 55.

Letter to the editor answering some of the criticisms of George Creel in his recently published book, *Rebel at Large.*

A2055 "EPIC Error," *Saturday Review of Literature*, XXXI (24 January), 23.

A2056* *To the Editor*, Monrovia, Calif: Upton Sinclair. 1 leaf.

Open letter to a New York publisher who had rejected *A Giant's Strength*, A2059; dated January.

A2057* "Recollections of Edward MacDowell," *Etude Music Magazine*, LXVI (July), 416, 444, 446, 451, 456.

Sinclair studied with MacDowell at Columbia for two years; see A1080, A1739.

A2058* *One Clear Call.* New York: Viking Press; Monrovia, Calif.: The Author, *c.* 27 August. 626 pp.

Includes figures on world circulation of series.

Foreign Editions: Dutch, English-Canada, English, German, Spanish, Swedish.

A2059* *A Giant's Strength.* Monrovia, Calif.: The Author; Girard, Kansas: Haldeman-Julius (B666), *c.* September. 52 pp.

Foreign Editions: English, German, Italian, Japanese, Swedish.

A2060* *Limbo on the Loose: A Midsummer Night's Dream.* Girard, Kansas: Haldeman-Julius (B675), *c.* October. 62 pp.

Includes, with addenda and postscript dated 1947, *The Way Out—What Lies Ahead for America*; see A1436, A2053.

Foreign Editions: German, Japanese.

A2061* *Marie and Her Lover.* Girard, Kansas: Haldeman-Julius (B708), *c.* November. 62 pp.

Preface by Upton Sinclair. Reprint of *Marie Antoinette*, A1945.

A2062* *Idea For A Radio Participation Show.* Monrovia, Calif.: The Author. 3 pp. Mimeographed.

A2063 *Upton Sinclair Answers Some Timely Questions.* Monrovia, Calif.: The Author, *c.* 1948. Leaflet, 4 pp.

1949

A2064* "The Best Policy," *Los Angeles Times*, 10 April, p. 4.

A2065* "Sinclair Hits Red Slavery," *Los Angeles Examiner*, 11 April, p. 6.

Also in *Los Angeles Daily News*.

A2066* "Reds Deceived Him," *New Leader* [London] XXXII (28 May), 9.

Denunciation of Russian Communism and exposé of how his novels have been misused.

A2067* Statement by Upton Sinclair on His Relations with the Communists, *Congressional Record*, XCV (21 July), 10109.

Letter from M. C. Sinclair to Senator Downey dated 7 May 1949, pp. 10108–10109.

1949 continued

A2068* *O Shepherd, Speak!* New York: Viking Press; Monrovia, Calif.: The Author, *c.* 30 July. 629 pp.

Iincludes an "Index to Lanny Budd Novels," figures on world circulation of series, and "World's End Impending."

Foreign Editions: Dutch, English-Canada, English, German, Spanish.

A2069* "Farewell to Lanny Budd," *Saturday Review of Literature*, XXXII (13 August), 18–19, 38.

A list of ten Lanny Budd novels, dates of publication and numbers sold in the U.S.

A2070* "My Ten Years' Hard," *John O'London's Weekly*, LVIII (30 September), 1–2.

A2071* *This World of 1949 and What to Do About It.* Girard, Kansas: Haldeman-Julius (B780), *c.* November. 64 pp.

"Revised letters to a Workingman on the Economic and Political Situation." Nineteen letters to Judd, essentially the same text as the publication *Letters to Judd*, A1089, with a few parenthetical additions dated 1948.

A2072* Foreword to *100%*, trans. Taiyo Sha and Koji Oiwa. Tokyo: Toranomon, Taiyosha, p. vii.

See Japanese edition. Printed letter from Upton Sinclair dated 10 November 1949.

1950

A2073* Upton Sinclair's Tribute. In *Testimonial Dinner in Honor of August Claessens. . . .* New York: [n.p.], p. 7.

The Sinclair telegram is dated 31 March.

A2074* "God and Birth Control: Why Priests Demand an Endless Stream of Dupes," *Critic and Guide*, IV (March), 61–63.

A2075* *Another Pamela: or Virtue Still Rewarded.* New York: Viking Press, *c.* 6 aMy. 314 pp.

Foreign Editions: English-Canada, English, French, German, Portuguese, Spanish.

A2076* "832 Years of Advice," *Pageant*, v (June), 59–63.

A2077* "Wanted: H-bomb-proof Library," *Saturday Review of Literature*, XXXIII (22 July), 25.

Letter to the editor expressing interest in placing his collected papers and manuscripts in suitable library.

A2078* *The Enemy Had It Too.* New York: Viking Press, 25 August. 127 pp.

Foreign Editions: English-Canada, Japanese.

A2079 "Los Intellectuales del Mundo en Defensa del Pueblo Español," *Las Españas* [Mexico], 29 August, p. 70.

Part of symposium.

A2080* "Confession of a Non-conformist," *City College Alumnus*, XLVI (October), 3–4.

Reminiscence about his days at City College.

A2081* "Pleasure and Profit in Self Portrait of Upton Sinclair," *Los Angeles Daily News*, 2 December, pp. 24, 27.

A2082* "A Letter to British Workers," *Tribune* [London], 29 December, pp. 9–10.

Changes in United States since publication of *The Jungle* have altered conditions. He also describes how the Russians have misused his works.

A2083* *Books by Upton Sinclair.* Girard, Kansas: Haldeman-Julius. 4 pp.

Advertising leaflet beginning with *Another Pamela.*

1950 continued

A2084* "Announcing Greeting to the L.I.D. from Upton Sinclair Founder of the I.S.S. Predecessor or L.I.D." In *Freedom and the Welfare State.* New York: League for Industrial Democracy, p. 36.

1951

A2085 "America Tells Her Story," *New Leader*, XXXIV (1 January), 25.

Review of *We Speak for Ourselves*, by Irving Stone and Richard Kennedy.

A2086* "Birthday Note," *Time*, LVII (8 January), 2.

Sinclair points out the error *Time* made in quoting his age.

A2087* "The Voice is the Voice of Evil . . . ," *New York Times Book Review*, 18 March, pp. 1, 20.

Review of *The Burned Bramble* by Manes Sperber, an exposé by an ex-Communist of the party's faults and excesses.

A2088* "To Er is Human," *Time*, LVII (7 May), 15.

Letter to the editor criticizing radio announcers who excessively interject "er" in their speech.

A2089* "With Mother Bloor in the Jungle," *Time*, LVIII (3 September), 6, 8.

Letter to the editor discussing Ella Reeve Bloor's role in his investigations of the Chicago stockyards which preceded *The Jungle*.

A2090* "Riddle of Modern Poetry," *New Republic*, CXXV (24 September), 2.

Letter to the editor criticizing William Carlos Williams's *Paterson*.

A2091* "Upton Sinclair Writes on the General Election," *Forward* [London], 20 October, 8.

A2092* "Upton Sinclair Sees Change in America Since *Jungle*," *New Leader* [London], XXXIV (22 October), 27.

Letter to the editor.

A2093 "Concerning Socialist Candidates," *New York Call*, 20 November.

A2094* Upton Sinclair Letter—In Memoriam, *Jewish Labor Bund Bulletin*, IV (November/December), 24.

A2095* "Behind the Times," *Tribune* [London], 14 December, p. 10.

He is now called a "Wall Street lacky" by the Russians.

A2096 "The Death of Roosevelt." In *Lucky Dip: A Miscellany From Divers Pens*. London: Werner Laurie, *c*. 1951, pp. 30–37.

1952

A2097* "Recipe for Co-existence," *Saturday Review of Literature*, XXXV (5 January), 23.

Letter to the editor.

A2098* "A Sermon on Democracy," *Unity*, CXXXVIII (May/June), 20–21.

Letter by Upton Sinclair prefacing another one by M. C. Sinclair to Ryô Namikawa, one of Sinclair's Japanese translators.

A2099* "Men of Extremes," *Saturday Review*, XXXV (21 June), 28.

Letter to the editor commenting on Professor Arthur Schlesinger's 24 May review of a book by Whittaker Chambers.

A2100* "An Open Letter to Stalin," *New Leader* [London], XXXV (30 June), 2–3.

Widely reprinted. See A2107.

A2101* "A New Unity," *New Republic*, CXXVII (14 July), 4.

Letter to the editor relating the message he recorded for the Congress for Cultural Freedom in Paris.

1952 continued

A2102* "Radicalism of Past Called Educational," *Arizona Republican*, 17 July, p. 6.

Guest columnist for Victor Riesel.

A2103 "Upton Sinclair Exposes Soviet Fake Democracy," *Oakland Tribune*, 20 July, p. A–9.

Guest columnist for Victor Riesel.

A2104* A Guest Column Substitution for Victor Riesel, *Daily News*, 21 July.

Sinclair discusses the Russian perversion of his books; he denounces the U.S.S.R., its constitution and social repression.

A2105* "A Peace Petition," *Peace News*, no. 842 (15 August), p. 2.

A2106 "A Changed America," *Trivandrum Letters* [Kerola, India], September, pp. 16–17.

Article on social changes in the U.S.A.

A2107* "Sinclair on Stalin," *Socialist Call*, XIX (31 October), 5.

Letter to the editor answering an open letter published in *Forward* by Gordon Schaeffer criticizing Sinclair's "Open Letter to Stalin," A2100.

A2108* "An Open Letter from Upton Sinclair," *Forward* [London], XLVI (1 November), 1.

A2109* "What about Lanny?" *Time*, LX (24 November), 11.

Letter to the editor claiming the Lanny Budd novels as the largest novel, some 3 million words.

A2110 *A Personal Jesus: Portrait and Interpretation.* New York and Philadelphia: Evans Publishing Co., November. 228 pp.

Reprinted: *The Secret Life of Jesus.* Philadelphia: Mercury Books, pa.; see A2245.

Foreign Editions: English, German, Malayalam.

A2111* "Twenty-five Candles—from Upton Sinclair," *Books Abroad*, XXVI (Winter), 11.

Tribute commemorating the magazine's silver jubilee.

A2112* "Communists in the Making," *Institute of Social Studies Bulletin*, I (Spring), 49, 56–57.

First in a series of memoirs by Upton Sinclair. He discusses Ella Reeve Bloor and the aftermath of *The Jungle*.

A2113* "Steffens: The Man and the Muckracker," *Institute of Social Studies Bulletin*, I (Summer), 62, 71–72.

Second in series of memoirs.

A2114* "*The Masses*," *Institute of Social Studies Bulletin*, I (Fall), 74, 80–81.

Third in series of memoirs. Sinclair discusses Max Eastman and *The Masses*.

A2115* "John Reed," *Institute of Social Studies Bulletin*, I (Winter), 86, 91–92.

Fourth in series of memoirs; see also A2131, A2134, A2140.

1953

A2116* "Upton Sinclair Answers His Critics," *Forward* [London], XLVII (17 January), 1.

An argument with Gordon Schaffer.

A2117* "Old Fogae," *New Republic*, CXXVIII (26 January), 4.

Letter to the editor.

A2118* "Upton Sinclair Replies to *Daily Worker* Open Letter," *New Leader*, XXXVI (16 February), 27.

Letter to the editor stating that he will not support the Rosenbergs.

A2119* "Reply to Review," *Zion's Herald*, CXXXI (18 February), 1.

Letter to the editor answering criticism of his *A Personal Jesus*.

1953 continued

A2120* "I Personally—," *Atlantic Monthly*, CXCI (February), 26.

Letter to the editor.

A2121* "The Pledge," *Progressive*, XVII (February), 37.

A letter to the editor defending the pledge of allegiance to the flag.

A2122* "Should Our Son Go to City College?" *City College Alumnus*, XLVIII (February), 15.

A2123* "Upton Sinclair and the Bolsheviks," *Thought* [Delhi], V (14 March), 8.

An answer to a letter to the editor referring to Sinclair's "Open Letter to Stalin," A2100.

A2124* "Upton Sinclair Seeks Aid to Translate Anti-Red Book," *New Leader* [London], XXXVI (30 March), 27.

Letter to the editor asking for aid in publishing *The Return of Lanny Budd* in backward countries which may not be able to pay the costs of translating and publishing the book. Another answer to the Communists' mis-representation of his books abroad. See A2129.

A2125 "We Must Win Asia to Win the Cold War," *Boston Globe*, 17 April.

A2126* " 'A Little Child Shall Lead Them,' " *The Progressive*, XVII (April), 26–27.

Reply to Peter Viereck's "The Peculiar Feebleness of Social Democrats."

A2127* *The Return of Lanny Budd*. New York: Viking Press, April.

Foreign Editions: Bengali, Dutch, English, German, Hebrew, Hindi, Japanese, Spanish.

A2128* "What Columbus Started: Richard Armour Finds History Hilarious," *Pasadena Star-News*, 17 May, p. 27.

Review of Armour's *It All Started with Columbus*.

A2129* "Indignation of People Building into Hate: Reds Use His Books for Propaganda," *Denver Post*, 7 June, p. 6.

A2130* "Hypocritical Oath," *New Republic*, CXXVIII (22 June), 4.

Letter to the editor.

A2131 "Millionaire Reds," *Institute of Social Studies Bulletin*, III (Spring), 2–3, 4, 8–12.

Fifth in series of memoirs, see A2112.

A2132* "Creator of Impassioned Prose Epics," *New York Times Book Review*, 9 August, p. 4.

Review of *Emile Zola* by F. W. J. Hemmings.

Reprinted in German: A2145.

A2133* "Journalese," *The New Statesman and Nation*, XLVI (26 September), 348.

Letter to the editor commenting on Colin Will's article "The Decline of Journalese" and discussing language and its growth and development.

A2134* "The Fish Peddler and the Shoemaker," *Institute of Social Studies Bulletin*, II (Summer), 13, 23–24.

Sixth of a series of memoirs; see A2112.

A2135* *The New Slavery*. New York: The Author, 9 October. 2 pp.

Mimeographed release in East Germany.

A2136* Letter to the Editor, *Socialist Call*, XXI (October), 23.

Replying to an unfavorable review of *The Return of Lanny Budd*, A2137.

A2137* "Says Rorty is a Square in Mathematical Circles," *New Leader*, XXXVI (30 November), 27.

Letter to the editor.

1953 continued

A2138* "What Didymus Did (Whether You Believe It or Not)," *Exposé*, II (November), 6–8.
Chapters 1 and 2 of a novel; see A2164, A2209.

A2139* "Our Secret Weapon: Love of Freedom," *Decatur Herald*, 16 December, p. 8.
See A2141.

A2140* "*Thunder Over Mexico*," *Institute of Social Studies Bulletin*, II (Winter), 42–43, 45–48.
Seventh in a series of memoirs; see A2112.

A2141* *America's Best Secret Weapon.* New York: The Author. 2 pp.
Mimeographed release. "Love of Freedom"; see A2139.

A2142* *Circular Letter.* Monrovia, Calif.: The Author. 2 pp.
Mimeographed release: "This Statement is being sent to individuals and organizations which may be interested in opposing the 'cold war' in the field of letters."

A2143* *Circular Letter.* Monrovia, Calif.: The Author. 2 pp.
Mimeographed; see A2127. "I am hereby submitting a proposal to assist publication in some of the more backward countries, of a novel, *The Return of Lanny Budd*, which is to be published in May by Viking Press."

1954

A2144* "Celestial Speculation," *Saturday Evening Post*, CCXXVI (2 January), 36.
Poem, Reprinted: A2179.

A2145* "Uber Emile Zola," *Neues Österreich* [Vienna], X (6 January), 12.
Book review originally appearing in *New York Times Book Review*, 9 August, 1953.

A2146* "For the Record: Upton Sinclair Can Claim Korea Victory Without Wanting Unification," *Enquirer-News* [Battle Creek, Michigan], 18 January.

A2147* "Sinclair's Advice," *Exposé*, III (January), 2.
Letter to the editor.

A2148* "Who Held the Bridge?" *New Republic*, CXXX (22 February), 23 .
Letter to the editor.

A2149* "Grounds for Separation," *Time*, LXIII (8 March), 8, 10.
Letter to the editor correcting a reference to him quoted in *Time*'s review of Harry Kemp's *Tramping on Life*, 8 February.

A2150* "Art vs. Propaganda: From Samuel Butler to Our Day," *New Leader*, XXXVII (10 May), 21–22.
See A2156.

A2151* "*When is a Communist?*" New York: Spadea Syndicate, 20 May. 2 pp.
Mimeographed release.

A2152* *Real and Phony Friends of Civil Liberties*. New York: The Author, 8 June. 2 pp.
Mimeographed release warning against Communism.

A2153* "Phony Friends of Liberty," *Evening Outlook* [Santa Monica, Calif.], 8 June, p. 4.
On the founding of the Southern California Chapter of the ACLU. Reprinted in *Greensboro Daily News*, 9 June, p. 11.

A2154* "Confusion in Credits," *New Republic*, CXXX (28 June), 23.
Letter to the editor.

A2155* "On Waldo Frank," *Nation*, CLXIX (3 July), 2.
Letter to the editor on anti-Communism in the U.S.

1954 continued

A2156* " 'Propaganda' Yesterday—But It's 'Art' Today," *Forward* [London], 3 July, 7.

See A2150.

A2157* "Guest Column by Upton Sinclair, Veteran of Civil Liberties Union, Warns of Communist Infiltration," *New Leader* [London], XXXVII (12 July), 19.

A2158 "Ending Poverty in California," *Institute of Social Studies Bulletin*, II (Summer), 65–72.

Eighth in series of memoirs. This one deals with the EPIC campaign in California and Communist infiltration into the Democratic party. See A2122.

A2159* " 'Spirits' in American Literature," *Listen*, VII (October–December), 11, 28.

Reprinted as offprint 1954 and in *Malibar Herald*, LI (8 October 1955).

A2160 *The Seamy Side of Social Drinking*. New York: Spadea Syndicate, 18 December. 2 pp.

Mimeographed release; see A2195.

A2161* Letter to the Editor, *New Republic*, CXXXI (27 December), 22–23.

Commenting on Mr. Henry Luce

A2162* "Life Without Liberty," *Institute of Social Studies Bulletin*, II (Winter), 86–87, 96.

Ninth in series of memoirs. Mentions Anna Louise Strong, Albert R. Williams, and Kate Crane-Gartz. See A2112.

A2163* *"Spirits" in American Literature*. Washington, D.C.: *Listen*. 8 pp.

Originally A2159.

A2164 *What Didymus Did*. London: Allan Wingate. 151 pp.

Published in U.S.A., 1958, as *It Happened To Didymus*; see A2138, A2209.

1955

A2165* "Jesus a Judge," *Saturday Review*, XXXVIII (1 January), 17.

Letter to the editor arguing for his *They Call Me Carpenter* (A880) as a convincing portrait of Christ and rebuffing Alan Paton and Liston Pope for their article "The Novelist and Christ" (November 4, 1954).

A2166* Letter to the Editor, *New Republic*, CXXXII (21 February), 30.

Concerning unfavorable comment of Dr. Carl Jung on Sinclair's novel *Our Lady*, A1913. Dr. Jung's reply follows, pp. 30–31.

A2167* Letter to the Editor, *Time*, LXV (7 March), 6.

How he introduced Freud to America.

A2168* "Enemy in the Mouth," *New Republic*, CXXXII (21 March), 21.

Plea for someone to publish his *Enemy in the Mouth* (*Cup of Fury*); see A2170, A2192, A2195.

A2169* "For the Record: A Resort to Rice Diet," *Buffalo Courier Express*, 8 April, p. 18.

A2170* "*Enemy in the Mouth*," *Friend's Intelligencer*, CXII (16 April), 221–222.

See A2168, A2192, A2195.

A2171* "Communists' 'International Hymn,' " *Malabar Herald*, 23 April, p. 7.

A2172* "For the 50th Anniversary of the L.I.D.," *50 Years of Democratic Education*, 23 April, pp. 8–9.

Sinclair remembers the past years and founding of the parent Intercollegiate Socialist Society.

A2173* "Does Capitalism Mean Freedom?" *New Leader* [London], XXVIII (2 May), 18.

Guest column by Upton Sinclair discussing Max Eastman's book *Reflections on the Failure of Socialism*; see A2176.

1955 continued

A2174* *Ike Splits His Party.* New York: Spadea Syndicate, 14 May. 2 pp.

Mimeographed release.

A2175* "Art vs. Propaganda; from Samuel Butler to Our Day," *Malabar Herald*, LI (9 July), 8.

See A2150, A2156.

A2176* "No—It Won't Do, Eastman," *Forward* [London], XLIX (9 July), 7.

Comment on Max Eastman's *Reflections on the Failure of Socialism*; see A2173.

A2177* "My Friends, the People of Japan," *Unity*, CXLI (September/October), 44–45.

A2178* Letter to the Editor, *Socialist Call*, XXIII (October), 26.

Tribute to Eugene Debs.

A2179* "Celestial Speculation," *Rhythm* [Calcutta], III (Autumn), 8.

See A2144.

A2180* "Fable for Our Time," *Exposé*, issue 49 (December), p. 7.

See A2198.

A2181* "A Letter." In *New World Writing*. New York: New American Library, pp. 280–281.

Letter to James T. Farrell condemning Farrell for reviving H. L. Mencken, whom Upton Sinclair says lied to him and about him, especially during the EPIC campaign.

A2182* *Radio Liberation Speech to the Peoples of the Soviet Union.* New York: American Committee for Liberation from Bolshevism, p. 19.

1956

A2183* "Mass Exodus from Mississippi," *New Republic*, CXXXIV (9 January), 23.

Letter to the editor on Mississippi's failure to indict the Emmett Till murderers.

A2184* "Credit Due," *New Leader*, XXXIX (23 January), 20.

A2185* "Singular and Plural," *Newsweek*, XLVII (30 January), 12.

A2186* "Workers Become Heroes When Depression Starts," *Labor's Daily*, 8 February, p. 5.

A2187* "No Time for People," *Collier's*, CXXXVII (17 February), 16.

Letter to the editor.

A2188* "Wunder," *Der Spiegel*, X (22 February), 7–8.

Letter to the editor about *What Didymus Did*, A2164.

A2189* "Memoirs of a Muckraker," *Exposé*, issue 51 (February), pp. 1, 8.

A2190* "Mr. Sinclair Elaborates," *Frontier: Voice of the New West*, VII (March), 24–25.

Letter to the editor referring to an article by Professor Bruce Mason, "After Two Decades" (August, 1955).

A2191* "Albert Einstein :Two Reminiscences," *Saturday Review*, XXXIX (14 April), 17–18, 56–58.

A2192* "*The Cup of Fury*; Book Condensation," *Pulpit Digest*, XXXVI (April), 81–97.

See A2195.

A2193* "Letter," *Chicago Review*, X (Spring), 131.

Letter to the editor commenting on Jean Bennett's review of Henry James's *The Ambassadors*.

1956 continued

A2194* "Ein Marchen fur unsere Zeit," *Neues Osterreich*, 1 May, p. 14.

See "A Fable for Our Time," A2180, A2198.

A2195* *The Cup of Fury*. Great Neck, New York: Channel Press, *c.* 7 May. 190 pp.

See A2168, A2170, A2192.

Reprinted: Great Neck, New York: Channel Press, 1957; Manhasset, New York: Channel Press, 1963; Westward, New Jersey: F. H. Revell, 1965 (Spire Book). Condensed: 1956. Excerpt: 1958, 1963.

Foreign Editions: English, Norwegian, Swedish.

A2196* "A Letter from Upton Sinclair," *The Dime Novel Round-up*, XXIV (August), 62.

Letter to the editor outlining his early career as a writer in response to an article by Ralph Adimari in June and July issues.

A2197* "Poet in a Hogshead: A Letter by George Sterling," *Westways*, XLVIII (September), 8.

A2198* "Fable for Our Time," *Rhythm* [Calcutta], IV (New Year Number), 20–23.

See A2180.

A2199* "The Seamy Side of Social Drinking," *Rhythm* [Calcutta], IV (New Year Number), 22.

Condemnation of drinking authors; see *The Cup of Fury*, A2195.

1957

A2200* "I Personally," *Atlantic Monthly*, CXCIX (February), 27.

Letter to the editor stating that he writes poetry as well as e.e. cummings.

A2201* "Light Up Unlucky," *New Republic*, CXXXVII (1 July), 23.

Letter to the editor deploring the poison in nicotine and alcohol.

A2202* "The Dark World," *Harper's Magazine*, CCXV (July), 8.

Letter to the editor replying to an article, "The Dark World of H. G. Wells."

A2203* "*Mental Radio*, a condensation . . . ," *Tomorrow*, V (Autumn), 105–123.

Tomorrow is a Quarterly Review of Psychical Research; see *Mental Radio*, A1254.

A2204* "Upton Sinclair Sends a New Year Message," *Forward* [London], LI (27 December), 2.

Letter to the editor expressing hope for the new year.

A2205* "Life in Letters Edited by Upton Sinclair," *Rhythm* [Calcutta], V, 54–55.

Describing his collection and the book of letters he proposes to publish.

A2206* Foreword to *Southern Belle*. New York: Crown Publishers, pp. vii–viii.

Reprinted: Phoenix, Arizona: Sinclair Press (Memorial Edition), 1962; see A2246.

A2207* Preface to *The Jungle*. Bombay, India: Jaico Publishing Co., p. 7.

See English editions.

1958

A2208* "Socialism Summed Up," *Socialist Call*, XXVI (February/March), 9–12.

Criticism of capitalism, the cold war and communism.

A2209* *It Happened to Didymus*. New York: Sagamore Press, *c*. 24 March. 151 pp.

See A2138 and A2164.

Foreign Editions: Danish, English-Canada, English (*What Didymus Did*, 1954), French, German, Spanish.

1958 continued

A2210* *Circular Letter.* Monrovia, Calif.: The Author, March. 4 pp.

Mimeographed letter begins "My fellow bookseller. . . ." Concerning the sale of *Southern Belle.*

A2211* Letter to the Editor, *Atlantic Monthly*, CCI (March), 31.

Comment on Fairfax M. Cone's article "Advertising Is Not a Plot," *Atlantic* (January).

A2212* "Greetings from Upton Sinclair," *New Leader* [London], XLI (7 April), 25.

An ad for *Southern Belle*, A2206.

A2213* "Ike is My Shepherd," *Independent*, issue 76 (April), p. 6.

A2214* "*The Cup of Fury*," *Alcohol Education Digest*, III (April/June), 17–21.

Excerpt from Chapter I. Sinclair believes this nation is threatened by "moderation" and "social" drinking. *The Cup of Fury* (A2195) is his crusading answer.

A2215* *Greetings from Upton Sinclair.* Monrovia, Calif.: The Author. 1 leaf.

Reprinted from 1958, promoting the sale of M. C. Sinclair's *Southern Belle*, A2206.

A2216* Introduction to *Lanny Budd Wereld in Beeld*, comp. Thee De Vries. The Hague: Servire, pp. viii, 1–4.

1959

A2217* *Theirs Be the Guilt: A Novel of the War Between the States*. New York: Twayne Publishers, February.

Reprinted: New York: Hillman Books, 1960, paper. A revised version of *Manassas*, A264. See Preface, pp. 4–5.

A2218* "The Wages of the Investor," *New Republic*, CXL (30 March), 24.

Letter to the editor commenting on an editorial in David Lawrence's magazine.

A2219* "Form Follows Function," *New Republic*, CXL (18 May), 23.

Letter to the editor in verse about Frank Lloyd Wright.

A2220* "The Datum Seeker," *Time*, LXXIV (7 September), 4.

Letter to the editor.

A2221* "Lanny Budd's Revenge," *Harper's Magazine*, CCXIX (October), 4.

Letter to the editor commenting on Irwin Ress's "The Supersalesmen of California Politics" (July).

A2222* Preface to *The Jungle*, trans. V. C. Narayanan. Trichur, India: The Mangalodayam, p. v.

Se Malayalam edition. Preface in the form of a letter dated 1956.

1960

A2223 "Could He Ask for More," *Time*, LXXV (11 January), 6.

Letter to the editor on the review of *Theirs Be the Guilt*, A2217.

A2224* "Hillybilly Ike," *California Liberal*, I (January), 3.

A2225* "Man of the World," *New Republic*, CXLII (15 February), 3.

Letter to the editor objecting to the bad review given to Neil Vanderbilt's *Man of the World* in the 18 January issue by Susan M. Black.

A2226* *My Lifetime in Letters*. Columbia, Mo.: University of Missouri Press, *c.* 15 February. 412 pp.

Introduction and commentary by Sinclair.

A2227* "Letters," *New York Times*, 28 February, p. 40.

Announcing the publication of his book *A Lifetime in Letters*.

1960 continued

A2228* "Letters," *New York Times Book Review*, 24 April, p. 49.

Letter to the editor concerning format of *My Lifetime in Letters.*

A2229* "Organizing Sinclair Letters," *New Republic*, CXLII (2 May), 24.

Letter to the editor about the review of *My Lifetime in Letters*, A2226.

A2230* "Upton Sinclair Tells Japan Affection," *Star-News* [Pasadena], 30 June, p. 9.

Open letter to the people of Japan.

A2231* Letter to the Editor, *Life*, XLIX (5 September), 14.

Sinclair bets *Life* will support Nixon.

1961

A2232* Letter to the Editor, *Look*, XXV (3 January), 5.

Disagreeing with McKinlay Kantor and his article "If the South Had Won the Civil War."

A2233* "Long Life That Led to *Cicero*," *New York Herald Tribune*, 5 February, p. 4.

On the genesis of his play *Cicero* and a summary review of his previous dramatic efforts.

A2234* "Mr. Upton Sinclair-Lewis," *Harper's Magazine*, CCXXII (March), 48.

How he has been mistaken for Sinclair Lewis.

A2235* Letter to the Editor, *Life*, C (28 April), 12.

Referring to an article on rocking chairs; suggests they include the platform rocker.

A2236* *Affectionately Eve*. New York: Twayne Publishers, *c.* 28 August. 215 pp.

Foreign Edition: German.

A2237* "Reuther," *Newsweek*, LVIII (25 September), 5.
Letter to the editor referring to an article on Walter Reuther.

A2238* "He's No Yankee," *Winston-Salem Journal*, 4 October, p. 4.
Letter to the editor commenting on the review of *Affectionately Eve*.

A2239* "A Tip from Upton Sinclair," *Modern Maternity*, IV (December/January 1961–1962), 43.

1962

A2240 "Controversy Continued," *Look*, XXVI (13 March), 12.
Letter to the editor; see A2232.

A2241 With R. Baldwin. "Ex Libris-Booklists," *Christian Century*, LXXIX (8 August), 962.
Weekly feature: famous figures give their answers to this question: "What books did most to shape your vocational attitude and your philosophy of life?"

A2242* "A Letter to the President," *Saturday Review*, XLV (18 August), 45.
About his ideas on language and spelling reform. Letter referred to at end of article available at Lilly Library.

A2243* *The Autobiography of Upton Sinclair*. New York: Harcourt, Brace & World, *c.* 3 December, 342 pp.
Foreign Edition: English.

A2244 *Mental Radio*. Springfield, Ill.: C. C. Thomas. 257 pp.
Revised edition with added material; see A1254.

A2245 *Secret Life of Jesus*. Philadelphia: Mercury Book. 192 pp.
Paperback reprint of *A Personal Jesus*, A2110.

A2246 "In Memoriam." In *Southern Belle*, by Mary Craig Sinclair. Phoenix, Arizona: Sinclair Press, p. vi.
The memorial edition; see A2206.

1962 continued

A2247* Preface to *Dzungle*. Prague: Statue Nakladatelstvi, p. 8.

See Czechoslovakian edition of *The Jungle*. Preface in the form of a letter dated 30 December 1958.

1963

A2248* "A Socialist Diet," *The New Statesman*, LXVI (23 August), 225.

A2249* "Corruption of the News," *Frontier*, XIV (September), 24.

Letter to the editor.

A2250 "*The Cup of Fury*," *Scientific Temperance Journal*, LXXI (October), 3–32.

Excerpts from the book comprise the entire issue of the journal; see A2195.

A2251 "Reference—Upton Sinclair's Memories of EPIC Campaign," *National Observer*, II (11 November), 12.

A2252* "My Anti-Headache Diet," *Harper's Magazine*, CCXXVII (December), 40–42.

A2253* Introduction to *The Russians Said It First*, by Simeon Aller. Los Angeles: Ward Ritchie Press, pp. v–viii.

A collection of proverbs selected and translated by Simeon Aller.

1964

A2254 "All Roads Lead to Reform," *Saturday Review*, XLVII (1 February), 35.

1965

A2255 "Mr. Sinclair Inquires," *Nation*, CC (4 January), back cover.

Letter to editor supporting American policy on Vietnam.

A2256* "Sinclair's Note on Dante," *Corriere del Popele* [Italy], 28 January, p. 4.

A2257 "SDS," *New Leader* [London], XLVIII (22 November), 33.

Letter to the editor.

A2258 *August 22nd.* New York: Universal Publishing & Distributing Corp.

Condensed edition of *Boston*; see A1195. Introduction by Michael A. Musmanno.

1966 Nothing recorded.

1967

A2259 Henry A. Christian. "Ten Letters to Louis Adamic," *The Princeton University Library Chronicle*, XXVIII (Winter), 76–94.

Two Sinclair letters.

See Part IV: Supplementary Material for further entries.

B. Tape and Disc Recordings and Films Featuring Upton Sinclair

Tape Recordings

(Lilly Library Code letters and numbers given where available)

B1 Speech, Introduction by Dr. Clarence MacIntosh, *c.* 1948, 40 min.

An afternoon speech on Armour, Ford and Rockefeller sponsored by the performing artists group of the college union. Further information not available.

B2 Statement for "This I Believe" Radio Program, *c.* 1949, 5 min.

In a capsule biography Sinclair discusses his early life and his love for the democratic process.

B3 Dorothy McKinney, Interview on "Concourse" T.V. Program, *c.* 1950, 30 min.

Sinclair discusses what advice he would give to youth, the Lanny Budd series, *The Brass Check*, and *The Gnomobile*.

B4 A Talk to the British Labor Movement, 1950, 17 min.

Sinclair discusses the conditions of American workers; notes that they are better than when he wrote *The Jungle*. He also remarks on the Soviets' misuse of his books.

B5 Voice of America Statement, 1950, 27 min.

Sinclair speaks for 5 minutes in German, then in English. He discusses Russian despotism, their misuse of his books, the 1923 Free Speech movement in California and the Lanny Budd series.

B6 Interview for Voice of America, May 1950, 10 min.

Sinclair discusses the Lanny Budd series and subsequent work, *Another Pamela, A Giant's Strength*.

B7 "Message from Upton Sinclair to the Cultural Congress in Paris," 1954, 27 min.

Contains "Open Letter to Stalin," *New Leader*, 30 June 1953. F745.

B8 "Comments on His 80th Birthday," 23 September 1958, 36 min.

Recorded for the "Voice of America." He comments on how the Communists have misused his books and how he came to write *The Jungle*. C662.

B9 Richard Lamparski, "Richard Lamparski Interviews Upton Sinclair," 2 February 1959, 75 min.

Sinclair discusses Communists, prohibition, biographical data and contemporary problems. I61.

B10 Harry W. Flannery, "As We See It: The Upton Sinclair Story I," 22 May 1960, 13 min.

Sinclair explains why he is interested in social reform and discusses his early life. Typescript. A9.

B11 Harry W. Flannery, "As We See It: The Upton Sinclair Story II," 12 June 1960, 13 min.

On the writing of *The Jungle*. Typescript.

B12 Harry W. Flannery, "As We See It: The Upton Sinclair Story III," 26 June 1960, 13 min.

On the writing of *King Coal*, *The Brass Check*, and *The Goose-Step*. Typescript.

B13 Harry W. Flannery, "As We See It: The Upton Sinclair Story IV," 10 July 1960, 13 min.

On the writing of *Oil*! and *The Flivver King*. Typescript. A91.

B14 Paul Coates, Interview, 1960, 30 min.

Sinclair talks about EPIC, prohibition, the Nobel Prize, and spiritualism. I603. Videotape.

B15 George E. Knutsen, "An Interview with Upton Sinclair," 8 July 1961, 103 min.

Sinclair discusses EPIC, *King Coal*, the memorial edition of his book, Eisenstein. Typescript. I609.

B16 "Changing America," Introduction by Richard Armour, 26 October 1961, 87 min.

A speech given at Pamona College, Claremont, California; Sinclair discusses Einstein, *The Jungle*, Ford, Gillett, and Theodore Roosevelt.

B17 "The Individual in a Troubled World," Introduction by Martha Bayals, 23 March 1962, 45 min.

Sinclair reviews some of his ideas and reminisces about life.

B18 News Conference with the Overseas Press Club, 27 April 1962, 47 min.

Sinclair discusses a wide variety of questions, *The Brass Check*, EPIC, telepathy, Lanny Budd, his ancestors.

B19 Harry Reasoner, Interview on CBS "Calender" with Norman Thomas, 1 May 1962, 12 min.

Reasoner asks Sinclair's opinion on J.F.K., Khrushchev, and whether he and Thomas have "mellowed" with time.

B20 Speech to Special Awards Banquet of the U.A.W., introduction by Walter Reuther, 6 May 1962, 22 min.

Sinclair speaks to the U.A.W. convention at Atlantic City about his acquaintance with Henry Ford.

B21 Bob Grant, Interview, 3 May 1962, 30 min.

Sinclair discusses collection and sale of papers to Indiana University, socialism and reform of Armour, Ford, and Rockefeller.

B22 Josef Kirigin, Interview, 15 August 1962, 80 min.

Kirigin, a correspondent with a Zagreb, Yugoslavia newspaper, interviews Sinclair on American writers James, Dreiser, Dos Passos, Adamic, Sterling, Lewis; also Helicon Hall and Mark Twain's meeting with him in Bermuda.

B23 Speech to California Library Association, 24 October 1962, 45 min.

Sinclair addresses the conference at Coronado. He discusses personalities he has known: Einstein, London, Steffens, Vanderbilt.

B24 Jack Linkletter, Interview, 18 January 1963, 30 min.

Sinclair discusses Common Market, his life as a Crusader, EPIC, and alcoholism.

B25 Jim Zahlian, Interview for program "Megalopolis," 21 January 1963, 20 min.

Sinclair discusses idea for an American-British common market and current problems, Red China, atomic attack.

B26 "Upton Sinclair Speaks at the University of Texas," 22 February 1963, 50 min.

Sinclair reminisces about Armour, Rockefeller, and Ford.

B27 Jere D. Witter, Interview for "Viewpoint," KNXT-TV, 6 April 1963, 30 min.

Sinclair appeared on half of this program and discussed his boyhood, democratic socialism, *The Jungle*.

B28 Speech at Los Angeles State College, 24 April 1963, 80 min.

The 3rd Annual Library Lecture (National Library Week). EPIC Campaign, Einstein.

B29 Looking Back at America at 85, 24 September 1963, 92 min.

Sinclair's lecture at Campbell Hall, University of California. He reminisces about *The Jungle*, his arrest for playing tennis, the coal strike. L794.

B30 Drew Cronin, "Front Page Challenge," 5 November 1963, 13 min.

Sinclair appears as a guest challenger on the CBC TV program. He discusses the Colorado Coal Strike in May 1914. F87.

B31 Mike Wallace, "Personal Close-Up—Upton Sinclair," 25 November 1963, 4 min.

Interviewed for "Dimension" on social drinking and his third marriage. P198.

B32 Ronald Gottesman, Interviews, 1963, 540 min.

An extensive interview for the Columbia Oral History Research Project. Tapes 8 and 9 are about the EPIC campaign. Typescript.

B33 Guy Nunn, Interview, 1963, 46 min.

Sinclair talks about the Eisenstein picture, the EPIC campaign, Debs, and Mrs. Jones. G95.

B34 Frank McGee, Interview for "Monitor," 15 January 1964, 10 min.

A discussion of the problems of unemployment, labor, and socialism. M82.

B35 Speech Given to Los Angeles County Federation of Labor, AFL & CIO, 10 June 1964, 75 min.

Sinclair talks about his adventures in California, with the *Los Angeles Times* and Henry Carr, Mrs. Kate Crane-Gartz, the founding of the Southern California Branch of the ACLU. L798.

B36 "Upton Sinclair," 13 September 1964, 55 min.

Sinclair discusses Jack London and George Sterling. U913.

B37 Hal Kauffman, "O, My America!" 1964 (?), 15 min.

Recorded by the Center for the Study of Democratic Institutions, Santa Barbara. Sinclair discusses his 1902 experience with a millionaire publisher, and his 1963 experience with an "automated monster." O108.

B38 Ted Kappel, Interview on ABC Radio News, 20 August 1965, 66 min.

Discussion of the racial situation, labor unions today, Vietnam. T35.

B39 Pierre Berton, Interview, 1965, 25 min.

Sinclair discusses Vietnam, the governor's race in California, and his earlier years.

B40 John Dryer, Interview, 1965, 200 min.

Sinclair discusses Ford, Rockefeller, Gillette, Reuther, T. Roosevelt, Norman Thomas, Woodrow Wilson. I608.

B42 Joe Toyoshima, Interview, 22 January 1966, 120 min.

Chiefly on California history.

B43 Miss Marilyn Paul and Mr. John Crane, Interview, 8 December 1966, 34 min.

Sinclair discusses primarily *The Jungle* for the Federal Drug Administration newspaper. Typescript.

Film

B44 "Upton Sinclair, A Documentary Film," KCET-TV, Hollywood, California, October 1964. Michael Vidor, producer, 35 min.

A biographical documentary film.

Disc Recordings

B45 "This I Believe," introduction by Edward R. Murrow, n.d., 4 min.

B46 "To the Conquered Peoples of Europe," 1941, 10 min.

Typescript. Published: A1984.

B47 "Talk to Friends of the League for Industrial Democracy," 1945, 15 min.

40th anniversary celebration. Sinclair talks about his early days.

B48 "Upton Sinclair Talk," 6 June 1949, 6 min.

Sinclair discusses how the Russians have misused his works. Now he criticizes the U.S.S.R. for their totalitarian methods.

Television Tape

B49 "Interview with Upton Sinclair," WMAL-TV, 13 October 1965.

The program is "Here's Barbara."

II. Upton Sinclair's Books and Pamphlets in Translation and Foreign Editions

Arabic: Syria

Oil! (1927)

C1 [*Oil!*] Damascus: Al-Talyah Magazine, [n.d.].

Armenian: U.S.A.

Singing Jailbirds (1924)

C2 [*Singing Jailbirds*]. Los Angeles: V. A. K. Tashjian, 1932. Listed in A1917 as in preparation; not located.

Armenian: U.S.S.R.

The Jungle (1906)

C3* *Dzhungli*. Moskva: Murch Mangakh ("Sickle and Hammer"), 1923, 1926. 196 pp. Translated by K. G.

A Captain of Industry (1906)

C4 *Komandir promyshlennosti*. Erevan: Armengiz, 1937. 92 pp. Translated by N. Vaganian.

Azerbaizhani (Asepo-Turkish): U.S.S.R.

The Jungle (1906)

C5 [*The Jungle.*] Baku: Krymgiz, 1931. 111 pp. Translated by I. Eiserezli.

100%: The Story of a Patriot (1920)

C6* [*100%.*] Baku: Azerpes'r, 1930. 171 pp. Translated by R. Safarov. Edited by M. S. Ordwati.

C7 [*100%.*] Baku: "Asgiz," 1931.

Bengali: India

The Jungle (1906)

C8* [*The Jungle.*] Calcutta: Mitra & Gotsh, [1906]. 571 pp.

The Return of Lanny Budd (1953)

C9 *Pratyavartan.* Calcutta: Prachi Prakasan, 1955. 368 pp. Translated by Vinodvihari Chakravarti.

Braille Editions

None of Sinclair's works is available in special large print editions or as talking books; *The Jungle* has since 1970 been available on magnetic tape at the Library of Congress, Division for the Blind and Physically Handicapped.

The Jungle (1906)

C10 *The Jungle.* New York: New York Public Library, 1934.

C11 *The Jungle.* Manchester, England: National Library for the Blind, 1935.

The Metropolis (1908)

C12 *Metropolis.* Manchester, England. National Library for the Blind, 1935.

The Brass Check (1920)

C13 *The Brass Check.* Janesville, Wisconsin: Wisconsin School for the Blind, [n.d.].

Oil! (1927)

C14 *Oil!* Manchester, England: National Library for the Blind, 1935.

Dragon's Teeth (1942)

C15 *Dragon's Teeth.* [n.p.]: Clovernook Printing House, 1942. 8 vols.

Presidential Agent (1944)

C16 *Presidential Agent.* [n.p.]: American Printing House, 1944. 9 vols.

Presidential Mission (1947)

C17 *Presidential Mission.* [n.p.]: American Printing House, 1947. 9 vols.

Bulgarian

The Jungle (1906)

C18 *Blatoto.* Sofia: peč. Edison, 1931. 144 pp. Translated by K.D.

A Captain of Industry (1906)

C19 *Kraljat na industrijata.* Sofia: Knigo-Lotos, 1945. 100 pp. Translated by Julij Genov.

The Metropolis (1908)

C20 *New York.* Sofia: Pravo, 1931. 172 pp. Translated by M.D.

C21 *Uolstrit.* Sofia: peč. Linotip, 1948. 389 pp. Translated by Vladimir Musakov.

King Coal (1917)

C22 *Car Văglen.* Sofia: peč. Napred, 1930. 294 pp. Translated by Rizor.

C23 *Car Văglen.* Sofia: peč. Pirin, 1941. 344 pp. Translated by Rizor.

Jimmie Higgins (1919)

C24 *Džimi Higins.* Sofia: Osvoboždenie, 1923. 283 pp. Translated by E. Dimitrova.

C25 *Džimi Higins.* Sofia: Globus, 1941. 283 pp.

C26 *Džimi Higins.* Sofia: ORPS, 1948. 364 pp. Translated by Zeni Hesapčieva.

100%: The Story of a Patriot (1920)

C27 *Sto prozenta.* Sofia: Zeml. koop. b-ka, 1924. 174 pp.

They Call Me Carpenter (1922)

C28 *Prorokăt ot Nju York.* Sofia: D. Madžarov, 1932. 164 pp. Translated by M. Mileva.

C29 *Hristos otnovo na zemjara.* Sofia: Vsemirna biblioteka, 1939. 202 pp. Translated by V. Jarski.

Mammonart (1925)

C30 *Moi săbratja po pero.* Sofia: peč. Napred, 1933. 48 pp. Translated by Simeon Andreev.

Oil! (1927)

C31 *Petrol.* Sofia: D. Maržarov, 1934. 276 pp. Translated by V. Manafova.

C32 *Petrol.* Sofia. Profizdat, 1970. 700 pp. Translated by Ivan Belčev. Preface by Maksim Naimovič.

Boston (1928)

C33 *Boston.* Sofia: Ignatov, 1933. 510 pp.
Translated by T.P. Trajanov.

Mountain City (1930)

C34 *Tăj se pečeljat pari*! Sofia: Azbuka, 1931. 333 pp.
Translated by P.K. Cinkov.

Roman Holiday (1931)

C35 *Rimski praznik.* Sofia: Br. Miladinovi, 1947. 263 pp.
Translated by Boris Tabakov.

Co-op (1936)

C36 *Koop.* Sofia: M.G. Smrikarov, 1939–1940. 2 vols. 440 pp.
Translated by P. K. Cinkov. Preface by G. Dikov.

The Flivver King (1937)

C37 *Kraljat na avtomobilite.* Sofia: Globus, 1939. 176 pp.
Translated by Pelin Velkov.

No Pasaran! (1937)

C38 *Te ne šte minat*! Sofia: peč. Br. Miladinovi, 1944. 206 pp.
Translated by Vasil Pavurdžiev. Illustrated by Ilija Petrov.

Little Steel (1938)

C39 *Stomana.* Sofia: M.G. Smrikarov, 1939. 288 pp.
Translated by P. K. Cinkov.

Your Million Dollars (Pamphlet; 1939)

C40 *Tvojat Milion Dolari.* Sofia: Hemus, 1946. 81 pp.
Translated by N. Pančev.

Presidential Agent (1944)

C41 *Agent na predsedatelja.* Sofia: peč. Far, 1946. 2 vols. Vol. 1, 472 pp.; vol. 2, 475 pp. Translated by Z. Dragneva and V. Dimitrieva.

Catalan

No Pasaran! (1937)

C42 *No Pasaran!* (*Una historia del seige de Madrid*). Barcelona: Comisariat de propaganda de la generalitat de Catalunya, 1937. 179 pp. Translated by Carme Montoriol Puig.

Ceylonese (Sinhalese)

Damaged Goods (1913)

C43 *Kunu Palatunu.* [n.p., n.d.]. Translated by J. Vijayatunga.

Chinese

The Jungle (1906)

C44 *Tu Chang.* Shanghai: Nan Chiang, [n.d.]. Translated by Mo-jo Kuo.

C45 *Tu Chang.* Shanghai: Nan Chiang, [n.d.]. Translated by Jêni Ching.

C46* [*The Jungle.*] Shanghai: [n.p.], 1931. 405 pp. Translated by Men-yo Kuo.

The Metropolis (1908)

C47* [*The Metropolis.*] Shanghai: [n.p.], 1931. 378 pp.

The Moneychangers (1908)

C48 [*The Moneychangers*]. Shanghai: Sui Mo, [n.d.]. Translated by Goshuen Chien.

C49. [*The Moneychangers*]. Hong Kong: Tien-ma, [n.d.]. Translated by Wei-ying Lin.

C50* [*The Moneychangers.*] Shanghai: [n.p.], 1929. 287 pp. Translated by Yao Mian Huang.

C51* [*The Moneychangers.*] Shanghai: Commercial Press, 1934. 112 pp. Translated by Kwang Kien Woo.

C52* [*The Moneychangers.*] Shanghai: [n.p.], 1937. 360 pp.

Samuel the Seeker (1910)

C53 *Dzooen ku dze.* Shanghai: [n.p., n.d.].

C54* [*Samuel the Seeker.*] Shanghai: Oriental Book Co., 1933. 350 pp.

King Coal (1917)

C55 *Shih hui wang.* Hong Kong: Hsien tai, [n.d.]. Translated by Jêni Ching.

C56 *Shih Tan Wang.* Shanghai: Lo Chun, 1928, 1929, 1930, 1932, 1947. 516 pp. Translated by Mo-jo Kuo.

C57 *Shih Tan Wang.* Shanghai: Hai Yen, 1938. Translated by Mo-jo Kuo.

C58 *Chan Shih Ti Hsin Niang.* [n.p.]: Le Hsin Book Store, 1940. Translated by Ko Chi'i Fu.

Jimmie Higgins (1919)

C59 *Kung Jen Jammie.* Shanghai: Chi Chih, [n.d.]. Translated by Yao Mian Huang.

C60* [*Jimmie Higgins.*] Shanghai: [n.p], 1929. 504 pp.

100%: The Story of a Patriot (1920)

C61 *Meet Tom.* Shanghai: Bei Sing, [n.d.].

C62* *100%*. Shanghai: Pei-hsin, 1930. 393 pp.

The Book of Life (1921)

C63 *Hüan ying yu shê hui*. Shanghai: Tien-ma, [n.d.]. Translated by Wên-jo.

The Book of Life: The Book of Love (1921)

C64 *Hsien tai lien an pi ping*. Shanghai: Shêng Chou, [n.d.]. Translated by Goshuen Chien.

The Book of Life: The Book of Society (1921)

C65 *Hsin ko lai shê hui lun*. Hong Kong: Hsin shêng ming, [n.d.]. Translated by Nei hsü Chang.

C66* *Zen Sen Kien*. Shanghai: World Book Company, 1929.

Hell! (1923)

C67 *Hell*! Shanghai: [n.p.], 1929. Translated by Goshuen Chien.

C68* *Hell*! Shanghai: [n.p.], 1930. 186 pp.

The Millennium (1924)

C69 *Wei Lai Dei Hei Chei*. Shanghai: Chien Char, [n.d.].

C70* [*The Millennium.*] Shanghai: Choochoo she, 1930. 238 pp.

Singing Jailbirds (1924)

C71 *Keo Siu*. [n.p., n.d.].

Oil! (1927)

C72 *Mai Yo*. Shanghai: Kong Hua, [n.d.]. Translated by Mo-jo Kuo.

C73* *Mai Yo*. Shanghai: [n.p.], 1930. 2 vols.

Money Writes! (1927)

C74 *Bi Kim Chu Yee.* Shanghai: The Modern Book Co., [n.d.].

Boston (1928)

C75 [*Boston.*] Shanghai: La Kneng, [n.d.].

C76 *Poshih Tou.* Shanghai: Kwang Hwa, [1929].

C77* [*Boston.*] Shanghai: [n.p.], 1931. 2 vols.

Mountain City (1930)

C78 *Shan Chien.* Shanghai: Modern Book Co., [n.d.].

C79* [*Mountain City.*] Shanghai: [n.p.], 1930, 1931, 1933. 386 pp.

The Roman Holiday (1931)

C80 *Loma ti chieh jih.* Hong Kong: Shih hsien, [n.d.]. Translated by Hsüan-hua Wang.

C81 [*Roman Holiday.*] Shanghai: Kwang Hwa, [n.d.].

The American Outpost (1932)

C82 *Ya-mei-li-chia ti chien shao.* Hong Kong: Chien-yeh, [n.d.]. Translated by Ch'un-hui Mei.

Upton Sinclair Presents William Fox (1933)

C83 *Dien Yin Wong.* Shanghai: Kwang Hwa, 1935.

World's End (1940)

C84* [*World's End.*] [n.p., n.d.]. 740 pp.

Czech (See Also Slovak)

Prince Hagen (1903)

C85* *Zlato.* Praha: Zora, 1925. 74 pp. Translated by R. Kocourek.

C86* *Princ Hagen, fantasie.* Praha: Družstevní práce, 1928. 134 pp. Translated by St. V. Klima.

Manassas (1904)

C87 *Otroctví.* Praha: Ustrední dělnické knihkupectví, 1925. 233 pp. Translated by F. Sadek.

C88 *Otroctví.* Praha: Družstevní práce, 1930. 381 pp. Translated by St. V. Klíma.

The Jungle (1906)

C89 *Obeti jatecních upíru.* Chicago: Aug. Geringer, [n.d.]. 294 pp. Translated by T. Vonásek.

C90 *Džungle.* Brno: Rovnost, 1906. 315 pp. Translated by A. Lomnický.

C91 *Džungle,* Vídeň: Dělniché listy, 1907. 428 pp. Translated by A. Lomnicky.

C92 *Jatky.* Praha: J. Laichter, 1909. 512 pp. Translated by Zdeněk Franta.

C93 *Džungle.* Praha: J. Havránek, 1922. 456 pp. Translated by J. Cihák.

C94 *Džungle.* Ceské Budějovice: Jihočeský dělník, 1925. 408 pp.

C95 *Jatky.* Praha: Družstevní práce, 1929, 1931. 371 pp. Translated by Zdeněk Franta.

C96* *Džungle.* Praha: Státní nakladatelství krásné literatury a umění, 1962. 385 pp. Translated by Emanuela and Emanuel Tilschovi. Afterword by Zdeněk Vancura.

C97 *Džungle.* Praha: Svoboda, 1967. 401 pp. Translated by Emanuela and Emanuel Tilschovi. Afterword by Zdeněk Vancura.

A Captain of Industry (1906)

C98 *V boji o miliony.* Praha: J. R. Vilímek, 1906. 149 pp. Translated by J. Zajícek - Horský.

C99 *Boj milionu.* Praha: B. Procházka, 1924. 100 pp. Translated by J. Vorcl.

A Captain of Industry (1906) — *Overman* (1907)

C100 *Kapitān prumyslu. Príběh civilizovaného muže a povídka Nadčlověk.* Praha: Družstevní práce, 1928. 88 pp. Translated by St. V. Klíma.

The Metropolis (1908)

C101 *Zlatý pól světa.* Plzeň: Nová doba, 1908. 322 pp. Translated by A. Sašek.

C102* *Metropole.* Praha: V. Petr, 1926. 250 pp. Translated by St. V. Klíma.

C103 *Metropole.* Praha: Družstevní práce, 1932. 266 pp. Translated by St. V. Klíma.

The Moneychangers (1908)

C104 *Penězoměnci.* Chicago: Slavie, 1910. 272 pp. Translated by J. E. S. Vojan.

C105 *Peněžní dravci.* Praha: Ustrední tiskové družstvo socialistické strany československého lidu pracujícího, 1921. 272 pp. Translated by J. E. S. Vojan.

C106 *Wall Street.* Praha: Družstevní práce, 1931. 1996 pp. Translated by J. E. S. Vojan.

Samuel the Seeker (1910)

C107 *Samuel hledající.* Praha: Ustrední dělnické knihkupectví, 1912, 1924. 228 pp.

C108 *Samuel hledající*. Praha: Družstevní práce, 1931. 191 pp. Translated by K. Jankovský.

Love's Pilgrimage (1911)

C109 *Pout lásky*. Praha: Komunistické nakladatelství, 1922. 351 pp. Translated by A. Macek.

C110 *Pout lásky*. Praha: Družstevní práce, 1931. Vol. 1, 232 pp.; vol. 2, 306 pp. Translated by St. V. Klíma.

The Second-Story Man (1912)

C111 *Jim Faraday*. Praha: Kniha, 1926. 19 pp. Translated by El. Ha.

The Blind Alley [The Machine?] (1912)

C112 *Slepá ulicka*. Praha: Družstevní práce, 1931, 95–114. pp. Bound with *Utajované zlo* (*Damaged Goods*) and *Prírodní žena* (*The Naturewoman*). Translated by St. V. Klíma.

The Naturewoman (1912)

C113 *Prírodní žena*. Praha: Družstevní práce, 1931, 115–177. pp. Bound with *Utajované zlo* (*Damaged Goods*) and *Slepá ulicka* (*The Blind Alley* [?]). Translated by St. V. Klíma.

Sylvia (1913)

C114* *Sylvie*. Praha: Družstevní práce, 1928. 270 pp. Bound with *Sylviino manželství* (*Sylvia's Marriage*). Translated by St. V. Klíma.

Damaged Goods (1913)

C115 *Utajované zlo*. Praha: Družstevní práce, 1931. 177 pp. Bound with *Slepá ulicka* (*The Blind Alley* [?] and *Prírodní žena* (*The Naturewoman*). Translated by St. V. Klíma.

Sylvia's Marriage (1914)

C116* *Sylviino manželství.* Praha: Družstevní práce, 1928. 210 pp. Bound with *Sylvie* (*Sylvia*). Translated by St. V. Klíma.

King Coal (1917)

C117 *Král uhlí.* Chicago: Ceské ústrední knihkupectví, 1917. 261 pp. Translated by Karel H. Beránek.

C118 *Král, Uhel.* Praha: Ustrední dělnické knihkupectví, 1920, 1927. 314 pp. Translated by A. Macek. Foreword by A. Macek.

C119 *Král Uhel.* Praha: Družstevní práce, 1932. 353 pp. Translated by A. Macek.

Jimmie Higgins (1919)

C120 *Jimmie Higgins.* Chicago: Vyd. Ceského ústrední knihkupectví, 1919. 302 pp. Translated by Karel H. Beránek.

C121 *Hrdina z davu.* Praha: Družstevní dělnické nakladatelství, 1921. 286 pp. Translated by A. Macek.

The Brass Check (1920)

C122 *Mosazná známka.* Praha: Družstevní práce, 1933. 415 pp. Translated by A. A. Hoch.

100%: The Story of a Patriot (1920)

C123* *100% vlastenec.* New York: Cesko-Americká knižnice, 1921. 279 pp. Translated by Jan Jirí Kárník.

C124 *Stoprocentní vlastenec.* Praha: Komunistické nakladatelství, 1921. 271 pp. Translated by A. Macek.

The Book of Life (1921)

C125 *Pohlaví-láska-manželství.* Praha: Kniha, 1923. 98 pp. Vol. 3 of *the Book of Life.* Translated by A. A. Hoch.

C126 *Kniha života.* Praha: Družstevní práce, 1930. 345 pp. Translated by A. A. Hoch.

The House of Wonder (1922)

C127 *Dum divu.* Praha: Orbis, 1922. 47 pp. 2 eds. Arranged by Otakar Zuna.

They Call Me Carpenter (1922)

C128 *Jsem tesar.* Praha: Komunistické knihkupectví a nakladatelství, 1923. 184 pp.

C129* *Nazývají mne tesar.* Praha: Ustrední dělnické knihkupectví, 1923. 181 pp. Translated by St. V. Klíma.

The Goslings (1924)

C130 *Houstata.* Praha: Knihovna Nový svět, 1927–1928. Vol. 1, 329 pp.; vol. 2, 260 pp. Translated by Junius.

The Millennium (1924)

C131 *Po katastrofě.* Praha: Právo lidu, 1925. 147 pp. Translated by F. Sádek.

C132* *Millennium.* Praha: Prulom, 1927. 185 pp. Translated by A. Viková.

Singing Jailbirds (1924)

C133 *Zpívající vězňové.* Praha: Prulom, 1927. 131 pp. Translated by Marie Hálová.

Mammonart (1925)

C134 *Umění a mamon.* Praha: Družstevní práce, 1930. 340 pp. Translated by M. Svozilová-Hokešová.

Oil! (1927)

C135* *Petrolej*. Praha: Družstevní práce, 1927, 1929, 1931. 2 vols. 1927: vol. 1, 274 pp.; vol. 2, 481 pp. 1929: vol. 1, 294 pp.; vol. 2, 307 pp. 1931: vol. 1, 294 pp.; vol. 2, 307 pp. Translated by St. V. Klíma.

Money Writes! (1927)

C136 *Peníze píší*. Praha: Družstevní prace, 1931. 148 pp. Translated by A. A. Hoch.

Boston (1928)

C137* *Boston. Soudobý historický román*. Praha: Družstevní práce, 1928. 2 vols. vol. 1, 423 pp., vol. 2, 416 pp.

C138 *Boston:* Praha: Svoboda, 1970. 778 pp. Translated by Lida Spackovă.

Mountain City (1930)

C139 *Horské město*. Praha: Družstevní práce, [n.d.]. Publication uncertain.

C140 *Město v horách*. Praha: Družtevní práce, 1930. 314 pp. Translated by St. V. Klíma and Z. Vancura.

Roman Holiday (1931)

C141* *Rímský svátek*. Praha: Družstevní práce, 1932. 213 pp. Translated by St. V. Klíma.

The Wet Parade (1931)

C142 *Prohibice*. Praha: Družstevní práce, 1931.

C143 *Alkohol*. Praha: Družstevní práce, 1933. 526 pp. Translated by St. V. Klíma.

The Flivver King (1937)

C144 *Automobilový král.* Praha: Práce, 1949. 262 pp. Translated by A. J. Stastný. Afterword by A. J. Stastný.

No Pasaran! (1937)

C145 *No Pasaran!* Praha: Družstevní práce, Lidová kultura, 1937. 174 pp. Translated by Ing. P. Schwarzkopf.

C146 *No Pasaran!* Detroit: Justice Printing and Publishing Co., 1937.

C147 *Neprojdou!* Praha: Práce, 1947. 31 pp. Published in the editions Románové novinky, no. 7. Translated by Ing. P. Schwarzkopf.

World's End (1940)

C148* *Konec světa.* Praha: Práce; London: Lincolns-Prager, 1946. Vol. 1, 386 pp.; vol. 2, 380 pp. Translated by G. Heyduk and M. Kottová.

C149 *Konec světa.* Praha: Práce; London: Lincolns-Prager, 1948. 732 pp. Translated by G. Heyduk and M. Kottová.

Between Two Worlds (1941)

C150* *Mezi dvěma světy.* Praha: Práce; London: Lincolns-Prager, 1947, 1948. 811 pp. Translated by Josef Schwarz.

Dragon's Teeth (1942)

C151* *Dračí zuby.* Praha: Práce; London: Lincolns-Prager, 1948. 876 pp. 3 eds. Translated by A. J. Stastný.

Wide Is the Gate (1943)

C152* *Brána je dokorán.* Praha: Práce; London: Lincolns-Prager, 1948. 876 pp. 2 eds. Translated by A. J. Urban and A. Sulc.

Presidential Agent (1944)

C153* *Presidentuv agent.* Praha: Práce; London: Lincolns-Prager, 1948. 887 pp. Translated by Zdenka Micková.

Dragon's Harvest (1945)

C154 *Dracî sklizeň.* Praha: Práce; London: Lincolns-Prager, 148. 785 pp. Translated by Zdenka Wattersonová.

A World to Win (1946)

C155* *Svět na váhách.* Praha: Práce; London: Lincolns-Prager, 1949. 823 pp. Translated by K. and M. Nigrínovi.

Danish

The Jungle (1906)

C156 *Junglen.* København: Lauritius Eiby, 1906. 608 pp.; København: Nyt Nordisk Forlag, 1918. 314 pp.; København: Nyt Nordisk Forlag, 1941. 296 pp. Translated by Ella Melbye.

A Captain of Industry (1906)

C157 *Industribaronen, En amerikansk Millionaers Saga.* København: Peter Hansen, 1906. 124 pp. Translated by Asl. Mikkelsen.

The Industrial Republic (1907)

C158 *Industri-Republiken, Et Billede af Amerika i 19.* København: Peter Hansen, 1907. 222 pp. Translated by Asl. Mikkelsen.

Love's Pilgrimage (1911)

C159 *Geniet i Laenker.* København: Hagerups Forlag, 1919. 236 pp.

The Fasting Cure (1911)

C160* *Faste-Kuren.* København: Pios Boghandel, 1920. 96 pp. Translated by Viggo Cavling.

King Coal (1917)

C161 *Kong Kul.* København: Gyldendals Forlag, 1918. 336 pp. Translated by Ellen Hørup-Nielson.

They Call Me Carpenter (1922)

C162 *Man kalder mig tømmermand.* København: Ny Tids Forlag, 1924. 152 pp.

The Millennium (1924)

C163 *Tusindaarsriget, En Roman fra Aar 2000.* København: Ny Tids Forlag, 1925. 126 pp.

C164 *The Millennium.* Køberhavn: Ny Tids Forlag, 1926.

Oil! (1927)

C165 *Olie.* København: H. Hagerups Forlag, 1928. 386 pp. Translated by Elise Koppel.

Money Writes! (1927)

C166 *Dollars, 2. Tus.* København: Nyt Nordisk Forlag, 1931. 310 pp. Translated by Børge Houmann.

Boston (1928)

C167 *Boston, En Roman om Sacco og Vanzetti.* København: Cai M. Woels Forlag, 1930. 564 pp. Translated by Elise Koppel.

Mountain City (1930)

C168 *Mountain City.* København: Cai M. Woels Forlag, 1931.

No Pasaran! (1937)

C169 *No Pasaran*! København: Socialdemokraten, 1937. Installment in the newspaper *Socialdemokraten*.

World's End (1940)

C170* *En verden gik under*. København: Thaning og Appels Forlag, 1946. 596 pp. Translated by H. C. Orsted.

Between Two Worlds (1941)

C171* *Mellem to verdener*. København: Thaning og Appels Forlag, 1947. 596 pp. Translated by H. C. Orsted.

Dragon's Teeth (1942)

C172* *Dragens taender*. København: Thaning og Appels Forlag, 1948. 518 pp. Translated by H. C. Orsted.

It Happened to Didymus (1958; What Didymus Did, 1954, England)

C173 *Didymus' gerninger*. København: Lund Madsens Forlag, 1956. 149 pp. Translated by Per Dorph-Petersen.

Dutch (and Flemish)

The Jungle (1906)

C174 *De Wildernis*. 's-Gravenhage: Servire, [n.d.]. Translated by H. Mendels-Stokvis.

C175 *De Wildernis*. Amsterdam: Wereldbibliotheek, 1907. 578 pp. Translated by H. Mendels-Stokvis. Introduction by F. N. Wibaut.

C176* *De Wildernis*. Amsterdam: van Goede en Goedekoope lectuur, [1927]. 556 pp. Translated by H. Mendels-Stovkis. Introduction by F. M. Wilbaut.

C177 *De Wildernis.* Amsterdam: Wereldbibliotheek, 1958; St. Denijs-Westrem: Uitgeverij Climax, [1958]. 350 pp. Translated by H. Mendels-Stovkis.

C178 *De Wildernis.* Antev: Wereld-Bibliotheek, 1958. Translated by H. Mendels-Stovkis.

A Captain of Industry (1906)

C179* *De millionnair, het leven van een man van beschaving.* Amsterdam: N.V. de Arbeiderspers, 1930. 100 pp.

The Moneychangers (1908)

C180* *Paniek in Wall Street.* Amsterdam: Republiek der Letteren (Zebra no. 24), [1946], 1948. 275 pp. Translated by Jac. V. D. Ster.

Samuel the Seeker (1910)

C181* *Samuel de zoeker.* Apeldoorn: De Zoonebloem, [1920]. 169 pp. Translated by Jo Arenburg.

The Second-Story Man (1912)

C182* *De inbreker, drama in éen bedriif.* Amsterdam: Ontwikkeling, 1928. 16 pp. Translated by Jo Arenberg.

Sylvia (1913)

C183* *Sylvia.* Amsterdam: J. T. Swartsenburg, [1919]. 256 pp. Translated by J. Kuylman.

Sylvia's Marriage (1914)

C184* *Sylvia's huweliik.* Zeist: J. T. Swartsenburg, [n.d.]. 166 pp. Translated by P. Kapteyn-Schröder.

King Coal (1917)

C185* *Koning kool, roman uit de amerikaansche kolenmijnen.* Amsterdam: W. Versluys, 1918. 2 vols. Translated by Th. Holdert, Foreword by Dr. Frederik van Eeden.

The Profits of Religion (1918)

C186* *Dr. voordeelen van den godsdienst; proeve van economische verklaring.* Rotterdam: N. V. Uitgevers-Maatschappij, De Tijdstroom, [1923]. Translated by Dr. J. v. d. Bergh van Eysinga-Elias.

Jimmie Higgins (1919)

C187* *Jimmy Higgins.* Amsterdam: Ontwikkeling, De Arbeiderspoers, 1927. 344 pp. Translated by Jo Arenberg.

100%: The Story of a Patriot (1920)

C188* *Een Volbloed Amerikaan, de geschiedenis van een patriot.* Amsterdam: W. Versluys, 1921. 346 pp.

They Call Me Carpenter (1922)

C189 *Men noemt mij timmerman.* 's-Gravenhage: Servire, [n.d.]. Translated by Willem Weeda, C. F. van der Horst

C190 *Men noemt mij timmerman.* Baarn: Hollandia Drukkerij, 1923.

The Millennium (1924)

C191* *Het duizendjarig rijk; een blijspel in het jaar 2000.* Amsterdam: Nederlandsche Uitgevers-Maatschap, 1930. 238 pp. Translated by Wm. J. Woltman.

Oil! (1927)

C192* *Petroleum.* Amsterdam: Ontwikkeling, 1928. 530 pp. Translated by Johanna E. Kuiper.

C193* *Petroleum. Vijfde druk.* Amsterdam: N. V. de Arbeiderspers, 1954. 562 pp. Translated by Johanna E. Kuiper.

Money Writes! (1927)

C194* *Geld.* Amsterdam: Arbeiderspers, 1931. 278 pp. Translated by H. J. Ankersmit.

Boston (1928)

C195* *Dr. Martelaren van Boston.* Amsterdam: Ontwikkeling, N. V. De Arbeiderspers, 1929; 's-Gravenhage: Servire, 1929. 993 pp. Translated by Willem Weeda, C. F. van der Horst.

Roman Holiday (1931)

C196* *Romeinsch Amerika.* Amsterdam: N. V. de Arbeiderspers, 1931. 269 pp. Translated by Johanna E. Kuiper.

The Wet Parade (1931)

C197* *Borrel Parade.* Amsterdam: N. V.. de Arbeiderspers, 1933. 529 pp. Translated by Johanna E. Kuiper.

The Way Out (1933)

C198* *De uitweg.* Groningen: R. Land, [1943]. 64 pp. Translated by W. L. van Warmelo.

We, People of America, and How We Ended Poverty (1934)

C199* *Wij, volk van Amerika, en hoe wij een einde maakten aan de annoede.* Groningen: R. Land, [1935]. 62 pp. Translated by W. L. van Warmelo.

Co-op (1936)

C200 *Co-operation.* Amsterdam: N. V. De Arbeiderspers, 1937.

C201* *De handen ineen.* Amsterdam: N. V. de Arbeiderspers, 1938. 400 pp. Translated by Johan Winkler.

The Flivver King (1937)

C202 *De Koning van de fordjes.* 's-Gravenhage: Servire, 1937. Translated by Willem Weeda, C. F. van der Horst.

C203* *Het gezond verstand ben ik, de geschiedenis van Ford, autokonig, idealist en werkgever.* Rotterdam: W. L. & J. Brusse, 1938. 207 pp. Translated by Wilha. F. H. ter Brugge.

C204* *Ford.* Amsterdam: Uitgeverij Pegasus, 1948. 269 pp. Translated by Wilha. F. H. ter Brugge.

No Pasaran! (1937)

C205* *No pasaran (zij zullen er niet doorkomen).* 's-Gravenhage: Servire, 1937. 205 pp. Translated by J. G. Schoup.

Our Lady (1938)

C206* *Onze Vrouwe.* Graveland: De Driehoek, [1933]. 87 pp. Translated by E. Engler van Bergen.

World's End (1940)

C207* *Einde van een Wereld.* 's-Gravenhage: Servire, [1946]. 575 pp. Translated by J. Maschmeyer-Buekers.

Lanny Budd, Collected Works (1940, 1942, 1944, 1946, 1948)

C208* *Lanny Bud; roman-cyclus van twee wereldoorlogen.* 's-Gravenhage: Servire, [1948]. 5 vols. Vol. 1—*Einde van* *een Wereld*; vol. 2—*Drakentanden*; vol. 3—*Geheim Agent nr. 103*; vol. 4—*Om een Nieuwe Wereld*; vol. 5—*Naar de Overwinning*. Translated by Rob J. Limburg.

Between Two Worlds (1941)

C209 *Tussen Twee werelden.* 's-Gravenhage: Servire, 1948. 687 pp. Translated by J. Maschmeyer-Buekers.

Dragon's Teeth (1942)

C210 *Drakentanden.* 's-Gravenhage: Servire, [1950]. 485 pp. Translated by Rob J. Limburg.

Wide Is the Gate (1943)

C211 *Wijd is de Poort.* 's-Gravenhage: Servire, 1949. 611 pp. Translated by J. Maschmeyer-Buekers.

Presidential Agent (1944)

C212 *Geheim Agent nr. 103.* 's-Gravenhage: Servire, 1950. 583 pp. Translated by Rob. J. Limburg.

Dragon Harvest (1945)

C213 *Wie Wind Zaait.* 's-Gravenhage: Servire, [n.d.].

C214* *Wie wind zaait.* 's-Gravenhage: Servire, 1950. 618 pp. Translated by Rob J. Limburg.

A World to Win (1946)

C215 *Om een Nieuwe Wereld.* 's-Gravenhage: Servire, 1950. 541 pp. Translated by J. L. van Tijn.

Presidential Mission (1947)

C216 *Met Geheims Zending.* 's-Gravenhage: Servire, 1951. 557 pp. Translated by Rob J. Limburg.

One Clear Call (1948)

C217* *Naar de Overwinning.* 's-Gravenhage: Servire, 1951. 540 pp. Translated by Rob J. Limburg.

The Return of Lanny Budd (1954)

C218* *Lanny Budd achter het ijzeren gordijn.* 's-Gravenhage: Servire, 1953. 463 pp. Translated by J. L. van Tijn.

Collected Works (1950)

C219 *Wereldberoemde Werken.* 's-Gravenhage: Servire, 1950. 4 vols. Vol. 1—*Uitstapje Naar Rome* (*Roman Holiday*); vol. 2—*Sylvia's Huweijk* (*Sylvia's Marriage*); vol. 3—*De Onschuld Beloond* (*Another Pamela; or, Virtue Still Rewarded*); vol. 4—*Kunst Als Handelwaar* (*Mammonart*). Translated by Johanna Kuiper (vol. 1); A. Van Onck (vol. 2); A. J. Gaastra (vol. 3); J. L. Van Tijn (vol. 4).

Southern Belle (1957) [By Mary Craig Sinclair]

C220 *Ridder Zonder Vrees en Blaam.* Den Haag: Servire, [n.d.]. 350 pp. Translated by A. Van Onck.

Dutch: Flemish

The Jungle (1906)

C221 *De Wildernis.* Antev: Wereld-Bibliotheek, 1958. 350 pp. Translated by H. Mendels-Stokvis.

Sylvia (1913)

C222 *Sylvia heeft lief.* Gent: Uitgeversbedrij Fiat, [1947]. 224 pp.

Sylvia's Marriage (1914)

C223 *Sylvia's huwelijk.* Gent: Uitgeversbedrij Fiat, [1947]. 224 pp.

English: Australia

The Jungle (1906)

C224 *The Jungle.* Melbourne: Geo. Robertson, 1906. 413 pp.

A Plea for Russia [*Russia: A Challenge* (1919)]

C225 *A Plea for Russia*; *a Boycotted Article.* Melbourne: Andrade's, [1919]. 16 pp.

The World of Economic Crisis (1931?)

C226 *The World of Economic Crisis.* Sydney: [n.p.], [1931?]. 12 pp. apparently a pamphlet; not available for checking.

English: Canada

The Jungle (1906)

C227 *The Jungle.* Toronto: McLeod & Allen, [1906]. 413 pp.

The Metropolis (1908)

C228 *The Metropolis.* Toronto: McLeod & Allen, [1908].

Samuel the Seeker (1910)

C229 *Samuel the Seeker.* Toronto: McLeod & Allen, [1910].

World's End (1940)

C230 *World's End.* Toronto: Macmillan, 1940, 740 pp.

Between Two Worlds (1941)

C231 *Between Two Worlds.* Toronto: Macmillan, 1941. 859 pp.

Dragon's Teeth (1942)

C232 *Dragon's Teeth.* Toronto: Macmillan, 1942. 631 pp.

Wide Is the Gate (1943)

C233 *Wide Is the Gate.* Toronto: Macmillan, 1943. 751 pp.

Presidential Agent (1944)

C234 *Presidential Agent.* Toronto: Macmillan, 1944. 655 pp.

Dragon Harvest (1945)

C235 *Dragon Harvest.* Toronto: Macmillan, 1945. 703 pp.

A World to Win (1946)

C236 *A World to Win.* Toronto: Macmillan, 1946. 581 pp.

Presidential Mission (1947)

C237 *Presidential Mission.* Toronto: Macmillan, 1947. 641 pp.

One Clear Call (1948)

C238 *One Clear Call.* Toronto: Macmillan, 1948. 626 pp.

O Shepherd, Speak! (1949)

C239 *O Shepherd, Speak*! Toronto: Macmillan, 1949. 629 pp.

Another Pamela (1950)

C240 *Another Pamela.* Toronto: Macmillan, 1950. 314 pp.

The Enemy Had It Too (1950)

C241 *The Enemy Had It Too.* Toronto: Macmillan, 1950. 127 pp.

English: France

King Coal (1917)

C242* *King Coal.* Paris: L. Conrad, 1918.

English: Germany

Mountain City (1930)

C243* *Mountain City.* Leipzig: B. Tauchnitz, 1930. Vol. 4940.

Roman Holiday (1931)

C244* *Roman Holiday.* Leipzig: B. Tauchnitz, 1931. Vol. 4982. 271 pp.

American Outpost (1932)

C245* *American Outpost, a Book of Reminiscences.* Leipzig: B. Tauchnitz, 1932. Vol. 5060. 286 pp.

English: Great Britain

King Midas (1901)

C246* *King Midas, a Romance.* London: Funk & Wagnalls, 1901. 388 pp. London: W. Heinemann, 1906. 388 pp. Illustrated by Charles M. Relyea.

The Journal of Arthur Stirling (1903)

C247* *The Journal of Arthur Stirling.* London: W. Heinemann, 1903. 1907. 356 pp.

C248* *The Journal of Arthur Stirling, The Valley of the Shadow.* London: T. Werner Laurie, [1933]. 209 pp.

Prince Hagen (1903)

C249 *Prince Hagen.* London: Chatto & Windus, 1903. 249 pp.

C250 *Prince Hagen.* London W. Heinemann, 1907. 250 pp.

Manassas (1904)

C251 *Manassas.* London: Macmillan, 1904.

C252* *Manassas.* London: T. Werner Laurie, [1933], 1934. 412 pp. Introduction by Arch Jamieson.

C253 *Manassas.* London: Mayfair, 1961. 288 pp. (paper). Anonymous introduction.

The Jungle (1906)

C254 *The Jungle.* London: W. Heinemann, 1906, 413 pp.; 1907, 164 pp. (paper).

C255* *The Jungle.* London: W. Heinemann, [1920]; London: T. Werner Laurie, [1929], 1931, [1933], 1946, 1949, 1952, 1955; London: Penguin Books, 1936, 320 pp.; [1965], 412 pp.

C256 *The Jungle.* London: World Distributors, 1959. 320 pp.

C257 *The Jungle.* Bath: Cedric Clivers, 1971.

A Captain of Industry (1906)

C258 *A Captain of Industry.* London: W. Heinemann, 1906. 90 pp.

The Industrial Republic (1907)

C259 *The Industrial Republic.* London: W. Heinemann, 1907. 284 pp.

The Metropolis (1908)

C260* *The Metropolis.* London: T. Werner Laurie, [1908]; London: E. Arnold, 1908. 342 pp.

C261 *The Metropolis.* London: Constable, 1913.

C262 *The Metropolis.* London: T. Werner Laurie, 1930, [1933], 1936, 1938, 1947. 342 pp.

The Moneychangers (1908)

C263 *The Moneychangers.* London: John Long, 1908. 318 pp.

Good Health and How We Won It (1909)

C264* *The Art of Health.* London: "Health & Strength," [1909], 1910. 250 pp.

Samuel the Seeker (1910)

C265* *Samuel the Seeker.* London: J. Long, [1910], 1923. 320 pp.

Love's Pilgrimage (1911)

C266 *Love's Pilgrimage.* London: W. Heinemann, 1912. 438 pp. With a note by Hall Caine, p. vii.

C267* *Love's Pilgrimage.* London: M. Kennerley, [1911]; London: T. Werner Laurie, 1927, 1933. 663 pp.

The Fasting Cure (1911)

C268* *The Fasting Cure.* London: W. Heinemann, 1911. 262 pp.

C269* *The Fasting Cure.* London: M. Kennerley, 1911, 1913. 153 pp.

C270 *The Fasting Cure.* London: T. Werner Laurie, 1934. 153 pp.

Sylvia (1913)

C271 *Sylvia.* London: John Long, 1914, 1917. 320 pp.

Damaged Goods (1913)

C272 *Damaged Goods.* London: Hutchinson, [1913], 1930.

C273* *Damaged Goods.* London: T. Werner Laurie, [1931]. 190 pp.

Sylvia's Marriage (1913)

C274* *Sylvia's Marriage.* London: T. Werner Laurie, [1915], 1917, 1918, 1921, 1927, 1931, [1934]. 211 pp.

King Coal (1917)

C275 *King Coal.* London: T. Werner Laurie, [1917]. 1920, 1931. 368 pp.

The Profits of Religion (1918)

C277 *The Profits of Religion.* London: T. Werner Laurie, 1936. 315 pp. (plus index).

Jimmie Higgins (1919)

C278* *Jimmie Higgins.* London: Hutchinson, 1918, [1919], 1929. 288 pp.

The Brass Check (1920)

C279 *The Brass Check.* London: T. Werner Laurie, [1919]. 443 pp.

100% (1920)

C280* *The Spy.* London: T. Werner Laurie, 1921, 1928, 1930, 1932, [1934], 1935. 255 pp.

The Book of Life (1921, 1922)

C281* *The Book of Life*, Part 1 (*The Book of the Mind*) and Part 2 (*The Book of the Body*). London: T. Werner Laurie, [1934]. 202 pp.

The Book of Life (1922)

C282* *The Book of Love*, Part 1 (*The Book of Love*) and Part 2 (*The Book of Society*). London: T. Werner Laurie, [1934]. 224 pp.

They Call Me Carpenter (1922)

C283* *They Call Me Carpenter.* London: T. Werner Laurie, 1922, 1928. 222 pp.

The Goose-Step (1923)

C284 *The Goose-Step.* London: T. Werner Laurie, 1923. 496 pp.

The Goslings (1924)

C285 *The Goslings.* London: T. Werner Laurie, [1930]. 454 pp.

The Millennium (1924)

C286* *The Millennium.* London: T. Werner Laurie, [1929], 246 pp.; 1934, 160 pp.

Singing Jailbirds (1924)

C287 *Singing Jailbirds.* London: T. Werner Laurie, 1930. 96 pp.

Mommonart (1925)

C288* *Mammonart.* London: T. Werner Laurie, 1934. 384 pp.

Oil! (1927)

C289* *Oil*! London: T. Werner Laurie, [1927], 1928, 1929, 1930, 1932, 1933, [1936], 1938, 1946, 1949. 527 pp.

C290 *Oil*! London: T. Werner Laurie, 1930. 80 pp.

C291 *Oil*! Bath: Cedric Chivers, 1971.

Money Writes! (1927)

C292* *Money Writes*! London: T. Werner Laurie, [1931]. 215 pp.

Boston (1928)

C293* *Boston*. London: T. Werner Laurie, [1929], 1930. 2 vols. 735 pp.

Mental Radio (1930)

C294* *Mental Radio*. London: T. Werner Laurie, [1930], 1951. 211 pp. Introduction by William McDougall.

Mountain City (1930)

C295* *Mountain City*. London: T. Werner Laurie, [1930], 1935. 312 pp.

Roman Holiday (1931)

C296* *Roman Holiday*. London: T. Werner Laurie, [1931], 1934. 248 pp.

The Wet Parade (1931)

C297* *The Wet Parade*. London: T. Werner Laurie, [1931], 1932. 449 pp. With a two page biographical summary by I. O. Evans.

American Outpost (1932)

C298* *Candid Reminiscences*; *My First Thirty Years*. London: T. Werner Laurie, [1932]. 249 pp.

The Way Out (1933)

C299* *The Way Out. A Solution of our Present Economic and Social Ills.* London: T. Werner Laurie, [1933]. 108 pp.

I, Governor of California, and How I Ended Poverty (1933)

C300* *I, Governor of California, and How I Ended Poverty; a True Story of the Future.* London: T. Werner Laurie, [1933]. 63 pp. Page 64, review of *The Way Out.*

An Upton Sinclair Anthology (1934)

C301* *An Upton Sinclair Anthology*, comp. I.O. Evans. London: T. Werner Laurie, 1934. 328 pp. Preface by Upton Sinclair.

Depression Island (1935)

C302* *Depression Island.* London: T. Werner Laurie, [1935]. 124 pp.

I, Candidate for Governor, and How I Got Licked (1935)

C303* *How I Got Licked and Why.* London: T. Werner Laurie, [1935]. 215 pp.

What God Means to Me (1936)

C304* *What God Means to Me; an Attempt at a Working Religion.* London: T. Werner Laurie, [1936]. 140 pp.

The Gnomobile (1936)

C305 *The Gnomobile.* London: T. Werner Laurie, 1936. 181 pp. Illustrated by John O'Hara Cosgrave II.

C306 *The Gnomobile.* London: Edmund Ward, 1963. 191 pp. Illustrated by Marcel Lillard.

C307 *The Gnome-mobile.* London: The New English Library (Four Square), 1967. 128 pp.

Co-op (1936)

C308* *Co-op, A Novel of Living Together.* London: T. Werner Laurie, [1936]. 415 pp.

The Flivver King (1937)

C309* *The Flivver King, a Story of Ford-America.* London: T. Werner Laurie, 1938, 1939, 1948. 236 pp.

C310 *The Flivver King.* Bath: Cedric Chivers, 1971.

No Pasaran! (1937)

C311* *No Pasaran! (They Shall Not Pass); A Story of the Battle of Madrid.* London: T. Werner Laurie, [1937]. 239 pp.

Our Lady (1938)

C312* *Our Lady.* London: T. Werner Laurie, [1938]. 158 pp.

Little Steel (1938)

C313* *Little Steel.* London: T. Werner Laurie, 1938, 1940, 1946. 282 pp.

Letters to a Millionaire (1939)

C314* *Letters to a Millionaire.* London: T. Werner Laurie, [1939]. 64 pp.

Marie Antoinette (1939)

C315* *Marie Antoinette.* London: T. Werner Laurie, 1939. 200 pp.

Telling the World (1939)

C316* *Telling the World.* London: T. Werner Laurie, [1939]. 211 pp.

World's End (1940)

C317* *World's End.* London: T. Werner Laurie, [1940], 1941, 1942, 1943, 1945. 627 pp.

C318 *World's End.* Bath: Cedric Chivers, 1970. 627 pp.

Between Two Worlds (1941)

C319* *Between Two Worlds.* London: T. Werner Laurie, [1941], [1943]. 691 pp.

C320 *Between Two Worlds.* Bath: Cedric Chivers, 1970. 691 pp.

Dragon's Teeth (1942)

C321* *Dragon's Teeth.* London: T. Werner Laurie, [1942], 1950. 624 pp.

C322 *Dragon's Teeth.* Bath: Cedric Chivers, 1970. 624 pp.

Wide Is the Gate (1943)

C323* *Wide Is the Gate.* London: T. Werner Laurie, 1943, [1944], 1948. 640 pp.

C324 *Wide Is the Gate.* Bath: Cedric Chivers, 1970. 640 pp.

Presidential Agent (1944)

C325* *Presidential Agent.* London: T. Werner Laurie, [1945], 1949. 615 pp.

C326 *Presidential Agent.* Bath: Cedric Chivers, 1970. 615 pp.

Dragon Harvest (1945)

C327* *Dragon Harvest.* London: T. Werner Laurie, 1945, [1946]. 639 pp.

C328 *Dragon Harvest.* Bath: Cedric Chivers, 1970. 639 pp.

A World to Win (1946)

C329* *A World to Win.* London: T. Werner Laurie, [1947]. 592 pp.

C330 *A World to Win.* Bath: Cedric Chivers, 1970. 592 pp.

Presidential Mission (1947)

C331* *Presidential Mission.* London: T. Werner Laurie, [1948]. 608 pp.

C332 *Presidential Mission.* Bath: Cedric Chivers, 1970. 608 pp.

A Giant's Strength (1948)

C333* *A Giant's Strength.* London: T. Werner Laurie, [1948]. 87 pp.

One Clear Call (1948)

C334* *One Clear Call.* London: T. Werner Laurie, [1949]. 711 pp.

C335 *One Clear Call.* Bath: Cedric Chivers, 1970. 711 pp.

O Shepherd, Speak! (1949)

C336* *O Shepherd, Speak*! London: T. Werner Laurie, [1950]. 645 pp.

C337 *O Shepherd, Speak*! Bath: Cedric Chivers, 1970. 645 pp.

Another Pamela (1950)

C338* *Another Pamela.* London: T. Werner Laurie, [1952]. 314 pp.

A Personal Jesus (1952)

C339* *A Personal Jesus.* London: G. Allen & Unwin, [1954]. 217 pp.

The Return of Lanny Budd (1953)

C340* *The Return of Lanny Budd*. London: T. Werner Laurie, [1953]. 528 pp.

C341 *The Return of Lanny Budd.* Bath: Cedric Chivers, 1970. 528 pp.

The Cup of Fury (1956)

C342* *The Cup of Fury*. London: Arco, [1957]. 190 pp.

It Happened to Didymus (1958)

C343 *What Didymus Did.* London: Wingate, [1954]. 151 pp.

The Autobiography of Upton Sinclair (1962)

C344 *The Autobiography of Upton Sinclair.* London: W. H. Allen, 1963. 350 pp.

English: India

The Jungle (1906)

C345* *The Jungle*. Bombay: Jaico publishing house, 1957. 308 pp.

English: U.S.S.R.

C346 *Upton Sinclair on Comrade Kautskii.* Moscow: Co-operative publ. society of foreign workers in the USSR, 1931. 16 pp.

C347 *Three Plays.* Moscow: Progress, 1965. 59 pp. Edited and preface by T. Shishkina. Preface and commentary in Russian.

Esperanto: England

Oil! (1927)

C348* *Petrolo!* London: The Esperanto Publishing Co., 1936. Translated by William Bailey.

Esperanto: France

Jimmie Higgins (1919)

C349* *Jimmie Higgins*. Paris: Sennacieca asocio Tutmonda, 1934. Translated by Karl Fröding.

Estonian

A Captain of Industry (1906)

C350 *Ameerika miljonääri elukäik*. Leningrad: [n.p.], 1924. 111 pp. Translated by K. Dixi.

C351 *Tööstusetuus*. Tartu: "Loodus," 1928. 62 pp. Translated by E. Oiderman. Foreword by Sinclair.

The Metropolis (1908)

C352* *Metropolis*. Tallinn: Ploompuu raamatukaupluse kirj., 1912. 168 pp. Translated by Mait Metsanurk.

The Money Changers (1908)

C353* *Rahavahetajad*. Viljandi: "Sakala" kirj., [1910]. 205 pp. Translated and introduction by H. Pöögelman.

100%: The Story of a Patriot (1920)

C354* *Sada protsenti*. Tallinn: Tööliste kirj. üh., 1927. 182 pp. Translated by H. Kiho.

The Millennium (1924)

C355* *Pärast veeuputust. Romaan aastast 2000*. Tallinn: "RahvaSöna," 1928. 79 pp.

Oil! (1927)

C356* *Oil*! Tartus: "Loodus," 1932. 2 vols. 496 pp. Translated by Alma Röigas. Forward by H. B.-P.

Finnish: Canada

Oil! (1927)

C357 *Kultainen mustavirta.* Port Arthur, Ontario: The Work People's College, 1933.

Finnish: Finland

The Jungle (1906)

C358 *Chikago.* Porvoo: Werner Söderström Oy., 1906. 406 pp. Translated by O. A. Joutsen.

A Captain of Industry (1906)

C359 *Pörssiylimys.* Tampere: K. Kaatra, 1907. 109 pp. Translated by H[anna] P[ispa].

C360 *Pörssiylimys.* Tampere: Isak Julin, 1912. 110 pp. Translated by H[anna] P[ispa].

The Metropolis (1908)

C361 *Maailmankaupunki.* Jyväskylä: Keski-Suomen Työväen Sanomalehti-osuuskunta, 1911. 339 pp.

The Moneychangers (1908)

C362 *Rahanvaihtajat.* Tampere: Tampereen Työväen Sanomalehti-Oy., 1915. 236 pp. Translated by Yrjö Sirola.

Samuel the Seeker (1910)

C363 *Estivä Samuel.* Pori: Osuusk. Kehitys, 1911. 370 pp.

King Coal (1917)

C364 *Kuningas kivihiili.* Helsinki: Kustannusoy, Kansanvalta, 1925. [2 vols.] Vol. 1, 270 pp.; vol. 2, 256 pp. Translated by J. Hollo.

Jimmie Higgins (1919)

C365* *Jimmie Higgins.* Helsinki: Oy. Työ, [1923]. 332 pp.

100%: The Story of a Patriot (1920)

C366 *100%.* Helsinki: Minerva Oy., 1924. 207 pp.

C367 *Urkkija.* Helsinki: Työväen Kirjallisuuden distämisyhdistys, 1924. 302 pp. Translated by Niilo V[älläri].

They Call Me Carpenter (1922)

C368 *Minua sanotaan puusepäksi.* Helsinki: Oy. Työ, 1926. 247 pp.

The Millennium (1924)

C369 *Tuhatvuotinen valtakunta.* Helsinki: Kustannusoy, Kansanvalta, 1925. Translated by Vilho Torniainen.

C369 *Tuhatvuotinen valtakunta.* Helsinki: Työväen kirjallisuuden edistämisyhdistys, 1925. 195 pp.

Mammonart (1925)

C370 *Taide ja mammona.* Helsinki: Tammi, 1946. 506 pp. Translated by Johan Helo.

Letters to Judd (1926)

C371 *Oikeus ja kohtuus.* Helsinki: Kustannusoy, Kansanvalta, 1929. 127 pp. Translated by Tauno Tainio.

Oil! (1927)

C372 *Öljyä!* Lahti: Mikko Taipale, 1951. 360 pp. Translated by Mikko Taipale. Part I only.

No Pasaran! (1937)

C373 *Ttaisele Madridista.* Helsinki: Kirjailijain Kustannusliike, 1937. 240 pp. Translated by N[iilo] W[adenströ]m.

Finnish: U.S.A.

The Last Judgment (?)

C374 *Viimeinen tuomio.* Hancock, Michigan: Työmiehen Kustannusyhtiö, 1906. 31 pp.

Pamphlet or portion of book unexamined. Deals with labor question.

100%: The Story of a Patriot (1920)

C375 *Sadan prosentin patriooti.* Duluth, Minnesota: Workers' Socialist Publishing, n.d. 261 pp.

Mountain City (1930)

C376 *Vuorikaupunki.* Fitchburg, Massachusetts: Raivaajan Kustannusyhtiö, 1932. 338 pp. Translated by Lauri Moilanen.

Finnish: U.S.S.R.

Jimmie Higgins (1919)

C377 *Jimmie Higgins.* Leningrad: Valtion Kustannusliike Kirja, 1934. 194 pp.

The Last Judgment (?)

C378 *Viimeinen tuomio.* Hämeenlinna: Hämeenlinnan uusi Kirjapaino, 1909. 32 pp.

Pamphlet or portion of book; unexamined. Deals with labor question.

French: France

Manassas (1904)

C379 *Manassas.* Paris: Éditions du Bateau Ivre, 1948. 473 pp. Translated by Roger Bertin.

C380 *Allan Montagu.* Paris: Éditions la Farandole, [1962]. 215 pp. Translated by Madeleine Gilard.

The Jungle (1906)

C381 *La Jungle, les empoisonneurs de Chicago.* Paris: Félix Juven, La Renaissance du Livre, 1905. 337 pp. Translated by Armand Fournier.

C382 *La fin de "La jungle" L'affranchi.* Paris: Félix Juven, La Renaissance du Livre, 1906. 290 pp. Translated by Armand Fournier.

The first edition concluded where Jurgis was blacklisted the second time. Unavailable for examination.

A Captain of Industry (1906)

C383 *Le roman d'un roi de l'or.* Paris: Hachette, 1907. 143 pp.

The Industrial Republic (1907)

C384 *La république industrielle.* Paris: Félix Juven, La Renaissance du Livre, [1907]. 301 pp. Translated by Armand Fournier.

The Metropolis (1908)

C385* *Métropolis* (*Les multimillionnaires à New-York*). Paris: Félix Juven, La Renaissance du Livre, [1909]. 304 pp. Translated and adapted by Armand Fournier.

The Moneychangers (1908)

C386 *Les brasseurs d'argent.* Paris: Félix Juven, La Renaissance du Livre, [1909], 1910. Translated by Armand Fournier.

Samuel the Seeker (1910)

C387* *Samuel le chercheur.* Paris: Georges Valois, 1931. 277 pp. Translated by Henri Delgove.

Love's Pilgrimage (1911)

C388 *Le pélerinage d'amour.* Paris: Albin Michel, [n.d.].

King Coal (1917)

C389 *Le roi charbon.* Paris: P. Ollendorff, Albin Michel, 1920. 2 vols. Vol. 1, 191 pp.; vol. 2, 185 pp. Translated by Victor Snell.

Jimmie Higgins (1919)

C390 *Jimmie Higgins, roman d'un ouvrier socialiste américain pendant la guerre.* Paris: Renaissance du livre, [1920]. 348 pp. Translated and a note by Henri Delgove.

100%: The Story of a Patriot (1920)

C391* *100 p. 100, Histoire d'un patriote.* Paris: Ernest Flammarion, 1924. 287 pp. Translated by David and M. L. Lamouroux.

They Call Me Carpenter (1922)

C392 *Le Christ à Hollywood.* Paris: Les Deux Sirènes, 1947. 311 pp. Translated and adapted by Yves Malartic.

Hell! (1923)

C393 *L'Enfer.* Paris: Albin Michel, [n.d.].

Oil! (1927)

C394 *Le pétrole.* Paris: Albin Michel, 1928. Part I. 333 pp. Translated by Henri Delgove and R. N. Raimbault.

C395* *La cité des anges.* Paris: Albin Michel, 1929. Part II. 318 pp. Translated by Henri Delgove and R. N. Raimbault.

C396* *La tête d'Holopherne.* Paris: Albin Michel, 1931. Part III. 345 pp. Translated by Henri Delgove and R. N. Raimbault.

Boston (1928)

C397 *Boston.* Paris: Albin Michel, 1932.

Mountain City (1930)

C398 *Mountain City.* Paris: Albin Michel, [n.d.].

Roman Holiday (1931)

C399* *Les jeux du cirque.* Paris: Éditions de Flore, 1947. 303 pp. Translated by R. N. Raimbault. Biographical sketch by Gilbert Sigaux.

American Outpost (1932)

C400* *Candides réminiscences.* Paris: A. Redier, Librairie de la Revue Francaise, 1933. 349 pp. Translated by R. N. Raimbault and Gwen Gilbert. Introduction by René Lalou.

What God Means to Me (1936)

C401* *Comment je crois en Dieu.* Paris: Editions Adyar, 1937. 163 pp. Translated by Henri Delgove and R. N. Raimbault.

The Gnomobile (1936)

C402* *L'étrange randonnée à travers l'Amérique.* Paris: Editions Bourrelier et Cie, [1937]. 193 pp. Translated by R. N. Raimbault and Henri Delgove. Preface by Charles Vildrac.

C403* *En Gnomobile à travers l'Amérique.* Paris: Bourrelier, 1959. 160 pp. Translated by Henri Delgove. Illustrated by Marcel Tillard.

The Flivver King (1937)

C404* *Le roi de l'auto: Henry Ford.* Paris: Editions Stock, Delarndin et Bontelleau, 1938. 302 pp. Translated by Henri Delgove.

No Pasaran! (1937)

C405* *No Pasaran! (Ils ne passeront pas!)* Paris: Editions de la Libraire populaire, 1937. 222 pp. Translated by Henri Delgove and R. N. Raimbault. Preface by Jean Longuet.

Our Lady (1938)

C406* *Notre-Dame, Marya de Nazareth.* Paris: Bernard Grasset, 1947. 233 pp. Translated by Yves Malartic.

World's End (1940)

C407* *La fin d'un monde.* Paris: Bruxelles: Éditions de la paix, 1947. 908 pp. Translated by R. N. Raimbault, Henri Delgove and Arlette Durand.

Between Two Worlds (1941)

C408* *Entre deux mondes.* Paris: Bruxelles: Éditions de la Paix, [1950]. 2 vols. Translated by Henri Delgove and Simone Chauveau.

Dragon's Teeth (1942)

C409* *Les griffes du dragon.* Bruxelles, Paris: Éditions de la Paix, [1950]. 2 vols. Vol. 1, 349 pp.; vol. 2, 333 pp. Translated by Eugène Rocart.

Wide Is the Gate (1943)

C410 *La grande porte.* Paris, Bruxelles: Éditions de la Paix, 1952. 576 pp. Translated by Eugène Rocart.

Presidential Mission (1944)

C411 *Mission secrète.* Paris, Bruxelles: Éditions de la Paix, 1952. 413 pp. Translated by Eugène Rocart.

Dragon Harvest (1945)

C412 *La Moisson du dragon.* Paris, Bruxelles: Éditions de la Paix, [1954]. 415 pp. Translated by Eugène Rocart.

Another Pamela (1950)

C413* *Pamela.* Paris: Del Duca, Les Éditions Mondiales, 1950. 349 pp. Translated by Michel Arnaud.

It Happened to Didymus (1958; What Didymus Did, 1954, England)

C414* *Saint Thomas d'Hollywood.* Paris: Colmann-Lévy, 1956. 211 pp. Translated by Benoît Braun.

French: Switzerland

The Jungle (1906)

C415 *La jungle.* Lausanne: Éditions Rencontre, 1965. 575 pp. Translated by Armand Fournier. Preface by Jacques Caban.

Georgian-Caucasian (see also Russian): U.S.S.R.

Samuel the Seeker (1910)

C416 *Samuil iskatel'.* Tiflis: Shroma, 1921. 218 pp.

King Coal (1917)

C417 *Korol' ugol'.* Tiflis: Shroma, 1926, 1927. 360 pp. Translated by K. Chichinadze.

Manassas (1904)

C418 *Sklaverei.* Wien: Renaissance, 1923. 265 pp. Translated by Hermynia zur Mühlen.

100%: The Story of a Patriot (1920)

C419 *100%, Roman eines Polizeispitzels.* Wien: Strom, 1929. 124 pp. Translated by Hermynia zur Mühlen.

Depression Island (1935)

C420 *Depression Island.* Wien: E. Prager, 1937.

The Gnomobile (1936)

C421 *Das Gnomobile.* Klagenfurt: Kaiser (Buchgemeinde Alpenland), 1966. 181 pp. Translated by Lisolette Julius.

World's End (1940)

C422 *Welt Ende.* Klagenfurt: Kaiser (Buchgemeinde Alpenland), 1965. 523 pp. Translated by Elizabeth Rotten.

A Giant's Strength (1948)

C423 *Eines Riesen Kraft, Drama in drei Akten.* Wien: R. Geist, 1948. 89 pp. Translated by Maria Zettl-Bayer.

Limbo on the Loose; a Midsummernight's Dream (1948)

C424 *Sie folgten meinem Ruf, Ein Mittsommernachtstraum.* Wien: R. Geist, 1948. 108 pp. Translated by Marie Zettle-Bayer.

Affectionately Eve (1961)

C425 *Eva entdeckt das Paradies.* Klagenfurt: (Buchgemeinde Alpenland), 1966. 275 pp. Translated by Dorothea Gotfurt.

German: Czechoslovakia

The House of Wonder (1922)

C426 *Das Haus der Wunder.* Praha: Orbis, 1922. 46 pp. Translated by Hermynia zur Mühlen. (Pamphlet.)

Mountain City (1930)

C427 *So macht man Dollars.* Praha, Berlin: Malik, 1931; Berlin: Buchergilde Gutenberg, 1931. 398 pp. Translated by Paul Baudisch.

I, Candidate for Governor, and How I Got Licked (1935)

C428 *Das Ende der Armut.* Bratislava, Wien: Donauverlag, 1937. 260 pp. Translated by Herbert Guggenbacher.

Co-op (1936)

C429* *Co-op.* Praha: Mercy, 1937. 411 pp.; Praha, Wien, Zürich: Büchergilde Gutenberg, 1937. 415 pp. Translated by Rudolf Jacob Humm.

German: Germany

Prince Hagen (1903; as play, 1910)

C430* *Prinz Hagen, Ein phantastisches Schauspiel in vier Aufzügen.* Berlin: Malik, [1921]. 56 pp. Translated by Hermynia zur Mühlen.

The Jungle (1906)

C431* *Der Sumpf, Roman aus Chicagos Schlachthäusern.* Hannover: A Sponholtz, 1906, 1907, 1922. 381 pp. Translated by Eduard Eugen Ritter.

C432* *Der Sumpf.* Berlin: Malik, [1923], [1924], 1928. 266 pp. Translated by Hermynia zur Mühlen.

C433 *Der Sumpf.* Berlin: Dietz, 1949. 251 pp. Translated by Hermynia zur Mühlen.

A Captain of Industry (1906)

C434 *Der Industriebaron.* Hannover: Sponholtz, 1906. 131 pp.

C435 *Der Industriebaron.* Berlin: Malik, 1925. 72 pp. Translated by Hermynia zur Mühlen.

The Industrial Republic (1907)

C436 *In 10 Jahren.* Hannover: A. Sponholtz, 1907. 191 pp. Translated by M. Enckhausen and E. von Kraatz.

Metropolis (1908)

C437 *Metropolis.* Hannover: A. Sponholtz, 1908. 400 pp. Translated by E. von Kraatz.

The Metropolis (1908)

C438* *Die Metropole.* Berlin: Malik, 1925. 171 pp. Translated by Hermynia zur Mühlen.

The Moneychangers (1908)

C439 *Die Börsenspieler.* Hannover: A. Sponholtz, 1909. 287 pp. Translated by Robert Müller.

C440* *Die Wechsler.* Berlin: Malik, 1925. 201 pp. Translated by Hermynia zur Mühlen.

Samuel the Seeker (1910)

C441 *Samuel der Suchende.* Berlin: Malik, 1909.

C442 *Samuel der Suchende.* Hannover: Sponholtz, 1911. 286 pp. Translated by Hermynia zur Mühlen.

C443* *Samuel der Suchende.* Berlin: Malik, [1924], [1928]. 206 pp. Translated by Hermynia zur Mühlen.

Love's Pilgrimage (1911)

C444* *Der Liebe Pilgerfahrt.* Potsdam: G. Kiepenheuer, 1922. 267 pp. Berlin: Malik, 1924, [1928]. 300 pp. Translated by Hermynia zur Mühlen.

C445* *Leidweg der Liebe.* Berlin: Malik, 1930. 661 pp. Translated by Elias Canetti.

The Second-Story Man (1912)

C446 *Der Fassadenkletterer.* Leipzig: Die Wölfe, 1924. 28 pp. Translated by Hermynia zur Mühlen.

King Coal (1917)

C447* *König Kohle.* Berlin: Malik, 1925, 1928. 392 pp. Translated by Hermynia zur Mühlen.

C448 *König Kohle.* Berlin: Dietz, [1949]. 381 pp. Translated by Hermynia zur Mühlen.

The Profits of Religion (1918)

C449* *Religion und Profit.* Leipzig: Der Neue Geist, 1922. 184 pp. Translated by Isidor Singer.

C450 *Religion und Profit.* Leipzig: P. Reinhold, 1924. 218 pp.

Jimmie Higgins (1919)

C451* *Jimmy Higgins.* Potsdam: G. Kiepenheuer, 1919. c.320 pp. Translated by Hermynia zur Mühlen.

C452* *Jimmie Higgins.* Berlin: Malik, 1924, [1928]; Berlin: Dietz, 1948. 338 pp. Translated by Hermynia zur Mühlen.

C453 *Jimmie Higgins.* Berlin: Freier Schulverlag, [1929].

The Brass Check (1920)

C454* *Der Sündenlohn, eine Studie über den Journalismus.* Leipzig: Der Neue Geist, 1921. 299 pp. Translated by Isidor Singer.

C455* *Der Sündenlohn, eine Studie über den amerikanischen Journalismus.* Berlin: Malik, 1928, 1929. 363 pp. Translated by Julian Gumperz.

100%: The Story of a Patriot (1920)

C456* *100%, Roman eines Patrioten.* Berlin: Malik, 1921. 337 pp. Translated by Hermynia zur Mühlen.

C457* *Hundert Prozent.* Berlin: Malik, 1923, [1928]. 288 pp. Translated by Hermynia zur Mühlen.

C458* *100%, Roman eines Patrioten.* Berlin: Dietz, 1948. 273 pp. Translated by Hermynia zur Mühlen.

The Book of Life (1921)

C459* *Das Buch des Lebens.* Berlin: Malik, 1922. 4 vols. Vol. 1—*Das Buch des Geistes.* 192 pp.; vol. 2—*Das Buch des Körpers.* 63 pp.; vol. 3—*Das Buch der Liebe.* 87 pp.; vol. 4—*Das Buch der Gesellschaft.* 182 pp. Translated by Hermynia zur Mühlen.

They Call Me Carpenter (1922)

C460* *Man nennt mich Zimmermann.* Berlin: Malik, 1922 187 pp. Translated by Hermynia zur Mühlen.

The Goose-Step (1923)

C461* *Der Parademarsch, eine Studie über amerikanische Erziehung.* Berlin: Malik, 1924. 252 pp. Translated by Hermynia zur Mühlen.

Hell (1923)

C462* *Die Hölle.* Berlin: Malik, 1925. 95 pp. Translated by Hermynia zur Mühlen.

The Goslings (1924)

C463* *Der Rekrut, eine Studie über amerikanische Erziehung.* Berlin: Malik, 1925. 252 pp. Translated by Hermynia zur Mühlen.

The Millennium (1924)

C464* *Nach der Sintflut, ein Roman aus dem Jahre 2000.* Berlin: Malik, 1925. 156 pp. Translated by Hermynia zur Mühlen.

C465 *Nach der Sintflut. Roman aus dem Jahre 2000.* Berlin: Sieben Stöbe, 1931. 243 pp. Translated by Hermynia zur Mühlen.

Singing Jailbirds (1924)

C466 *Singende Galgenvögel.* Berlin: Malik, 1925. 72 pp. Translated by Hermynia zur Mühlen.

C467* *Singende Galgenvögel.* Berlin: Malik, 1927. 104 pp. Translated by Hermynia zur Mühlen.

Mammonart (1925)

C468 *Die Goldene Kette; oder, Die Sage von der Freiheit der Kunst.* Berlin: Malik, 1927. 422 pp. Translated by Hermynia zur Mühlen.

The Machine (1925)

C469 *Die Maschine, Schauspiel.* Berlin: Malik, 1921. 48 pp. Translated by Hermynia zur Mühlen.

Letters to Judd (1926)

C470* *Briefe an einen Arbeiter.* Leipzig, Wien: E. Prager, 1932. 186 pp. Translated by Tibor Barta.

The Spokesman's Secretary (1926)

C471* *Präsident der USA, Roman aus dem Weissen Hause.* Berlin: Universum-Bücherei für alle, 1927; Berlin: Robinson, 1928. 274 pp. Translated by Hermynia zur Mühlen.

Oil! (1927)

C472* *Petroleum.* Berlin: Malik, 1927. 638 pp. Translated by Hermynia zur Mühlen.

C473* *Petroleum.* Berlin, Praha: Malik, 1931. 618 pp. Translated by Hermynia zur Mühlen.

Money Writes! (1927)

C474* *Das Geld schreibt*; *Eine Studie über die Amerikanische Literatur.* Berlin: Malik, 1930. 215 pp. Translated by Elias Canetti.

Boston (1928)

C475 *Boston.* Berlin: Büchergilde Gutenberg, 1929.

C476* *Boston.* Berlin: Malik, 1929. 797 pp. Translated by Paul Baudisch.

Mountain City (1930)

C477 *So macht man Dollars.* Berlin: Malik Verlag, 1931. 399 pp. Translated by Paul Baudisch.

C478 *So macht man Dollars.* Frankfurt am Main: Büchergilde Gutenberg, 1931. 371 pp. Translated by Paul Baudisch.

C479* *So macht man Dollars*. Hannover: Verlag für literatur und zeitgeschehen, [1960]. 372 pp. Translated by Paul Baudisch.

C480 *So macht man Dollars*. Frankfurt: Büchergilde Gutenberg, 1961.

C481* *So macht man Dollars*. München: Goldman, [1963]. 331 pp. Translated by Paul Baudisch.

Mental Radio (1930)

C482 *Mental Radio*. Berlin: Malik, 1930.

The Wet Parade (1931)

C483* *Alkohol*. Berlin: Malik, 1932. 479 pp. Translated by Elias Canetti.

Roman Holiday (1931)

C484* *Römische Vision*. Stuttgart: Union deutsche, 1932, 1933. 357 pp. Translated by Lyonel Dunin.

American Outpost (1932)

C485* *Auf Vorposten*. Berlin, Praha, London: Malik, 1934, 1935, 1936. 316 pp. Translated by Bolder Olden.

Gnomobile (1936)

C486 *Das Gnomobil*. München, Bern: A Scherz, 1964. 181 pp. Translated by Liselotte Julius.

Co-op (1936)

C487* *Co-op*. Hamburg: F. Oetinger, 1948. 446 pp. Translated by Hermann W. Michaelson.

The Flivver King (1937)

C488* *Das Fliessband, ein Roman aus Ford-Amerika.* Hamburg: F. Oetinger, 1948. 173 pp. Translated by Heinz Jens.

Our Lady (1938)

C489* *Unsere liebe Frau.* Düsseldorf: Progress-Verlag, J. Fladung, [n.d.]. 106 pp. Translated by Katherine and Heinrich Arndt.

World's End (1940)

C490 *Welt-Ende.* Hamburg: Toth, [1949]. 717 pp. Translated by Elizabeth Rotten.

Another Pamela (1950)

C491* *Eine neue Pamela.* Stuttgart: Diana, 1951. 366 pp. Translated by Ernst Bucher.

C492 *Eine neue Pamela.* Stuttgart: Europäischer Buchklub, 1952. 420 pp. Illustrated. Translated by Ernst Bucher and Felix Strössinger.

C493 *Eine neue Pamela.* Stuttgart: Diana, 1960. 287 pp. Translated by Ernst Bucher.

A Personal Jesus (1952)

C494* *Jesus wie ich ihn fand und sah.* Zürich: Steinberg, 1957. 255 pp. Translated by Ursula von Wiese.

Affectionately Eve (1961)

C495 *Eva entdeckt das Paradies.* Stuttgart: A. Scherz, 1962, 1966. 275 pp. Translated by Dorothea Gotfurt.

Collected Works

C496* *Gesammelte Romane.* Berlin: Malik, 1924–1925. 5 vols. Vol. 1—*Der Sumpf.* 266 pp. *Hundert Prozent.* 286 pp.; vol. 2— *Jimmie Higgins.* 338 pp. *Man nennt mich Zimmerman.* 90 pp.; vol. 3—*Samuel der Suchende.* 207 pp. *Der Liebe Pilgerfahrt.* 301 pp.; vol. 4—*Der Industrie-Baron.* 72 pp. *König Kohle.* 393 pp.; vol. 5—*Die Metropole.* 171 pp. *Der Wechsler nach der Sintflut.* 156 pp. Translated by Hermynia zur Mühlen.

C497 *Gesammelte Werke.* Berlin, Praha: Malik, 1927–1930. 12 vols.
Unavailable for examination.

German: Great Britain

Upton Sinclair Presents William Fox (1933)

C498* *William Fox.* London: Malik, 1936, 1937. 591 pp. Translated by Paul Baudisch.

No Pasaran! (1937)

C499* *Drei Freiwillige.* London: Malik, 1937. 289 pp. Translated by Peter Bauer.

The Flivver King (1937)

C500* *Autokönig Ford.* London: Malik, 1938. 271 pp. Translated by Peter Bauer.

German: Switzerland

King Coal (1917)

C501 *König Kohle.* Zürich, Bern: Internationaler, 1918. Davos, 1920. 349 pp. Translated by Hermynia zur Mühlen. Introduction by Georg Brandes.

World's End (1940)

C502* *Welt-Ende.* Bern: A Scherz, [1942], 1943, 1947. 721 pp. Translated by Elizabeth Rotten.

C503* *Welt-Ende.* Bern, Stuttgart, Wien: A. Scherz, [1963]; Zurich: Schweizer Druch-und Verlagshaus, 1963; Zurich: Büchergilde Gutenberg, 1963; Klagengurt: Kaiser, 1965; 524 pp. Translated by Elizabeth Rotten.

Between Two Worlds (1941)

C504* *Zwischen zwei Welten.* Bern: A. Scherz, 1945. 792 pp. Translated by Ursula von Wiese.

Dragon's Teeth (1942)

C505* *Drachenzähne.* Bern: A. Scherz, 1946. 645 pp. Translated by Ursula von Wiese.

C506 *Drachenzähne.* Bern: A. Scherz, 1948. 693 pp. Translated by Ursula von Wiese.

Wide Is the Gate (1943)

C507* *Weit ist das Tor.* Bern: A. Scherz, 1947, 1948. 693 pp. Translated by N. O. Scorpi.

Presidential Agent (1944)

C508* *Agent des Präsidenten.* Bern: A. Scherz, [1948], 1957. 705 pp. Translated by N. O. Scorpi.

Dragon Harvest (1945)

C509* *Teufelsernte.* Bern: A. Scherz, [1949]. 717 pp. Translated by N. O. Scarpi.

A World to Win (1946)

C510* *Schicksal im Osten.* Bern: A. Scherz, 1950. 660 pp. Translated by N. O. Scarpi.

Presidential Mission (1947)

C511* *Im Auftrag des Präsidenten.* Bern: A. Scherz, 1951. 671 pp. Translated by N. O. Scarpi.

One Clear Call (1948)

C512* *Die elfte Stunde.* Bern: A. Scherz, [1952]. 647 pp. Translated by N. O. Scarpi.

O Shepherd Speak! (1949)

C513* *A Schäfer, sprich!* Bern: A. Scherz, [1953]. 596 pp. Translated by N. O. Scarpi.

Another Pamela (1950)

C514 *Eine neue Pamela.* Zürich: Konstanz, 1951. 366 pp. Translated by Ernst Bucher.

The Return of Lanny Budd (1953)

C515* *Lanny Budd kehrt zurück.* Bern: A. Scherz, [n.d.]. 582 pp. Translated by N. O. Scarpi.

It Happened to Didymus (1958) (In England as *What Didymus Did, 1954)*

C516* *Die Wundertaten des Didymus, ein Gleichnis unserer Zeit.* Bern: A. Scherz, 1955. 196 pp. Translated by Werner DeHaas.

Gujarathi: India

Samuel the Seeker (1910)

C517 [*Samuel the Seeker*]. Ranpur: Fulchhab, 1932.

C518 *Satyani Sodhman.* Ahmedabad: Gurjar Grantharatna Karyalay, 1946. 226 pp. Translated by Jhaverchand Kalidas Meghani.

C519* [*Samuel the Seeker*]. Bombay: Bharathi Sahitya Sangh, 1947. 240 pp.

Love's Pilgrimage (1911)

C520* [*Love's Pilgrimage*]. Bombay: R. R. Sheth, 1946. 272 pp.

Damaged Goods (1913)

C521* [*Damaged Goods*]. Bombay: Nalini, 1938. 190 pp.

The Millennium (1924)

C522 *Vaheti Ganga*. Bombay: R. R. Sheth, 1962. 235 pp. Translated by Gunavantray Acharya.

Hebrew (and Ladino): Israel

Manassas (1904)

C523 *Manassas*. Jerusalem–Tel-Aviv: Mizpah, [1930].

The Jungle (1906)

C524* *Ha-Jungle*. Jerusalem–Tel-Aviv: Mizpah, [n.d.]. 324 pp.

C525 *Ha-Jungle*. Jerusalem–Tel-Aviv: Mizpah, 1929. 326 pp. Translated by Aharon Reuveni.

King Coal (1917)

C526* *Ha-Melekh peham*. Tel-Aviv: Mizpah, 1930–1931. 2 vols. Translated by Efraim Broida.

100% (1920)

C527 *Mea Ahuz*. Tel-Aviv: Mizpah, 1932. 199 pp. Translated by Menahem Zalman Wolfowski.

Oil! (1927)

C528* *Neft*. Jerusalem–Tel-Aviv: Mizpah, 1929–1930. 2 vols. Translated by Aharon Reuzeni.

The Flivver King (1937)

C529 *Melekh ha-mekhoniyyot; roman al America shel Ford.* Tel-Aviv: Tevel, 1952. 243 pp. Translated by Nehemya Porat.

No Pasaran! (1937)

C530 *No Pasaran!* Nathanya, Palestine: The Nations Editions, 1938.

Return of Lanny Budd (1953)

C531 *Lanny Budd.* Tel-Aviv: Tevel, 1955. 743 pp. Translated by Zeev Hartavi.

Hebrew: Poland

Oil! (1927)

C532 *Neft.* Warszawa: Medura, 1929. Translated by M. Avishai.

Hebrew: U.S.S.R.

The Moneychangers (1908)

C533 *Den'gi.* Minsk: Belgosizdat, 1929. 188 pp.

Samuel the Seeker (1910)

C534 *Samuel'-iskatel'.* Kyiv: Kul 'tur-Liga, 1928. 224 pp. Translated by D. Hofshtein.

King Coal (1917)

C535 *Korl' ugol'.* Moskva: Emes, Shkola i Kniga, 1925. 389 pp. Translated by A. Veviurko.

No Pasaran! (1937)

C536 *No Pasaran*! Kyiv: Ukrderzhnatsmenvydav, 1939. 112 pp.

C537 *Oni ne proidut.* Moskva: Der-Emes, 1939. 212 pp.

Hebrew: Ladino (Judeo-Spanish dialect in Hebrew characters) Greece

100% (1920)

C538 *100% Patriota, o la Istoria de un mangoroforo.* Salonica: la Vara, 1922.

Oil! (1927)

C539 *Petrolio*; *romanso de la vida moderna.* Salonica: Edicion del Avante, 1928.

Hindi: India

The Jungle (1906)

C540 [*Jungle*]. Patna: Hindi Sahitya Karyalay, [1936]. 360 pp. Translated by Chavinath Pandey.

Oil! (1927)

C541 *Tel.* Patna: Hindi Sahitya Karyalay, 1936. 408 pp. Translated by Chavinath Pandey.

Boston (1928)

C542 *Boston.* [n.p., 1930]. Translated by N. K. Nigam.

The Return of Lanny Budd (1953)

C543 [*The Return of Lanny Budd*]. Ranpur: Fulchhab, [n.d.]. 2 vols.

C544 *Pratyavartan.* Calcutta: Praciprakasan, 1955. 2 vols. Translated by Nandakumar Pandey.

Cup of Fury (1956)

C545 *Sangharsh.* Patna: Kalaniketan, 1957. 430 pp. Translated by Chavinath Pandey.

Hungarian: Austria

Jimmie Higgins (1919)

C546* *Jimmie Higgins.* Wien: Bécsi Magyar Könyvkiadó, [1922, 1923?]. 280 pp. Translated by Zoltán Franyó.

Hungarian: Czechoslovakia

Upton Sinclair Presents William Fox (1933)

C547 *William Fox.* Praha: Eugen Prager-Verlag, 1937.

Hungarian: Hungary

Manassas (1904)

C548 *Rabszolgák.* Budapest: Nova, 1946. 186 pp. Translated by Pál Sándor.

The Jungle (1906)

C549 *A posvány.* Budapest: Commission of Patria, 1907. 232 pp. Translated by Károlyné Baross.

C550 *A mocsár.* Budapest: Nova Irodalmi Intézet, 1934, 224 pp.; 1944, 1946, 269 pp. Translated by Dr. Soma Braun.

A Captain of Industry (1906)

C551 *Az imparbáró.* Budapest: Commission of Patria, Ltd., 1908. 95 pp. Translated by Károlyné Baross.

C552 *Az imparbáró, Egy amerikai milliomos életének története.* Budapest: Athenaeum, Ltd., 1915, [1919]. 76 pp. Translated by Bella Sárosi. Bound with *Az elitélt: The Convict.*

The Moneychangers (1908)

C553 *Parážnapenz.* Budapest: Kultura, 1918. 256 pp. Translated by Andor Halasi.

C554 *A mindenható pénz.* Budapest: Nova, 1948. 214 pp. Translated by Andor Halasi.

Samuel the Seeker (1910)

C555* *Kutató Sámuel.* Budapest: Népszava Könyvkereskedés, 1913, 293 pp.; 1919, 324 pp.; 1924, 320 pp. Translated by Dezsö Schöner.

C556 *Kutató Sámuel.* Budapest: [n.p.], 1924. 324 pp. Translated by Dezsö Schöner.

C557 *Kutató Sámuel.* Budapest: Arkádia, 1914. 253 pp. Translated by Dezsö Schöner.

Love's Pilgrimage (1911)

C558 *A szerelem zarámdokutja.* Košice: Munkás Könyvkereskedés, 1924. 174 pp. Translated by Jenö Fried. Košice, the former Kassa, was given to Czechoslovakia in 1920.

C559 *A szerelem kálváriája.* Budapest: Európa, 1942. 240 pp. Translated by Ferenc Kollár.

C560* *A szerelem tövises útja.* Budapest: Táncsics Könyvkiadó, [1958], 1960. 593 pp. Translated by Olga Abel and Sándor Benamy. Introduction by Tibor Lutter. Poems by Miklós Vidor.

The Second-Story Man (1912)

C561 *Az elitélt.* Budapest: Athenaeum, Ltd., [1913]. 68 pp. Translated by Dezsö Schöner.

C562* *Az elitélt.* Budapest: Athenaeum, [1919]. 67 pp. Translated by Dezsö Schöner. Bound with *Az iparbáró* (*A Captain of Industry*).

Sylvia (1913)

C563 *Amerikai házasság.* Budapest: Szikra, 1949. 318 pp. Translated by Mária Kilényi.

King Coal (1917)

C564* *Szén öfelsége. A bánya regénye.* Budapest: Kultura Könyvkiadó, 1920. 2 vols. Translated by Pál Bodó and László Sas.

Jimmie Higgins (1919)

C565* *Jimmie Higgins.* Budapest: Nova Irodalmi Intézet, 1945. 251 pp. Budapest: Szikra, 1949. 256 pp. Translated by Mihály Tábori.

100%: The Story of a Patriot (1920)

C566* *100%.* Budapest. Népszava-Könyvkereskedés, 1928. 262 pp. Translated by Kornél Nagy.

C567* *100%.* Budapest: Nova Irodalmi Intézet, [1944]. 280 pp. Translated by Kornél Nagy.

C568* *100%.* Budapest: Európa Könyvkiadó, 1964. 269 pp. Translated by György Déri. Afterword by Miklós Vásárhelyi.

They Call Me Carpenter (1922)

C569* *Az ács fiának hivnak.* Budapest: Népszava-Könyvkereskedés, 1925. 186 pp. Translated by Kornél Nagy.

C570* *Az ács fiának hivnak.* Budapest: Nova Irodalmi Intézet, [1946]. 200 pp. Translated by Kornél Nagy.

The Millennium (1924)

C571* *Az özönviz után, komédia a kétezredik évből.* Budapest: Népszava-Könyvkereskedés, 1928. 172 pp. Translated by Soma Braun.

C572* *Az özönviz után.* Budapest: Nova Irodalmi Intézet, [1946]. 165 pp. Translated by Soma Braun.

Mammonart (1925)

C573* *Irodalom története.* Budapest: Epocha Könyvkiadö, 1938, 244 pp.; 1944, 272 p. Translated by Sándor Benamy.

Oil! (1927)

C574 *Petróleum.* Budapest: Commission of Saly, 1928. 2 vols.; Budapest: Népszava-Könyvkereskedés, 1929; 5th ed. 1943; new ed. 1944. Translated by Soma Braun.

C575 *Petróleum.* Budapest: Nova, 1943, 530 pp.; 1949, 529 pp. Translated by Soma Braun.

Mountain City (1930)

C576* *Hajsza a pénz után.* Budapest: Nova Irodalmi Intézet, [1933], 330 pp.; 1944, 340 pp. Translated by Soma Braun.

Roman Holiday (1931)

C577 *Római látomás.* Budapest: Nova Irodalmi Intézet, 1934, 234 pp.; 1944, 254 pp. Translated by Emmy B. Karinthy.

The Wet Parade (1931)

C578* *Alkohol.* Budapest: Nova Irodalmi Intézet, 1933; 2nd ed. 1943. 469 pp. Translated by Emmy B. Karinthy.

American Outpost (1932)

C579* *Önéletrajza.*. Budapest: Epocha Könyvkiadó, 1938. 211 pp. Translated by Sándor Benamy.

C580 *Amerikai elöörs.* Budapest: Epocha-Csokonai, 1947. 176 pp. Translated by Sándor Benamy.

Co-op (1936)

C581 *Munka nélkül.* Budapest: Nova, 1944. 476 pp. Translated by János Sándor and Kornél Tábori.

The Flivver King (1937)

C582 *A tragacskirály.* Budapest: Fovárosi Könyvkiadó, 1944. 257 pp. Translated by Jenö Vértes.

Little Steel (1938)

C583* *Acél.* Budapest: Nova Irodalmi Intézet, [1944]. 315 pp. Translated by Kornél Tábori and János Sándor.

World's End (1940)

C584 *Letünt világ.* Budapest: Renaissance, 1942, 798 pp.; 1943, 841 pp.; 1944, 2 vols.; 1945, 3 vols. Translated by Andor Gaál and Gizella Takács.

C585 *Letünt világ.* Budapest and London: Nova-Lincolns Prager, 1948, 2 vols. Translated by Andor Gál and Gizella Takács.

Between Two Worlds (1941)

C586 *Két világ között.* Budapest: Renaissance, 1945, 1947. 2 vols. Translated by Elek Máthé.

C587 *Két világ között.* Budapest and London: Nova-Lincolns Prager, 1948. 2 vols. Translated by Elek Máthé.

Dragon's Teeth (1942)

C588 *A sárkány fogia.* Budapest and London: Nova-Lincolns Prager, 1946. 2 vols. Translated by Janka Gergely.

Wide Is the Gate (1943)

C589* *Tág a kapu.* Budapest and London: Nova-Lincolns Prager, 1947. 2 vols. Translated by Janka Gergely.

Presidential Agent (1944)

C590 *Az elnök ügynöke.* Budapest: Nova, 1947. 2 vols. Translated by Janka Gergely.

Dragon Harvest (1945)

C591 *Arat a sárkány.* Budapest and London: Nova-Lincolns Prager, 1945, 1948. 2 vols. Translated by Janka Gergely.

A World to Win (1946)

C592 *Megnyerhetitek a világot.* Budapest: Nova-Lincolns Prager, 1949. 2 vols. Translated by Janka Gergely.

Icelandic

The Jungle (1906)

C593 *A refilstigum.* Eyrarbakki: Prentsmidja Sudurlands, 1913. 289 pp.

C594 *A refilstigum.* Eyrarbakki: Prentsmidjan Gutenberg, 1914. 289 pp. (Same as C593?)

King Coal (1917)

C595 *Koli konungur.* Reykjavík: Althydubladid, 1919–1920. (Serial: 17 Nov. 1919–12 Oct. 1920.)

Jimmie Higgins (1919)

C596 *Jimmy Higgins. Jafnadarmadur í heimsstyrjöld.* Reykjavík: Bókmentafélag jafnadarmanna, 1931. 623 pp. Translated by Ragnar E. Kvaran.

C597 *Thjódnyting atvinnutækjanna eöa fasismi í Bandaríkjunum.* Reykjavík: Althydubladid, 1935.

C598 *Baráttan gegn nazismanum.* Reykjavík: Althydubladid, [n.d.].

They Call Me Carpenter (1922)

C599 *Smidur er ég nefndur.* Reykjavík: Althyduprentsmidjan, 1926. 396 pp. Translated by Ragnar E. Kvaran.

The Millennium (1924)

C600 *Thúsundárakíkid.* Reykjavík: Althyduprentsmidjan, 1941. 135 pp. Translated by Gudjón Gudjónsson.

Letters to Judd (1926)

C601 *Bréf til Judds.* Akureyri: Réttur, 1926, pp. 56–62. (Letter 11).

C602 *Bréf til Judds.* Isafjördur: Skutull, 1926. (Letter 14).

No Pasaran! (1937)

C603 *Orustan um Madrid.* Reykjavík: Althydubladid, 1937. (Serial: 24 June–25 August.)

Sinclair-McNeal: Debate on Socialism (1931)

C604 *Deilt um jafnadarstefnuna.* Akureyi and Reykjavík: Réttur, 1924, pp. 102–113, 124–136.

Indian (see Bengali, Gujarati, Hindi, Malayalam, Marathi)

Italian: Italy

The Jungle (1906)

C605 *La giungla.* Milano: Cooperativa del libro popolare, 1954. Translated by Ida Ombani.

The Metropolis (1908)

C606 *La metropoli.* Milano: Edizione Monanni, 1928. 230 pp. Translated by Angelo Treves.

Jimmie Higgins (1919)

C607 *Il faticone.* Milano: Edizione Avanti, 1922. 383 pp. Translated by Arturo Caroti.

The Brass Check (1920)

C608* *Il gettone della prostituta.* Rome: Casa editrice Rassegna internazionale, 1922. 489 pp. Translated and with a preface by Anita Dobelli Zampetti.

100 %:The Story of a Patriot (1920)

C609* *100%, storia di un patriotta.* Milano: Società editrice avanti, 1921. 368 pp. Translated by A. Caroti.

C610 *Cento per cento.* Milano: Baldini and Castoldi, 1945. Translated by A. Caroti.

What God Means to Me (1936)

C611* *Cos' è Dio per me; un tentativo di porre le basi di una religione razionale.* Verona: Casa editrice Europa, 1949. 175 pp. Translated by Pasquale Brazzini.

World's End (1940)

C612* *Fine del mondo.* Milano: A. Mondadori, 1950. 717 pp. Translated by Luigi Berti.

Between Two Worlds (1941)

C613* *Fra due mondi.* Milano: A. Mondadori, 1952. 826 pp. Translated by Luigi Berti.

Dragon's Teeth (1942)

C614* *I denti del drago.* Milano: A. Mondadori, 1953. 673 pp. Translated by Giorgio Guzzelli.

Wide Is the Gate (1943)

C615* *Larga è la porta.* Milano: A. Mondadori, 1955. 728 pp. Translated by Giorgio Guzzelli.

Presidential Agent (1944)

C616* *Agente segreto del presidente.* Milano: A. Mondadori, 1957. 861 pp. Translated by Bruno Oddera.

Dragon Harvest (1945)

C617* *La messe del drago.* Milano: A. Mondadori, 1957. 942 pp. Translated by Bruno Oddera.

Giant's Strength (1948)

C618 *La forza di un gigante.* Torino: S. E. I., 1949. 127 pp.

Italian: U.S.A.

No pasaran! (1937)

C619 *No pasaran!* New York: Edizioni Labor Press, 1937. 200 pp.

Japanese

Prince Hagen (1903)

C620 *Purinsu Hâgen.* Tokyo: Kinseidô, 1927, 1930 (as part of multi-volume edition?), Translated by Hiro Sano.

Manassas (1904)

C621 *Manasasu* (*Nanboku-sensô*). Tokyo: Arusu, 1941. Translated by Saburô Asano.

The Jungle (1906)

C622 *Janguru.* Tokyo: Sŏbunkaku, 1925. 554 pp. Translated by Kôichirô Maedagawa.

C623* *Janguru.* Tokyo: Shunyôdô, 1932. 2 vols. Translated by Kôichirô Maedagawa.

C624* *Janguru.* Tokyo: Mikasa-shobô, 1946, 1950. 360 pp. Translated by Shôji Kimura.

The Metropolis (1908)

C625 [*The Metropolis*]. [n.p., n.d.]. Translated by Ryôichi Nakagawa.

The Naturewoman (1912)

C626 *Shizen no Onna.* Tokyo: Sekai Gikyoku Zenshu Kankôkai, 1928. Translated by Kihachi Kitamura.

The Machine (1912)

C627 [*The Machine*]. [n.p., n.d.]. Translated by Ryôichi Nakagawa.

The Second-Story Man (1912)

C628 *Nikai no Otoko:* Tokyo: Sekai Gikyoku Zenshu Kankôkai, 1928. Translated by Kihachi Kitamura.

King Coal (1917)

C629 *Sekitan O.* Tokyo: Hakuyôsha, 1925. 534 pp. Translated by Toshihiko Sakai.

C630 *Soko ni Ugoku.* Tokyo: Hakuyôsha, 1926. 534 pp. Translated by Toshihiko Sakai.

Profits of Religion (1918)

C631 *Skûkyô no Rijun.* Tokyo: Heibonsha, 1928. Translated by Masamichi Kazu.

C632 *Shukyô Shinzubeki Ka.* Tokyo: Arusu, 1930. Translated by Tsutomu Suyama and Takehito Ono.

Jimmie Higgins (1919)

C633 *Gijin Jimii.* Tokyo: Kaizôsha, 1926. 449 pp. Translated by Kôichirô Maedagawa.

C634* [*Jimmy Higgins*]. Tokyo: [n.p.], 1927. 462 pp. Translated by H. Maidako.

The Brass Check (1920)

C635 *Aka Kuro Shiro.* Tokyo: [n.p.], 1924. Translated by Sôkun Kamiyana.

C636* *Shinchu no Teisôkippu.* Tokyo: Shinchosha, 1929. 642 pp. Translated by Jirô Hayasaka. Prefatory letter by Sinclair.

100%: The Story of a Patriot (1920)

C637 *Supai.* Tokyo: Kyôseikaku, 1928. Translated by Toshihiko Sakai.

C638 *Supai.* Tokyo: Shunyôdô, 1932. Translated by Jirô Hayasaka.

C639 *Ogon Jidai.* Tokyo: Shunyôdô, 1933. Translated by Jirô Hayasaka.

C640* *Hyaku-pâsento Aikokusha.* Tokyo: Taiyôsha, 1949. 339 pp. Translated by Jirô Hayasaka.

The Book of Life (1921)

C641* *Gendai-jin no Seikatsu Geijutsu.* Tokyo: Shinchôsha, 1930. 578 pp. Translated by Jirô Hayasaka.

The Book of Love (1922)

C642 *Ren'aidokuhon.* Tokyo: Shinchôsha, 1937. 256 pp. Translated by Jirô Hayasaka.

C643 *Ren'aidokuhon.* Tokyo: Shinchôsha, 1937. Translated by Jirô Hayasaka. Apparently same book as C642.

They Call Me Carpenter (1922)

C644 *Hito Ware wo Daiku to Yobu.* Tokyo: Shinchôsha, 1930. Translated by Jôji Tani.

The Goose-Step (1923)

C645 [*The Goose-step*]. [n.p., n.d.]. Translated by Kazuo Fujita.

C646 [*The Goose-step*]. [n.p., n.d.]. Translated by Mataichi Hirose.

C647 *Daigaku Hyakkaten.* Tokyo: Shinchôsha, 1931.

Hell! (1923)

C648 *Jigoku.* Tokyo: Nanso Shoin, 1928. 216 pp. Translated by Kihachi Kitamura.

C649* *Jigoku.* Tokyo: Sekai Gikyoku Zenshu Kankôkai, 1929. 226 pp. Translated by Kôichirô Maedagawa.

The Goslings (1924)

C650 [*The Goslings*]. [n.p., n.d.]. Translated by Ryôichi Nakagawa.

Singing Jailbirds (1924)

C651 [*Singing Jailbirds*]. Tokyo: Tsukiji Little Theatre, [n.d.]. Translated by Kihachi Kitamura.

Mammonart (1925)

C652 *Haikin Geijutsu*. Tokyo: Kinseido, [1927]. 198 pp. Translated by Shôji Kimura.

C653 *Shin Sekai Bungakushi*. Tokyo: Arusu, 1940. 162 pp. Translated by Sen Shimizu. See C656.

C654 [*Mammonart*]. [n.p., n.d.]. Translated by Masafumi Tomita.

C655 *Haikin Geijutsu*. Tokyo: Kinseidô, 1927. Translated by Shôji Kimura.

C656 *Shin Sekai Bungakushi*. Tokyo: Aurusu, 1940. Translated by Nobu Shimizu. Apparently same as C653.

Bill Porter (1925)

C657 [*Bill Porter*]. [n.p., n.d.]. Translated by Ryôichi Nakagawa.

Letters to Judd (1926)

C658 *Hito wa Naze Bimbô Suru Ka*. Tokyo: Kurarasha, 1927, 1930. Translated by Shirô Koike.

Oil! (1927)

C659 *Oiru!* (*Sekiyu*) Tokyo: Heibonsha, 1927, 1930. 635 pp. Translated by Paul S. Cate and Masamichi Takatsu.

Money Writes! (1927)

C660 *Beikoku Gendai Bungaku Hihan.* Tokyo: Society for International Culture (Chûgai Bunka Kyôkai), 1928. Translated by Issaku Oka.

C661* *Kane ga Kaku.* Tokyo: Shinchôsha, 1930. 356 pp. Translated by Masafumi Tomita.

Boston (1928)

C662* *Bosuton.* Tokyo: Kaizosha, Atagoshita-machi, Shiba, 1930. 2 vols. Translated by K. Maedagawa and K. Nagano.

Mountain City (1930)

C663* *Shihon.* Tokyo: Nihonhyôronsha, 1930. 499 pp. Translated by Koichirô Maedagawa.

Upton Sinclair Presents William Fox (1933)

C664 *Seirin Bakugeki.* Tokyo: Genkai Shobô, 1935. 2 vols. Translated by Ryô Namikawa.

C665 *Eiga-ô Fokkusu.* Tokyo: Genkai shobô, 1936. 602 pp. Translated by Giichi Itô and others.

C666* [*Upton Sinclair Presents William Fox*]. Tokyo: [n.p.], 1937. 648 pp.

Co-op (1936)

C667* *Kyôdôkumiai.* Tokyo: Dai Ichishobô, 1937. 400 pp. Translated by Kôichirô Maedagawa.

World's End (1940)

C668 *Chohenshôsetsu Sekai no Owari.* Tokyo: Kaizôsha, 1942. Translated by Mitsuo Shôno and Shotarô Shimada.

C669* *Rani Baddo (I) Sekai no Owari.* Tokyo: Kyôwa Shuppansha, 1949. 407 pp. Translated by Ryô Namikawa.

C670 *Sekai no Matsujitsu.* Tokyo: Chûôkôronsha, 1950. 139 pp. Translated by Ryô Namikawa.

Between Two Worlds (1941)

C671* *Ranii Baddo (II) Futatsu no Sekai.* Tokyo: Kyôwa Shuppansha, 1949. 420 pp. Translated by Ryô Namikawa.

Dragon's Teeth (1942)

C672 *Ranii Baddo (III)* Kyôwa Shuppansha, Tokyo: 1942. 2 vols.

C763* *Ranii Baddo no Junrei.* Tokyo: Risunâshâ, 1948; Tokyo: Kyôwa Shuppansha, 1949; Kyôwa Shuppansha, 1949–1950. 413 pp. Translated by Ryô Namikawa.

Wide Is the Gate (1943)

C674* *Ranii Baddo (IV) Mon wa Hirakaretari,* Tokyo: Kyôwa Shuppansha, 1950. 398 pp. Translated by Ryô Namikawa.

Presidential Agent (1944)

C675* *Ranii Baddo (V) Jigoku e no Michi.* Tokyo: Kyôwa Shuppansha, 1950. 393 pp. Translated by Ryô Namikawa.

A World to Win (1946)

C676* *Shôri no Sekai.* Tokyo: Kokusai Shuppansha, 1948. 2 vols. Translated by Ryô Namikawa.

Presidential Mission (1947)

C677 *Ranii Baddo (VI) no Junrei.* Tokyo: Risunâsha, 1948. 2 vols. Translated by Ryô Namikawa.

A Giant's Strength (1948)

C678* *Sekai no Matsujitsu.* Tokyo: Chûôkôronsha, 1950. 144 pp. Translated by Ryô Namikawa. Same as C670?

Limbo On the Loose: Midsummer Night's Dream (1948)

C679 *Sabaku no Yo no Yume: Daisanji Sekai Taisen no Kyofu.* Tokyo: Nichitetsusha, 1955. 232 pp. Translated by Ryô Namikawa.

The Return of Lanny Budd (1953)

C680* *Ranii Baddo no Seikan.* Tokyo: Tôen Shobô, 1954. 368 pp. Translated by Ryô Namikawa.

The Enemy Had It Too (1950)

C681* *Teki mo Motte Ita.* Tokyo: Nichigetsusha, 1955, 1957. 175 pp. Translated by Ryô Namikawa.

Lettish: (Latvian)

The Jungle (1906)

C682* *Džungela.* Riga: E. Poišs, 1912. 2 vols. 473 pp. Translated by R. K[roders].

A Captain of Industry (1906)

C683* *Ruhpniecibas karalis.* Liepaja: M. Ukstinš, 1907. 58 pp. Translated by Zyl. Cpl.

The Metropolis (1908)

C684* *Nujorka (četri simti).* Riga: "Saule," 1924. 303 pp. Translated by Janis Grots.

The Second-Story Man (1912)

C685* *Uzbrukums nakti.* Riga: "Kulturas Balss," 1928. 23 pp. Translated by Janis Grots.

Sylvia (1913)

C686* *Silvija.* Riga: Isdewejs "Leta," 1925. 192 pp.

Jimmie Higgins (1919)

C687 *Dzhimmi Khiggins.* Riga: Latgosizdat, 1946. 260 pp. Translated by A. Araias-Bertse and A. Bauga.

Oil! (1927)

C688* *Nafta.* Riga: "Gramata Draugs," [1933]. 211 pp. Translated by A. Mezsēts.

The Flivver King (1937)

C689 *Automobilu karalis.* Riga: Latgosizdat, 1946. 159 pp. Translated by P. Gurvičs.

[*Title. unknown*]

C690 *Arestants karbodi.* Riga: Pipe [n.d.]. 48 pp. Translated by A. Tannenbergs.

Lithuanian: Lithuania

The Jungle (1906)

C691 *Pelkes. Iš lietuviu darbininku gyvenimo Amerikoje.* Vilnius: Isleista Bielskio lesomis, 1908. 468 pp. Translated by K. Puida.

C692 *Džiungles.* Kaunas: Valst, grož. 1948. 462 pp. Translated by A. Milukas.

100% (1920)

C693 *Provokatorius.* Kaunas: Sakalas, [1936]. 269 pp. Translated by J. Simkus.

C694 *100%.* Vilnius: "Vaga," 1965. 251 pp. Translated by J. Simkus.

The Flivver King (1937)

C695 *Automobiliu karalius.* Kaunas: Kulturos Svietimo D-ja, 1939. 271 pp. Translated by P. Rotomskis.

No Pasaran! (1937)

C696* *Savanoriai Ispanijos kare.* Kaunas: Varpas, 1937. 228 pp. Translated by J. Simkus.

Lithuanian: U.S.A.

The Jungle (1906)

C697* *Raistas. 2-a laida.* Chicago: sp. "Lietuvos," Janas Naujokas, 1908, 1912. 355 pp.

C698 *Raistas, pataisytas ir papildytas lietuviu kalbon vertimas.* Brooklyn: Dienrascio "Laisvēs" leidinys, 1939. 450 pp.

A Captain of Industry (1906)

C699 *Pramones Kapitonas.* Brooklyn: Nanjoji Gadyne Cooperation, 1932.

The Second-Story Man (1912)

C700* *Vagis, vienaveiksmis dramatiškas paveiksla.* Chicago: M. G. Valaskas, 1914. 21 pp. Translated by K. Varonas.

King Coal (1917)

C701* *Karalius anglis, apysaka.* Brooklyn: "Laisvēs" spanda, 1924. 590 pp. Translated by J. Pašešupys.

100%: The Story of a Patriot (1920)

C702* *100%*: Chicago: Lithuanian Daily News, 1924.

The Millennium (1924)

C703* *Kaip zmonēs be ponu gyveno, komedija ivykusi 2000 metais.* Brooklyn: "Laisvēs" spanda, 1926. 249 pp. Translated by J. Pašešupys.

Oil! (1927)

C704* *Aliejus*! Brooklyn: Laisvēs spanda, 1931. 800 pp. Translated by Jonas Kaškaitis.

Macedonian: (see also Serbo-Croatian and Slovene) Yugoslavia

Jimmie Higgins (1919)

C705 *Dzimi Higinz.* Skopje: Kultura, 1950. 332 pp. Translated by Blagoj Korubin from the Serbian of Miloš Morinović.

Malayalam: India

The Jungle (1906)

C706* [*Jungle*]. Trichur: Mangalodayam, 1959. 350 pp. Translated by S. Sanmukham.

Damaged Goods (1913)

C707 *Takarnna Jivitangal.* Madras: Lokavani, [n.d.]. 89 pp. Translated by K. Surendran.

A Personal Jesus (1952)

C708* *Ente svantam Yesu.* Madras: Sarika, 1957. 199 pp.

Marathi: India

The Jungle (1906)

C709 [*Jungle*]. Bombay: Abhinav Prakasan, 1950. 244 pp. Translated by Vasant Poredi.

Damaged Goods (1913)

C710 *Viralele Vasant.* Poona: Viswanath Ganesh Tamhankar, 1935. 120 pp. Translated by Sadashiv.

C711 [*Damaged Goods*]. Bombay: Maharashtra Grantha Bhandar, 1949. 139 pp. Translated by Sa. Hriday.

No Pasaran! (1937)

C712 [*No Pasaran!*] Bombay: Lokasahitya, 1943. 176 pp.

Norwegian

The Jungle (1906)

C713 *Junglen.* Kristiania: P. Aas and Co., 1906; Oslo: "Frémtiden," 1931.

King Coal (1917)

C714 *Kong Kull.* Oslo: Frams Forlag, 1934. 157 pp. Translated by Hakon Erang.

Jimmie Higgins (1919)

C715 *Jimmy Higgins.* Oslo: Aschehoug, 1930. Translated by Charles Kent.

The Brass Check (1920)

C716 *Messingskiltet.* Oslo: N. S. F. S. Forlag, 1929. Translated by Rolf Groll.

They Call Me Carpenter (1922)

C717 *Man kalder mig Tömmermand.* Kristiania: Det norske Arbeiderparti, 1924.

The Millennium (1924)

C718 *Tusindaarsriget, en Roman for Aar 2000.* Oslo: Det norske Arbeiderparti, 1925.

Letters to Judd (1926)

C719* *Breve til Judd.* Oslo: N. S. V. s. Forlag, 1927. 136 pp. Translated by Nils Jontvedt. Preface by Johan Bojer.

Oil! (1927)

C720 *Oljen.* Oslo: Aschehoug, 1928–1929. 2 vols. Translated by Gunnar Larsen.

Roman Holiday (1931)

C721 *Veddelopet i Rivertown og Circus Maximus.* Oslo: Aschehoug. 1932. Translated by Hans Heiberg.

The Wet Parade (1931)

C722 *Den vate Parade.* Trondheim: Globus-forlaget, 1933. 437 pp. Translated by Johan B. Rian.

Upton Sinclair Presents William Fox (1933)

C723 *Historien om William Fox.* Oslo: Nasjonalforlaget, 1933. 420 pp. Translated by Leif Scheen.

No Pasaran! (1937)

C724 *No Pasaran*! Oslo: Tiden, Norsk Forlag, 1937.

The Flivver King (1937)

C725 *Bilkongen.* Oslo: Tiden, Norsk Forlag, 1938. 260 pp.

World's End (1940)

C726* *En verden går under.* Oslo: H. Aschehoug, 1948. 680 pp. Translated by Odd Feydt.

Between Two Worlds (1941)

C727* *Mellom to verdener.* Oslo: H. Aschehoug, 1949. 791 pp. Translated by Odd Feydt.

Dragon's Teeth (1942)

C728* *Dragetenner.* Oslo: H. Aschehoug, 1950. 600 pp. Translated by Odd Feydt.

Wide Is the Gate (1943)

C729* *Veien til fortapelse.* Oslo: H. Aschehoug, 1951. 702 pp. Translated by Fridtjof Dahl.

Presidential Agent (1948)

C730* *Presidentens hemmelige agent.* Oslo: H. Aschehoug, 1952. 737 pp. Translated by Fridtjof Dahl and Anders Hagerup.

Cup of Fury (1956)

C731* *Vanviddets beger.* Bergen: A. S. Lunde, 1957. 177 pp. Translated by Ragnar Kvam.

Polish: Poland

The Jungle (1906)

C732 *Grzesawisko.* Warszawa: Biblioteka Dzieł Wyborowych, 1907. 2 vols. Translated by J. P.

C733 *Grzesawisko.* Warszawa: Ksiegarnia Powszechna, 1907. 295 pp. Translated by Andrzej Niemojewski.

C734 *Grzesawisko.* Warszawa: "Przeglad Społeczny," 1907. 227 pp. Translated by Antonina Brzozowska.

C735 *Grzesawisko.* Warszawa: Ksiazka i Wiedza, 1949. 371 pp. Translated by Andrzej Niemojewski.

A Captain of Industry (1906)

C736 *Baron Przemysłu.* Warszawa: Ksiegarnia Powszechna, 1907. 149 pp. Translated by S. F.

C737 *Baron Przemysłowy.* Warszawa: Ksiazka i Wiedza, 1949. 120 pp. Translated by S. F.

The Metropolis (1908)

C738 *Stolica.* Warszawa: "Rój," 1932. 304 pp. Translated by St. Stande.

The Moneychangers (1908)

C739 *Giełdziarze.* Lwów: Kurier Lwowski, 1909. 316 pp.

C740 *Giełdziarze.* Lwów: Ksiegarnia H. Altenberga, 1911. 350 pp.

C741 *Spekulanci.* Warszawa: "Rój," 1932. 260 pp. Translated by St. Stande.

Samuel the Seeker (1910)

C742 *Poszukiwanie prawdy.* Kraków: G. Gebethner, 1914. 246 pp.

C743 *Emil poszukujacy prawdy.* Lwów: "Lektor," 1918. 246 pp. Preface by W. Witwicki.

C744 *Człowiek, który szuka prawdy.* Warszawa: Biblioteka Dzieł Wyborowych, [1924]. 189 pp. Translated by Bernard Szarlitt.

C745 *Człowiek, który szuka prawdy.* Warszawa: Ksiazka i Wiedza, 1949. 182 pp. Translated by Bernard Szarlitt.

Love's Pilgrimage (1911)

C746 *Pielgrzymka miłosci.* Warszawa: "Rój," 1955. 285 pp. Translated by Antonina Sokolicz.

C747 *W niewoli miłosci.* Warszawa: "Rój," 1935. 356 pp. Translated by Antonina Sokolicz.

The Second-Story Man (1912)

C748 *Kryminalista.* Warszawa: "Ksiazka," 1928. 21 pp. Translated by Antonina Sokolicz.

C749 *Kryminalista.* Warszawa: Ksiazka i Wiedza, 1949. 34 pp. Translated by Antonina Sokolicz.

Sylvia (1913)

C750 *Sylwja.* Warszawa: "Rój," 1932, 1934. 327 pp. Translated by Antonina Sokolicz.

Sylvia's Marriage (1914)

C751 *Małzenstwo Sylwii.* Warszawa: "Rój," 1933. 310 pp. Translated by J. P. Zajaczkowski.

King Coal (1917)

C752 *Król wegiel.* Warszawa: "Rój," "Ksiazka," 1931, 1947, 1948. 461 pp. Translated by Antonina Sokolicz.

C753 *Walka w kopalni.* Warszawa "Prasa Wojskowa," 1949. 150 pp. Translated by Janina Skarzyńska.

Jimmie Higgins (1919)

C754 *Dzym Higgins.* Lwów: Ludowe Spółdzielcze Towarzystwo Wydawnicze, 1922. 384 pp. Translated by Felicj Nossig.

C755 *Dzym Higgins.* Warszawa: "Ksiazka," 1922. 359 pp.

C756 *Dzym Higgins.* Warszawa: Ksiazka i Wiedza, 1949. 325 pp.
Translated by Felicja Nossig.

C757 *Dzym Higgins.* Warszawa: Ksiazka i Wiedza, 1949. 255 pp.

100% (1920)

C758 *Rdzenny Amerykanin.* Warszawa: Ksiazka," 1923. 282 pp.

C759 *100%.* Warszawa: Rój," 1936. 329 pp. Translated by A. Sokolicz and M. Kwiatkowski.

They Call Me Carpenter (1922)

C760 *Nazywaja mnie cieslarz.* Lwów: Ludowe Spółdzielcze Towarzystwo Wydawnicze, 1925, 1928. 158 pp.

The Millennium (1924)

C761 *Kataklizm w roku 2000–ym.* Warszawa: "Rój," 1930. 197 pp. Translated by Antonina Sokolicz.

Oil! (1927)

C762 *Nafta.* Warszawa: "Rój," 1930. 2 vols. Vol. 1, 407 pp.; vol. 2, 307 pp. Translated by Antonina Sokolicz.

C763 *Nafta.* Warszawa: "Ksiazka," 1946, 1949. 2 vols. Vol. 1, 430 pp.; vol. 2, 322 pp. Translated by Antonina Sokolicz.

Boston (1928)

C764 *Boston, współczesna powieść historyczna.* Warszawa: "Ksiazka," 1929–1931. 4 pts. Pt. 1, 171 pp.; pt. 2, 175 pp.; pt. 3, 184 pp.; pt. 4, 169 pp. Translated by Antonina Sokolicz.

C765 *Boston.* Warszawa: Ksiazka i Wiedza, 1949. 2 vols. Vol. 1, 365 pp.; vol. 2, 369 pp. Translated by Antonina Sokolicz.

C766 *Sacco i Vanzetti.* Warszawa: Ksiazka i Wiedza, 1950. 72 pp. Translated by Antonina Sokolicz. Set for the stage by Anna Milska. Excerpt from *Boston.*

C767 *Boston.* Warszawa: Ksiazka i Wiedza, 1957. 2 vols. Vol 1, 418 pp.; vol. 2, 418 pp. Translated by Antonina Sokolicz.

Mountain City (1930)

C768 *Zawrótna kariera Amerykanina.* Warszawa: "Rój," 1933. 369 pp. Translated by Antonina Sokolicz.

The Wet Parade (1931)

C769 *Mokra parada.* Warszawa: "Rój," 1932. 327 pp. Translated by Antonina Sokolicz.

C770 *Słuzba panstwowa.* Warszawa: "Rój," 1932. 367 pp. Translated by Antonina Sokolicz.

The Way Out (1933)

C771 *Z kryzysu jest wyjscie!* Warszawa: "Rój," 1933. 108 pp. Translated by Antonina Sokolicz.

I, Candidate for Governor, and How I Got Licked (1935)

C772 *Jak kandydowałem na Guberntora Kalifornji.* Warszawa: "Rój," 1936. 326 pp. Translated by Pomian.

Co-op (1936)

C773 *Socializm na raty.* Warszawa: "Rój," 1938. 474 pp. Translated by Antonina Sokolicz.

Polish: U.S.A.

The Flivver King (1937)

C774 *Król Taradajek.* Detroit: [n.p.], 1938. Translated by Jan Zygmunt. Published serially in *Głos Ludowy.*

Portuguese: Brazil

Jimmie Higgins (1919)

C775 *Jimmie Higgins.* Rio de Janeiro: Minha Livraria Editôra, [1938].

Oil! (1927)

C776* *Petróleo.* Rio de Janeiro: Minha livraria, 1937. 288 pp. Translated by J. A. de Moraes.

C777 *Petróleo.* Rio de Janeiro: Irmãos Pangetti ed., 1944. 255 p. Translated by Jorge Jobinsky.

Roman Holiday (1931)

C778* *Feriado Romano.* Rio de Janeiro: Flores & Mano, 1932, 1933. 224 pp.

The Wet Parade (1931)

C779 *The Wet Parade.* Rio de Janeiro: Instituto Central do Povo, [n.d.].

American Outpost (1932)

C780 *American Outpost.* Rio de Janeiro: Instituto Central do Povo, [n.d.].

What God Means to Me (1936)

C781 *What God Means to Me.* Rio de Janeiro: Instituto Central do Povo, [n.d.].

The Flivver King (1937)

C782* *Ford, o Rei dos Automóveis Baratos.* Porto Alegre: Edição da livraria do Globo, [1940]. 219 pp. Translated by Casemiro M. Fernandes.

World's End (1940)

C783 *O fin do mundo.* Rio de Janeiro: J. Olympio, 1941. 521 pp. Translated by Lucio Cardoso.

Wide Is the Gate (1943)

C784* *O Caminho da Perdição.* Rio de Janeiro: Cruzeiro, 1945. 446 pp. Translated by Olívia Krahenbul and Aurélio Buarque de Holanda.

Presidential Agent (1944)

C785 *Agente secreto do presidente.* São Paulo: Liv. Exposição do Livro, 1965. Translated by Aydano Arruda.

Another Pamela (1950)

C786* *Pamela e Satã.* São Paulo: Melhoramentos, 1956. 234 pp. Translated by Agenor Soares Santos.

Portuguese: Portugal

The Gnomobile (1936)

C787 *Um Gnomo na Corte do Rei Dólar.* Porto: Civilização Editôra, [1937]. 226 pp. Translated by Maria I. Morna Dias Braga and Mário A. de Almeida Braga.

Romanian

The Jungle (1906)

C788 *Discursul unui agitator socialist.* Bucuresti: Biblioteca "România muncitoare," 1912; Bucuresti: Biblioteca Socialistă, 1920.

C789* *Mocirla.* Bucuresti: Ed. Modernă, 1945. 304 pp. Translated by George Demetru Pan.

C790 *Jungla.* [Bucuresti]: Ed. pentru literatură universală, 1967. Translated by Sorina Stănescu.

A Captain of Industry (1906)

C791* *Regele aurului.* Bucuresti: Ed. I. Brănisteanu, [n.d.]. 93 pp.

The Metropolis (1908)

C792 *Metropola.* Bucuresti: E. Cultura Românească, 1941. Translated by Constantin Apostol.

Samuel the Seeker (1910)

C793 *In căutarea adevărului.* Bucuresti: "Cultura Românească," [n.d.]. Translated by Constantin Apostol.

C794* *In căutarea adevărului.* Bucuresti: "Cultura Româneacă," [1945]. 379 pp. 2nd ed. Translated and with preface by Paul B. Marian.

Love's Pilgrimage (1911)

C795 *Iubire.* Bucuresti: Ed. "Cultura Românească," 1926. 1942. Translated by R. Donici.

C796 *Iubire.* Bucuresti: Ed. "Cultura Românească," 1940. Translated by Bar S. Bar.

King Coal (1917)

C797 *Regele Cărbune.* Bucuresti: Editura Pentru Literatura, 1969. Translated by Virgil Florea. Preface by Nicolae Minei.

Jimmie Higgins (1919)

C798* *Jimmie Higgins.* Bucuresti: Ed. I. Brănisteanu, [1925]. 200 pp. Translated by Ion Pas.

C799* *Jimmie Higgins.* Bucuresti: Ed. Partidului Social-Democrat, 1946. 376 pp. Translated by Ion Pas.

They Call Me Carpenter (1922)

C800 *Mi se spune Dulgherul.* Bucuresti: Ed. Socec, [n.d.]. Translated by St. Freamăt.

C801* *Mi se spune Dulgherul.* Bucuresti: "Cultura românească," 1940. 349 pp. Translated by Bar S. Bar.

The Millennium (1924)

C802* *Cataclismul, roman din anul 2000.* Bucuresti: "Adevărul," [n.d.]. 203 pp. Translated by Dr. A. Mibashan.

C803 *Gradul trei American.* Bucuresti: Ed. pentru literatură si artă a Societătii Scriitorilor din RSN, [n.d.].

Oil! (1927)

C804* *Petrolul.* Adevărul. Bucuresti: "Vatra," [1931]. 2 vols. 575 pp. Translated by Dr. A. Mibashan.

Mountain City (1930)

C805* *Asa se fac dolarii.* Bucuresti: Veritas, [1946]. 338 pp. Translated by St. Freamăt.

The Wet Parade (1931)

C806* *Casa Tarleton.* Bucuresti: "Vatra," [1946]. 476 pp. Translated by St. Freamăt.

Our Lady (1938)

C807* *Madona.* Bucuresti: "Vatra," [n.d.]. 109 pp. Translated by D. Libette and F. Violette.

Dragon Harvest (1945)

C808* *Balaurul.* Bucuresti: "Cultura natională," 1946. 2 vols. Translated by L. Leu and D. Dutescu.

A World to Win (1946)

C809* *O lume de cîstigat.* Bucuresti: "Cultura natională," 1947. 2 vols. Translated by Viola Dutescu and Rodu Vasiliu.

Russian (see also Azerbaizhani [Asepo-Turkish], Georgian-Caucasian, Tajik, Tatar, Turkmen, Ukranian, Uzbek, White-Russian): Bulgaria

Your Million Dollars (1939)

C810 *Tvolat milion dolari.* Sofi: Khemus, 1946. 81 pp. Translated by N. Pančev.

Russian: Imperial and Soviet

King Midas (1901)

C811 *Tsar' Midas.* [Sankt-Peterburg]: State Publ. House Prometei, 1913. 319 pp. Translated by E. Khuravskaia. (Vol. 4 of Collected Edition.)

C812 *Korol' Midas.* Leningrad: Mysl', 1924. 195 pp. Translated by M. N. Matveeva. Introduction by A. Danilov.

C813 *Korol' Midas.* Leningrad: Mysl', 1925. 208 pp. Translated by M. N. Matveeva. Introduction by A. Danilov. 2 eds.

Prince Hagen (1903)

C814* *Prints Gagen.* Petrograd-Moskva: Petrograd Biblioteka kudozectrennoj literatury: 1923. 99 pp. Translated by A. V. Luchinskii.

The Journal of Arthur Stirling (1903)

C815 *Artur Stirling.* Leningrad-Moskva: Mysl', 1924, 200 pp.; 1925, 172 pp. Translated by V. I. Smetanina.

C816 *V severnoi doline*. Kharkiv-Kiev: Ukrhosnatsmenizdat, 1932. 54 pp. Translated by A. Veviurko.

Manassas (1904)

C817* *Iug i sever*. Leningrad: Priboi, 1924, 1925. 212 pp.

C818 *Manassas*. Leningrad, Moskva: [n.p.], 1924. 252 pp. Translated by I. E. Kharodchinskaia.

C819* *Sever i iug*. Moskva: Zemlia i fabrika, 1928. 168 pp. Translated with notes by Rud. Bershadskii.
Supplement to magazine *30 dneĭ* in 1928.

C820 *Iug i sever*. Leningrad: "Krasnaia gazeta," 1929. 2 vols. Vol. 1, 162 pp.; vol. 2, 148 pp.

The Jungle (1906)

C821 *Chashcha. Amerikanskii roman*. Sankt-Peterburg: [n.p., 1906]. 278 pp. Translated by V. K. Shneur.

C822 *Debri*. Kiev: S. I. Ivanov i Ko, 1906. 318 pp.

C823 *Debri khishchvichestva i bezzakoniia*. Sankt-Peterburg: [n.p.], 1906. 166 pp. Translated by Z. A. Rogozina.
In [*New Journal of Literature, Art and Science*].

C824 *Debri*. Moskva: [n.p.], 1907. 451 pp. Translated by K. Zh.

C825 *V tiskakh. Iz zhizni amerikanskikh rabochikh*. Sankt-Peterburg: [n.p.], 1907, 1911, 1920. In 3 pts. Pt. 1, 150 pp.; pt. 2, 166 pp.; pt. 3, 141 pp. Translated by A. Ostrogorskaia-Malkina.

C826 *Dzhungli*. Sankt-Peterburg: Prometei, 1912. 254 pp. Translated by A. N. Kudriavtseva. (Collected works, vol. 2.)

C827 *Debri*. Kharkiv-Kiev: Proletarii, 1923. 306 pp.

C828* *Dzhungli.* Moskva-Petrograd: Gos. izd-vo, 1923. 179 pp. Translated by D. M. Gorfinkel'.

C829 *Dzhungli.* Moskva: Gos. izd-vo, 1956. 352 pp. Translated by D. M. Gorfinkel' and E. L. Linetskaia.

C830* *Chashcha.* Moskva: Krasnaja Nov', 1923. 148 pp. Translated by P. Konstantinov. Illustrated.

C831 *Okovy sbrosheny. Konets dzhunglei.* Petrograd: Mysl', 1923. 237 pp. Translated by Zin. L'vovskii.

C832 *Dzhungli.* Ekaterinburg: Granit, Uralskava Kniga, 1924. 288 pp. Preface by N. Raivid.

C833 *Debri.* Moskva-Leningrad: Trud i kniga, Mysl', 1924, 1925. 236 pp. Translated by I. D. Markuson.

C834 *Debri.* Moskva: V.Ts.S.P.S., 1925. 155 pp. Translated by P. Zaitsef.

C835 *Debri.* Leningrad: Priboi, 1925. 269 pp.

C836* *Dzhungli.* Moskva-Leningrad: Gos. izd-vo, 1928. 142 pp. Translated by D. M. Gorfinkel'. (Abridged.)

C837 *Dzhungli.* Moskva: Gudok, 1928. 365 pp.
Supplement to nos. 29–30, 31–32, 33–34 of the newspaper *Gudok.*

C838* *Dzhungli.* Moskva, Tashkent: Goslitizdat, 1956, 1957. 352 pp. Translated by D. M. Gorfinkel' and E. L. Linetskaia.

A Captain of Industry (1906)

C839 *Tsar' promyshlennosti.* [n.p.]: Novy, 1907, 102 pp. Translated by I. G.

C840 *Promyshchlehki foedal.* [n.p.]: Volnaia Tipografiia, 1907. 80 pp. Translated by V. K.

C841* *Istoriia amerikanskogo millionera.* Petrograd: Poliarnaia zvezda, 1923. 85 pp.

C842 *Istoriia odnogo (amerikanskogo millionera)*, Leningrad: Krasnaia Nov'; Moskva: Gosizdat, 1924. 85 pp. Translated by S. K-ova.

The Industrial Republic (1907)

C843 *Promshlennaia respublika.* Leningrad: Mysl', 1925. 192 pp. Translated by A. M. Karnaukhova. Preface by D. O. Zaslavskii.

The Metropolis (1908)

C844 *5-oe Aveniu.* Moskva, Kharkiv, Kherson: Gos. Iz., 1924. 239 pp. Translated by M. Simokovich. Edited by K. B. Barkhin.

C845* *Chetyresta. (N'iu-Iork).* Petrograd, Leningrad, Moskva: Gosizdat, 1924, 1925. 2nd and 3rd eds. 228 pp. Translated by V. A. Azov.

C846 *Stolitsa.* Leningrad: Mysl', 1925. 271 pp. Translated by M. V. Vatson and M. S. Titova.

C847* *Stolitsa.* Moskva: Goslitizdat, 1957. 280 pp. Translated by L. Mirtsevaia and L. Slonimskaia.

The Moneychangers (1908)

C848 *Den'gi.* Sankt-Peterburg: Prometei, 1912. 236 pp. Translated by E. V. Sviatlovski. (Collected works, vol. 3.)

C849* *Amerikanskie birzheviki.* (*Den'gi*). Petrograd, Moskva, Leningrad: Petrograd, 1923, 200 pp. 1924, 198 pp. Translated by E. K. Pimenova.

C850* *Den'gi.* Petrograd, Leningrad: Priboi, 1923–1924. 144 pp.

C851 *Den'gi.* Moskva-Leningrad: Trud i kniga, Mysl', 1925. 201 pp. Translated by V. F. Sofronova.

C852 *Spekulianty*. Leningrad-Moskva: Gosizdat khud. lit-ry, 1932. 248 pp. Translated by E. I. Patterson.

Samuel the Seeker (1910)

C853 *Samuel' Iskatel'*. Leningrad: Mysl', 1924. 264 pp. Translated by D. E. Keikhtenberg.

C854 *Samuel' Iskatel'*. Moskva: Novaia Moskva, 1924. 284 pp. Translated by A. V. Krivtsova. Edited by E. Lann.

C855* *V poiskakh pravov*. Leningrad: Priboi, 1924. 130 pp.

C856 *Samuel' Iskatel'*. Leningrad: Mysl', 1924, 1925. 228 pp. Translated by D. E. Leikhtenberg. Edited by D. O. Glickman.

C857 *Samuel' Iskatel'*. Moskva: Izd-vo V. Ts. S. P. S., 1925. 129 pp.

C858* *Samuel' Iskatel'*. Moskva: Gudok, 1925. Preface by A. Ts.

C859 *Za khlebom i schast'em*. Moskva-Leningrad: Gos. izd-vo, 1926. 61 pp. Translated by A. Ostrogorska-Malkina.

Love's Pilgrimage (1911)

C860 *Ispytaniia liubvi*. [n.p.]: Prometei, 1912. 512 pp. Translated by M. I. Bruslanina. (Collected works, Vol. 1.)

C861 *Ispytanie liubvi*. Petrograd, Moskva, Leningrad: Vsemirnaia literatura, Gosizdat, 1923. 261 pp. Translated by M. I. Bruslianina. Edited by Stanelberg-Popovaya. (Abridged.)

C862 *Ispytanie liubvi*. Leningrad: Mysl', 1925. 295 pp. Translated by I. D. Markuson.

C863* *Ispytaniia liubvi*. Leningrad-Moskva: Lengikhl, 1932. 352 pp. Translated by M. G. Volosov.

The Machine (1912)

C864* *Mashina.* Moskva-Leningrad: Gosizdat, 1923. 84 pp. Translated by O. Mandel'stam.

C865 *Mashina.* Moskva: ZIF, 1924. 85 pp. Translated by A. V. Krivtsova.

The Second-Story Man (1912)

C866 *Chelovek Vtorykh Etazhe.* [n.p.]: "Mol. Gvard," 1926. No. 6, pp. 3–10. Translated by N. Galperin.

C867 *Vor.* Moskva: Teakinopechat', 1929. 16 pp. Translated by Zelikova.

Sylvia (1913)

C868 *Sil'viia.* Moskva-Petrograd: Gosizdat, 1922, 1923. 272 pp. Translated by A. F. Damanskaia.

C869 *Sil'viia.* Voronezh: [Gov't. Section for Public Health,] 1925. 32 pp.

C870 *Sil'viia.* Leningrad-Moskva: Petrograd, 1925. 352 pp. Translated by L. Vsevolodskaia.

C871 *Sil'viia.* Leningrad: Priboi, 1927. 376 pp. Translated by A. F. Damanskaia.

Damaged Goods (1913)

C872 *Porchenye.* Leningrad: Mysl', 1925. 167 pp. Translated by D. P. Nosovich. Introduction by L. M. Vasilevski.

Sylvia, Sylvia's Marriage (1913, 1914)

C873 *Sil'viia. Zamuzhestvo Sil'vii.* Tashkent: Goslitizdat, 1957. 439 pp. (2 vols. in one.)

Sylvia's Marriage (1914)

C874 *Zamuzhestvo Sil'vii.* Moskva: Gos. izd-vo, 1924. 338 pp. Translated by E. Blagoveshchenskaia.

C875 *Zamuzhestvo Sil'vii.* Leningrad-Moskva: Petrograd, 1924. 240 pp. Translated by E. K. Pimenova.

C876 *Sil'viia zamuzhem.* Leningrad: Mysl', 1925. 232 pp. Translated by N. D. Vol'pin.

The Cry for Justice (1915)

C877 *V poiskakh pravdy.* Leningrad: Priboi, 1924. 130 pp. Apparently the same as C855.

C878 *Kirk o spravedlivosti.* Leningrad: Mysl', 1925. 296 pp. Translated by E. K. Pimenova and T. A. Bogdanovich.

C879 *Vopl' o spravedlivosti.* Leningrad-Moskva: Petrograd, 1925. 286 pp. Translated by T. L. Shchepkinoi-Kupernik.

King Coal (1917)

C880 *Korol' ugol'.* Moskva-Petrograd: Gos. izd-vo, 1923. 437 pp. Translated by S. S. Nesterova.

C881 *Korol' ugol'.* Kharkiv: Proletarii, 1923. 285 pp. Translated by Gr. Petnikov and B. Ianovskii.

C882 *Korol' ugol'.* Moskva-Leningrad: Mysl', Trud i kniga, Publ. House of Mosps, 1924, 1925. 420 pp. Translated by B. Ianovskii.

C883 *Tsarstvo korolia uglia.* Moskva: Novaia Moskva, 1924. 248 pp. Translated by Iarko.

C884 *Korol' ugol'.* Moskva: V.Ts. S. P. S., 1925. 211 pp. Translated by B. Ianovskii.

C885 *Korol' ugol'.* Leningrad: Priboi, 1925. 260 pp. Introduction by Georg Brandes.

C886 *Korol' ugol'*. Moskva: Rabochaia gazeta, 1925. 208 pp. Translated by Z. V.

Appeared as a supplement.

C887 *Korol' ugol'*. Klyntsy?: [Publ. House of the Newspaper Trud,] 1925. 288 pp. Translated by S. S. Nesterova.

C888 *Chernyi vlastelin*. Moskva: Ts. K.S.T., 1928. 103 pp. Supplement to "Golos tekstilei." (Abridged.)

C889 *Korol' ugol'*. Moskva-Leningrad: Ogiz-gos. izd. khud. lit-ry, 1931. 415 pp. Translated by S. G. Zaimovskii.

C890* *Korol' ugol'*. Moskva: Goslitizdat, 1958. 383 pp. Translated by N. Mandel'stam. Postscript by Ia. Zasurskii.

Profits of Religion (1918)

C891 *Vygody religii*. Moskva-Leningrad: Krasnaia Nov', 1924. 152 pp. Translated by A. I. Iakovlev. Preface by V. S. Rozhitsyn.

C892 *Imenem religii*. Leningrad-Moskva: Petrograd, 1925. 391 pp. Translated by E. Fortunato.

C893 *Religiia i nazhiva*. Leningrad: Mysl', 1925. 256 pp. Translated by S. A. Adrianov.

Jimmie Higgins (1919)

C894* *Dzhimmi Khiggins*. Petrograd: Gosizdat, 1921. 328 pp. Translated by M. S. D'yakonova.

C895* *Dzhimmi Khiggins*. Moskva: Krasnia Nov', 1922. 242 pp. Translated by M. A. D'yakonova.

C896 *Dzhimmi Khiggins*. Moskva-Petrograd: Gos. izd., 1923. 315 pp. Translated by M. A. D'yakonova. 2nd ed. Moskva: Krasnaia Nov', 1923. 236 pp. 3rd ed. Moskva-Leningrad: Gos. izd., 1927. 320 pp.

C897 . . . *Krasyni bielyi Dzhimmi Khiggins*. Moskva: Moskovskii rabochii, 1923. 361 pp.

C898 *Dzhimmi Khiggins*. Klyntsy?: Trud, 1925. 2 vols. 273 pp. Translated by M. A. D'yakonova.

C899 *Dzhimmi Khiggins*. Moskva-Leningrad: Priboi, Gos. izd-vo., 1925. 224 pp. Translated by E. K. Brodersen.

C900 *Dzhimmi Khiggins*. Leningrad: Mysl', 1925. 357 pp. Translated by E. K. Pimenova.

C901 *Dzhimmi Khiggins*. Moskva: Izd-vo V.Ts.S.P.S., 1925. 155 pp. Translated by P. Zaitsev. (Abridged?)

C902 *Prikliucheniia malen'kogo sotsialista*. (*Dzhimmi Khiggins*). Moskva: Rabochaia Moskva, 1926. 68 pp. Translated by Iu. Slezkin. (Abridged.)

C903 *Dzhimmi Khiggins*. Moskva-Leningrad: Gos. izd-vo, 1928. 181 pp. Translated by M. A. D'yakonova (Abridged.)

C904 *Dzhimmi Khiggins*. Moskva: Ts. K.S.T., 1928. 111 pp.

C905 *Dzhimmi Khiggins*. Moskva-Leningrad: Gosizdat, 1930. 364 pp. Translated by M. A. D'yakonova. Preface by G. Munblit.

C906 *Dzhimmi Khiggins*. Leningrad: Priboi, 1930. Translated by D. M. Gorfinkel.

C907* *Dzhimmi Khiggins*. Leningrad: Priboi, [1930]. 398 pp. Translated by M. A. D'yakonova. Edited by V. A. Aleksandrov and A. N. Gormin. (Collected works, vol. 1.)

C908 *Dzhimmi Khiggins*. Moskva-Leningrad: Gosizdat, 1933. 200 pp. Translated by M. A. D'yakonova.

C909 *Dzhimmi Khiggins*. Leningrad: OGIZ, 1933. 198 pp.

C910* *Dzhimmi Khiggins*. Moskva: Gosizdat, 1937. 296 pp. Translated by V. Limanovska and L. Navrosov.

The Brass Check (1920)

C911 *Mednaia marka*. Kharkiv: Proletarii, 1924. 77 pp. Translated by S. Sredinskii.

100% (1920)

C912 *Sto protsentov. Istoriia amerikanskogo patriota*. Moskva: Moskovskii rabochii, 1922. 230 pp. Translated by S. S. Zaiaitskii.

C913 *Sto protsentov. Istoriia odnogo patriota*. Petrograd, Moskva, Leningrad: Vsemirnaia literatura, 1922, 1924; Petrograd, Moskva, Leningrad: Gosizdat, 1923, 1924, 1925. 315 pp. Translated by L. M. Gausman.

C914 *Amerikanskaia krov'—Sto protsentov*. Moskva: Krasnia Nov', 1923. 110 pp. Translated by I. I. Iasinskii.

C915 *100%, Amerikanskaia krov'. Sto protsentov*. Bakhmut: Rabochii Donbass, 1924. 48 pp. Translated by I. I. Iasinskii. Supplement to newspaper *Kochegarda* (apparently Ukrainian).

C916 *Sto protsentov*. Moskva-Leningrad: Mysl', Trud i kniga, 1924/1925. 293 pp. Translated by K. N. Chetverikova.

C917 *Predatel'*. Moskva: Gosizdat, 1925. 64 pp. Translated by Petrova. Adapted by V. G. Shershenevich.

C918 *Sto protsentov*. Moskva: [Russian Theater Society,] 1925. 86 pp.

C919 *Sto protsentov*. (*Istoriia odnogo patriota*). Moskva: V.Ts.S.P.S., 1925. 161 pp. Foreword by G. Yakubovskii. (Abridged.)

C920 *Sto protsentov*. Moskva-Leningrad: Gos. izd-vo, 1928. 178 pp.

C921* *100%*. Leningrad: Priboi, 1930. 396 pp. Translated by I. R. Gerbach. Published with *Istoriia amerikanskogo millionera* [*A Captain of Industry*, 1906]. Volume in Collected Works edited by V. A. Aleksandr and A. N. Gormin.

C922* *100% Biografiia patriota*. Moskva: Goslitizdat, 1957. 362 pp. Translated by E. Birukova and M. Shishkanova.

[Peter Gudge Becomes A Secret Agent] (from 100%)

C923 *Rasskaz dlia nachal'nogo chteniia na angl. iaz.* Moskva-Leningrad: Gos. izd., 1927. 35 pp. Edited by A. Vikstid.

Book of Life (1921)

C924 *Kniga o obshchestve*. Leningrad: Seiatel' E. V. Vysotskogo, 1925. 160 pp. Translated by L. M. Vaisenberg and E. M. Kaluzhskii.

C925 *Kniga zhizni*. Leningrad-Moskva: Petrograd, 1925. 312 pp. Translated by A. V. and I. I. Andreevye.

They Call Me Carpenter (1922)

C926 *Prishestvie Khrista v leto 1921–3*. Moskva: Molodaia gvardiia, 1924. 148 pp.

C927* *Khristos v Uestern-Siti*. Petrograd-Moskva: Petrograd, 1923. 132 pp. Translated by A. Ostrogorskaia.

C928* *Menia zovut? plotnikom*. Petrograd-Moskva: Kniga, 1923. 252 pp. Translated by S. I. Tsederbaum.

C929* *Mob.* Moskva [Moscow Theatre publications,] 1924. 126 pp.

C930 *Menia zovut? plotnikom.* Leningrad: Mysl', 1924/1925. 171 pp. Translated by M. M. Birinskii.

The Goose-Step (1923)

C931 *Gusinyi shag. (Mushtrovka v amerik. universitetakh).* Moskva: Krasnaia Nov', 1924. 210 pp.

C932 *Shkola v Amerike.* Kharkiv: Proletarii, 1925. 93 pp. Translated by Shtuser. (Abridged.)

Hell (1923)

C933* *Ad.* Moskva: Krasnaia Nov', [n.d.]. 158 pp. Translated by V. I. Morits. Foreword by P. S. Kogan.

C934* *Ad.* Petrograd, Moskva, Leningrad: Vsemirnaia lit-ra, Gosizdat, 1926. 165 pp. Translated by S. V. Sh. Edited by M. Lozinskii and E. Zamiatin.

The Goslings (1924)

C935* *Gusiata. Narodnoe obrazovanie v Amerike* Leningrad: Seiatel' E. V. Vysotskogo, [n.d.]. 182 pp. Translated by E. I. Fortunato.

The Pot-Boiler (1924)

C936* *Kipiashchii gorshok.* Moskva: Vsemir, Lit., Gosizdat, 1925. 111 pp. Translated by K. Zhikhareva.

C937* *Otets semeistva.* Moskva: Mezhrabpom, 1925. 180 pp.

The Millennium (1924)

C938 *2000-i god. (Komicheskaia utopia).* Moskva: Mezhrabkom, [n.d.]. 174 pp. Translated by M. Iu. Levidov.

C939* *2000-i god. (Svetoprestavlenie)*. Moskva: Vsemirnaia literatura, Gosizdat, [n.d.]; Leningrad: Seiatel', 1924/1925. 207 pp. Translated by I. S. Fortunato.

C940 *I votsarilos' na tysiachu let.* Leningrad-Moskva: Kniga, 1924/1925. 148 pp.

C941* *Zhizn' na razvalinakh.* Leningrad: Priboi, 1925. 109 pp. Translated by A. D'Aktil'.

C942 *Isbrannye rasskazy dlia nachalnogo chtenia na Angliiskom iazyke.* Moskva: Gosizdat, 1930. Translated by A. Wiksteed and N. Settingsona.

The Golden Age (Novels and Stories 1924)

C943 *Zolotoi vek. Romany i povesti.* Moskva-Leningrad: Gosizdat, 1927. 598 pp.
Translated by N. M. Rachinskaia and others.

Singing Jailbirds (1924)

C944 *Tiuremnye solovushki.* Petrograd: Gos. izd-vo, 1925. 150 pp. Translated by V. A. Azov and A. N. Gorlin.

C945* *Poiushchie uzniki.* Moskva: Krug, 1925. 108 pp. Translated by B. I. Iarkho.

C946 *Tiuremnye ptitsy poiut.* Moskva: Trud i kniga, 1925. 94 pp. Translated by A. Shtuser. Songs translated by D. Gorbov. Foreword by V. Friche. Afterword by Upton Sinclair.

Mammonart (1925)

C947 *Iskusstvo mannony.* Leningrad: Priboi, 1925/1926. 278 pp.

Bill Porter (1925)

C948* *Bil' Porter.* (*O. Genri*). Moskva-Leningrad: Gos. izd., 1926. 95 pp.
(Universal'naia b-ka NN 11–12.)

Letters to Judd (1926)

C949* *Pis'ma k rabochemu.* Moskva-Leningrad: Gos. izd-vo, 1927. 108 pp. Translated by M. B. Volosov.

The Spokesman's Secretary (1926)

C950 *Sekretar' govoruna.* (*Pis'ma Mem k mame*). Moskva-Leningrad: Gos. izd-vo, 1927. 192 pp. Translated by L. N. Vsevolodskaia.

Oil! (1927)

C951 *Neft'.* Moskva-Leningrad: Gos. izd., 1926 (?). 307 pp. Translated by V. A. Barbasheva and E. K. Gdaleva.

C952 *Neft'.* Moskva-Leningrad: Gos. izd., 1928. 539 pp. Translated by V. A. Barbasheva and E. K. Gdaleva. Edited by Z. A. Vershinina.

Money Writes! (1927)

C953 *Den'gi pishut. Etiud o vliianii ekonomiki na literaturu.* Moskva-Leningrad: Gosizdat, 1928. 296 pp. Translated by B. Ia. Zhukhovetskii. Preface by S. S. Dinamov.

Boston (1928)

C954* *Boston.* Moskva-Leningrad: Gosizdat, 1930. 2 vols. Vol. 1, 468 pp.; vol. 2, 443 pp. Translated by Z. A. Vershinina and A. V. Krivtsova. Preface by D. Dzhermanetto.

Mountain City (1930)

C955* *Maunten-Siti.* (*Gorod v gorakh*). Moskva-Leningrad: Ogiz-Gos. izd-vo, 1931. 481 pp. Translated by M. Volosov.

Roman Holiday (1931)

C956* *Rimskie kanikuly.* Leningrad-Moskva: Lengikhl, (Gosizdat), 1933. 290 pp. Introduction by S. Rodzevich.

The Wet Parade (1931)

C957 [*The Wet Parade.*] Moskva-Leningrad: Gosizdat, 1933.

Upton Sinclair on "Comrade" Kautskii (1931)

C958 *Upton Sinclair on "Comrade" Kautskii.* Moskva: Izd-vo inostrannykhrabochikh v SSSR, 1931. 16 pp.

American Outpost (1932)

C959 [*American Outpost.*] Moskva-Leningrad: Gosizdat, 1933.

The Flivver King (1937)

C960 *Avtomobil'nyi korol'*. Moskva: Goslitizdat, Vsemirnaia b-ka, 1938. 220 pp. Translated by S. Gurevich.

C961* *Avtomobil'nyi korol'*. Moskva: Gosizdat, 1939, 268 pp.; 1957, 195 pp. Translated by M. Urnov.

No Pasaran! (1937)

C962 *No pasaran*! (*Oni ne proidut*!). Moskva: Gosizdat, [n.d.]. 159 pp. Translated by A. Gavrilova.

C963* *No pasaran*! (*Oni ne proidut*!). Moskva: "Khudozhestvennaia literatura," "Romangazette," [n.d.]. 67 pp.

C964 *No pasaran*! (*Oni ne proidut*!) Arkhangel'sk: Obligiz, [n.d.]. 147 pp. Translated by A. Gavrilova.

C965* *No pasaran!* Stalinsk: Ogiz Archoblgiz, [n.d.]. 144 pp.

C966 *No pasaran!* (*Oni ne proidut!*). Moskva: Zhurn.-gaz. ob "edinenie," [n.d.]. 208 pp. Translated by S. Gurevich. Postscript by A. Mingulin.

C967 *No pasaran!* Moskva: Znamia, [n.d.]. 97 pp. Translated by A. Gavrilova.

World's End (1940)

C968 *Krushenie mira.* Moskva: Gos. izd-vo inostr. lit., 1947. 708 pp. Translated by V. Toper and O. Kholmskaia. Preface by B. Izakov. Edited by O. Galperina. (Abridged.)

Between Two Worlds (1941)

C969 *Mezhdu dvukh mirov.* Moskva: Gos. izd-vo inostr. lit., 1948. 552 pp. Translated by R. Rozental' and V. Stanevich. Preface by V. Rubin Kholmskaia. (Abridged.)

Dragon's Teeth (1942)

C970 *Zuby drakona. Glavy iz knigi.* Magadan: Sov. Kolyma, 1943. 192 pp. Translated by D. Gorbov and V. Kurell. (Abridged.)

Presidential Agent (1944)

C971 *Agent Prezidenta.* Moskva: Novy Mir, 1946, nos. 7–8, pp. 137–183. Translated by V. Stanevich. (Abridged.)

Collected Works

C972 *Sobranie sochinenii.* Sankt-Peterburg: Prometei, 1912–1913. 2 vols. Edited by A. N. Kudriavtseva.

C973 *Sobranie sochinenii.* Sankt-Peterburg: Prometei, 1915. 2 vols. Edited by A. N. Kudriavtseva.

C974 *Sobranie sochinenii. Romany.* Moskva: Gosizdat, 1922. 5 vols.

C975 *Sobranie sochinenii.* Leningrad: Gos. isd-vo, 1924–1927. 12 vols. Edited by V. A. Azov and A. N. Gorlin.

Vol. 1. *Dzhimmi Khiggins.* (*Jimmie Higgins*). 1924. 320 pp. Translated by M. A. Dyakonova. 2nd ed.; 1927.

Vol. 2. *Sto protsentov.* (*100%*). 1925. 299 pp. Translated by L. M. Gausman.

Vol. 3. *Iskatel' pravdy.* (*Samuel the Seeker*). Translated by V. A. Azov. *Tiuremnye solovushki.* (*Singing Jailbirds*). Translated by V. A. Azov and A. N. Gorlin. 1925. 334 pp.

Vol. 4. *Dzhungli.* (*The Jungle*). 1925. 384 pp. Translated by D. M. Gorfinkel'.

Vol. 5. *Stolitsa.* (*The Metropolis*). 1925. Translated by I. R. Gerbach. *Prints Gagen.* (*Prince Hagen*). 1925. Translated by M. N. Matveeva. 432 pp.

Vol. 6. *Chernyi vlastelin.* (*King Coal*), 1926. 424 pp. Translated by D. I. Nosovich. Foreward by G. Brandes. 2nd ed.; 1927.

Vol. 7. *Strannoe proisshestvie v Uestern-Siti.* (*They Call Me Carpenter*). 1926. Translated by D. M. Gorfinkel'. *Spekulianty* (*The Moneychangers*). 1926. Translated by E. I. Patterson and N. M. Rachinskii. *Moe sobratiia po peru.* (*The Brass Check*). 1926. Translated by D. M. Gorfinkel'. 498 pp. 2nd ed.: 1927.

Vol. 8. *Ispytaniia liubvi* (*Love's Pilgrimage*). 1926. Translated by M. I. Brusianina. *Ad.* (*Hell*). 1926. Translated by S. V. Sh. *Gvozd'.* 1926. Translated by K. M. Zhikhareva. 544 pp. 2nd ed.: 1927.

Vol. 9. *Kniga o zhizni.* (*The Book of Life*). 1926. Translated by O. Ia. Skitalets-Iakovlev. *Vopl' o spravedlivosti* (*Antologiia sotsial' nogo protesta*). (*The Cry for Justice*). 1926. Translated by E. I. Vygodska. 464 pp. 2nd ed.: 1927.

Vol. 10. *Sil'viia* (*Sylvia*). 1926. Translated by A. F. Damanski. *Zamuzhestvo Syl'vii.* (*Sylvia's Marriage*). 436 pp. 2nd ed.: 1927.

Vol. 11. *Sever i iug.* (*Manassas*). 1926. Translated by N. F. Davydova. 368 pp. 2nd ed.: 1927.

Vol. 12. *Tsar' Midas.* (*King Midas*). 1927. *Zolotoi vek.* (*The Millennium*). 1927. Translated by N. M. Rachinskaia, M. N. Matveeva, I. P. Gerbach, Ye. K. Gdaleva, V. A. Barbasheva. *Istoriia amerikanskogo millionera.* (*A Captain of Industry*). 1927. *Neft'* (*Oil!*). 1926. 631 pp. 2nd ed.: 1927. With an essay by L. M. Weissenberg.

C976 *Sobranie sochinenii.* Moskva-Leningrad: Priboi and Gosizdat, 1930–1932. Edited by V. A. Aleksandrov and A. N. Gorlin.

Vol. 1. *Dzhimmi Khiggins.* (*Jimmy Higgins*). 1930. 400 pp. Illustrated. Translated by M. A. D'jakonova.

Vol. 2. *Sto protsentov* (*100%*). 1930. Translated by L. M. Tausman. *Istoriia amerikanskogo millionera.* (*A Captain of Industry*). 1930. Translated by I. R. Grebach. 396 pp. Illustrated.

Vol. 3. *Chernyi vlastelin.* (*King Coal*). 1930. 432 pp. Illustrated by D. I. Nosovich. Introduction by Georg Brandes.

Vol. 4. *Dzhungli.* (*The Jungle*). 1930. 456 pp. Illustrated. Translated by D. M. Gorfinkel'.

Vol. 5. *Stolitsa.* (*The Metropolis*). 1930. 372 pp. Illustrated. Translated by I. R. Grebach.

Vol. 6. *Iskatel' pravdy.* (*Samuel the Seeker*). 1930. Translated by Aleksandrov. *Tsar' Midas.* (*King Midas*). 1930. Translated by M. N. Matveeva. 416 pp. Illustrated.

Vol. 7. *Sil'viia.* (*Sylvia*). 1931. Translated by A. N. Gorlin. *Sil'viia zamuzhem.* (*Sylvia's Marriage*). 1931. Translated by N. F. Davydova. 510 pp. Illustrated.

Vol. 8. *Sever i iug.* (*Manassas*). 1931. 444 pp. Illustrated. Translated by N. F. Davydova.

Vol. 9. *Strannoe proisshestvie v Uestern Siti.* (*They Call Me Carpenter*). 1931. *Zolotoi vek.* (*The Millennium*). 1931. *Solovyi tiuremnye.* (*Singing Jailbirds*), 1931. Translated by D. M. Gorfinkel'. 469 pp. Illustrated.

Vol. 10. *Mounten-Siti.* (*Gorod v gorakh*). (*Mountain City*). 1932. 444 pp. Illustrated. Translated by M. G. Volosov.

Vols. 11 and 12. *Neft'.* (*Oil!*). 1932. 793 pp. Illustrated. Translated by V. A. Barbasheva.

Serbo-Croatian (see also Macedonian and Slovene): Austria

King Coal (1917)

C977* *Car ugalj.* Wien, Beograd: Edition Slave, 1922. 371 pp.

Serbo-Croatian: U.S.A.

The Jungle (1906)

C978 [*The Jungle.*] Chicago: Prolitiarec, 1909.

They Call Me Carpenter (1922)

C979 *Tesarom me zovu.* Pittsburgh: nakl. Prosvjetnog odbora, 1925. 162 pp. Translated by Vinko Solić.

Serbo-Croatian: Yugoslavia

The Jungle (1906)

C980 *Močvara.* [n.p.]: Biblioteka baklja, 1921. 388 pp.

C981 *Močvara, roman iz čikaških klaonica.* U Sidu: Pravo Naroda, 1921. 333 pp.

C982 *Kaljuga.* Beograd, Zagreb: "Tipografija," 1931. 276 pp. Translated by D. Mihajlović.

Captain of Industry (1906)

C983 *Industrijski velikan.* Zagreb: "Naša snaga," 1909, 1912. 113 pp. Translated by Vanda Novosel.

C984* *Industrijski baron.* Beograd: "Tucović," 1927. 84 pp. Translated by Sofija Celebi-Arandjelović.

The Metropolis (1908)

C985* *Metropola.* Beograd: "Nolit," 1929, 1930. 199 pp. Translated by Bogdan Bilbija.

The Moneychangers (1908)

C986* *Menjači.* Beograd: "Nolit," 1930. 244 pp. Translated by Desanka Andjelković.

Love's Pilgrimage (1911)

C987* *Hodočašće ljubavi.* Zagreb: "Narodne novine," 1930. 291 pp. Translated by Ljubomir Ivanković.

King Coal (1917)

C988 *Car Ugalj.* Beograd: "Prosveta," 1946. 378 pp. Translated by Stevan J. Milović.

The Profits of Religion (1918)

C989 *Religija i profit.* Zagreb: "Glas Rada," 1951. 204 pp. Translated by Marijan Krleža.

Jimmie Higgins (1919)

C990 *Džimi Higins.* Zagreb: Biblioteka Novinarske Zadruge, 1931. 346 pp. Translated by Branko Kojić.

C991 *Džimi Higins.* Beograd, Zagreb: Kultura, 1947, 1948. 316 pp. Translated by Miloš Marinković.

C992 *Džimi Higins.* Novi Sad: Bratstvo-Jedinstvo, 1949. 295 pp. Translated by Franjo Zoltán.

C993 *Džimi Higins.* Sarajevo: "Svjetlost," 1965. 368 pp. Translated by Miloš Marinović.

C994 *Ratovanje.* Beograd: "Privredni pregled," 1940. 20 pp. (Excerpt.)

100% (1920)

C995 *Konfident.* Zagreb: M. Kelović, 1935, 1936. 207 pp.

C996 *Sto proocenta.* Zagreb: M. Kelović, 1936.

C997 *Patriot.* Zagreb: Nakladni Hrvatski tiskarski zavod D.D., 1946, 1964. 228 pp. Translated by Vlado Smiljan.

They Call Me Carpenter (1922)

C998* *Tesarom me zovu.* Zagreb: Edition Prosvjetni Odbor, 1925. 162 pp. Translated by Vinko Solić.

C999 *Zovu me drvodjelja.* Naklada. Prosvjetnog Odbora, 1925.

C1000* *Tesarom me zovu.* Zagreb. "Final," 1928. 127 pp. Translated by M. Martić.

C1001 *Zovu me drvodelja.* Beograd: Rad, 1952. 232 pp. Translated by Ljubicu Vuković.

The Millennium (1924)

C1002 [*The Millennium.*] Beograd: Nolit, [1930]. 209 pp. Translated by Bogdan Bilbija.

Mammonart (1925) and *Money Writes!* (1927)

C1003* *Zlatni lanac.* Zagreb: Biblioteka Savremenih pisaca, 1932. 116 pp. Translated and with preface by S. Galogaža. (Selections.)

Oil! (1927)

C1004 *Petrolej.* Zagreb: Edicija Socialna misao, 1931.

C1005 *Petrolej.* Beograd: Atheneum; Zagreb, Beograd: Vjesnik, 1945. 601 pp.

C1006 *Petrolej.* Zagreb: Nakladni Hrvatski tiskarski zavod D.D., 1946, 1964. 2 vols. Vol. 1, 299 pp.; vol. 2, 334 pp. Translated by Vlado Smiljan.

C1007 *Petrolej.* Beograd: Rad, 1953. 479 pp. Translated by A. Andjelić.

Money Writes! (1927)

C1008* *Novac piše.* Zagreb: Biblioteka "Epoha," 1936. 227 pp. Translated by Ante Donković.

Mountain City (1930)

C1009 *Novi grad.* Zagreb: "Obzor," 1931.

Roman Holiday (1931)

C1010 *Rimski praznik.* Zagreb: "Novosti," [n.d.].

American Outpost (1932)

C1011 *Amerika sutra.* Beograd: "Svetlost," 1934. 112 pp. Translated by Lazar P. Vukičević.

The Flivver King (1937)

C1012* *Kralj automobila Ford.* Zagreb: Hrvatska književna Naklada, 1938. 274 pp. Translated with preface by Mirko Kus-Nikolajev.

Presidential Mission (1947)

C1013 *U Predsjednikovoj misiji*. Zagreb: Grafički zavod Hrvatske "Zora," 1954. 762 pp. Translated by Elza Grin.

Slovak (see also Czech): Czechoslovakia

The Jungle (1906)

C1014 *Džungl'a*. Bratislava: Tatran, 1966. 344 pp. Translated by J. Simo. Afterword by Zuzana Bolshová.

They Call Me Carpenter (1922)

C1015 *Volajú ma tesárom*. Kosice: Svojet, 1948. 203 pp. Translated by Z. Kubisová.

The Millennium (1924)

C1016 *Po potope*. Bratislava: Tlačový výbor KSC, 1926. 181 pp. Translated by M. C. Biss.

Oil! (1927)

C1017 *Petrolej*. Bratislava: Slovenský spisovatel, 1959. 599 pp. Translated by V. Szathmáry - Vlčková. Afterword by Ján Vilikovský.

The Flivver King (1937)

C1018 *Král' tragăcov*. Bratislava: Práca, 1948. 221 pp. Translated by P. Orth.

Slovene (see also Macedonia and Serbo-Croatian): U.S.A.

Jimmie Higgins (1919)

C1019 *Jimmy Higgins*. Chicago: Slovene National Benefit Society, 1921. 482 pp. Translated by Ivan Molek.

The Moneychangers (1908)

C1020 *Menjolci.* Ljubljana: Ljubljanski Dnevnik, 1952. 113 pp. Translated by Jože Zupančič.

Samuel the Seeker (1910)

C1021 *Samuelovo iskanje.* Ljubljana: Delavska založba, [1930], 1931. 221 pp. Translated by France Acko.

They Call Me Carpenter (1922)

C1022 [*They Call Me Carpenter.*] Ljubljana: Cankarjeva Družba, [1930].
Publication uncertain.

The Millennium (1924)

C1023 [*The Millennium.*] Ljubljana: Cankarjeva Družba, [1930].
Publication uncertain.

Oil! (1927)

C1024* *Petrolej.* Ljubljana: Cankarjeva založba, 1955. 691 pp. Translated by August Petrišič.

Mountain City (1930)

C1025 *Dolarji.* Ljubljana: Delavska založba, 1933, 1934. 2 vols. Vol. 1, 169 pp.; vol. 2, 175 pp. Translated by Mirko Javornik.

The Wet Parade (1931)

C1026* *Alkohol.* Ljubljana: Založba "Prijatelj," 1933. 288 pp. Translated and abridged by Pavel Breznik.

Spanish: Argentina

The Jungle (1906)

C1027 *Los envenenadores de Chicago.* Buenos Aires: Tor, [1939].

Samuel the Seeker (1910)

C1028* *Samuel busca la verdad.* Buenos Aires: Ed. del Portico, [1952–1953?]. 205 pp. Translated by A. Torilla.

Love's Pilgrimage (1911)

C1029 *Peregrinación de amor.* Buenos Aires: Santiago Rueda, 1955. 329 pp. Translated by Aristides Gregori.

The Book of Life (1921)

C1030 *El libro de la revolución.* Buenos Aires: [n.d.].

Letters to Judd (1926)

C1031 *Letters to Jud.* Buenos Aires: [n.p., n.d.].

Oil! (1927)

C1032* *Petroleo*! Buenos Aires: Americana, 1955. 375 pp. Translated by F. Aláiz.

Upton Sinclair Presents William Fox (1933)

C1034 [*Upton Sinclair Presents William Fox.*] Buenos Aires: Claridad, [n.d.].

The Way Out (1933)

C1034* *El final de la crisis, como resolver los males economics y sociales de la actualidad.* Buenos Aires: Tor, [n.d.]. 170 pp. Translated by Cesar Klug.

The Flivver King (1937)

C1035 [*The Flivver King*]. Buenos Aires: Claridad, [n.d.]. Publication uncertain.

No Pasarán! (1937)

C1036* *Brigada internacional* (*No pasarán*!). Buenos Aires: "Acento," 1937. 202 pp.

Our Lady (1938)

C1037 *Nuestra Señora.* Buenos Aires: Schapíre, 1942. 217 pp. Translated by Manuel Sendra.

World's End (1940)

C1038* *El fin del mundo.* Buenos Aires: Claridad, 1941. 651 pp. Translated by Antonio Gallo.

C1039 *El fin del mundo.* Buenos Aires: Claridad, 1948 [1952, 1956?]. 543 pp. Translated by S. M. Neuschoosz.

Between Two Worlds (1941)

C1040* *Entre dos mundos, historia novelada.* Buenos Aires: Claridad, 1945, 1951, 1955. 668 pp. Translated by Antonio Gallo.

Dragon's Teeth (1942)

C1041* *Los dientes del dragón, novela.* Buenos Aires: Claridad, 1947, 1952, 1960. 480 pp. Translated by Luisa Rivaud.

Wide Is the Gate (1943)

C1042* *El ancho camino*; *historia novelada.* Buenos Aires: Claridad, 1949, 1952. 558 pp. Translated by Juan Rodríguez Chicano.

Presidential Agent (1944)

C1043* *Agente presidencial*; *historia novelada.* Buenos Aires: Claridad, 1950, 1953. 576 pp. Translated by Juan Rodríguez Chicano.

Dragon Harvest (1945)

C1044* *La cosecha del dragón*; *historia novelada.* Buenos Aires: Claridad, 1951, 1954. 604 pp. Translated by Juan Rodríguez Chicano.

A World to Win (1946)

C1045* *Un mundo que ganar*; *historia novelada.* Buenos Aires: Claridad, 1952, 1955. 542 pp. Translated by Juan Rodríguez Chicano.

Presidential Mission (1947)

C1046* *Misión presidencia*; *historia novelada.* Buenos Aires: Claridad, 1952, 1954. 566 pp. Translated by Juan Rodríguez Chicano.

One Clear Call (1948)

C1047* *Una clara llamada*; *historia novelada*; *serie Lanny Budd.* Buenos Aires: Claridad, 1953, 1955. 357 pp. Translated by Juan Rodríguez Chicano.

O Shepherd Speak! (1949)

C1048* *Habla, oh pastor! historia novelada*; *serie Lanny Budd.* Buenos Aires: Claridad, 1953, 1955. 520 pp. Translated by Juan Rodríguez Chicano.

Another Pamela (1950)

C1049 *Otra Pamela.* Buenos Aires: Kraft, [n.d.]. 285 pp. Translated by Luis Echavari.

The Return of Lanny Budd (1953)

C1050* *El regreso de Lanny Budd; historia novelada, serie Lanny Budd*. Buenos Aires: Claridad, 1956, 1963. 479 pp. Translated by Juan Rodríguez Chicano.

It Happened to Didymus (1958; What Didymus Did, England, 1954)

C1051* *Lo que hizo Dídimus*. Buenos Aires: J. Muchnik, 1956; Fabril Editora, 1962. 189 pp. Translated by Clara Santos.

Spanish: Brazil

The Jungle (1906)

C1052* *Los envenenadores de Chicago*. Rio de Janeiro, Buenos Aires: Editorial Tor, [n.d.]. 286 pp. Translated by Vicente Vera Y López.

The Flivver King (1937)

C1053* *El rey del automóvil*. Rio de Janeiro, Buenos Aires: Tor, [1939]. 238 pp. Translated by Leonardo A. Wadel.

Spanish: Chile

Jimmie Higgins (1919)

C1054 *Jimmy Higgins* [selections]. [n.p., n.d.].

No Pasarán! (1937)

C1055 *No Pasarán*! Santiago: George V. Duncan, [n.d].

They Call Me Carpenter (1922)

C1056* *Cristo ya regresó*. Mexico City: "Cima," 1940. 364 pp. Translated by S. Jesús Querada.

Spanish: Mexico

No Pasarán! (1937)

C1057* *No Pasarán*! Mexico City: Masas, 1937. 144 pp. Translated by Pedro Zuloaga.

Our Lady (1938)

C1058 *Nuestra señora.* [n.p.]: Schapire, [n.d.]. Translated by Manuel Sendra. See C1037.

Spanish: Spain

The Jungle (1906)

C1059 *La Jungle.* Madrid: Ruiz, 1907. 395 pp. Translated by Vicente Very y López.

C1060* *Los envenenadores de Chicago.* Barcelona: B. Bauzá, 1932. 338 pp. Translated by F. Alaiz.

A Captain of Industry (1906)

C1061 *El caudillo de la industria*; *Ola historia de un millonario.* Barcelona: Salvat, 1907. 138 pp.

Samuel the Seeker (1910)

C1062* *Samuel busca la verdad.* Barcelona: B. Bauzá, [1928]. 256 pp. Translated by Filipe Aláiz.

King Coal (1917)

C1063* *Carbón*! *novela de la cuenca carbonífera del Colorado.* Barcelona: B. Bauzá, [1929; ed. Elite?]. 362 pp. Translated by F. Alaiz. Introduction by G. Brandes.

100%: The Story of a Patriot (1920)

C1064* *Un patriota 100 por 100*; *novela.* Madrid: Cenit., 1930; Establecimientos Tip, 1932. 300 pp. Translated by Manuel Pumarega.

Oil! (1927)

C1065* *Petroleo!* Barcelona: B. Bauzá, 1929, [1930?]. 500 pp. Translated by F. Aláiz.

Boston (1928)

C1066* *Boston* (*El proceso Sacco-Vanzetti*). Barcelona: B. Bauzá, 1930. 640 pp. Translated by F. Alaíz.

Mountain City (1930)

C1067* *Su majestad el rico.* Barcelona: B. Bauzá, 1930. 406 pp. Translated by Manuel Vallvé.

Mental Radio (1930)

C1068* . . . *Radio mental* . . . Barcelona: B. Bauzá, [1933]. 239 pp. Illustrated.

The Wet Parade (1931)

C1069 [*The Wet Parade.*] [n.p.], [1932]. Translated by M. Rodriguez de Aumente.

The Gnomobile (1936)

C1070 *El gnomomóvil.* Barcelona: Toray, 1964. 189 pp. Translated by Mariano Orto. Illustrated by Marcel Tillard.

No Pasarán! (1937)

C1071 *No pasarán! un relato del sitio de Madrid.* Barcelona: Comissariat de Propaganda, 1937. 197 pp. Translated by F. Sussana Montaner(?).

Spanish: Uruguay

Mountain City (1930)

C1072 *Ciudad en la montaña.* Montevideo: Elite, 1946. 317 pp. Translated by Monteverde.

Socialism and Culture (1931)

C1073 "Socialismo y cultura," in *Enciclopedia pequeña socialista.* Vol. I

Apparently a translation of pamphlet *Socialism and Culture* (A1327).

Swedish

Manassas (1904)

C1074* *Manassas, en roman om amerikanska inbördeskriget.* Stockholm: Axel Holmström, 1929. 494 pp. Translated by Johannes Lindberg.

The Jungle (1906)

C1075 *Vildmarken.* Stockholm: Björck & Börjesson, 1906.

C1076 *Vildmarken.* [n.p.]: Excelsior, [n.d.]. Translated by Algot Sandberg.

C1077 *Vildmarken.* Stockholm: Axel Holmström, 1906.

C1078 *Vildmarken.* Stockholm: Axel Holmström, 1926.

C1079* *Vildmarken, Chicagoroman.* Stockholm: Folket i bild, [1950]. 409 pp.

A Captain of Industry (1906)

C1080 *Börsbaronen.* Stockholm: Silén Bokförlag, 1906. Translated by Hugo Gyllander.

C1081 *Börsbaronen.* Stockholm: B. Wahlström, 1913. Translated by Hugo Gyllander.

C1082* *Börsbaronen.* Stockholm: Axel Holmström, 1923, 1928. 118 pp. Translated by Hugo Gyllander.

The Industrial Republic (1907)

C1083* *Industri-republiken, eller, Amerika om tio år.* Stockholm: Björck & Börjeson, [1909]. 245 pp. Translated by Henry V. Kraemer.

The Moneychangers (1908)

C1084* *Wall Street.* Stockholm: Axel Holmström, [1927]. 263 pp. Translated by Eugen Albàn.

Samuel the Seeker (1910)

C1085* *Ett problem.* Stockholm: Nordiska förlaget, [1911]. 190 pp. Translated by Tom Wilson.

C1086 *Ett problem.* Stockholm: Axel Holmström, 1925, 1928. Translated by Tom Wilson.

C1087* *Samuel Sökaren.* Stockholm: Axel Holmström, [1925]. 229 pp. Same as C1086?

Love's Pilgrimage (1911)

C1088* *Kärlekens pilgrimsfärd.* Stockholm: Axel Holmström, [1927]. 2 vols. Translated by Eugen Albàn.

King Coal (1917)

C1089* *Kung Kol.* Stockholm: Axel Holmström, 1917, [1923]. 556 pp.

C1090* *Kung Kol.* Stockholm: Folket i bild, [1950]. 381 pp. Translated by Eugen Albàn.

The Profits of Religion (1918)

C1091* *Under Religionens Täckmantel.* Stockholm: Axel Holmström, 1920–1921, [1926]. 3 vols. Translated by Eugen Albàn.

Jimmie Higgins (1919)

C1092* *Jimmie Higgins.* Stockholm: Axel Holmström, [1924]. 400 pp.

C1093* *Jimmie Higgins.* Stockholm: Tidens Folket i Bild, [1946, 1950]. 326 pp. Translated by Ture Nerman.

100%: The Story of a Patriot (1920)

C1094* *Hundra procent, en patriots historia.* Stockholm: Axel Holmström, [1921]. 334 pp. Translated by Eugen Albàn.

They Call Me Carpenter (1922)

C1095* *Man kallar mig timmerman; en historia om Kristi återkomst.* Stockholm: Axel Holmström, [1926]. 210 pp. Translated by Eugen Albàn.

The Millennium (1924)

C1096* *Det tusenåriga riket.* Stockholm: Axel Holmström, [1924], 1928. 160 pp. Translated by Ture Nerman.

Singing Jailbirds (1924)

C1097* *Sjungande fängelsefåglar.* Stockholm: Axel Holmström, [1929]. 128 pp. Translated by Ture Nerman.

Mammonart (1925)

C1098* *Gyllene länkar.* Stockholm: Axel Holmström, [1928]. 544 pp. Translated by Eugen Albàn.

Letters to Judd (1926)

C1099* *Brev till Judd.* Stockholm: Axel Holmström, [1928]. 123 pp. Translated by Eugen Albàn.

Oil! (1927)

C1100* *Bunny Ross* (*Olja*). Stockholm: Axel Holmström, Folket i bild, [n.d.], 1950. 276 pp. Translated by Eugen Albàn.

C1101* *Olja.* Stockholm: Folket i bild, [1950]. 293 pp. Translated by Eugen Albàn.

Money Writes! (1927)

C1102* *Så gör man dollars.* Stockholm: Axel Holmström, [1931]. 422 pp. Translated by Eugen Albàn.

C1103* *Så gör man dollars.* Stockholm: Tiden, [1950]. 291 pp.

Boston (1928)

C1104* *Boston.* Stockholm: Axel Holmström, [1928–1929]. 3 vols. Translated by Eugen Albàn.

Mental Radio (1930)

C1105 *Mental Radio.* Stockholm: Axel Holmström, [n.d.].

C1106 *Mental Radio.* Stockholm: Silèn Bokförlag, 1938. Translated by Tira Helberg.

The Wet Parade (1931)

C1107* *Våta paraden.* Stockholm: Axel Holmström, [1934]. 571 pp. Translated by Eugen Albàn.

The Gnomobile (1936)

C1108 *Gnomobilen.* Stockholm: Bonnier, 1966. Translated by Claes Gripenberg.

Co-op (1936)

C1109 *Co-op.* Stockholm: Axel Holmström, 1938.

The Flivver King (1937)

C1110* *Bilkungen, en roman om Henry Ford.* Stockholm: Axel Holmström, 1938. 224 pp. Translated by Arne Holmström.

C1111 *Bilkungen, en roman om Henry Ford.* Stockholm: Folket i bild, 1960. 253 pp. Translated by Arne Holmström.

No Pasaran! (1937)

C1112 *Våra Liv för Spanien.* Stockholm: A. Holmström, 1937. 212 pp. Translated by Arne Holmström.

Little Steel (1938)

C1113**Kämpande stål.* Stockholm: Axel Holmström, [1939]. 310 pp. Translated by Arne Holmström.

World's End (1940)

C1114* *De sådde vind.* Stockholm: Axel Holmström, 1944, 1949. 799 pp. Translated by Arne Holmström.

Between Two Worlds (1941)

C1115* *Mellan två världar.* Stockholm: Axel Holmström, 1942, [1946]. 864 pp. Translated by Karl Vennberg.

Dragons' Teeth (1942)

C1116* *Drakens tänder.* Stockholm: Axel Holmström, 1943. 696 pp. Translated by Karl Vennberg.

C1117 *Drakens tänder.* Stockholm: Tiden, 1950. 603 pp. Translated by Erik Lindegren and Karl Vennberg.

Wide Is the Gate (1943)

C1118* *Förtappelsens väg.* Stockholm: Axel Holmström, [1944]. 765 pp. Translated by Karl Vennberg.

Presidential Agent (1944)

C1119* *Presidentens agent.* Stockholm: Axel Holmström, [1945]. 785 pp. Translated by Karl Vennberg.

Dragon Harvest (1945)

C1120* *Drakskörd.* Stockholm: Axel Holmström, 1946. 854 pp. Translated by Arne Holmström.

A World to Win (1946)

C1121 *En värld att vinna.* Stockholm: Axel Holmström, 1947. 562 pp. Translated by Arne Holmström.

Presidential Mission (1947)

C1122* *Presidentens uppdrag.* Stockholm: Tidens förlag, [1949]. 622 pp. Translated by Maud Adlercreutz.

A Giant's Strength (1948)

C1123 *Allmänheten måste bereda sig på det värsta.* Stockholm: Alb. Bonnier, 1949. 81 pp. Translated by Börje Lindell.

One Clear Call (1948)

C1124* *Signal till uppbrott.* Stockholm: Tiden, [1950]. 714 pp. Translated by Knut Stubbendorff.

The Cup of Fury (1956)

C1125 *Giftbägaren.* Stockholm: Central Press, 1958. 198 pp. Translated by Erik Janson.

Tajik (see also Russian): U.S.S.R.

100% (1920)

C1126 *Sto protsentov.* Dushanbe-Samarkand: Tadzhikgosizdat, 1932. 156 pp. Translated by S. Ali-Zade.

Tamil: India

The Jungle (1906)

C1127* *Mirugavalkai.* [Madras?]: Tirunelveli, [1945]. 200 pp. Translated by S. Sanmukham.

The Fasting Cure (1911)

C1128 *Upavaca cikiccai.* Madras: Sutantiraccanku karyalayam, 1937. 87 pp. Translated by S. Ganesan.

The Millennium (1924)

C1129 *Putu Yukam, kipi Irantayirattil.* Madras: Allied, 1958. 138 pp. Translated by S. Sanmukham.

Boston (1928)

C1130 *Puratci Virar Sacco-Vanzetti.* Tiruchirapalli: Star pracuram, 1946. 190 pp. Translated by S. Sanmukham.

The Wet Parade (1931)

C1131 [*The Wet Parade.*] Madras: P. G. Sundarajan, 1937.

Tatar (see also Russian): U.S.S.R.

The Jungle (1906)

C1132 *Dzhungli.* Simferopol': Krymgiz, 1930. 111 pp. Translated by I. Aiserezli.

Jimmie Higgins (1919)

C1133* *Dzhimmi Khiggins.* Kazan': Tatgosizdat, 1934. 158. pp. Translated by G. Habib.

100% (1920)

C1134 *Pletka o dvukh kontsakh. Otryvok iz romana "Sto protsentov."* Kazan': Ianalif, 1929. 16 pp. (Excerpt.)

Turkish

The Jungle (1906)

C1135 [*The Jungle.*] Constantinople: Son Saat, [n.d.].

Mammonart (1925)

C1136* *Altin zincir* (*Sanat tarihi*). Istanbul: Numune Matbaasi, 1940. 235 pp. Translated by Emin Türk Eliçin.

C1137 *Altin Zincir.* [n.p.]: "May Yayinlari," 1966. 308 pp. Translated by Emin Türk Eliçin.

C1138 *Sanayi Kirali.* Izmir: Gutenberg Matbaasi, 1962. 91 pp. Translated by Cevat Sakir Kabaagacli. (Excerpt.)

Turkmen (see also Russian): U.S.S.R.

King Coal (1917)

C1139 *Korol' ugol'.* Ashkhabad: Turkmengosizdat, 1938. 408 pp.

Ukrainian (see also Russian): Canada

The Jungle (1906)

C1140* *Netrv.* Winnipeg: "Rus'ka Knyharnia," 1919. 332 pp.

A Captain of Industry (1906)

C1141 *Heroi kapitalu.* Winnipeg: K., druk I-i Kiivs'k druk spilki; Kiev-L'viv: [n.p.], 1911, 1918. 60 pp. Translated by N. Romanovych.

Ukrainian: U.S.S.R.

The Jungle (1906)

C1142* *Netry.* Kiev: K., druk I-i Kiivs'k druk spilki, 1908. 308 pp. Translated by M. Levyts'kyi.

C1143 *Netry*. Kharkiv: "Ukrainskii robotnik," 1930. 202 pp. Translated by M. Levyts'kyi.

C1144 *Netry. (Dzhungli) (Debry)*. Kharkiv: "Ukrainskii robotnik," 1930, 1931. 130 pp. Translated by M. Levyts'kyi.

A Captain of Industry (1906)

C1145 *Heroi kapitalu*. Kiev: Vseukr. Derzh Vid-vo, 1920, 1921. 102 pp. Translated by N. Romanovych.

C1146 *Heroi kapitalu*. Kharkiv: Derzh. Vid. Ukr., 1927. 392 pp. Translated by N. Romanovych. 2nd ed.

Samuel the Seeker (1910)

C1147* *Samuel'-iskatel'*. Kiev: Derzh. Vid. Ukr., 1927. 316 pp. Translated by N. T. Kuchma.

C1148* *Khobo. p'iesa na p'iat' dii*. Kharkiv: Derzhvydav Ukrainy, 1926. 121 pp. Translated by A. Panov. Adapted by P. S. Hlaholin.

Hobo. A Play in Five Acts: an adaptation of the novel *Samuel the Seeker*.

King Coal (1917)

C1149* *Korol' ugol'*. Kharkiv: Ukrgiz, 1927. 428 pp. Translated by N. T. Kuchm. Edited by M. Johansen.

Jimmie Higgins (1919)

C1150 *Kzhimmi Khiggins*. Kharkiv-Kiev: Literatura i mistatstvo, 1933. 400 pp. Translated by D. Egorova.

100% (1920)

C1151* *Sto protsentov. Istoriia odnogo patriota*. Kharkiv: Derzh. Vid-vo Ukrainy, 1928. 316 pp. Translated by L. Skripnik.

They Call Me Carpenter (1922)

C1152* *Mene zovut' tesleiu. Povist' pro druhe prishestia.* Kharkiv, Katerynoslav: Derzhvydav Ukrainy, 1925. 157 pp. Translated by Ie. Kas'ianenko.

C1153 *Mene zovut' tesleiu. Povist' pro druhe pryshestia.* Kharkiv-Kyiv: Literatura i mystetstvo, 1932. 196 pp. Translated by Ie. Kas'ianenko.

The Millennium (1924)

C1154 *Kinets' staroho svitu.* Kharkiv: "Knyhospilka," 1925. 91 pp. Translated by H. Borysovych.

Uzbek (see also Russian): U.S.S.R.

King Coal (1917)

C1155 [*King Coal.*] Tashkent-Samarkand: Gosizdat, 1933.

C1156* *Korol' ugol'.* Tashkent-Samarkand: Gosizdat, 1933. Same as C1555?

White Russian (see also Russian): U.S.S.R.

The Second Story Man (1912)

C1157 *Vor.* Minsk: Belgosizdat, 1930. 16 pp.

Hell! (1923)

C1158 *Zlodzei. P'esa u adnei dzei.* Minsk: Belar. dzerzd. vid., 1930. 15 pp.

Translation of the adaptation by Naz. B.

The Flivver King (1937)

C1159 *Avtomobil'nyi korol'.* Minsk: DUB Mastatskaia lit., 1939. 92 pp.

No Pasaran! (1937)

C1160 *No pasaran!* (*Oni ne proidut.*) Minsk: Dziarzh. vid. Belarusi Mastatskaia lit-ra, 138. 208 pp. Translated by V. A. Liaudanskii.

Yiddish: Poland

Prince Hagen (1903)

C1161 [*Prince Hagen.*] [n.p.]: Lowicz, 1932.

The Jungle (1906)

C1162 *Zump.* Warszawa: Sh. Goldfarb, 1928. 2 vols. 476 pp. Translated by Mark Fogelman.

A Captain of Industry (1906)

C1163 *Der Americaner Millioner.* Warszawa: Romanzeitung, 1924. 98 pp.

Samuel the Seeker (1910)

C1164 *Der Sucher fun Emes.* Warszawa: Sh. Goldfarb, 1927. 250 pp. Translated by Mark Fogelman.

King Coal (1917)

C1165 *Kenig Koyl un zeyne msharsim.* Warszawa: Sh. Goldfarb, 1931.

Jimmie Higgins (1919)

C1166 *Dzimi Hugiens.* Warszawa: Sh. Goldfarb, 1927, 1930. 409 pp. Translated by Mark Fogelman.

100% (1920)

C1167 *100%. Roman fun a patriot.* Warszawa: "Die Welt," 1923, 1927. 249 pp. Translated by Y. S. Szapir.

The Book of Life (1921)

C1168 *Dos Buch fun Leben.* Warszawa: Jackowski, 1929, 312 pp. Translated by Y. Rapaport.

They Call Me Carpenter (1922)

C1169 *Tyszler.* Warszawa: Sh. Goldfarb, 1929. 245 pp. Translated by Mark Fogelman.

The Millennium (1924)

C1170 *Der Suf. Fantastiszer roman funjar 2000.* Warszawa: Sh. Goldfarb, 1930. 212 pp. Translated by Jechiel Sztajn.

Mammonart (1925)

C1171 *Kunst und Gelt.* Warszawa: Sh. Goldfarb, 1930. 230 pp. Translated by Mark Fogelman.

Letters to Judd (1926)

C1172 [*Letters to Judd.*] Warszawa: "Pol," 1929, 1932. 113 pp.

C1173 *Briv tsv Arbeter.* Warszawa: Jackowski, 1930. 113 pp. Translated by Elim Borzsztajn.

Oil! (1927)

C1174 *Petroleum.* Warszawa: Sh. Goldfarb, 1928–1929. 2 vols. 896 pp. Translated by A. Erlikh. 2nd ed.: 1932.

Boston (1928)

C1175 *Boston, di tragedje fun Sacco un Wanzetti.* Warszawa: Farleg J. A. Cuker, 1929. 357 pp. Translated by Mark Fogelman.

C1176 *Boston.* Warszawa: Miedzynardowa Ajencja Dziennikow, 1930.

C1177 *Boston.* Warszawa: Sh. Cukier, 1930. 182 pp.

C1178 *Boston.* Warszawa: Die Welt, 1930. 3 vols. 1193 pp. Translated by Mark Fogelman.

C1179 *Boston, di tragedje fun Sako un Wancete.* Warszawa: J. A. Cuker, 1931. 874 pp. Translated by Mark Fogelman.

Yiddish: U.S.S.R.

The Moneychangers (1908)

C1180 *Wallstreet.* Minsk: [n.p.], 1929. 188 pp.

C1181 *Geld.* Minsk: White-Russian Verlag, 1929. 190 pp.

Samuel the Seeker (1910)

C1182 *Samuel Der Emes-Zukher.* Kiev: Kulturlige, 1928. 223 pp. Translated by D. Hofshtein.

King Coal (1917)

C1183 *Kenig Koil.* Moskva: School and Book, 1925. 389 pp. Translated by A. Veviurko.

III. Publications about Upton Sinclair

D. Selected Bibliographical Sources

D1 Upton Sinclair. *Books of Upton Sinclair in Translations and Foreign Editions.* Pasadena: The Author, August 1930. 36 pp.

A bibliography of 525 titles in 34 countries. See D5.

D2 Upton Sinclair. *Books of Upton Sinclair in Russia: Proceedings of Literary Groups and Workers' Clubs of the Metal Workers of Leningrad.* Pasadena: The Author, May 1931. 35 pp.

Printing of young Russian workers' comments on Sinclair's novels.

D3 *Checklist of the Morse Collection.* Typescript, [*c.* 1932]. 34 pp.

Part of the *Sinclair Collection from the Library of Dr. and Mrs. Elmer Belt,* Occidental College Library, Pasadena, Calif.
Pt. I—Books by Upton Sinclair, 15pp.
Pt. III—Periodical articles by Upton Sinclair, 19pp.
Three other parts contain references to book and magazine references to Sinclair and his books. See D11.

D4 Joseph Gaer, ed. *Upton Sinclair: Bibliography and Biographical Data.* California Literary Research Project (Monograph #6), Mimeograph, 1935. 55 pp.
Recently reprinted.

D5 Upton Sinclair. *Books of Upton Sinclair in Translations and Foreign Editions.* Pasadena: The Author, August 1938. 48 pp.

A bibliography of 772 titles in 47 languages, 39 countries.

D6 Fred B. Millett, *Contemporary American Authors.* New York: Harcourt, Brace and World, 1940, pp. 579–586.

An excellent if understandably incomplete listing of major works.

D7 Elizabeth Bantz. "Upton Sinclair: Book Reviews and Criticism Published in German and French Periodicals and Newspapers," *Bulletin of Bibliography*, XVIII (January/April 1946), 204–206.

D8 Upton Sinclair. *Upton Sinclair Anthology.* Preface by Upton Sinclair. Introduction by Irving Stone and Lewis Browne. Culver City, California: Murray and Gee, 1947. Bibliography pp. 347–351.

D9 *We Have Made Arrangements to Sell the Works of Upton Sinclair Brought Out by Other Publishers.* Girard, Kansas: Haldeman-Julius Publications, 1948. 8 pp.

D10 Albert Mordell. "Haldeman-Julius and Upton Sinclair," *The Critic and Guide*, IV (February 1950), 94–119.

Many leads and references.

D11 Kate Trauman Steinitz and Margot Archer. *The Upton Sinclair Collection from the Library of Dr. and Mrs. Elmer Belt.* Typescript, 1950. 52 pp.

Next to the Lilly Library's, the best publicly available collection.

D12 Arnold Biella. *Upton Sinclair: Crusader.* Dissertation, Stanford University, 1954. Bibliography pp. 297–333.

Bibliography incomplete but helpful.

D13 Glenora W. and Deming B. Brown. *A Guide to Soviet Russian Translations of American Literature.* New York: King's Crown Press (Columbia University), 1954, pp. 38, 178–192.

D14 Lewis Leary. *Articles on American Literature, 1900–1950.* Durham, North Carolina: Duke University Press, 1954, pp. 274–275.

D15 Harry Laidler. "Upton Sinclair at Eighty; List of Books, Pamphlets and Leaflets by Upton Sinclair in the Tamiment Institute Library," *The Tamiment Institute Library* no. 17 (September 1958), pp. 1–7.

D16 I.O. Evans. *Upton Sinclair: A Bibliography.* Typescript, 1960. 36 pp.

Copy at the Lilly Library.

D17 Frederic Litto. *The Dramatic World of Upton Sinclair, a Survey of the Published and Unpublished Plays.* From unpublished Ms., Indiana University, 1960. 21 pp.

Copy at the Lilly Library.

D18 Richard Mummendey. *Belle Lettres of the United States of America in German Translation.* Charlottesville, Virginia: Bibliographical Society of the University of Virginia, 1961, pp. 148–152.

D19 Edward Allatt. *A Classified Checklist of a Collection of Upton Sinclair Material in England.* Holograph, March 1963. 36 pp.

Copies of several supplements at the Lilly Library. Allatt's collection is superb and carefully maintained; supplements prepared frequently.

D20 Ronald Gottesman. *A Catalogue of Books, Manuscripts, and Other Materials from the Upton Sinclair Archives.* Bloomington, Indiana: Lilly Library, 1963. 56 pp.

D21 Robert Spiller, *et al. Literary History of the United States: Bibliography.* 3rd ed., rev. New York: Macmillan, 1963, pp. 723–725 and Supplements.

D22 Ronald Gottesman. "The Upton Sinclair Dime Novels," *Dime Novel Round-up*, XXXIII (15 March 1964), 20–23.

D23 Ronald Gottesman. *Upton Sinclair: an Annotated Bibliographical Catalogue, 1894–1932.* Dissertation, Indiana University, 1964. 409 pp.

D24 Valentin A. Libman (comp.), Robert V. Allen (trans.), and Clarence Gohdes (ed.). *Russian Studies of American Literature.* Chapel Hill, N.C.: University of North Carolina Press, 1969.

Pages 164–173 list reviews, mentions, articles, prefaces, dissertations, etc., devoted to Sinclair. Arranged chronologically (1906–1963) and very useful.

D25 Ronald Gottesman and Charles Silet. *The Literary Manuscripts of Upton Sinclair.* Ohio State University Press, forthcoming 1972. Includes unpublished as well as published manuscripts.

For more intensive bibliographies, including secondary material, see bibliographies in dissertations listed below and in other compilations such as D24.

E. Selected Reviews of Upton Sinclair's Books

King Midas (Springtime and Harvest 1901)

E1 *Literary Digest*, XXIII (26 October 1901), 509.

E2 *Outlook*, LXIX (20 November 1901), 839.

E3 *Argonaut*, L (10 February 1902), 89.

The Journal of Arthur Stirling (1903)

E4 *Independent*, LV (12 March 1903), 625–626.

E5 Arthur Bartlett Maurice. *Bookman*, XVII (March 1903), 84–85.

E6 *Literary World*, XXXIV (March 1903), 51.

E7 *Dial*, XXXIV (1 May 1903), 311.

E8 *Athenaeum*, 20 June 1903, pp. 778–779.

E9 *Literary Digest*, XXXVI (20 June 1908), 908.

E10 *Spectator*, CLI (16 September 1933), 352.

E11 Hamish Miles. *The New Statesman*, n.s. VI (23 September 1933), 357.

E12 *Times Literary Supplement* [London], 28 September 1933, p. 652.

E13 *Public Opinion* [London], CXLIV (27 October 1933), 412.

E14 *Punch*, CLXXXV (15 November 1933), 560.

Prince Hagen (1903)

E15 *Literary World*, XXXIV (June 1903), 137–38.

E16 Quentin MacDonald. *Book News Monthly*, XXI (July 1903), 868.

E17 *International Socialist Review*, IV (August 1903), 124.

E18 *Independent*, LV (24 September 1903), 2292.

As Play (1910)

E19 *Progress Magazine*, X (June 1910).

Manassas (1904)

E20 *Independent*, LVII (17 November 1904), 1149–1151.

E21 *Bookman*, XX (November 1904), 178–179.

E22 *Nation*, LXXIX (1 December 1904), 441.

E23 *Outlook*, LXXVIII (3 December 1904), 872.

E24 *Arena*, XXXII (December 1904), 676–677.

E25 W. M. Payne. *Dial*, XXXVIII (1 January 1905), 15.

E26 *International Socialist Review*, V (February 1905), 507.

E27 *American Review of Reviews*, XXXI (January 1905), 117.

E28 *Current Literature*, XXXVIII (February 1905), 184.

E29 *Saturday Review* [London], CLV (1 April 1933), 317.

E30 *Times Literary Supplement* [London], 20 April 1933, p. 274.

E31 *Public Opinion* [London], CXLIII (28 April 1933), 403.

E32 *Public Affairs*, II (April 1924), 26.

The Jungle (1906)

E33 Jack London. *Chicago Socialist*, 25 November 1905, p. 2.
Review of the serial version.

E34 *Louisville Courier-Journal*, 24 February 1906, p. 5.

E35 *Chicago Record-Herald*, 26 February 1906, p. 5.

E36 *Arena*, XXXV (February 1906), 186–187.

E37 *New York Times Saturday Review*, 3 March 1906, p. 128.

E38 *Independent*, LX (24 March 1906), 740.

E39 *Outlook*, LXXXII (31 March 1906), 758.

E40 *Athenaeum*, I (14 April 1906), 446.

E41 *Public Opinion*, XL (14 April 1906), 476.

E42 William M. Payne. *Dial*, XL (16 April 1906), 262.

E43 Edward C. Marsh. *Bookman*, XXIII (April 1906), 195.

E44 *Book News Monthly*, XXIV (April 1906), 575.

E45 *Reader*, VII (April 1906), 564.

E46 *Literary Digest*, XXXII (5 May 1906), 679.

E47 *Spectator*, XCVI (19 May 1906), 793.

E48 *Saturday Review*, CI (26 May 1906), 661.

E49 *Critic*, XLVII (May 1906), 476.

E50 *Current Literature*, XL (May 1906), 562–563.

E51 *Everybody's Magazine*, XIV (May 1906), 712–713.

E52 *Times Literary Supplement* [London], 1 June 1906, p. 201.

E53 *New York Times Saturday Review*, 16 June 1906, p. 384.

E54 Winston Churchill. *P.T.O.*, I (16 June 1906), 25–26; I (23 June 1906), 65–66.

E55 *Arena,* XXXV (June 1906), 651.

E56 *North American Review*, CLXXXII (June 1906), 925.

E57 *American Review of Reviews*, XXXIII (June 1906), 759.

E58 Eugene V. Debs. *Appeal to Reason*, 21 July 1906, p. 3.

E59 *Critic*, XLIX (July 1906), 4.

E60 H. Norman. *World's Work*, VIII (July 1906), 163.

E61 Jack London. *New York Evening Journal*, 8 August 1906, p. 2.

E62 Frederick Boyd Stevenson. *Wilshire's Magazine* [London], X (August 1906), 12.

E63 Jack London. *Wilshire's Magazine* [London], X (August 1906), 10.

E64 *Bookman*, XXIV (September 1906), 2–3.

E65 *Critic*, XLIX (September 1906), 195.

E66 Literary Digest, XXXIII (7 October 1906), 595.

E67 *Independent*, LXI (15 November 1906), 1158.

E68 Madeleine Z. Doty. *Charities*, XVII (15 December 1906), 480.

E69 *American Library Association Booklist*, III (January 1907), 27.

E70 Mary Moss. *Atlantic Monthly,* XCIX (January 1907), 122.

E71 The *New Statesman*, XXXIII (1 June 1929), 246, 248.

E72 Herbert Abrams. *Chicago News,* 19 June 1929, p. 13 (Midweek Features).

E73 R. Duffus. *New York Times Book Review*, 13 October 1946, p. 3.

E74 James T. Farrell. *New Republic*, CXV (4 November 1946), 601.

E75 L.L.L. Golden. *Saturday Review*, XLIX (12 November 1966), 103.
As much about Sinclair as book.

The Industrial Republic (1907)

E76 *Times Literary Supplement* [London], 19 July 1907, p. 229.

E77 *New York Times Saturday Review*, 20 July 1907, p. 451.

E78 *Academy*, LXXIII (3 August 1907), 746.

E79 *Spectator*, XCIX (17 August 1907), 231.

E80 *Independent*, LXIII (31 October 1907), 1060–1061.

E81 *Journal of Political Economy*, XV (November 1907), 572.

The Overman (1907)

E82 *New York Times Saturday Review*, 5 October 1907, p. 600.

E83 *New York Times Saturday Review*, 19 October 1907, p. 652.

E84 *San Francisco Call*, 20 October 1907.

The Metropolis (1908)

E85 *Nation*, LXXXVI (19 March 1908), 263–264.

E86 *Saturday Review*, CV (28 March 1908), 409.

E87 *Athenaeum*, no. 4197 (4 April 1908), p. 413.

E88 *Spectator*, C (4 April 1908), 544.

E89 *Literary Digest*, XXXVI (11 April 1908), 528.

E90 William Morton Payne. *Dial*, XLIV (16 April 1908), 246–247.

E91 *Current Literature*, XLIV (May 1908), 569–570.

E92 *Independent*, LXV (30 July 1908), 264–265.

E93 Johan Barrett. *Everybody's Magazine*, XIX (July 1908), 138–139.

The Moneychangers (1908)

E94 *New York Times Saturday Review*, 19 September 1908, p. 506.

E95 *Nation*, LXXXVII (22 October 1908), 389.

E96 *New York Times Saturday Review*, 24 October 1908, p. 615.

E97 *Bookman*, XVIII (October 1908), 111–115.

E98 *Saturday Review*, CVI (7 November 1908), 581.

E99 B. O. Flower. *Arena*, XL (December 1908), 623–625.

Good Health and How We Won It (1909)

E100 *New York Times Saturday Review*, 6 March 1909, p. 134.

E101 *Literary Digest*, XXXVIII (20 March 1909), 474.

E102 H. L. Mencken. *The Smart Set*, XXVII (March 1909), 154.

E103 *Independent*, LXVII (11 November 1909), 1092.

Samuel the Seeker (1910)

E104 *New York Times Saturday Review*, 16 April 1910, p. 214.

E105 *Book News Monthly*, XXVIII (10 June 1910), 775–776.

E106 *Nation*, XC (23 June 1910), 629.

E107 *Athenaeum*, II (23 July 1910), 93.

E108 *Spectator*, CV (30 July 1910), 178.

E109 *Bookseller* [London], DCCVII (12 August 1910), 1028, 1032.

E110 *Saturday Review* [London], CX (17 September 1910), 365.

Love's Pilgrimage (1911)

E111 J. B. Kerfoot. *Life*, LVII (4 May 1911), 890.

E112 *Independent*, LXX (11 May 1911), 1010.

E113 B. Russell Herts. *Book News Monthly*, XXIX (May 1911), 600.

E114 G. F. Douglas. *San Francisco Chronicle*, 4 June 1911, p. 6.

E115 *New York Times Book Review*, 2 July 1911, p. 424.

E116 G. Middleton. *Bookman*, XXXIII (11 July 1911), 549.

E117 R. Burton. *Bellman* [Milwaukee], XI (12 August 1911), 210.

E118 *American Review of Reviews*, XLIV (September 1911), 382.

E119 *The New Statesman*, XXXIII (1 June 1929), 246, 248.

Plays of Protest (1912)

E120 *New York Times Book Review*, 18 February 1912, p. 83.

E121 R. Burton. *Bellman* [Milwaukee], XII (16 March 1912), 339.

E122 *Independent*, LXXII (25 April 1912), 897.

E123 Albert S. Henry. *Book News Monthly*, XXXI (December 1912), 288.

Sylvia (1913)

E124 R.B. *Boston Transcript*, 17 May 1913, p. 6.

E125 L.M.F. *New York Times Book Review*, 25 May 1913, p. 310.

E126 *Book News Monthly*, XXXI (June 1913), 756.

E127 *Nation*, XCVII (10 July 1913), 34.

E128 *Current Opinion*, LV (July 1913), 51.

E129 H. L. Mencken. *The Smart Set*, XL (August 1913), 160.

E130 *Wilshire's Magazine*, XVII (October 1913), 8.

E131 Wilkinson Sherren. *Bookman*, XLVI (July 1914), 180.

Damaged Goods (1913)

E132 *Times Literary Supplement* [London], 17 September 1931, p. 708.

Sylvia's Marriage (1914)

E133 *New York Times Book Review*, 25 October 1914, p. 463.

E134 *Nation*, XCIX (25 October 1914), 463.

The Cry for Justice (1915)

E135 Emanuel [Haldeman-] Julius. *New York Call*, 25 July 1915, Sect. 2, pp. 8–9.

E136 *Outlook*, CX (18 August 1915), 931.

E137 *American Review of Reviews*, LII (September 1915), 379.

E138 Alexandar Mackendrick. *Dial*, LIX (28 October 1915), 376.

E139 *New York Times Book Review*, 28 November 1915, p. 479.

E140 M.H.B. Mussey. *Survey*, XXXV (11 December 1915), 302.

E141 J.H.T. *International Journal of Ethics*, XXVI (January 1916), 305.

E142 *New Republic*, VI (5 February 1916), 26.

King Coal (1917)

E143 *New York Times Book Review*, 23 September 1917, p. 354.

E144 D. P. Berenberg. *New York Call*, 7 October 1917, p. 14.

E145 *Times Literary Supplement* [London], 11 October 1917, p. 493.

E146 *Nation*, CV (11 October 1917), 403.

E147 R.T.P. *Boston Transcript*, 16 October 1917, p. 6.

E148 Georg Brandes. *Appeal to Reason*, 20 October 1917, p. 3.

E149 *Literary Digest*, LV (27 October 1917), 42.

E150 R.B. *New Republic*, XII (27 October 1917), 359.

E151 *American Library Association Booklist*, XIV (November 1917), 63.

E152 *Athenaeum*, no. 4623 (November 1917), p. 596.

E153 H. W. Boynton. *Bookman*, XLVI (November 1917), 338.

E154 J. A. Fitch. *Survey*, XXXIX (1 December 1917), 257.

E155 Francis Wilson Wyatt. *Dial*, LXIII (1 December 1917), 587.

E156 *Spectator*, CIX (8 December 1917), 681.

E157 *Cleveland Open Shelf*, 17 December 1917, 133.

The Profits of Religion (1918)

E158 Upton Sinclair. *Chicago Daily News*, 12 February 1919, p. 12.

E159 A. H. Howland. *New York Call*, 16 February 1919, p. 10.

E160 Alexander Mackendrick. *Public*, XXII (February 1919), 114.

E161 *Nation*, CVIII (15 March 1919), 404.

E162 H. L. Mencken. *The Smart Set*, LVIII (March 1919), 143–144.

E163 *New Republic*, XVIII (12 April 1919), 352.

Jimmie Higgins (1919)

E164 Francis Hackett. *New Republic*, XIX (31 May 1919), 154.

E165 *New York Times Book Review*, 1 June 1919, p. 306.

E166 H. W. Boynton. *Weekly Review*, I (21 June 1919), 126–127.

E167 *Springfield* [Mass.] *Republican*, 22 June 1919, p. 17.

E168 *Nation*, CVIII (28 June 1919), 1017.

E169 H. W. Boynton. *Bookman*, XLIX (July 1919), 578.

E170 *Athenaeum*, no. 4660 (22 August 1919), p. 800.

E171 L. H. Joachim. *Public*, XXII (23 August 1919), 910.

E172 *Catholic World*, CIX (August 1919), 687.

E173 Frank Harris. *Pearson's Magazine*, XLII (August 1919), 467.

E174 E.F.E. *Boston Transcript*, 17 September 1919, p. 4.

The Brass Check (1920)

E175 *Springfield* [Mass.] *Republican*, 22 February 1928, p. 13A.

E176 Heywood Broun. *New York Tribune*, 28 March 1920, sect. 7, p. 9.

E177 H. L. Mencken. *The Smart Set*, LXI (April 1920), 138–140.

E178 J. G. McDonald. *Survey*, XLIV (29 May 1920), 307.

E179 M. C. Crook. *Socialist Review*, VIII (May 1920), 382.

E180 E. H. Gruening. *Nation*, CXI (17 July 1920), 72.

E181 *International Journal of Ethics*, XXXI (October 1920), 116.

E182 H. L. West. *Bookman*, LII (October 1920), 116.

E183 W. J. Ghent. *Weekly Review*, III (3 November 1920), 420.

E184 *Times Literary Supplement* [London], 4 November 1920, p. 712.

E185 Edwin Bjorkman. *Freeman*, II [10 November), 212.

E186 *Literary Digest*, LXVIII (15 January 1921), 30–31.

E187 J. J. Smertenko. *Grinnell* [Iowa] *Review*, XVI (January 1921), 329.

100% (1920)

E188 *Nation*, CXI (27 October 1920), 481.

E189 *New Republic*, xxv (12 January 1921), back cover.

E190 G. H. *World Tommorow*, iv (January 1921), 30.

E191 H. L. Mencken. *The Smart Set*, LXIV (February 1921), 143–144.

The Book of Life: Vol. I (1921)

E192 *New York World*, 8 October 1921, p. 9.

E193 J. J. Smertenko. *New York Post Literary Review*, 18 February 1922, p. 426.

The Book of Life: Vol. II (1922)

E194 *New York Times Book Review*, 11 June 1922, p. 25.

E195 H. L. Mencken. *The Smart Set*, LXVIII (July 1922), 138–144.

E196 Dorothy Brewster. *Nation*, cxv (23 August 1922), 193.

E197 A. E. R. *New Age*, xxxi (3, 10, 17, 24 August 1922), 174–175, 186–187, 199–200, 214–215.

E198 *Bookman*, LVI (September 1922), 105.

E199 Frank Harris. *Pearson's Magazine*, XLVII (September 1922), 26–28.

E200 Robert Herrick. *New Republic*, XXXII (18 October 1922), 203.

They Call Me Carpenter (1922)

E201 E. L. Pearson. *Independent*, CIX (30 September 1922), 167.

E202 *Springfield* [Mass.] *Republican*, 8 October 1922, p. 7A.

E203 *Survey*, XLIX (1 November 1922), 210 (supplement).

E204 *New York Post Literary Review*, 18 November 1922, p. 219.

The Goose-Step (1923)

E205 *Springfield* [Mass.] *Republican*, 23 March 1923, p. 12.

E206 L.S. *New York World*, 25 March 1923, p. 9E.

E207 John Macy. *Nation*, CXVI (11 April 1923), p. 433. (supplement).

E208 C. Merz. *New Republic*, XXXIV (11 April 1923), p. 8. (supplement).

E209 H. S. Canby. *New York Post Literary Review*, 14 April 1923, p. 602.

E210 *Boston Transcript*, 21 April 1923, p. 4.

E211 *The New Statesman*, XXI (12 May 1923), 150.

E212 *Dial*, LXXIV (May 1923), 523.

E213 J.W.F. *Double Dealer*, V (May 1923), 174–175.

E214 H. L. Mencken. *The Smart Set*, LXXI (May 1923), 141–144.

E215 H. L. Stuary. *Freeman*, VII (13 June 1923), 332.

E216 J.K.H. *Survey*, L (15 June 1923), 353.

E217 *Bookman*, LVII (June 1923), 464.

E218 *American Library Association Booklist*, IX (July 1923), 301.

E219 E. L. Talbot. *School and Society*, XVIII (27 October 1923), 491–497.

The Goslings (1924)

E220 H. L. Mencken. *Baltimore Evening Sun*, 23 February 1924, p. 6.

E222 *Springfield* [Mass.] *Republican*, 4 April 1924, p. 12.

E223 J. W. Crawford. *New York Times Book Review*, 6 April 1924, p. 10.

E224 D.R. *Boston Transcript*, 19 April 1924, p. 5.

E225 *The New Statesman*, XXIII (19 April 1924), 50.

E226 J. K. Hart. *New Republic*, XXXVIII (21 May 1924), 343.

E227 *Public Affairs*, II (May 1924), 32.

E228 *Bookman*, LIX (July 1924), 609.

E229 C. H. Grattan. *Nation*, CIX (1 October 1924), 340.

Singing Jailbirds (1924)

E230 Charles Norman. *New York Post Literary Review*, 6 September 1924, p. 9.

E231 Max Beerbohm. *New York Times Book Review*, 5 October 1924, p. 2.

E232 G. H. Pouder. *Baltimore Evening Sun*, 11 October 1924, p. 8.

E233 John W. Crawford. *New York World*, 14 December 1924, p. 8E.

E234 J.S. *Manchester Guardian*, 10 February 1930, p. 15.

E235 H.H. *Observer* [London], 16 February 1930, p. 15.

Singing Jailbirds Performance (1928—)

E236 Ernest W. Gross. *New York Herald-Tribune Books*, 6 November 1928, p. 2.

E237 Robert Littell. *New York Post Literary Review*, 5 December 1928, p. 12.

E238 Arthur Ruhl. *New York Herald-Tribune Books*, 9 December 1928, p. 1.

E239 Upton Sinclair. *New York Times Book Review*, 23 December 1928, p. 4.

E240 Gladys E. Meyerand. *World Tomorrow*, XII (March 1929), 112.

E241 J. E. Sewell. *The New Statesman*, XXXIV (1 March 1930), 666.

The Millennium (1924 England—1929)

E242 *Manchester Guardian*, 27 September 1929, p. 7.

E243 E. K. Wakeford. *Bookfinder Illustrated* [London], III (October 1929), 14 .

E244 *Times Literary Supplement* [London], 10 October 1929, p. 796.

E245 *Public Opinion* [London], CXXXVI (11 October 1929), p. 356.

E246 Stanley E. James. *Catholic Times* [London], 18 October 1929.

Mammonart (1925)

E247 *Milwaukee Leader*, 12 January 1925, p. 7.

E248 J. D. Adams. *New York Times Book Review*, 22 March 1925, p. 12.

E249 B.P.H. *Boston Transcript*, 28 March 1925, p. 10.

E250 Ernest Boyd. *Independent*, CXIV (11 April 1925), 418.

E251 *Independent*, CXIV (11 April 1925), 422.

E252 Edwin Seaver. *New York Post Literary Review*, 11 April 1925, p. 7.

E253 V. F. Calverton. *Nation*, CXX (15 April 1925), 440.

E254 Edmund Wilson. *New Republic*, XLII (22 April 1925), 236–237.

E255 C. W. Thompson. *International Book Review*, III (May 1925), 406.

E256 W. L. Phelps. *Scribner's Magazine*, LXXVII (May 1925), 546.

E257 *Outlook*, CXL (17 June 1925), 268.

E258 Floyd Dell. *Bookman*, LXI (June 1925), 480.

E259 H. L. Mencken. *American Mercury*, V (June 1925), 252–253.

E260 *Double Dealer*, VII (June 1925), 198.

E261 Helen Sahler. *World Tomorrow*, VII (July 1925), 220.

E262 *Saturday Review*, CXL (19 September 1925), 315.

E263 *Dial*, LXXIX (September 1925), 262.

E264 *Times Literary Supplement* [London], 1 October 1925, p. 642.

E265 Raymond Weaver. *New York Herald-Tribune Books*, 13 December 1925, p. 14.

E266 Joseph T. Shipley. *New York Leaders*, 23 January 1926, p. 11.

E267 G. W. Stonier. *The New Statesman and Nation*, n.s. VIII (8 September 1934), 300, 302.

Bill Porter (1925)

E268 *Washington* [D.C.] *Herald*, 20 September 1925, p. D3.

E269 R. W. Thompson. *Literary Review*, VI (7 November 1925), 9.

E270 Joseph T. Shipley. *New Leader*, 23 January 1926, p. 11.

E271 *Independent*, CXVI (27 February 1926), 257.

E272 *Boston Transcript*, 26 June 1926, p. 5.

E273 *Public Affairs*, V (November 1925), 21–22.

Letters to Judd (1926)

E274 *Washington* [D.C.] *Herald*, 11 April 1926, p. D5.

E275 *New York Herald-Tribune Books*, 5 September 1926, p. 15.

E276 *Nation*, CXXIII (29 September 1926), 301–302.

The Spokesman's Secretary (1926)

E277 *New York Times Book Review*, 15 August 1926, p. 13.

E278 *Milwaukee Leader*, 28 August 1926, p. 6.

E279 *Public Affairs*, VII (November 1926), 20.

E280 Tom White. *Overland Monthly*, Ser. 2, LXXXV (June 1927), 20.

Oil! (1927)

E281 *Huntington* [W.Va.] *Advertiser*, 27 March 1927.

E282 *Independent*, CXVIII (9 April 1927), 393.

E283 W.E.H. *Boston Transcript*, 30 April 1927, p. 5.

E284 *New York Times Book Review*, 8 May 1927, p. 22.

E285 J. W. Wise. *New York Post Literary Review*, 21 May 1927, p. 5.

E286 Johan Smertenko. *Nation*, CXXIV (8 June 1927), 643.

E287 Floyd Dell. *New York Herald-Tribune Books*, 12 June 1927, p. 7.

E288 W. McFee. *New Republic*, LI (15 June 1927), 104.

E289 Vern Smith. *The Daily Worker*, 15 June 1927, p. 6.

E290 R. G. Tugwell. *Saturday Review of Literature*, III (2 July 1927), 942.

E291 *World Tomorrow*, X (July 1927), 316.

E292 *Public Affairs*, IX (July 1927), 15.

E293 *Spectator*, CXXXIX (13 August 1927), 261.

E294 *Times Literary Supplement* [London], 21 August 1927.

E295 Geoffrey West. *London Daily Herald*, 26 August 1927, p. 3.

E296 Willis J. Ballinger. *Washington* [D.C.] *Evening Star*, 28 August 1927.

E297 James Fuchs. *New Masses*, III (August 1927), 27.

E298 *Times Literary Supplement* [London], 20 September 1927, p. 644.

E299 Floyd Dell. *Forum*, LXXVIII (September 1927), 479.

E300 Leon Whipple. *Survey*, LIX (1 October 1927), 52.

E301 L. P. Hartley. *Saturday Review*, CXLIV (8 October 1927), 482.

E302 G. R. Stirling Taylor. *Bookman*, LXXIII (October 1927), 34–35.

E303 B.W. *Springfield* [Mass.] *Republican*, 6 November 1927, p. 7F.

Money Writes! (1927)

E304 Sender Garlin. *The Daily Worker*, 26 October 1927, p. 4.

E305 Harry Hansen. *New York World*, 19 November 1927, p. 11.

E306 Elmer Davis. *New York Herald-Tribune Books*, 22 November 1927, p. 23.

E307 *New York Herald-Tribune Books*, 27 November 1927, p.27.

E308 Herschel Brickell. *New York Evening Post*, 30 November 1927, p. 13.

E309 Heywood Broun. *Nation*, CXXV (7 December 1927), 622–623.

E310 Ernest Boyd. *Independent*, CIX (10 December 1927), 579.

E311 *New Yorker*, III (10 December 1927), 122–123.

E312 Donald Douglas. *New York Herald-Tribune Books*, 18 December 1927, p. 1.

E313 Leon Whipple. *Survey*, LIX (1 January 1928), 464.

E314 Joseph T. Shipley. *New Leader* [London], I (7 January 1928), 5.

E315 Robert Herrick. *New Republic*, LIII (11 January 1928), 227.

E316 *Boston Transcript*, 25 January 1928, p. 4.

E317 H. R. Massey. *Nation*, CXXVI (8 February 1928), 163.

E318 C. W. Wood. *New York Evening Post*, 18 February 1928, p. 11.

E319 H. L. Mencken. *American Mercury*, XIII (February 1928), 253–254.

E320 *Saturday Review*, CXLVI (21 July 1928), 88.

E321 *Times Literary Supplement* [London], 2 August 1928, p. 562.

E322 *World Tomorrow*, XI (September 1928), 375.

E323 Bernard Smith. *New Masses*, III (November 1928), 20–21.

E324 *Times Literary Supplement* [London], 4 June 1931, p. 442.

E325 *Manchester Guardian*, 10 June 1931, p. 5.

E326 *Spectator*, CXLVII (11 July 1931), 64.

E327 *Public Opinion* [London], CXL (7 August 1931), 134.

Boston (1928)

E328 John Clair Minot. *Boston Herald*, 28 January 1928, p. 5.

E329 *Boston Transcript*, 28 January 1928, Sect. 5, p. 5.

E330 Courtney Ferrett. *New York Telegram*, 28 January 1928, p. 3.

E331 Sender Garlin. *The Daily Worker*, 4 February 1928, p. 7.

E332 *New Leader* [London], I (4 February 1928), 5.

E333 *New York Times Book Review*, 5 February 1928, p. 22.

E334 Heywood Broun. *New York World*, 8 February 1928.

E335 Floyd Dell. *New York Herald-Tribune Books*, 11 November 1928, p. 3.

E336 R. M. Lovett. *New Republic*, LVI (14 November 1928), 354.

E337 Horace Gregory. *New York Evening Post*, 17 November 1928, p. 8M.

E338 S. A. DeWitt. *New Leader* [London], VII (17 November 1928), 5.

E339 Edwin H. Blanchard. *New York Sun*, 17 November 1928, p. 26.

E340 *New York Times Book Review*, 18 November 1928, p. 6.

E341 Bernard Smith. *New York World*, 25 November 1928, p. 10M.

E342 K.S. *Boston Transcript*, 1 December 1928, p. 4.

E343 Joseph T. Shipley. *New Leader* [London], VII (1 December 1928), 4.

E344 R. N. Linscott. *Saturday Review of Literature*, V (1 December 1928), 425.

E345 Arthur G. Hays. *Survey Graphic*, LXI (1 December 1928), 315.

E346 James Rorty. *Nation*, CXXVII (5 December 1928), 618 (supplement).

E347 Arthur Hays. *Survey Graphic*, LXI (December 1928), 315–318.

E348 *Washington* [D.C.] *Herald*, 1 January 1929.

E349 *Times Literary Supplement* [London], 24 January 1929, p. 60.

E350 *Public Opinion* [London], CXXXV (11 January 1929), 37.

E351 *Spectator*, XLII (19 January 1929), 93.

E352 Gerald Gould. *Observer* [London], 20 January 1929, p. 8.

E353 *Times Literary Supplement* [London], 24 January 1929, p. 60.

E354 B.K.M. *Manchester Guardian*, 15 February 1929, p. 7.

E355 *American Library Association Booklist*, XXV (February 1929), 214.

E356 T. S. Matthews. *Bookman*, LXVIII (February 1929), 688.

E357 A. W. Taylor. *Christian Century*, XLVI (14 March 1929), 359.

E358 *Dial*, LXXXVI (March 1929), 264.

E359 L. W. Legge. *World Tomorrow*, XII (April 1929), 183.

E360 *The New Statesman*, XXXIII (1 June 1929), 248.

E361 Joseph North. *New Masses*, V (October 1929), 24–25.

Mountain City (1930)

E362 G.B. *New York Telegram*, 7 March 1930, p. 5.

E363 Bernard Smith. *New York Evening Post*, 8 March 1930, p. 11M.

E364 *New York Times*, 9 March 1930, p. 9.

E365 *The Rocky Mountain News* [Denver], 23 March 1930, Sect. 3, p. 6.

E366 Halle Schaffner. *New York Herald-Tribune Books*, 6 April 1930, p. 15.

E367 L. W. Dodd. *Saturday Review of Literature*, VI (19 April 1930), 944.

E368 *The New Statesman*, XXXV (17 May 1930), 192.

E369 R.M.L. *New Republic*, LXIII (28 May 1930), 54.

E370 V. F. Calverton. *Nation*, CXXX (11 June 1930), 680.

E371 *Times Literary Supplement* [London], 19 June 1930, p. 512.

E372 *Spectator*, CLXIV (21 June 1930), 1019.

E373 Stirling Bowen. *Bookman*, LXXI (August 1930), 543.

E374 *American Library Association Booklist*, XXVII (September 1930), 30.

E375 *World Tomorrow*, XIII (November 1930), 375.

E376 *Christian Century*, XLVII (10 December 1930), 1531.

Mental Radio (1930)

E377 *Philadelphia Record*, 19 April 1930, p. 11.

E378 *New York Sun*, 2 May 1930, p. 30.

E379 *Saturday Review*, CXLIX (10 May 1930).

E380 *New York Times Book Review*, 15 June 1930, p. 20.

E381 *Times Literary Supplement* [London], 3 July 1930, p. 548.

E382 *New York Herald Books*, 6 July 1930, p. 15.

E383 *Springfield* [Mass.] *Republican*, 6 July 1930, p. 5E.

E384 *Survey*, LXIV (15 August 1930), 448.

E385 Albert Einstein. *South Bend* [Ind.] *Times*, 21 September 1930.

E386 *American Mercury*, XXI (October 1930), xxxvi, xxxviii.

E387 *Bookman*, LXXII (October 1930), xv.

Roman Holiday (1931)

E388 Ida Gilbert Hyers. *Washington* [D.C.] *Star*, 4 January 1931, sect. 7, p. 20.

E389 Harry Hansen. *New York World*, 8 January 1931, p. 13.

E390 *New York World-Telegram*, 9 January 1931, p. 9.

E391 Mary Ross. *New York Herald-Tribune Books*, 11 January 1931, p. 5.

E392 *New York Times Book Review*, 11 January 1931, p. 15.

E393 F. L. Robbins. *Outlook*, CLVII (14 January 1931), 67.

E394 Arthur Ruhl. *Saturday Review of Literature*, VII (17 January 1931), 532.

E395 V. F. Calverton. *Nation*, CXXXII (4 February 1931), 132–133.

E396 James Rorty. *New Republic*, LXV (11 February 1931), 358.

E397 Gerald Gould. *Observer* [London], 15 February 1931, p. 6.

E398 *Times Literary Supplement* [London], 19 February 1931, p. 132.

E399 H. C. Harwood. *Saturday Review*, CLI (21 February 1931), 276.

E400 *Spectator*, CXLVI (21 February 1931), 281.

E401 I.W.L. *Boston Transcript*, 25 February 1931, p. 2.

E402 *Christian Century*, XLVIII (25 February 1931), 274.

E403 *Public Opinion* [London], CXXXIX (6 March 1931), 234.

E404 *Wisconsin Library Bulletin*, XXVII (March 1931), 83.

E405 *American Library Association Booklist*, XXVII (May 1931), 409.

E406 *Bookman*, LXXIII (July 1931), iv.

E407 *World Tomorrow*, XIV (November 1931), 376.

The Wet Parade (1931)

E408 *Chicago Tribune*, 10 September 1931, p. 17.

E409 Isabel Paterson. *New York Herald-Tribune Books*, 10 September 1931, p. 19.

E410 *Christian Science Monitor*, 12 September 1931, p. 12.

E411 Stanley Walker. *New York Herald-Tribune Books*, 13 September 1931, p. 1.

E412 P.H. *Christian Century*, XLVIII (16 September 1931), 1145.

E413 Ben Blumenburg. *New Leader* [London], XIII (19 September 1931), 5.

E414 *New York Times Book Review*, 20 September 1931, p. 6.

E415 H. L. Mencken. *Nation*, CXXXIII (23 September 1931), 310.

E416 A. W. Porterfield. *Outlook*, CLIX (23 September 1931), 120.

E417 *New Yorker*, VII (26 September 1931), 79–81.

E418 Robert Herrick. *New Republic*, LXVIII (7 October 1931), 213.

E419 H. C. Harwood. *Saturday Review*, CLII (10 October 1931), 463.

E420 *Times Literary Supplement* [London], 29 October 1931, p. 838.

E421 Arthur Kellogg. *Survey*, LXVII (1 November 1931), 151.

E422 L. A. Strong. *Spectator*, CXLVII (7 November 1931), 616.

E423 Basil Davenport. *Saturday Review of Literature*, VIII (28 November 1931), 327.

E424 *North American Review*, CCXXXII (November 1931), 474.

E425 *American Library Association Booklist*, XXVIII (November 1931), 106.

E426 Emily Newell Blair. *Good Housekeeping*, XCIV (January 1932), 165.

E427 A. Elistratova. *International Literature*, II–III (1932), 134–35.

American Outpost (1932)

E428 C. H. Grattan. *Nation*, CXXXIV (13 April 1932), 432.

E429 Lewis Gannett. *New York Herald-Tribune Books*, 14 April 1932, p. 15.

E430 *New York Times Book Review*, 14 April 1932, p. 19.

E431 Fanny Butcher. *Chicago Daily Tribune*, 16 April 1932, p. 16.

E432 William MacDonald. *New York Herald-Tribune Books*, 17 April 1932, p. 3.

E433 *New Yorker*, VIII (23 April 1932), 75–77.

E434 John Chamberlain. *New York Times Book Review*, 1 May 1932, p. 5.

E435 L. W. Dodd. *Saturday Review of Literature*, VIII (7 May 1932), 709.

E436 *Times Literary Supplement* [London], 16 June 1932, p. 444.

E437 Newton Arvin. *New Republic*, LXXI (22 June 1932), 160.

E438 *American Library Association Booklist*, XXVIII (June 1932), 433.

E439 John Strachey. *Spectator*, CXLIX (9 July 1932), 55.

E440 *Pittsburgh Monthly Bulletin*, XXXVII (July 1932), 49.

E441 Leon Whipple. *Survey*, LXVIII (July 1932), 312.

E442 Edmund Wilson. *New Republic*, LXXII (28 September 1932), 173–175.

E443 *American Mercury*, XXVII (September 1932), xxvi, xxviii.

E444 H. S. Tigner. *Christian Century*, XLIX (19 October 1932), 1276.

Upton Sinclair Presents William Fox (1933)

E445 Lewis Gannett. *New York Herald-Tribune Books*, 14 February 1933, p. 15.

E446 S. A. Dewitt. *New Leader* [London], XV (18 February 1933), 9.

E447 Roy Chansler. *New York Evening Post*, 4 March 1933, p. 9.

E448 Edward Kennedy. *Saturday Review of Literature*, IX (11 March 1933), 475.

E449 J. T. Flynn. *Nation*, CXXXVI (15 March 1933), 291.

E450 A. A. Heist. *Christian Century*, L (5 April 1933), 462.

E451 K.P. *World Tomorrow*, XVI (12 April 1933), 356.

E452 H. P. Fairchild. *New Republic*, LXXIV (19 April 1933), 287.

E453 D.C.S. *Churchman*, CXLVII (1 May 1933), 34–35.

E454 *New York Times Book Review*, 14 May 1933, p. 4.

E455 *Public Opinion* [London], CXLIII (26 May 1933), 496.

E456 *Catholic World*, CXXXVII (May 1933), 242.

E457 *Springfield* [Mass.] *Republican*, 18 June 1933, p. 73.

E458 H. L. Mencken. *American Mercury*, XXIX (June 1933), 252–254.

E459 Herschel Brickell. *North American Review*, CCXXXV (June 1933), 573.

E460 *American Library Association Booklist*, XXIX (July 1933), 340.

The Way Out (1933)

E461 William Soskin. *New York Post Literary Review*, 31 May 1933, p. 11.

E462 *New Republic*, LXXV (28 June 1933), 189.

E463 *Boston Transcript*, 12 July 1933, p. 2.

E464 *Public Opinion* [London], CXLIV (28 July 1933), 86.

E465 *American Library Association Booklist*, XXIX (July 1933), 329.

E466 *Times Literary Supplement* [London], 3 August 1933, p. 526.

E467 Leon Whipple. *Survey Graphic*, XXII (August 1933), 427.

E468 *Review of Reviews [London]*, LXXXIV (August 1933), 77.

E469 Louis Rich. *Saturday Review of Literature*, X (16 September 1933), 118.

I, Governor of California, and How I Ended Poverty (1933)

E470 Lewis Gannett. *New York Herald-Tribune Books*, 15 December 1933, p. 23.

E471 *New York Times Book Review*, 31 December 1933, p. 5.

E472 Arthur Warner. *Nation*, CXXXVIII (21 February 1934), 226.

An Upton Sinclair Anthology (1934)

E473 *Times Literary Supplement* [London], 29 March 1934, p. 231.

E474 Lewis Gannett. *New York Herald-Tribune Books*, 18 June 1934, p. 13.

E475 A.B.T. *Boston Transcript*, 7 July 1934, p. 1.

E476 Eric Ely-Estorich. *Nation*, CXXXIX (12 September 1934), 308.

I, Candidate for Governor, and How I Got Licked (1935)

E477 *San Francisco Chronicle*, 14 November 1934, p. 1.

E478 H. L. Mencken. *Baltimore Evening Sun*, 28 January 1935, 2nd sect., p. 15.

E479 Edward Angly. *New York Herald-Tribune Books*, 10 February 1935, p. 18.

E480 *Boston Transcript*, 16 February 1935, p. 5.

E481 *Times Literary Supplement* [London], 21 February 1935, p. 99.

E482 *Saturday Review of Literature*, XI (13 April 1935), 625.

E483 W. E. Garrison. *Christian Century*, LII (1 May 1935), 577.

What God Means to Me (1936)

E484 *Time*, XXVII (27 January 1936), 58.

E485 Alfred Kazin. *New York Times Book Review*, 2 February 1936, p. 2.

E486 Lincoln Steffens. *Pacific Weekly*, 17 February 1936.

E487 J. H. Holmes. *New York Herald-Tribune Books*, 15 March 1936, p. 26.

E488 *Cleveland Open Shelf*, March 1936, p. 7.

E489 *Manchester Guardian*, 28 April 1936, p. 8.

E490 *American Library Association Booklist*, XXXII (April 1936), 220.

E491 *Times Literary Supplement* [London], 6 June 1936, p. 483.

Co-op (1936)

E492 F. T. Marsh. *New York Herald-Tribune Books*, 27 September 1936, p. 8.

E493 Garrett Mattingly. *Saturday Review of Literature*, XIV (3 October 1936), 10.

E494 S.Y. *New York Times Book Review*, 4 October 1936, p. 6.

E495 *Time*, XXVIII (5 October 1936), 68.

E496 Fred T. Marsh. *Epic News*, III (5 October 1936), 7.

E497 William Phillips. *Nation*, CXLIII (10 October 1936), 422.

E498 B.B.F. *Christian Science Monitor*, 12 October 1936, p. 14.

E499 W. E. Harris. *Boston Transcripts*, 24 October 1936, p. 6.

E500 J. D. Beresford. *Manchster Guardian*, 13 November 1936, p. 7.

E501 *Times Literary Supplement* [London], 14 November 1936, p. 925.

E502 *American Library Association Booklist*, XXXIII (November 1936), 84.

E503 *Wisconsin Library Bulletin*, XXXII (November 1936), 111.

E504 Helen Marsh. *Canadian Forum*, XVI (December 1936), 36.

E505 Mary Ross. *Survey Graphic*, XXVI (January 1937), 44.

The Gnomobile (1936)

E506 E. M. Mack. *Boston Transcript*, 21 November 1936, p. 4.

E507 *Wisconsin Library Bulletin*, XXXIII (January 1937), 12.

The Flivver King (1937)

E508 P.H. *Saturday Review of Literature*, XVII (13 November 1937), 11.

E509 Robert Cantwell. *New Republic*, XCII (22 December 1937), 203.

E510 Mark Farrell. *Canadian Forum*, XVII (January 1938), 362.

E511 Margaret Marshall. *Nation*, CXLVI (19 February 1938), 222.

E512 V. S. Pritchett. *The New Statesman and Nation*, XV (12 March 1938), 43.

E513 *Times Literary Supplement* [London], 12 March 1938, p. 172.

E514 *Wisconsin Library Bulletin*, XXXIV (March 1938), 47.

E515 R. C. Feld. *New York Herald-Tribune Books*, 22 May 1938, p. 8.

E516 F. T. Marsh. *New York Times Book Review*, 22 May 1938, p. 7.

Our Lady (1938)

E517 Norah Hoult. *New York Times Book Review*, 12 June 1938, p. 14.

E518 J. H. Holmes. *New York Herald-Tribune Books*, 3 July 1938, p. 10.

E519 *Brooklyn Daily Eagle*, 11 July 1938, p. 5.

E520 *Times Literary Supplement* [London], 14 January 1939, p. 27.

Terror in Russia? Two Views (1938; with Eugene Lyons)

E521 V.M.D. *Saturday Review of Literature*, XVIII (19 July), 21.

E522 *New Republic*, XCVI (10 August 1938), 28.

E523 D.B. *Christian Science Monitor*, 7 September 1938, p. 16.

E524 *Foreign Affairs*, XVII (January 1939), 445.

Little Steel (1938)

E525 *Boston Transcripts*, 24 September 1938, p. 3.

E526 *American Library Association Booklist*, XXXV (1 October 1938), 48.

E527 *New Yorker*, XIV (1 October 1938), 78.

E528 F. T. Marsh. *New York Herald-Tribune Books*, 2 October 1938, p. 10.

E529 John Chamberlain. *New Republic*, XCVI (5 October 1938), 246.

E530 *Saturday Review of Literature*, XVIII (8 October 1938), 21.

E531 R. C. Feld. *New York Times Book Review*, 16 October 1938, p. 16.

E532 J. A. Breig. *Commonweal*, XXIX (28 October 1938), 23.

E533 John Mair, *The New Statesman and Nation*, XVI (10 December 1938), 1010.

E534 *Times Literary Supplement* [London], 10 December 1938, p. 783.

E535 Helen Marsh. *Canadian Forum*, XVIII (January 1939), 316.

E536 C. M. Kirk. *Survey Graphic*, XXVIII (January 1939), 34.

Marie Antoinette (1939)

E537 W. P. Eaton. *New York Herald-Tribune Books*, 23 July 1939, p. 11.

E538 K.W. *New York Times Book Review*, 30 July 1939, p. 9.

E539 *Times Literary Supplement* [London], 9 September 1939, p. 531.

E540 Byron Dexter. *New Republic*, C (27 September 1939), 223.

World's End (1940)

E541 H. T. Moore. *Saturday Review of Literature*, XXII (15 June 1940), 5.

E542 F. T. Marsh. *New York Herald-Tribune Books*, 16 June 1940, p. 3.

E543 R. L. Duffus. *New York Times Book Review*, 16 June 1940, p. 1.

E544 Lewis Gannett. *Boston Transcript*, 18 June 1940, p. 11.

E545 E. B. Gulick. *Boston Transcript*, 22 June 1940, p. 1.

E546 Clifton Fadiman. *New Yorker*, XVI (22 June 1940), 68.

E547 Granville Hicks. *New Republic*, CII (24 June 1940), 863.

E548 *Time*, XXXV (24 June 1940), 92.

E549 W. J. Grace. *Commonweal*, XXXII (5 July 1940), 234.

E550 *American Library Association Booklist*, XXXVI (15 July 1940), 430.

E551 John Chamberlain. *Nation*, CLI (20 July 1940), 54.

E552 *Catholic World*, CLI (July 1940), 503.

E553 *Cleveland Open Shelf*, July 1940, p. 16.

E554 *Wisconsin Library Bulletin*, XXXVI (July 1940), 127.

E555 *Times Literary Supplement* [London], 24 August 1940, p. 409.

E556 Wilfred Gibson. *Manchester Guardian*, 30 August 1940, p. 6.

E557 G. E. Shipler, Jr. *Churchman*, CLIV (1 September 1940), 20.

E558 W. E. Garrison. *Christian Century*, LVII (4 September 1940), 1079.

E559 Brian Howard. *The New Statesman and Nation*, XX (7 September 1940), 243.

E560 George Orwell. *The Tribune* [London], 13 September 1940, p. 14.

E561 Marguerite Wyke. *Canadian Forum*, XXVII (September 1940), 188.

Between Two Worlds (1941)

E562 Esther Johnston. *Library Journal*, LXVI (15 March 1941), 265.

E563 *New Yorker*, XVII (22 March 1941), 84.

E564 H. T. Moore. *Saturday Review of Literature*, XXIII (22 March 1941), 9.

E565 R. L. Duffus. *New York Times Book Review*, 23 March 1941, p. 4.

E566 *Springfield* [Mass.] *Republican*, 23 March 1941, p. 7E.

E567 *Time*, XXXVII (24 March 1941), 90.

E568 L. B. Saloman. *Nation*, CLII (29 March 1941), 386.

E569 Milton Rugoff. *New York Herald-Tribune Books*, 30 March 1941, p. 4.

E570 *American Library Association Booklist*, XXXVII (1 April 1941), 360.

E571 W. C. Derry. *Boston Transcript*, 5 April 1941, p. 2.

E572 Lloyd Eshleman. *Commonweal*, XXXIII (11 April 1941), 326.

E573 G. E. Shipler, Jr. *Churchman*, CLV (15 April 1941), 18.

E574 *Wisconsin Library Bulletin*, XXXVII (April 1941), 77.

E575 M.I.T. *Canadian Forum*, XXI (May 1941), 59.

E576 Harold Brighouse. *Manchester Guardian*, 17 October 1941, p. 3.

E577 *Times Literary Supplement* [London], 18 October 1941, p. 517.

E578 Anthony West. *The New Statesman and Nation*, XXII (15 November 1941), 427.

Dragon's Teeth (1942)

E579 Lena Ruppert. *Library Journal*, LXVII (1 January 1942), 41.

E580 R. J. Conklin. *Springfield* [Mass.] *Republican*, 4 January 1942, p. 7E.

E581 Milton Rugoff. *New York Herald-Tribune Books*, 4 January 1942, p. 2.

E582 *Time*, XXXIX (5 January 1942), 68.

E583 *New Yorker*, XVII (10 January 1942), 59.

E584 John Cournos. *New York Times Book Review*, 11 January 1942, p. 4.

E585 *Nation*, CLIV (17 January 1942), 73.

E586 R. R. Plant. *Saturday Review of Literature*, XXV (24 January 1942), 7.

E587 Kay Boyle. *New Republic*, CVI (26 January 1942), 125.

E588 *Commonweal*, XXXV (30 January 1942), 372.

E589 *American Library Association Booklist*, XXXVIII (1 February 1942), 190.

E590 *Wisconsin Library Bulletin*, XXXVIII (February 1942), 32.

E591 Wilson Follett. *Atlantic Monthly*, CLXIX (March 1942), 17.

E592 *Canadian Forum*, XXI (March 1942), 381.

E593 G. E. Shipler, Jr. *Churchman*, CLVI (1 April 1942), 16.

E594 *Catholic World*, CLV (May 1942), 254.

E595 *Times Literary Supplement* [London], 18 July 1942, p. 357.

E596 Harold Brighouse. *Manchester Guardian*, 24 July 1942, p. 3.

E597 Philip Toynbee. *The New Statesman and Nation*, XXIV (22 August 1942), 129.

Wide Is the Gate (1943)

E598 F. T. Marsh. *New York Herald-Tribune Books*, 3 January 1943, p. 2.

E599 E. W. Watts. *Boston Globe*, 6 January 1943, p. 15.

E600 R. Duffus. *New York Times Book Review*, 10 January 1943, pp. 2, 21.

E601 Malcolm Cowley. *New Republic*, CVIII (11 January 1943), 58.

E602 *American Library Association Booklist*, XXXIX (15 February 1943), 253.

E603 Joseph McSorley. *Catholic World*, CLVI (March 1943), 754.

E604 *Library Journal*, LXVIII (1 September 1943), 670.

E605 L. E. Grinter. *Chicago Sun Book Week*, 3 October 1943, p. 10.

E606 *Canadian Forum*, XXIII (November 1943), 191.

Presidential Agent (1944)

E607 *Virginia Kirkus Bookshop Service*, XII (1 April 1944), 148.

E608 H. S. Taylor. *Library Journal*, LXIX (1 June 1944), 502.

E609 *New Yorker*, XX (3 June 1944), 82.

E610 Sterling North. *Chicago Sun Book Week*, 4 June 1944, p. 1.

E611 R. L. Duffus. *New York Times Book Review*, 4 June 1944, p. 1.

E612 F. T. Marsh. *New York Herald-Tribune Weekly Book Review*, 4 June 1944, p. 3.

E613 Struthers Burt. *Saturday Review of Literature*, XXVII (10 June 1944), 7–8.

E614 Lee Varley. *Springfield* [Mass.] *Republican*, 11 June 1944, p. 4D.

E615 Margaret Marshall. *Nation*, CLIX (15 June 1944), 74.

E616 Francis Downing. *Commonweal*, XL (30 June 1944), 258.

E617 *American Library Association Booklist*, XL (15 July 1944), 390.

E618 L.A.S. *Christian Science Monitor*, 29 July 1944, p. 12.

E619 Allan Spalding. *New Republic*, CXI (16 October 1944), 499.

E620 *Wisconsin Library Bulletin*, XL (October 1944), 131.

Dragon Harvest (1945)

E621 *Virginia Kirkus Bookshop Service*, XII (15 April 1945), 162.

E622 E. B. Burgum. *New York Times Book Review*, 10 June 1945, p. 5.

E623 F. T. Marsh. *New York Herald Tribune Weekly Book Review*, 10 June 1945, p. 2.

E624 *American Library Association Booklist*, XLI (15 June 1945), 302.

E625 Hamilton Basso. *New Yorker*, XXI (16 June 1945), 60.

E626 H. M. Jones. *Saturday Review of Literature*, XXVIII (16 June 1945), 9.

E627 Sterling North. *Chicago Sun Book Week*, 17 June 1945, p. 2.

E628 *Springfield* [Mass.] *Republican*, 17 June 1945, p. 4D.

E629 Joseph McSorley. *Catholic World*, CLXI (June 1945), 363.

E630 *New Republic*, CXIII (23 July 1945), 111.

E631 *Cleveland Open Shelf*, September 1945, p. 20.

A World to Win (1946)

E632 *Virginia Kirkus Bookshop Service*, XIV (1 May 1946), 201.

E633 L. R. Etzkorn. *Library Journal*, LXXI (15 May 1946), 759.

E634 *New Yorker*, XXII (25 May 1946), 93.

E635 P. W. Ferris. *Chicago Sun Book Week*, 26 May 1946, p. 3.

E636 *American Library Association Booklist*, XLII (1 June 1946), 318.

E637 Perry Miller. *New York Times Book Review*, 2 June 1946, p. 4.

E638 *Time*, XLVII (3 June 1946), 106.

E639 W. S. Lynch. *Saturday Review of Literature*, XXIX (15 June 1946), 18.

E640 *Springfield* [Mass.] *Republican*, 16 June 1946, p. 4D.

E641 F. T. Marsh. *New York Herald-Tribune Weekly Book Review*, 16 June 1946, p. 5.

E642 *Christian Science Monitor*, 22 June 1946, p. 14.

E643 John Farrelly. *New Republic*, CXIV (24 June 1946), 910.

E644 J. C. Cort. *Commonweal*, LXIV (28 June 1946), 265.

E645 Eleanor McNaught. *Canadian Forum*, XXVI (July 1946), 94.

E646 H. M. Jones, *Atlantic Monthly*, CLXXVIII (August 1946), 148.

Presidential Mission (1947)

E647 *Virginia Kirkus Bookshop Service*, XV (15 March 1947), 169.

E648 *American Library Association Booklist*, XLIII (15 May 1947), 291.

E649 L. R. Etzkorn. *Library Journal*, LXXII (15 May 1947), 810.

E650 H. M. Robinson. *Saturday Review of Literature*, XXX (17 May 1947), 9.

E651 P. W. Ferris. *Chicago Sun Book Week*, 18 May 1947, p. 3.

E652 Perry Miller. *New York Times Book Review*, 18 May 1947, p. 5.

E653 *New Yorker*, XXIII (24 May 1947), 105.

E654 *Time*, XLIX (26 May 1947), 106.

E655 Milton Rugoff. *New York Herald-Tribune Weekly Book Review*, 15 June 1947, p. 10.

E656 Marvin Sargent. *San Francisco Chronicle*, 22 June 1947, p. 15.

E657 Eleanor McNaught. *Canadian Forum*, XXVII (14 August 1947), 18.

One Clear Call (1948)

E658 *Virginia Kirkus Bookshop Service*, XVI (1 July 1948), 313.

E659 Maxwell Geismar. *Saturday Review of Literature*, XXXI (28 August 1948), 13.

E660 Perry Miller. *New York Times Book Review*, 29 August 1948, p. 5.

E661 E. D. Doyle. *San Francisco Chronicle*, 29 August 1948, p. 19.

E662 L. R. Etzkorn. *Library Journal*, LXXIII (August 1948), 1091.

E663 *American Library Association Booklist*, XLV (1 September 1948), 14.

E664 *New Yorker*, XXIV (4 September 1948), 80.

E665 Emmett Dedmon. *Chicago Sun Book Week*, 5 September 1948, p. 7X.

E666 F. H. Bullock. *New York Herald-Tribune Weekly Book Review*, 5 September 1948, p. 7.

E667 *Time*, LII (6 September 1948), 90.

E668 *Springfield* [Mass.] *Republican*, 19 September 1948, p. 7B.

E669 *Wisconsin Library Bulletin*, XLIV (October 1948), 166.

O Shepherd, Speak (1949)

E670 *Virginia Kirkus Bookshop Service*, XVII (15 May 1949), 255.

E671 *American Library Association Booklist*, XLV (1 June 1949), 326.

E672 Jack Conroy. *Chicago Sun-Times*, 21 July 1949, p. 41. (under column "Book Days.")

E673 F. H. Bullock. *New York Herald-Tribune Weekly Book Review*, 24 July 1949, p. 4.

E674 Perry Miller. *New York Times Book Review*, 24 July 1949, p. 5.

E675 E. D. Doyle. *San Francisco Chronicle*, 24 July 1949, p. 16.

E676 *Time*, LIV (25 July 1949), 84–85.

E677 Edmund Fuller. *Saturday Review of Literature*, XXXII (30 July 1949), 17.

E678 L. R. Etzkorn. *Library Journal*, LXXIV (July 1949), 1026.

E679 *New Yorker*, XXV (6 August 1949), 61.

E680 O. D. Hormel. *Christian Science Monitor*, 11 August 1949, p. 11.

E681 *Springfield* [Mass.] *Republican*, 14 August 1949, p. 7B.

E682 Eleanor McNaught. *Canadian Forum*, XXIX (October 1949), 165.

Another Pamela (1950)

E683 *American Library Association Booklist*, XLVI (15 February 1950), 194, 262.

E684 *Virginia Kirkus Bookshop Service*, XVIII (15 February 1950), 115.

E685 E. S. Brown. *Library Journal*, LXXV (1 April 1950), 561.

E686 Granville Hicks. *New York Times Book Review*, 23 April 1950, p. 30.

E687 Robert Halsband. *Saturday Review of Literature*, XXXIII (29 April 1950), 14.

E688 Lorine Pruette. *New York Herald-Tribune Book Review*, 30 April 1950, p. 9.

E689 *San Francisco Chronicle*, 4 May 1950, p. 20.

E690 *Time*, LV (8 May 1950), 98.

E691 *Chicago Sunday Tribune*, 14 May 1950, p. 9.

E692 *New Yorker*, XXVI (20 May 1950), 119.

E693 *Christian Science Monitor*, 3 June 1950, p. 6.

E694 *Chicago Sun Book Week*, 13 June 1950, p. 15.

E695 *U. S. Quarterly Booklist*, VI (September 1950), 284.

The Enemy Had It Too (1950)

E696 *Virginia Kirkus Bookshop Service*, XVIII (1 July 1950), 378.

E697 Saul Colin. *New York Times Book Review*, 24 September 1950, p. 26.

E698 *Springfield* [Mass.] *Republican*, 1 October 1950, p. 8D.

E699 Frank Jones. *San Francisco Chronicle*, 8 October 1950, p. 13.

E700 W. P. Eaton. *New York Herald Book Review*, 15 October 1950, p. 23.

E701 *American Library Association Booklist*, XLVII (1 November 1950), 92.

E702 George Freedly. *Library Journal*, LXXV (15 November 1950), 2014.

A Personal Jesus (1952)

E703 L. R. Miller. *Library Journal*, LXXVII (1 December 1952), 2070.

E704 A. P. Davies. *New York Times Book Review*, 25 January 1953, p. 18.

E705 W. L. Caswell. *Churchman*, CLXVII (1 February 1953), 15.

E706 C. G. Jung. *New Republic*, CXXVIII (27 April 1953), 18.

The Return of Lanny Budd (1953)

E707 *Virginia Kirkus Bookshop Service*, XXI (1 March 1953), 155.

E708 Leo Etzkorn. *Library Journal*, LXXVIII (15 April 1953), 730.

E709 Charles Lee. *Saturday Review*, XXXVI (18 April 1953), 23.

E710 R. L. Duffus. *New York Times Book Review*, 19 April 1953, p. 5.

E711 E. D. Doyle. *San Francisco Chronicle*, 19 April 1953, p. 21.

E712 *Christian Science Monitor*, 23 April 1953, p. 7.

E713 *New Yorker*, XXIX (25 April 1953), 133.

E714 William Yates. *Chicago Sunday Tribune*, 26 April 1953, p. 9.

E715 *Springfield* [Mass.] *Republican*, 24 May 1953, p. 7C.

E716 F. H. Bullock. *New York Herald-Tribune Book Review*, 31 May 1953, p. 9.

E717 *Christian Century*, LXX (10 June 1953), 692.

E718 H. C. Webster. *New Republic*, CXXVIII (15 June 1953), 21.

E719 Riley Hughes. *Catholic World*, CLXXVII (July 1953), 312.

E720 John Metcalf. *Spectator*, CLXC (20 November 1953), 612.

E721 *Times Literary Supplement* [London], 18 December 1953, p. 813.

Cup of Fury (1956)

E722 *Time*, LXVII (30 April 1956), 116.

E723 *American Library Association Booklist*, LII (15 May 1956), 375.

E724 Seymour Krim. *Commonweal*, LXIV (10 August 1956), 474.

E725 H.E.F. *Christian Century*, LXXIII (15 August 1953), 951.

E726 H. Springer. *Baptist Layman*, IX (September 1963), 3.

It Happened to Didymus (1958 What Didymus Did—England, 1954)

E727 *Library Journal*, LXXXIII (1 April 1958), 1088.

E728 R. H. Glauber. *New York Herald-Tribune Book Review*, 20 April 1958, p. 3.

E729 R. L. Duffus. *New York Times Book Review*, 20 April 1958, p. 34.

E730 *American Library Association Booklist*, LIV (15 May 1958), 536.

My Lifetime in Letters (1960)

E731 William Hogan. *San Francisco Chronicle*, 1 February 1960, p. 23.

E732 J. Hutchens. *New York Herald-Tribune Book Review*, 11 February 1960, p. 21.

E733 H. T. Moore. *New York Times Book Review*, 21 February 1960, p. 26.

E734 C. W. Mann. *Library Journal*, LXXXV (1 April 1960), 1449.

E735 Ronald Sanders. *New Republic*, CXLII (18 April 1960), 19.

E736 Lewis Gannett. *New York Herald-Tribune Book Review*, 8 May 1960, p. 9.

E737 A. P. Biella. *American Literature*, XXXIII (November 1961), 390–391.

Affectionately Eve (1961)

E738 Warren Carrier. *Los Angeles Times*, 3 September 1961, p. 14 (in a "calendar" supplement).

E739 R. L. Duffus. *New York Times*, 20 August 1961.

The Autobiography of Upton Sinclair (1962)

E740 E. T. Smith. *Library Journal*, LXXXVII (1 November 1962), 4012.

E741 *Christian Century*, LXXIX (14 November 1962), 1390.

E742 H. T. Moore. *New York Times Book Review*, 18 November 1962, p. 20.

E743 G. W. Johnson. *New Republic*, CXLVII (1 December 1962), 23.

E744 Howard Fast. *Saturday Review*, XLV (1 December 1962), 34.

E745 J. K. Hutchens. *New York Herald-Tribune Books*, 9 December 1962, p. 3.

E746 *Time*, LXXX (14 December 1962), 94.

E747 *Critic*, XXI (December 1962/January 1963), 82.

E748 *New Yorker*, XXXVIII (12 January 1963), 113.

E749 William Barrett. *Atlantic Monthly*, CCXI (January 1963), 110.

E750 J. Moynahan. *Observer Weekend Review* [London], 21 April 1963.

E751 David Williams. *Punch*, CCXLIV (22 May 1963), 754.

E752 *Times Literary Supplement* [London], 24 May 1963, p. 374.

E753 David Marquand. *The New Statesman*, LXV (21 June 1963), 943.

E754 *Virginia Quarterly Review*, XXXIX (Spring 1963), lxii.

E755 Ronald Gottesman. *American Literature*, XXXV (November 1963), 388–389.

F. Selected Books and Articles about Upton Sinclair

1903

F1 "Comments on 'My Cause,' " *Independent*, LV (11 May), 1160–1161.

1904

F2 Mrs. Lundy H. Harris. "Novels and Novelists," *Independent*, LVII (17 November), 1131–1135.

1905

F3 Jack London. "What Jack London Says of *The Jungle*," *The Chicago Socialist*, 25 November, p. 2.

1906

F4 "Portrait," *Arena*, XXXV (February), 187.

F5 "The Truth About Packing Towns," *Collier's*, XXXVI (17 March), 30.

F6 "President Hunts in the Jungle," *Chicago Tribune*, 10 April, pp. 1, 4.

F7 "The Jungle Hunt to Produce Game," *Chicago Tribune*, 11 April, pp. 1, 6.

F8 "Portrait," *Bookman*, XXIII (April), 130.

F9 "A Novelist of Temperament," *The Book News*, XXIV (April), 564.

F10 "Mr. Sinclair's Grave Charges," *Literary Digest*, XXXII (19 May), 746–747.

F11 Mrs. Lundy H. Harris. "The Walking Delegate Novelist," *Independent*, LX (24 May), 1213–1216.

F12 "Packers Fear Publicity More Than New Bill," *Chicago Examiner*, 28 May.

F13 "Witnessed Doctoring of Putrid Meat," *Chicago Examiner*, 29 May.

F14 "A Remarkable Man, A Remarkable Book," *Chicago American*, 30 May, p. 12.

F15 "Upton Sinclair and *The Jungle*," *Chicago American*, 1 June.

F16 "Demand for Clean Meat," *Literary Digest*, XXXII (9 June), 1–2.

F17 "The Meat Scare and Its Results," *Independent*, LX (14 June), 1438–1440.

F18 "Upton Sinclair's Dream of Home," *Literary Digest*, XXXII (23 June), 931–932.

F19 "The Inferno of Packingtown Revealed," *Arena*, XXXV (June), 651–658.

F20 "Mr. Sinclair's Colony: Author Outlines Plan for Co-operative Community," *New York Tribune*, 16 July, p. 7.

F21 "Anxious to Colonize," *New York Tribune*, 18 July, p. 14.

F22 Edward Clark Marsh. "*The Jungle* Vindicated," *Bookman*, XXIII (July), 481–483.

1906 continued

F23 "Portrait—America is Cleaning Its Sewers," *Current Literature*, XLI (July), 3.

F24 "Packingtown Sensation," *Review of Reviews*, XXXIV (July), 6.

F25 "The Packers in Reply," *World Today*, XI (July), 676.

F26 "The Fight for Clean Meat," *The World's Work*, XII (July), 7700.

F27 Frederick Boyd Stevenson. "Sinclair, The Beef Trust Griller," *Wilshire's Magazine* [London], X (1 August), 12.

Reprinted from *Brooklyn Daily Eagle*.

F28 "Mr. Sinclair's Colony: Plan for Co-operative Settlement Has Had Many Predecessors," *New York Tribune*, 12 August, Sect. V, p. 8.

F29 "Discuss Sinclair Plan: Home Colony Members Listen to Reports of Committees," *New York Tribune*, 13 August, p. 5.

F30 "Sinclair Colony Plan: Cost of Institution Project Estimated to Be $275,000," *New York Tribune*, 14 August, p. 5.

F31 "The Novel as an Instrument of Reform," *Current Literature*, XLI (August), 163–164.

F32 "Portrait," *Reader Magazine*, VIII (August), 322.

F33 "Portrait," *Independent*, LXI (6 September), 559.

F34 "He Aimed At the Heart of the Public," *Chicago American*, 21 September, p. 16.

F35 "Upton Sinclair As an Actor," *New York Tribune*, 4 October, p. 7.

F36 "What Life Means to Upton Sinclair," *Literary Digest*, XXXIII (27 October), 606.

F37 Harry E. Maule and Melville H. Cane, eds. *The Man from Main Street: A Sinclair Lewis Reader.* New York: Random House, 1953.

Reprints newspaper piece on Helicon Hall by Lewis written in 1906.

F38 Fra Elburtus [Elbert Hubbard]. *The Jungle Book, A Criticism.* East Aurora, Erie County, New York: The Roycrofters, 1906.

1907

F39 Robert Blatchford. "What Upton Sinclair Meant," *The Clarion*, no. 798 (22 March), p. 1.

F40 Mrs. Lundy H. Harris. "Upton Sinclair and Helicon Hall," *Independent*, LXII (28 March), 711–713.

F41 "The Burning of Helicon Hall," *The Reader*, IX (May), 678–679.

F42 "Helicon Hall and the Beef Trust," *American Magazine*, LXIV (June), 220–221.

F43 "Helicon Hall," *Pearson's Magazine*, XXII (June), 710–711.

F44 "Helicon Hall," *Putmans' Monthly*, II (July), 506.

1908

F45 "How Sinclair Knows the Smart Set," *Literary Digest*, XXXVI (9 May), 687–688.

F46 Mrs. Lundy H. Harris. "Advance of Civilization in Fiction," *Independent*, LXV (19 November), 1167–1172.

1909

F47 Robert Blatchford. "The Grim Logic of Facts," *The Clarion*, no. 926 (3 September), p. 1.

1910

F48 Mrs. Ella Reeve Bloor. "*The Jungle*'s Aftermath, with an Introduction by Upton Sinclair," *Physical Culture*, XXIII (June), 547–554.

F49 "Upton Sinclair and the Sunday Law," *Independent*, LXXI (10 August), 326–328.

1911

F50 "Note on Sinclair's Article 'Fasting, the Foe of Sickness,' " *Cosmopolitan*, L (February), 433.

F51 Meta H. (Fuller) Sinclair, "Plea for Freer Divorce," *World Today*, XXI (October), 1202–1205.

1913

F52 Gaylord Wilshire. "Upton Sinclair Against the One-Leg Dance," *Wilshire's Magazine* [London], XVII (August/September), 1–2.

1914

F53 "Court Deals a Blow to 'Sinclair Pickets,' " *New York Times*, 8 July, p. 20.

F54 Samuel Gompers. "Upton Sinclair's Mental Workmanship," *American Federationist*, XXI (April), 293–302.

1917

F55 "Socialists Enunciate New Principle," *New Republic*, X (31 March), 262–263.

Statement signed by several authors.

F56 Frank Harris. "Upton Sinclair," *Pearson's Magazine*, XXXVIII (December), 252–254.

Reprinted in *Contemporary Portraits*, Third Series. New York: The Author, 1920, pp. 15–30.

F57 Dr. Georg Brandes. "Introduction," *King Coal*. New York: Macmillan, pp. ix-xi.

1918

F58 Clement Wood. "Upton Sinclair," *New York Call*, 31 March, p. 20, mag. sect.

1919

F59 "Upton Sinclair Reproved for Swatting Venerable Heads," *Current Opinion*, LXVI (June), 386.

F60 Charles C. Baldwin. *The Men Who Make Our Novels*. New York: Moffat, Yard, pp. 450–459.

F61 Percy H. Boynton. *A History of American Literature*. Boston: Ginn, pp. 117–131, 257–259.

1920

F62 William Bross Lloyd. "Upton Sinclair's Newspaper," *Nation*, CX (21 February), 369.

F63 "Upton Sinclair's Indictment of the American Press," *Current Opinion*, LXVIII (May), 669–671.

F64 "Upton Sinclair is a Prophet Who is Not Without Power Abroad," *Living Age*, XX (30 October), 281.

F65 "Sinclair Makes Great Showing," *Appeal to Reason*, 13 November, p. 1.

F66 Isaac F. Marcosson. *Adventures in Interviewing*. New York: Lane, pp. 280–289.

1921

F67 "Truth and Upton Sinclair," *Weekly Review*, IV (9 February), 128–129.

F68 W. J. Ghent. "The Singular Case of Upton Sinclair," *Weekly Review*, IV (27 April), 393–397.

F69 Curtis N. Hitchcock. "*The Brass Check*," *Journal of Political Economy*, XXIX (April), 336–348.

F70 Carl Van Doren. "Contemporary American Novelists: Upton Sinclair," *Nation*, CXIII (28 September), 347–348.
Reprinted in *Contemporary American Novelists*. New York: Macmillan, 1922, pp. 65–74.

1922

F71 Alexander Marky. "A Challenge: Introduction to Upton Sinclair's House of Wonder," *Pearson's Magazine*, XLVIII (June), 6–8.
Concerning Dr. Albert Abrams.

F72 Harry Kemp. *Tramping on Life*. New York: Boni and Liveright.
In this fictionalized account of Kemp's relations with Upton and Meta, Upton is Penton, and Meta is Hildreth Baxter.

F73 John Mathews Manly. *Contemporary American Literature*. New York: Harcourt, Brace and Co., pp. 139–140.

1923

F74 Frank Harris. "Portrait of Upton Sinclair," *Haldeman-Julius Weekly*, 27 January, p. 2.

F75 Editorial—About Upton Sinclair, *Nation*, CXVI (23 May), 585.

F76 "Foes of Freedom—Editorial," *New Republic*, XXXV (13 June), 60–61.

F77 Upton Sinclair, comp. *Upton Sinclair: Biographical and Critical Opinions*. Pasadena: The Author. Pamphlet, 32 pp.

1924

F78 "About Upton Sinclair," *The Progressive*, VII (1 October), 28.

F79 "Lenin Brands Upton Sinclair," *Sunday Boston Advertiser*, 2 November, p. 5M.

1925

F80 "Upton Sinclair Is Honored By Soviet," *Washington Times*, 9 July, p. 6.

F81 "Sinclair Says California Act Would Have Jailed Lincoln," *St. Louis Post Dispatch*, 6 November, p. 39.

F82 Paul Jordan-Smith. "Upton Sinclair," *World Tomorrow*, VIII (December), 378.

F83 Carl and Mark Van Doren. *American and British Literature Since 1890*. New York: The Century Co., pp. 79–81, 319.

1926

F84 E. Haldeman-Julius. *Culture and Its Modern Aspects: A Series of Essays*. Girard, Kansas: Haldeman-Julius Company (Big Blue Book no. B-15, Old Series; no. B-246, New Series), 18 January. 128 pp.

F85 E. Haldeman-Julius. *Iconoclastic Literary Reactions*. Girard, Kansas: Haldeman-Julius Company (Big Blue Book no. B-16, Old Series; no. B-811, New Series), 27 January. 128 pp.

1926 continued

F86 "Upton Sinclair As Governor of California," *Boston Transcript*, 10 March.

F87 V. F. Calverton. "Sinclair—An American Don Quixote," *Haldeman-Julius Monthly*, III (April), 532–536.

F88 H. L. Mencken. *Prejudices—Fifth Series*. New York: Alfred Knopf, p. 133.

F89 E. Haldeman-Julius. *A Book of Persons And Personalities: Paragraphs and Essays*. Girard, Kansas: Haldeman-Julius Company (Big Blue Book no. B-19, Old Series; no. B233, New Series), *c.* 1926. 128 pp.

1927

F90 Floyd Dell. "The Artist in Revolt," *Bookman*, LXV (27 May), 316–322.

F91 Goeffrey West. "America's Greatest Socialist Writer," *London Daily Herald*, 24 August, p. 9.

F92 Harry Salpeter. "Sinclair on George Sterling," *New York World*, 27 August, p. 11.

F93 "Upton Sinclair and George Sterling," *Argonaut*, CII (10 September), 3–4.

F94 Haldeman-Julius. "The Haters of Upton Sinclair," *Haldeman-Julius Weekly*, 17 September, pp. 2, 4.

F95 "The Vogue of Upton Sinclair," *Holyoke* [Mass.] *Transcript*, 17 September, p. 12.

F96 Isaac Goldberg. "Upton Sinclair's Book Fight in Boston," *Haldeman-Julius Monthly*, VI (September), 105–110.

F97 Louis Adamic. "Upton Sinclair—A Prophet of Red Dawn," *Open Forum*, IV (26 November), 1–2.

F98 Charles R. Walker. "Business in the American Novel," *Bookman*, LXVI (December), 401–405.

F99 Van Wyck Brooks. *Emerson and Others*. New York: E. P. Dutton, pp. 209–217.

F100 Floyd Dell. *Upton Sinclair: A Study in Social Protest*. New York: George H. Doran; Long Beach: Upton Sinclair; New York: A. & C. Boni.

Still the best biographical source, even though it carries Sinclair's life only through 1915 in any detail. Leon Harris is preparing a full-length biography for Holt, Rinehart and Winston.

F101 Mark Sullivan. *Our Times*, vol. II. New York: Scribners, p. 471.

1928

F102 "Rumford Press Drops *Bookman*," *Boston Herald*, 25 January, p. 9.

F103 James S. Hodges. "Book Urchins," *Forum*, LXXIX (February), 318.

F104 Walter Lippmann. "Upton Sinclair," *Saturday Review of Literature*, IV (3 March), 641–643.

F105 "Diagnosis of Upton Sinclair—Editorial," *Boston Herald*, 6 March, p. 12.

F106 Laurence S. Morris. "Upton Sinclair, The Way of the Reformer," *New Republic*, LIV (7 March), 90–93.

F107 Harry Hansen. "Did Upton Sinclair's Dog Bite Jim Tully?" *New York World*, 30 June, p. 11.

F108 Jay E. House. "On Second Thought," *New York Post*, 30 July, p. 9.

1928 continued

F109 Floyd Dell. "Upton Sinclair in America," *Haldeman-Julius Quarterly*, II (July/September), 74–75.

F110 Lew Blumenfeld. "Upton Sinclair on the Jews," *Jewish Tribune*, 2 November, pp. 5, 32.

F111 Roger Baldwin. "A Unique Socialist," *New Masses*, III November, 7.

F112 Floyd Dell. "Upton Sinclair in America," *New Masses*, III (November), 6–7.

F113 Michael Gold. "In Foggy California," *New Masses*, III (November), 10–12.

F114 John Haynes Holmes. "Sinclair's Flaming Youth," *New Masses*, III (November), 17.

F115 Robert Morss Lovett. "Upton Sinclair," *English Journal*, XVII (November), 706–714.

F116 Scott Nearing. "Sinclair's One Hangover," *New Masses*, III (November), 7.

F117 Robert Wolf. "An Upper Class Prophet," *New Masses*, III (November), 7.

F118 Art Young. "Upton Never Laughs," *New Masses*, III (November), 7.

F119 David Karsner. *Sixteen Authors to One*. New York: Lewis Copeland Co., pp. 265–278.

1929

F120 Joseph P. Lash. "About Sinclair," *New York World*, 8 January, p. 19.

F121 "Sinclair's Suit Against *News* Resumes Monday," *Denver News*, 16 June.

F122 "Evidence Ends in Sinclair's Suit," *Denver News*, 19 June.

F123 "*News* is Winner in Libel Suit of Upton Sinclair," *Denver News*, 20 June.

F124 "Upton Sinclair Loses $200,000 Libel Suit," *Editor and Publisher*, LXII (22 June), 12.

F125 "Upton Sinclair—British Estimate of American Writer," *Springfield* [Mass.] *Republican*, 27 June, p. 8.

F126 "About Suit vs. *Denver News*," *Fort Wayne News Sentinel*, 28 June.

F127 Geoffrey West. "Upton Sinclair," *The Millgate*, XXIV (June), 515–519.

F128 Floyd Van Buren. "About Sinclair—*Boston* and *Oil*!" *Milwaukee Journal*, 17 August.

F129 Meyer Levin. "A Protest Against *The Jungle*," *Chicago Daily News*, 2 October, p. 12, Midweek Features.

F130 Michael Gold. "On Upton Sinclair, Letter," *New Masses*, V (December), 23.

1930

F131 "Letter about *The Jungle*," *Publisher's Weekly*, CXVII (18 January), 342.

F132 "Upton Sinclair and Pity," *Survey*, LXIII (15 February), 600.

F133 Jim Kerr. "Sinclair and Good Beer—Letter," *New Masses*, V (May), 22.

F134 "1,500 in L.A. Urge Release for Mooney," *New Leader* [London], XI (16 August), 2.

1930 continued

F135 "The Week: About Sinclair's Opinion of *Literary Digest* Poll," *New Republic*, LXV (19 November), 2.

F136 M. Kus-Nikolajev. [*A Biography of Upton Sinclair.*] Zagreb, Yugoslavia. 55 pp.
In Serbo-Croatian.

1931

F137 "Upton Sinclair Near Death Through Attack of Hiccoughs," *London News Chronicle*, 21 June.

F138 Albert Mordell. Letter about Sinclair's Ancestors, *Saturday Review of Literature*, VIII (29 August), 92.
See also Mordell's unpublished book Ms., "The Fighting Sinclairs," dealing with his naval ancestors, in Lilly Library.

F139 "Upton Sinclair to Put his Books in Charity Trust," *New York Herald Tribune*, 3 September, p. 13.

F140 Karl Kautsky. "The Bolshevik Dromedary—a Reply to Upton Sinclair I," *New Leader* [London], XII (24 October), 4.

F141 Karl Kautsky. "The Russian Dromedary—a Reply to Upton Sinclair II," *New Leader* [London], XII (31 October), 4.

F142 Paul G. Hayes. "Upton Sinclair Challenges Chinese Thought," *Chinese Recorder*, LXII (December), 747–758.

F143 Robert Morss Lovett. *Preface to Fiction*: *A Discussion of Great Modern Novels*. Chicago: Thomas S. Rockwell Co., pp. 97–112.
Analysis of *Boston*.

1932

F144 "Notables Back Upton Sinclair for Nobel Prize," *Chicago Tribune*, 11 January, p. 17.

F145 "Upton Sinclair Urged for Nobel Prize," *Baltimore Sun*, 11 January, p. 7.

F146 Robert E. Rogers. "Sinclair True Idealist for Nobel Prize," *Boston American*, 12 January, p. 11.

F147 Harry Hansen. "Upton Sinclair for Nobel Prize," *New York World-Telegram*, 13 January, p. 23.

F148 Gilbert Seldes. "Nobel Candidate," *New York Evening Journal*, 15 January, p. 19.

F149 Ernest S. Greene. "About Upton Sinclair and the Nobel Prize," *Galveston News*, 24 January.
See F161.

F150 Walter Franklin Prince. "Mrs. Sinclair's 'Mental Radio,'" *Scientific American*, CXLVI (March), 135–138.

F151 J. H. Whyte. "Upton Sinclair—Puritan and Socialist," *Modern Scot*, II (First Quarter), 149–155.

F152 C. H. Gratten. "Upton Sinclair and Current Literature, Summary of a Conversation," *Bookman*, LXXV (April), 61–64.

F153 The Research Officer. "The Sinclair Experiments Demonstrating Telepathy," *Bulletin of Boston Society for Psychic Research*, XVI (April), 1–86.

F154 Edmund Wilson. "Lincoln Steffens and Upton Sinclair," *New Republic*, LXXII (28 September), 173–175.

F155 David Sinclair. "Upton Sinclair: Reply to E. Wilson," *New Republic*, LXXII (12 October), 236.
By his son.

F156 H. S. Tigner. "Story of Upton Sinclair," *Christian Century*, IL (19 October), 1274–1275.

1932 continued

F157 Seymour Stern. "*Que Viva Mexico*!—The Fate of Eisentein's American Film," *Cinema Quarterly* [Edinburgh], I (Winter), 73–80.
See also Geduld and Gottesman, F342.

F158 Joseph Warren Beach. *The Twentieth Century Novel: Studies in Technique*. New York: Century, p. 445.

F159 Van Wyck Brooks. *Sketches in Criticism*. New York: E. P. Dutton, pp. 291–298.

F160 V. F. Calverton. *The Liberation of American Literature*. New York: Scribner's, p. 391.

F161 Ernest Greene. *The Candidacy of Upton Sinclair for The Nobel Prize for Literature*. New York: Published by the Committee. Pamphlet, 40 pp.
770 signers from 55 countries including Nobel Prize Winners Shaw, Rolland, Einstein; Algiers to Uruguay.

F162 Grant C. Knight. *American Literature and Culture*. New York: R. Long and R. R. Smith, pp. 431–433.

F163 Ludwig Lewisohn. *Expression in America*. New York: Harper and Bros., pp. 469–473.

1933

F164 James Francis Crow. "Backers Face Bitter Attack in Manifesto," *Hollywood Citizen News*, 13 May, p. 4.

F165 "Communists See Red [Over *Que Viva* Mexico!] But Control Selves," *Variety*, 16 May.

F166 T. A. Jackson. "Upton Sinclair: Free-Lance of Journalism," *The Plebs*, XXV (May), 104–107.

F167 A. A. Leiva. " 'Viva Mexico' y 'Rayos y Truenos Sobre Mexico' Palabra Final in el caso Eisenstein-Sinclair," *El Nacional* [Mexico City], 10 June.

F168 Bernarr MacFadden. "Why Mr. Sinclair is All Wrong," *Liberty*, x (17 June), 20–22.

F169 [Seymour Stern.] "Manifesto on *Que Viva Mexico!*," *Experimental Cinema*, no. 4 (June).
See also Geduld and Gottesman, F352.

F170 Seymour Stern and Herman G. Weinberg. Letters to Editor, *Modern Monthly*, VII (July), 373–375.

F171 William Troy. "The Eisenstein Muddle," *Nation*, CXXXVII (19 July), 83–84.

F172 Ivor Montagu. "Eisenstein and Upton Sinclair," *New Clarion*, III (5 August), 142.

F173 "La Pelicula de Eisenstein Salio Sin Haberse Aprobado . . . ," *El Nacional* [Mexico City], 9 August.

F174 Seymour Stern, A. A. Leiva and H. W. L. Dana. "More Thunder Over Eisenstein," *New Republic*, LXXV (9 August), 344–345.

F175 Kirk Bond. "Destruction of a Masterpiece," *Adelphi* [London], VI (August), 372–374.
Concerning *Que Viva Mexico!*

F176 Marie Seton. "Eisenstein Aims at Simplicity," *Film Art* [London], I (Summer), 27–28.

F177 Kate Crane-Gartz. "More About Eisenstein," *New Republic*, LXXVI (6 September), 104.

F178 "Upton Sinclair, Democrat, Joins Governor Race," *Sacramento* [Calif.] *Bee*, 14 September, p. 10.

F179 "Upton Sinclair in Race," *Los Angeles Times*, 15 September, Sec. 2, p. 1.

1933 continued

F180 "Sinclair Ruined Eisenstein Film, Mexicans Hold," *New York Herald Tribune*, 16 September.

F181 "Upton Sinclair Critic 'Bounced' at Film Debut," *New York Herald Tribune*, 19 September.

F182 Frank L. Hayes. "Sinclair Tells How He Will Rout Poverty in California," *Chicago Daily News*, 20 September, p. 13.

F183 "Socialists Fire Upton Sinclair," *Los Angeles Times*, 22 September, sect. 2, p. 5.

F184 "Mexican Movie Evokes Thunder Over Sinclair . . . ," *The Daily Worker*, 26 September, p. 5.

F185 Seymour Stern et al. "Manifesto," *Close-up* [London], X (September), 248–254.

F186 William Troy. "Selections from Eisenstein," *Nation*, CXXXVII (4 October), 391–393.
Review of *Thunder Over Mexico*.

F187 Helen Woodward. "Eisenstein and Upton Sinclair," *Nation*, CXXXVII (11 October), 410.

F188 Seymour Stern. "The Greatest Thing Done This Side of the Atlantic," *Modern Monthly*, VII (October), 525–532.

F189 Kenneth Macpherson and Upton Sinclair. "Letters to the Editor," *Close-up* [London], X (28 December), 361.

F190 Albert Parry. *Garrets and Pretenders*. New York: Covici, Friede, pp. 197–198.

F191 Granville Hicks. *The Great Tradition*. New York: Macmillan, pp. 196–203.

1934

F192 Ivor Montagu. "The Sinclair Tragedy; Eisenstein's *Thunder Over Mexico*," *New Statesman and Nation*, VII (20 January), 85–86.

F193 A. Goulding. "Democracy in California," *Canadian Forum*, XIV (February), 172–173.

F194 Chapin Hall. "Upton Sinclair Out for Governor," *New York Times*, 1 April, p. 6E

F195 Mark Van Doren. "The Art of American Fiction," *Nation*, CXXXVIII (25 April), 471–474.

F196 Reuben Borough. "Upton Sinclair for Governor," *Nation*, CXXXVIII (9 May), 535.

F197 Sender Garlin. "Upton Sinclair, Reactionary Utopian," *New Masses*, XXIX (22 May), 10–12.

F198 Sinclair Campaign Committee. *End Poverty in California*, 15 June.
Leaflet.

F199 Chapin Hall. "California, Oregon, Face Turn to Left as Radical Campaigns Tempt Voters," *New York Times*, 24 June, p. 6E.

F200 Oswald Garrison Villard. "Upton Sinclair Startles California," *Nation*, CXXXIX (11 July), 35.

F201 "Sinclair Says He's Not Red," *Los Angeles Times*, 15 July, p. 18.

F202 "Germany Bans Sinclair Books," *Los Angeles Times*, 20 July, p. 6.

F203 Mark Sullivan. "California Race May Face Issue," *Los Angeles Times*, 19 August, Sect. 2, p. 5.

1934 continued

F204 Carey McWilliams. "Upton Sinclair and his EPIC," *New Republic*, LXXX (22 August), 37–41.

F205 "California Press Attacks Sinclair," *New York Times*, 31 August, p. 3L.

F206 H. L. Mencken. "40 Acres and a Mule," *Baltimore Evening Sun*, 10 September.

F207 "EPIC Nominations: Political Importance of the Sinclair Victory," *Christian Century*, LI (12 September), 1135–1136.

F208 "Upton Sinclair's Victory," *Nation*, CXXXIX (12 September), 285–286.

F209 Carey McWilliams. "Upton Sinclair's Chances," *New Republic*, LXXX (12 September), 117.

F210 George West. "Sinclair Modifies Some of His Plan," *New York Times*, 16 September, pp. [1E,] 6E.

F211 S. J. Woolf. "Upton Sinclair Describes His Evolution," *New York Times Magazine*, 16 September, pp. 9, 17.

F212 "California Issue Held Clear Cut," *Los Angeles Times*, 22 September, p. 4.

Local prominent citizens quote from Sinclair's writing to prove forthcoming election a contest between Americanism and Communism.

F213 "Cotten Calls Democratic Platform 'Fairy Tales,' " *Los Angeles Times*, 22 September, p. 4.

F214 "Unions Follow Sinclair Lead," *Los Angeles Times*, 22 September, p. 4.

F215 "Sinclair Tells New Deal Aims," *Los Angeles Times*, 22 September, p. 4.

EPIC platform will help bring New Deal to entire nation.

F216 "Harrison Not to Aid Sinclair," *Los Angeles Times*, 22 September, p. 4.

F217 "Sinclair's Aim Scored by Hatfield," *Los Angeles Times*, 22 September, p. 4.

F218 "Nine-Tenths of State's Papers Oppose Sinclair," *Los Angeles Times*, 22 September, p. 4.

F219 Madeline Matzen. "*The Jungle's* Author: Times Caught Up With Upton Sinclair," *Psychology*, XX (September), 29, 55.

F220 George West. "California Sees Red," *Current History*, XL (September), 658–662.

F221 Raymond Gram Swing. "EPIC and the Ohio Plan," *Nation*, CXXXIX (3 October), 379–381.

F222 "Stand Up and Be Counted [As Republicans]," *Los Angeles Times*, 5 October, sect. 2, p. 1.

F223 Raymond Moley. "Looking Backward with Mr. Sinclair and Mr. Hoover," *Today*, II (6 October), 12–13.
Also in *San Francisco Chronicle*, 7 October.

F224 "California Climax," *Time*, XXIV (22 October), 13–16.

F225 "700 Miles of Debate Over Sinclair in California," *Newsweek*, IV (27 October), 9–10.

F226 "M'Adoo Partner Bolts Sinclair," *New York Times*, 30 October, pp. [1,] 8.

F227 H. C. Herring. "California Votes for God," *Christian Century*, LI (31 October), 1370–1372.

F228 Raymond Gram Swing. "Last Look at the Campaign," *Nation*, CXXXIX (7 November), 529–530.

1934 continued

F229 George Creel. "Utopia Unlimited," *Saturday Evening Post*, CCVII (24 November), 5–7.

F230 Harold Laski. "On Sinclair," *Living Age*, CCCXLVII (November), 276–277.

F231 Frank Scully. "Author! Author! For Governor," *Esquire*, II (November), 32, 177–179.

Also in his *This Gay Knight*. Philadelphia and New York: Chilton Co., 1962, pp. 52–60.

F232 "They Stood Out from the Crowd in 1934," *Literary Digest*, CXVIII (29 December), 7.

F233 Theodore Dreiser. "The Epic Sinclair," *Esquire*, II (December), 32–33, 178–179.

F234 I. O. Evans. *An Upton Sinclair Anthology: a Biographical Note*, pp. 317–322.

F235 Harry Hartwick. *The Foreground of American Fiction.* New York: American Book Company, pp. 231–249.

F236 Frederick W. Nelson. "The Great Gubernatorial Campaign of California, 1934," *EPIC California,* 1934, vols. 1–5.

Comprehensive scrapbooks of published material at Lilly Library.

F237 Thomas E. Pickerill. *I, Assemblyman From Orange County And How I Supported Upton Sinclair*. Santa Ana: [Upton Sinclair?]. 24 pp.

1935

F238 H. L. Mencken. "Storm Damage in Utopia," *Baltimore Evening Sun*, 28 January.

F239 George West. "Sinclair in Eclipse; Fights on for EPIC," *New York Times*, 17 March, p. 6E.

F240 Hanson W. Baldwin. "Sinclair at Work on a Bigger EPIC," *New York Times*, 5 May, p. 6E.

F241 Newton Arvin. "Fiction Trends in America," *Current History*, XLII (September), 610–616.

F242 E. Haldeman-Julius. *Questions and Answers*, Series 1, 1st ed. Girard, Kansas: Haldeman-Julius Company, p. 43.
Refutes description of Sinclair as fascist in Communist press.

F243 Harlan Hatcher. *Creating the Modern American Novel.* New York: Farrar, Rinehart, pp. 127–132.

F244 Granville Hicks. *The Great Tradition: An Interpretation of American Literature Since the Civil War.* Rev. ed. New York: Macmillan, pp. 196–203.

1936

F245 Harold M. King. "Sinclair and Marx," *Pacific Weekly*, IV (6 January), 3–4.

F246 Andres J. Steiger. "American Authors Popular in Soviet Russia," *International Literature*, III (March), 98–103.

F247 Percy H. Boynton. *Literature and American Life.* Boston: Ginn, pp. 746, 755, 757–758, 759, 871, 889.

F248 Joseph McCabe. *Upton Sinclair Finds God.* Girard, Kansas: Haldeman-Julius Company. (Pamphlet.)

F249 E. Haldeman-Julius. *Questions and Answers*, Series 8, 1st ed. Girard, Kansas: Haldeman-Julius Company, p. 11.
Sinclair an emotional, not a logical thinker.

F250 Arthur H. Quinn. *American Fiction: An Historical & Critical Survey.* New York: Appleton-Century-Crofts, pp. 652–656.

1936 continued

F251 Luther Whiteman and Samuel L. Lewis. *Glory Roads: The Psychological State of California.* New York: Thomas Y. Crowell, pp. 203–252.

F252 Marcet Haldeman-Julius. *Famous and Interesting Guests of a Kansas Farm.* Girard, Kansas: Haldeman-Julius Publications (Reviewer's Library no. 8; Big Blue Book no. B-204), *c.* 1936. 31 pp.

1937

F253 "Portrait," *Time*, xxx (1 November), 60.

F254 Robert Cantwell. "Upton Sinclair." In *After the Genteel Tradition*, ed. Malcolm Cowley. New York: W. W. Norton, pp. 37–51.

Originally published in part in *New Republic*, xc (24 February), 69–71.

1938

F255 Douglas Churchill. "Upton Sinclair 60, Looks Back on His Crusades," *New York Times Magazine*, 18 September, pp. 7, 22.

F256 James L. Harte. *This Is Upton Sinclair*. Emmaus, Pa.,: Rodale Press, 206 pp.

Absurdly adulatory book.

1939

F257 "Soviet Views of Some American Books," *International Literature*, II (February), 101–104.

1940

F258 Theodore Dreiser. "Upton Sinclair," *The Clipper*, I (September), 3–4.

F259 Carl Van Doren. *The American Novel, 1789–1939.* New York: Macmillan, pp. 240–242.

F260 William B. Seabrook. *Witchcraft, Its Power in the World Today*. New York: Harcourt, Brace, pp. 233–246.

1941

F261 Joseph Warren Beach. *American Fiction 1920–1940.* New York: Macmillan, p. 237.

1942

F262 Max Eastman. "Proletarian Novelists, Old and New," *American Mercury*, LIV (April), 496–498.

F263 Alfred Kazin. *On Native Grounds.* New York: Reynal and Hitchcock, pp. 116–121.

1943

F264 Granville Hicks. "The Survival of Upton Sinclair," *College English*, IV (January), 213–220.

F265 Frank Scully. *Rogues Gallery.* Hollywood: Murray and Gee, pp. 193–209.

1944

F266 Jacob Blanck. "News From the Rare Book Sellers: *The Jungle*," *Publisher's Weekly*, CXLVI (30 September), 1431.

1946

F267 Howard Mumford Jones. "The Confused Case of Upton Sinclair," *Atlantic Monthly*, CLXXVIII (August), 148.

F268 Irving Stone. "Upton Sinclair," *Book Find News*, II (August), 6–7.

1946 continued

F269 Carey McWilliams. *Southern California Country*. New York: Duell, Sloane, p. 290.

1948

F270 Leon Spitz. "Upton Sinclair and Nazism," *American Hebrew*, CLVIII (22 October), 2.

F271 Leon Spitz. "Upton Sinclair on Zionism," *American Hebrew*, CLVIII (31 December), 6, 15.

F272 Stan Lee Kapustka. "The Universal Understanding of Upton Sinclair," *Kapustkan Magazine*, IX (December), 22–25.

Extensive discussion of Sinclair and quotations from *Limbo on the Loose*.

1949

F273 James Baldwin. "Everybody's Protest Novel [*The Jungle*]," *Partisan Review*, XVI (June), 578-585.

F274 E. Haldeman-Julius. *My Second 25 Years*. Girard, Kansas: Haldeman-Julius Company (Blue Book no. 814).

1950

F275 Albert Mordell. "Haldeman-Julius and Upton Sinclair," *The Critic and Guide*, IV (February), 94–119.

Also as pamphlet: *Haldeman-Julius and Upton Sinclair: The Amazing Record of a Long Collaboration*. Girard, Kansas: Haldeman-Julius Publications, pp. 3–28. An important biographical-bibliographical source.

F276 P. P. Rogers. "Francisco Rojas Gonzalez and *The Jungle*," *Modern Language Forum*, XXXV (March/June), 39–41.

1951

F277 Jo Davidson. *Between Sittings*. New York: Dial Press, pp. 28–32.

F278 John Fischer. Introduction to *The Jungle*. New York: Harcourt, Brace, 1951, pp. xiii-xviii.

1952

F279 Marie Seton. *Eisenstein, A Biography*. London: The Bodley Head. Chapters 8 and 9 and Appendices 5 and 6 especially.

1955

F280 Quentin Reynolds. *The Fiction Factory, or From Pulp Row to Quality Street*. New York: Random House, pp. 103, 104.

On Sinclair's nickel novels.

1956

F281 J. D. Koerner. "The Last of the Muckrake Men," *South Atlantic Quarterly*, LV (April), 221–232.

F282 Ralph Adimari. "Upton Sinclair, Last of the Dime Novelists," *Dime Novel Round-Up*, XXIV (15 June), 41–44.

F283 ———. "Upton Sinclair, Last of the Dime Novelists," *Dime Novel Round-Up*, XXIV (15 July), 51–52.

F284 Walter Rideout. *The Radical Novel in the United States, 1900–1954*. Cambridge, Mass.: Harvard University Press, pp. 130ff.

Excellent discussions of several Sinclair novels.

1957

F285 Howard H. Quint. "Upton Sinclair's Quest for Artistic Independence—1909," *American Literature*, XXIX (May), 194–202.

F286 Griesha Alexandrov and Eduard Tissé, "About an Unfinished Film," *Iskkustvo Kino* [Moscow], no. 5 (May), pp. 104–117.

F287 R. M. Posner. "A. P. Giannini and the 1934 Campaign in California," *Historical Society of Southern California*, XXXIX (June), 190–201.

F288 Mary Craig Sinclair. *Southern Belle*. New York: Crown Publishers.
His second wife's account of forty-five years with him.

F289 Carl Anderson. "Swedish Criticism Before 1920: The Reception of Jack London and Upton Sinclair." In *The Swedish Acceptance of American Literature*. Philadelphia: University of Pennsylvania Press, pp. 33–44.

1958

F290 Charles E. Larsen. "The EPIC Campaign of 1934," *Pacific Historical Review*, XXVII (May), 127–147.

F291 William E. Bohn. "Sinclair—The Writer as a Good Man," *New Leader* [London], XLI (22 September), 23.

F292 "Upton Sinclair at 80," *New Republic*, CXXXIX (29 September), 6.

F293 Harry Laidler. "Upton Sinclair at Eighty," *Tamiment Institute Library Bulletin*, no. 17 (September), p. 1.
Tribute and bibliography.

1959

F294 George J. Becker. "Upton Sinclair, Quixote in a Flivver," *College English*, XXI (December), 133–140.

1960

F295 Anne Marie Springer. "Jack London and Upton Sinclair." In *The American Novel in Germany: A Study of the Critical Reception of Eight American Novelists Between the Two World Wars*. Hamburg, West Germany: Cram. de Gruyter & Co., pp. 39–46.

F296 Robert B. Downs. Afterword to *The Jungle*. New York: New American Library, pp. 343–350.

F297 Bernard Kreissman. *Pamela-Shamela*. Lincoln, Nebraska: University of Nebraska Press, pp. 75–80.

1961

F298 Bill Becker. "Upton Sinclair—A Crusade at 83," *New York Times*, 22 April, p. 60.

F299 "Upton Sinclair, Author, Takes a Bride at 83," *Los Angeles Times*, 15 October, p. 16A.

Sinclair's marriage to May Hard.

F300 Harvey Swados. "The World of Upton Sinclair," *Atlantic Monthly*, CCVIII (December), 96, 98, 100, 102.

F301 Daniel Aaron. *Writers on the Left: Episodes in American Literary Communism*. New York: Harcourt, Brace and World.

An important study.

1962

F302 Wesley Marx. "Upton Sinclair: The Rebel in Retirement," *Los Angeles*, III (June), 41–44.

1962 continued

F303 "Banquet Honors 3 Who Led," *U.A.W. Solidarity*, v (June), 7–8.

Eleanor Roosevelt, Mary Heaton Vorss, and Sinclair were honored.

F304 "Sinclair, Upton," *Current Biography*, XXIII (December), 23–26.

More reliable than most accounts, but far from accurate or complete.

F305 Deming B. Brown. *Soviet Attitudes Toward American Writing.* Princeton: Princeton University Press, 1962.

Chapter viii, pp. 202–219, sums up an important—and fluctuating—relationship.

F306 S. Gorley Putt. "World Without End: Upton Sinclair and Lanny Budd." In *Scholars of the Heart.* London: Faber and Faber, pp. 87–109.

1963

F307 Ronald Gottesman. *Sinclair Exhibit Brochure.* Bloomington, Indiana: Lilly Library, 20 September. 3 pp.

F308 Ronald Gottesman. *A Catalogue of Books, Manuscripts, and Other Materials from the Upton Sinclair Archives.* Bloomington, Indiana: Lilly Library. 56 pp. (Second printing: 1964.)

F309 "Upton Sinclair Here," *Bloomington Herald Telephone*, 18 October.

F310 Sean Fitzpatrick. "Sinclair Tells Tales of Reform," *Bloomington Herald Telephone*, 19 October.

F311 Kathryn Gibson. "Reception Renews Old Friendships," *Milwaukee Journal*, 21 October sect. 2, p. 9.

F312 Larry Van Gelder. "Sinclair Hacks Away at the Social Jungle," *New York World*, 28 October, p. 9.

F313 Sue Solet. "Upton Sinclair Still a Firebrand," *New York Herald Tribune*, 30 October, p. 23.

F314 "Upton Sinclair Revisits City College," *New York Times*, 31 October, p. 23.

F315 "Wrath From the Time Past," *Portland Reporter*, 2 November, p. 18.

F316 J. O. Brice. "Upton Sinclair Reflects on 85 Years," *Portland Reporter*, 9 November, p. 4.

F317 "Upton Sinclair'[s] Miracle Diet," *Boston Globe*, 28 November, p. 13A.

F318 Robert Spiller. *Literary History of the United States*, vol. III. New York: Macmillan, pp. 995–999.

1964

F319 Ronald Gottesman. "The Upton Sinclair Dime Novels," *Dime Novel Round-Up*, XXXIII (15 March), 20–23.

F320 "Neo-Surrealist Interview—Upton Sinclair," *Limbo*, I (April), 14–15.
Question and answer interview.

F321 David M. Chalmers. *The Social & Political Ideas of the Muckrakers*. New York: Citadel Press, pp. 88–103.

F322 Max Eastman. *Love and Revolution: My Journey Through an Epoch*. New York: Random House, p. 15.

1965

F323 Reuben W. Borough. "Upton Sinclair's EPIC, 1934," *Occidental Review*, IV (Summer), 29–41.

F324 Ronald Gottesman. "Sergei Eisenstein and Upton Sinclair," *Sight and Sound*, XXXIV (Summer), 142–143.

1965 continued

F325 Ronald Gottesman. "Upton Sinclair and the Sinclair Archives," *Manuscripts*, XVII (Fall), 11–20.

F326 John Dorsey. "Upton Sinclair Relives His Baltimore Childhood," *The* [Baltimore] *Sun Magazine*, 10 October, pp. 16–18.

1966

F327 Boris Yaro. "Civil Libertarian Sinclair Honored," *Los Angeles Times*, 21 March.

F328 "ACLU Chapter Honors Upton Sinclair," *Open Forum*, XLIII (March), 1–6.

F329 Ion Barna. *Eisenstein*. Bucharest, Romania.
In Romanian; English translation forthcoming.

F330 Joseph Blotner. *The Modern American Political Novel*. Austin: University of Texas Press, pp. 113–117, 286–290.

1967

F331 Henry A. Christian. "Ten Letters to Louis Adamic," *The Princeton University Library Chronicle*, XXVIII (Winter), 76–94.
With commentary and annotation.

F332 Tom Dolan. "Upton Sinclair Relives Glories of a Life of Social Reformation," *Buffalo Evening News*, 6 March, p. 19.

F333 Abraham Blinderman. "The Social Passions of Upton Sinclair," *Chicago Jewish Forum*, XXV (Spring), 203–208.

F334 Edward Ainsworth. "Remembering 'Uppie,' " *Saturday Review*, L (30 September), 32–33.

1968

F335 Edward Allatt. "Jack London and Upton Sinclair," *Jack London Newsletter*, I (January-June), 22–27.

F336 Henry Lee. "Upton Sinclair, America's Mightiest Muckraker," *Coronet*, 6 (May), 120–125.

F337 Edward Allatt. "An Upton Sinclair Collection in England," *Book Collecting & Library Monthly* [England], II (June), 20–21.

F338 "Once a Nation's Conscience, Upton Sinclair Looks Back," *The Sunday Oregonian*, 15 September, p. 11.

F339 Abraham Blinderman. "Upton Sinclair at 90," *Christian Century*, LXXXV (25 September), 1200–1203.

F340 R. A. McConnell. "ESP Without Cards," *The Science Teacher*, XXXV (September), 29–33.

Sinclair's experiments with Mary Craig Sinclair in extrasensory perception.

F341 Ronald Gottesman. "Louis Adamic and Upton Sinclair: the Record of a Friendship," *Acta Neophilologica* [Ljubljana], I (November), 41–65.

Mostly letters, with introduction and notes on their relationship.

F342 James B. Gilbert. *Writers and Partisan: A History of Literary Radicalism in America.* New York: Wiley and Sons, pp. 10–12.

Contains analytic bibliography of literary radicalism and socialism in America.

F343 Herbert L. Phillips. *Big Wayward Girl: An Informal Political History of California.* Garden City, N.Y.: Doubleday, pp. 66–73.

F344 "Is This Jack London?" In *The First Occult Review Reader*, ed. Bernhardt J. Hurwood. New York: Award Books, pp. 13–26.

1969

F345 Lorna D. Smith. "Upton Sinclair, Dreiser, Etc.," *Book Collecting & Library Monthly* [England], III (April), 360–363.

F346 R. A. McConnell. "ESP and Credibility in Science," *American Psychologist*, XXIV (May), 531–538.
About Sinclair's experiments in "mind reasoning."

F347 Edward Allatt. "Upton Sinclair on Jack London in 1963," *Jack London Newsletter*, II (September–December), 77–78.

F348 Martin Zanger. "Politics of Confrontation: Upton Sinclair and the Launching of the ACLU in Southern California," *Pacific Historical Review*, XXXVIII (November), 383–406.

F349 Ivor Montagu. *With Eisenstein in Hollywood*. New York: International Publishers.
See Postscript on Mexican (*Que Viva Mexico!*) adventure.

1970

F350 James C. Duram. *Upton Sinclair's Realistic Romanticism*. Wichita, Kansas: Wichita State University, 1970. 11 p.
University Studies no. 83 (May).

F351 Harry M. Geduld and Ronald Gottesman. *Sergei Eisenstein and Upton Sinclair: The Making and Unmaking of "Que Viva Mexico!"* Bloomington: Indiana University Press; London: Thames and Hudson.
Extensive annotated bibliography, pp. 429–443, lists scores of items dealing with Sinclair.

G. Unpublished Material about Upton Sinclair

G1 Ronald E. Chinn. "The Sinclair Campaign of 1934." M.A. thesis, Stanford University, June 1937. 136 pp.

G2 Charles E. Larsen. "The EPIC Movement in California Politics, 1933–1934. M.A. thesis, University of California at Los Angeles, December 1945. 64 pp.

G3 Earl N. Lockard. "Technique in the Novels of Upton Sinclair." Ph.D. dissertation, University of Chicago, August 1947. 287 pp.

G4 Glynn B. Lee. "A Study of the Zenith of Evolutionary Socialism. . . ." M.A. thesis, Chicago State College, August 1951. 127 pp.

G5 George F. Ashton. "Upton Sinclair." M.A. thesis, University of California at Los Angeles, August 1951. 176 pp.

G6 R. J. Riley. "Upton Sinclair and the 1934 California Gubernatorial Elections." M.A. thesis, Chicago State College, June 1952. 111 pp.

G7 Richard B. Fisher. "The Last Muckraker." Ph.D. dissertation, Yale University, March 1953. 636 pp.

G8* John H. Duke. "The Prophet in Politics." Course paper, University of Southern California, June 1953. 93 pp.

G9* Arnold P. Biella. "Upton Sinclair: Crusaders." Ph.D. dissertation, Stanford University, May 1954.

G10 Clarence F. McIntosh. "Upton Sinclair and the EPIC Movement, 1933–1936." Ph.D. dissertation, Stanford University, May 1955. 374 pp.

G11 Robert M. Gordon. "The EPIC Movement and the California Election of 1934." M.A. thesis, College of the Pacific, June 1957. 225 pp.

G12 David E. Montgomery. "Upton Sinclair: His Characteristics and Significance as an Exponent of Reform, with particular emphasis on the period from 1905 to 1938." B.A. thesis, Princeton University, June 1958.

G13* Frederic Litto. "The Dramatic World of Upton Sinclair." Course paper, Indiana University, 1960. 22 pp.

G14* Abraham Blinderman. "Upton Sinclair's Criticism of Higher Education in America." Ph.D. dissertation, New York University, October 1963. 453 pp.

G15 Donald L. Singer. "Upton Sinclair and the California Gubernatorial Campaign." Course paper, University of Southern California, January 1964. 54 pp.

G16* Ronald Gottesman. "Upton Sinclair: An Annotated Bibliographical Catalogue, 1894–1932." Ph.D. dissertation, Indiana University, May 1964. 409 pp.

G17* R. R. Morris. "Upton Sinclair and the Social Novel." Course paper, Nottingham College of Education, 1965. 56 pp.

G18 Norton B. Eastman. "Upton Sinclair: A Social Crusader Views American Education." Ph.D. dissertation, State University of New York at Buffalo, 1965. 230 pp.

G19 George E. Knutsen. "Upton Sinclair: The Urge to Reform." M.A. thesis, University of Southern California, June 1965. 120 pp.

G20 Donald L. Singer. "Upton Sinclair and the California Gubernatorial Campaign." M.A. thesis, University of Southern California, January 1966. 153 pp.

G21* Alfred J. Albrecht. "A Rhetorical Study of Upton Sinclair's 1934 Campaign. . . ." Ph.D. dissertation, Indiana University, September 1966. 227 pp.

G22* David R. Yale. "From Mugwump to Socialist." Course paper, University of Minnesota, Spring 1967. 26 pp.

G23* David A. Remley. "The Correspondence of H. L. Mencken and Upton Sinclair." Ph.D. dissertation, Indiana University, July 1967. 488 pp.

G24* Charles C. Heimerdinger. "Propagandist in the Theater: the Career of Upton Sinclair as an American Dramatist." Ph.D. dissertation, Indiana University, August 1968. 436 pp.

G25 Mary M. Whipple. "Upton Sinclair: A Study of his Works of Social Criticism, 1918–1933." M.A. thesis, George Washington University, 1969. 80 pp.

G26 Lewis A. Fretz. "Upton Sinclair: The Don Quixote of American Reform." Ph.D. dissertation, Stanford University, August 1970.

In Progress:

G27 Martin Zanger. "Upton Sinclair's Reform Activities in California, 1915–1930." Department of History, Indiana University.

Title as of 1966.

G28 Christine Scriabine. "Upton Sinclair and the Literature of Protest." Ph.D. dissertation, Brown University.
Listed in *American Literature*, May 1969.

See also: Lawrence F. McNamee. *Dissertations in English and American Literature: Theses Accepted by American, British and German Universities, 1865–1964.* New York and London: R. R. Bowker, 1968.

IV. Supplementary Material

Compiled with the assistance of Edward Allatt

Supplement to Section A: Upton Sinclair's Publications

1905

SA1 *Circular Letter*. Princeton: The Author. 1 p.

1907

SA2 "Upton Sinclair Praises the President But Will Vote as a Socialist," *New York World*, 29 August.
Letter to editor.

1909

SA3 "Repudiates an Interview," *New York Times*, 16 February.
Letter to editor denying interview on "free love."

SA4 Marriage Is Nothing But Legalized Slavery," *Gazette* [Charleston, W. Va.], 28 February.
Short piece on marriage.

1910

SA5 Letter to the Editor, *New Age* [London], VI (3 February), 333.
Congratulating magazine on its success and socialistic outlook.

1910 continued

SA6 "The New Fourth," *New York Call*, 10 July, p. 16.
An address delivered by Upton Sinclair in Edgemore, Delaware, on 4 July 1910.

SA7 "Upton Sinclair's Statement," *Springfield Republican*, 23 July.
Letter to the editor on Fred D. Warren's conviction; see A371.

SA8 "Defends Wilshire Methods," *Social Democratic* [Milwaukee], 6 August.
Letter to the editor on Bishop Creek Mine and Gaylord Wilshire.

SA9 "The Coming Crisis," *New York Call*, 14 August, p. 16.

SA10 "Mr. Upton Sinclair and the New York *Outlook*," *New Age* [London], VII (18 August), 381.
Letter to editor concerning *Outlook*'s editorial in previous issue of that magazine.

SA11 "Rally to the *Appeal*," *New York Call*, 25 November.
Article on the Fred Warren case.

SA12 "New Conspiracy of Silence," *Appeal to Reason*, 24 December, p. 2.
Article on press, silence over Fred Warren case.

1911

SA13 "The Referendum," *New Age* [London], 12 January, p. 263.
Letter to editor on referendum in England.

SA14 "Jim Faraday Drame en 1 acte" (Beginning), *Les Temps Nouveaux, Supplement Litteraire*, VI, no. 16 (14 January), 433–435.
Completed in nos. 17 and 18, (21 and 28 January), pp. 443–444 and 450–452.

SA15 "*The Chasm*," *New York Call*, 4 February.
Letter to editor on George Cram Cook's book of that name.

SA16 "Taft and an Editor," *New York Evening Post*, 5 or 6 February.

Letter to editor on Fred Warren case.

SA17 "On Fasting," *New York Call*, 9 February.

Another letter in the correspondence with Dr. Robinson.

SA18 "On Fasting," *New York Call*, 19 February.

Letter to editor.

SA19 "On Fasting," *New York Call*, 23 February.

Letter to editor on fasting controversy.

SA20 "What Have the British Suffragettes Accomplished," *New York Call*, 26 February.

Letter to editor of *New Age* [London].

SA21 "Two Kinds of Fasting," *New York Call*, 27 February.

Letter to editor dated 22 February replying to letter from a correspondent in a previous issue.

SA22 "Advertising Claims," *New York Tribune*, 28 February.

Letter to editor on misleading nature of advertising claims.

SA23 "Literature and Economics," *New York Call*, 9 April, p. 10.

SA24 "From a Faster," *Life*, LVII (1 June), 1084.

Letter to the editor denying that his advice on fasting caused death of man who fasted for 15 days.

SA25 "Bringing Up a Boy," *News Tribune* [Detroit], 9 July.

SA26 "Sinclair, Freed, Wires World of Prison's Lessons," *World* [New York], 3 August, p. 1.

Telegraphed letter to the editor.

SA27 "A Card from Upton Sinclair," *New York Times*, 6 August.

Letter to the editor denying that he is a Single Taxer.

1911 continued

SA28 "A Suggested Plan," *Appeal to Reason*, 19 August, p. 2.
On Socialists' plans if successful at polls.

SA29 *America's Greatest Newspaper*. Girard, Kansas: *Appeal to Reason*. 4 pp.
Reprint of article which appeared in *Appeal to Reason* in June.

1912

SA30 "From the Author of *The Jungle*," *The Syndicalist* [England], I (March/April).
Letter to the editor on Tom Mann's imprisonment.

1913

SA31 "Genius and Privacy," *Chicago Evening Post*, 21 February, pp. 1, 14.
Review of Morley Robert's *The Private Life of Henry Maitland*.

SA32 "Sinclair with Sulzer," *Journal* [Ogdensburg, New York], 30 May.
Letter to editor of Albany Knickbocker Press offering support to Governor Sulzer.

SA33 "Sinclair Tells Story of Strike Mass-Drama," *Evening Journal* [New York], 6 June.
Article on Paterson, New Jersey, strike.

SA34 "Mr. Upton Sinclair's Local Illustration," *The Hertfordshire Express*, 1 November.
Letter to the editor in answer to criticism of his Letchworth speech.

1914

SA35 "Author of *The Jungle* Has Beauty Sleep Disturbed by Burglar," *Bermuda Colonist*, 4 February, p. 2.
Open letter to the burglar.

SA36 "Colorado, a Football for Big Business Interests, Sinclair Writes," *News* [Toledo, Ohio], 5 June.
On the Ludlow massacre.

SA37 "Sinclair Criticises Report," *New York Herald*, 10 June, p. 22.
Letter to editor on report of Tarrytown meeting.

SA38 "Colorado War Spreads . . ." and "A Challenge to the Associated Press," *Appeal to Reason*, 13 June, p. 2.
Articles on the Ludlow incident.

SA39 "Free Speech Fight in John D's Town," *Appeal to Reason*, 20 June, p. 2.
Article on speech following picketing of Rockefeller offices.

SA40 " 'No War Shall Curse this Land,' is the Socialist Demand," *Appeal to Reason*, 15 August.
Article on World War I.

SA41 "Literature of Protest," *American Socialist*, (19 September).
Letter to editor on collecting material for *Cry for Justice*.

SA42 "About *Samuel the Seeker*," *New York Call*, 13 October.
Letter to the editor explaining that this was not a new book.

SA43 "A Letter on the War," *New York Call*, 19 November.
Letter to unnamed German-American friend on the War situation.

1915

SA44 "Upton Sinclair Discusses 'Quack Novelists' in a Letter to Owen Wister," *New York Sundal Call*, 19 June, p. 11.
In response to Wister's article in *Atlantic Monthly*.

SA45 "The Wisdom of Mercy," *The Clarion* [London], no. 1229 (25 June), p. 3.
Article in reply to Robert Blatchford's article on conduct of the War.

1915 continued

SA46 "A Review by Upton Sinclair," *New York Sunday Call*, 27 June, p. 2.

An article on Scott Nearing.

SA47 "Spontaneous Combustion," *International Socialist Review*, xv (June), 723.

Article on Negro servant's understanding of Socialism.

SA48 "The Cry for Justice," *Weekly People*, 21 August.

Correspondence with Arnold Petersen about Sinclair's book. Further letter from Petersen in *Weekly People*, 28 August.

SA49 "The Lesson of the War," *Appeal to Reason*, 28 August, p. 4.

1916

SA50 "*Sylvia's Marriage*," *The Clarion* [London], no. 1257 (7 January), p. 2.

Letter to the editor taking issue with reviewer of his novel in earlier number of magazine.

SA51 "Punitive Tax on Wealth," *Philadelphia Public Ledger*, 18 February.

Letter to editor on income tax.

1917

SA52 "The Millionaire Socialist," *The Clarion* [London], no. 1321 (30 March), p. 3.

Long article on men of goodwill arising to save civilization.

1918

SA53 "Canning the Kaiser," *Mercury Herald* [San José], 26 March.

A poem; appeared in many other papers at same time.

SA54 "The New Book That Interested Me Most," *New York Sun*, 21 April.

1919

SA55 "*Jimmie Higgins*," *New York Times*, 24 August, p. 434.

SA56 "The Russian Tangle," *The Clarion* [London], no. 1460 (5 December), p. 6.

Letter to editor in reply to remark in 26 September issue of magazine.

1920

SA57 "The Russian Riddle," *The Clarion* [London], no. 1468 (30 January), p. 10.

Letter to editor continuing debate on Allied governments' interference in Russian affairs.

SA58 "Every Strike is Right," *World Tomorrow*, III (June), 176.

Short article on striking.

SA59 *Circular Letter*. Pasadena, 6 September. 1 leaf.

Beginning: "Dear Sirs. We beg to call your attention to a new novel . . . entitled *100%*."

SA60 "American Journalism and Mr. Upton Sinclair," *The Bookman's Journal* [London], 12 November.

Letter to the editor concerning *The Brass Check*.

SA61 "*The Brass Check* Once More," *The Weekly Review*, III (24 November), 498.

Letter to the editor concerning W. J. Ghent's review of *The Brass Check* in 3 November issue.

SA62 "Should the United States Have a Mandate over Mexico?" *Pittsburgh Dispatch*, 27 November, p. 4.

A symposium by well-known people.

SA63 " 'Suppressing' Upton Sinclair," *Globe & Commercial Advertiser* [New York], 21 December.

Letter to editor answering W. J. Ghent.

1920 continued

SA64 *Circular Letter*. Pasadena, 1920.

A "Notice to Dealers," beginning: "Increasing costs makes it impossible for us to give trade discounts. . . ."

1921

SA65 "Debs and the Poets," *New York Call*, 17 January, p. 8.

Letter to the editor concerning David Karsner's review of Ruth Le Prade's *Debs and the Poets*, published by Sinclair.

SA66 "Upton Sinclair Writes," *New York Herald*, 26 January.

Letter to the editor complaining of *New York Herald* editorial poking fun at Sinclair's need for capital to publish his books.

SA67 "Ghent vs. Sinclair," *New York Evening Globe*, 4 February.

Letter to the editor concerning the continuing correspondence between Sinclair and W. J. Ghent.

SA68 "Upton Sinclair Writes Another," *Editor & Publisher*, 12 February.

Letter to the editor pointing out errors of fact in statements about *The Brass Check* in previous issue.

SA69 "Swift & Company Advertising," *The Golden Age*, 16 February, pp. 290–292.

Letter to magazine at their request to answer letter from Swift & Co.

SA70 "Frank Harris and England," *Pearson's Magazine*, XLVII (February), 259.

SA71 "Concerning God," *Appeal to Reason*, 16 April, p. 2.

SA72 *Circular Letter*. Pasadena, 1921. 1 leaf.

"A Proposition to Reprint the Early Books of Upton Sinclair"; printed on brown 'kraft' paper.

1923

SA73 Letter to President David P. Barrows, University of California, Berkeley, *Laughing Horse*, no. 5 (January), pp. 7–11.

Sinclair takes Barrows to task for his suppression of material published in University magazine. Dated 14 December 1922.

SA74 "Upton Sinclair's Arrest," *New Age* [London], XXXIII (2 August).

Reprint of Sinclair's letter in *New Republic*, 11 July.

SA75 "As We Grow Old We Realize That Human Motives Are Mixed and That Characters are Complicated," *Baltimore American*, 2 December.

Review of *Damaged Souls* by Gamaliel Bradford.

SA76 "We Have Developed Our Material Power Marvelously But We Have Not Equally Developed Our Moral Power," *New York American*, 9 December, L11, p. 3.

Review of *The Ship* by St. John G. Ervine.
Also in *Boston Advertiser*, 16 December, and *Los Angeles Examiner*, 23 December.

SA77 "Modern Psychology Is Exploring the Subconscious Mind and Discovering Mechanism by Which Miracles are Wrought," *New York American*, 16 December.

Review of *Oh Doctor* by Harry Leon Wilson.
Also in *Boston Advertiser*, 23 December, and *San Francisco Examiner*, 30 December.

SA78 "Another Great International War Is Coming Quickly; It Will be a Desperate Struggle for the World's Oil," *New York American*, 23 December.

Review of *Oil and the Germs of War* by Scott Nearing.
Also in *Baltimore American*, 23 December, *Washington Herald*, 30 December and *Syracuse American*, 30 December.

1923 continued

SA79 "Gandhi's Undertaking to Deliver Idea from British Oppression Is World's Most Colossal Experiment in Political Idealism," *New York American*, 30 December.

Review of *Gandhi the Apostle* by H. T. Muzumdar.
Also in *Rochester American*, 6 January 1924, and *Syracuse American*, 6 January 1924.

1924

SA80 "Coming Into Power of the Labor Party in Britain Is a Great Event in the History of Mankind," *New York American*, 20 January.

Review of *The Case for Nationalization* by A. Emil Davies.
Also in *Baltimore American*, 20 January, *Milwaukee Telegram*, 27 January, and *Los Angeles Examiner*, 3 February.

SA81 "Bok Plan Will Not End War Because It Is Political, Whereas Causes of Modern War Are Economic," *New York American*, 3 February.

Review of *The History of the French People* by Guy de Batut and Georges Friedmann.
Also in *Baltimore American*, 3 February.

SA82 "Our Policy Toward Russia Has Been One of Stupid Reactionism and Bigotry, Poor Aid to a People Educating Themselves to Rule," *New York American*, 17 February, L, p. 13.

Review of *Cross Currents in Europe Today* by Charles A. Beard.
Also in *Baltimore American*, 17 February, *Boston Advertiser*, 24 February, *Washington Herald*, 2 March, and *Seattle Post Intelligencer*, 16 March.

SA83 "*Literary Digest* Third Week," *Union Record* [Seattle], 9 October.

Letter to editor on polls concerning Prohibition.

1925

SA84 "My Dear Madam," *Open Forum*, II (11 April), 3.

Letter on Prohibition, probably to a German woman, as Sinclair apologises at having difficulty in reading German script.

SA85 Letter to the Editor, *New York Times*, 26 April.

On review of *Mammonart*.

SA86 "Mr. Sinclair Replies," *Independent*, CXIV (23 May), 596–597.

Letter to editor on review of *Mammonart*.

SA87 "The Faith Betrayed," *The Alert* [Queensland], 19 June.

A poem.

SA88 "The Total Amount of Drinking is Less Then It Was . . . ," *Manufacturers' Record*, 30 July, p. 74.

Letter to editor on Prohibition.

SA89 "Der Ungekronte König," *Frankfurter Zeitung*, 12 August.

On Mark Twain, part of Chapter C in *Mammonart*, 326–333.

SA90 "Sinclair Talks Back," *New York Telegraph*, 16 August.

Letter to G.D.E. on his review of *Mammonart*.

SA91 "Brief Von Upton Sinclair," *Stachelschwein* [Frankfurt], 31 August, pp. 15–19.

German translation of Sinclair's circular letter dated 20 May 1925 regarding Co-operative Organization for the publishing of his books.

1926

SA92 "Mr. Sinclair to Mr. Jordan-Smith: A Copy," *World Tomorrow*, IX (January), 19.

Letter to Paul Jordan-Smith on article in December 1925 issue of magazine.

1926 continued

SA93 "Meeting the Attacks of the Small Town Dictator," *Haldeman-Julius Weekly*, no. 1584 (13 April), p. 4.
Letter to editor of *Evening Journal* [Lisbon, Ohio].

SA94 "Upton Sinclair Declares Himself an Agnostic," *Haldeman-Julius Weekly*, no. 1585 (17 April), p. 3.
Letter to Woolsey Teller, New York City.

SA95 "Upton Sinclair and the Ohio Censors," *Haldeman-Julius Weekly*, no. 1587 (1 May), p. 1.
Letter to editor of *Evening Journal* [Lisbon, Ohio] on library throwing out his books.

SA96 "Upton Sinclair's Letter to a Poet," *Haldeman-Julius Weekly*, no. 1587 (1 May), p. 1.
Letter to William Ellery Leonard.

SA97 "Rises to Tell," *Time*, VII (28 June), 10.
Letter to editor on Bernarr Macfadden's cures.

SA98 "Mencken and Sinclair," *San Francisco News*, 15 October.
Letter to editor on rumors of Mencken visiting with him.

1927

SA99 "Man, Not Monkey," *Nation*, CXXIV (2 March), 336.
Letter to editor on symposium in current *New Masses*.

SA100 "Sinclair Assails War Plot Against Soviets," *The Daily Worker*, 14 April.
Letter to editor of *Vetchernava Moskva*.

SA101 "That Foreman," *Nation*, CXXIV (1 June), 611.
Letter to editor on magazine's "Prize Poems."

1928

SA102 Letter to the Editor, *Banner of Life* [Boston], 7 April, p. 2.
Explaining what he "believes" about psychic phenomena.

SA103 "Personal Immortality," *New York Times*, 8 April, sect. 9, p. 1.

A symposium on the question of "life after death."

SA104 "Socialist Denounces War," *Indian National Herald* [Bombay], 15 October.

Article on poverty and war.

1929

SA105 "A *Brass Check* Footnote," *Boston Herald*, 9 February.

Letter to editor on review of *Boston*.

SA106 "The S.L.P. in Boston," *New Leader* [London], VIII (16 March).

Letter to editor on Sacco-Vanzetti case.

SA107 "From Abroad," *New Leader* [London], VIII (3 May), 7.

Messages from Upton Sinclair and Leon Blum.

SA108 "The Pulitzer Prize and 'Special Pleading,' " *Minnesota Daily*, 7 May, p. 2.

Article on awarding of prize.

1930

SA109 "The Curse of Unlimited Breeding," *The American Freeman*, no. 1787 (1 March), p. 4.

Letter on birth control "to the editor of *Janmabhumi*, a paper devoted to the freedom of India."

SA110 "Yes, We Have Bread Lines, " *The American Freeman*, no. 1789 (15 March), p. 3.

Letter to George S. Viereck; see SA112.

SA111 "Upton Sinclair on Free Speech," *The American Freeman*, no. 1790 (22 March), p. 3.

Letter to Julius Mosner on Communism.

1930 continued

SA112 "About Food—Therefore Highly Important," *The American Freeman*, no. 1791 (29 March), p. 2.

An additional note to George S. Viereck; see SA110.

SA113 "Radicals and Police Clubs," *The American Freeman*, no. 1795 (26 April), p. 2.

Correspondence between Sinclair and Horton on Communism.

SA114 " 'Reform Society, Not the Rebel'—Sinclair," *The American Freeman*, no. 1811 (16 August), p. 1.

Letter to State Board of Prison Directors, San Quentin.

SA115 "Upton Sinclair," *Sierra Educational News*, August, p. 16.

Letter to editor explaining platform as Socialist candidate for Governor of California.

SA116 "A Sinclair Bibliography," *Saturday Review of Literature*, VII (27 September), 171.

Letter to editor.

SA117 "Can Mr. Pepper Speeka da Engleesh?" *New Republic*, LXIV (8 October), 259.

Letter to editor on Communism in America.

1931

SA118 "Upton Sinclair and the Communists," *Forward* [Glasgow], 31 January.

Letter to International Defense Organization.

1932

SA119 "The Sportsmanship of Mr. Pope," *The Star* [London], 13 October.

Letter to editor on review of *Candid Reminiscences* (*American Outpost*).

SA120 "Success of Socialism in USSR Means End of Capitalism, Says Upton Sinclair," *Moscow Daily News*, 8 November, p. 2.
Letter to editor on 15th Anniversary of Soviet Union.

SA121 "Go Slow in Denouncing the Rabble, Dr. Larkin," *Open Forum*, IX (17 December), 2.
Letter to Secretary of California State Church Federation.

SA122 "Hell Next," *Open Forum*, IX (17 December), 2.
Letter to the editor concerning Prohibition.

1933

SA123 "Marx & Labor," *Scribner's Magazine*, XCIII (April), 14–15.
Letter to editor on Max Nomad's article in previous issue. Nomad replies on page 15.

SA124 *The EPIC Plan: (E)nd (P)overty (I)n (C)alifornia.* n.p., *c.* 1933.
Broadside: the 12 points of the End Poverty plan.

1934

SA125 "The Nation's Largest 'Pork Barrel,'" *The Young Democrat*, February, pp. 10–11.
Article on "Production for Use."

SA126 "Upton Sinclair Explains Basis of His Plan to End Poverty," *Citizen Register* [Ossining, New York], 31 August, p. 2.
Article on EPIC Plan.

SA127 "To the Editor of the *Literary Digest*," *Literary Digest*, CXVIII (8 September), 6.
Congratulates editor on fine piece of journalism in previous week's issue.

1934 continued

SA128 "Upton Sinclair's Position," *Christian Science Monitor*, October.

Letter to editor on editorial in paper dated 11 October 1934.

SA129 "The Power of Your Subconscious Mind," *Modern Living*, IX (October), 172–173, 192–194.

SA130 "Sinclairiana," *Time*, XXIV (5 November), 2.

Letter to editor on Helicon Hall misstatement in 22 October issue of magazine.

SA131 "Upton Sinclair Writes Poem-Prayer," *Christian Century*, LI (14 November), 1467.

Reprint of poem in *New Republic*, 7 November.

SA132 "An Apology," *Nation*, CXXXIX (26 December), 741.

Letter to editor concerning misleading statement in Sinclair's article in *Nation*, 28 November.

SA133 *The EPIC Plan. What Is It?* Los Angeles, West Branch: Upton Sinclair. 4 pp.

Outlines the EPIC Plan.

1935

SA134 "A Retraction from Mr. Sinclair," *Nation*, CXL (16 January), 131.

Letter to the editor withdrawing allegations of preachers receiving money to vote against him.

SA135 Letter to Editor, *Daily Record* [Coalinga, California], September.

Letter dated 5 September 1935 in reply to editorial in previous issue of newspaper.

SA136 "A Letter from Upton Sinclair," *The American Freeman*, no. 1957 (October), p. 4.

Letter to E. Haldeman-Julius, dated 1 August 1935, concerning EPIC Plan. (*The American Freeman* was a monthly by this time; thus no day of the month is given.)

SA137 *Circular letter*. Pasadena: The Author. 1 p.

"I put this statement in writing in order to avoid hurting the feelings of many friends. . . ."

1936

SA138 "Calls Fascism: a Reply," *Pacific Weekly*, IV (9 March), 127.

Letter to the editor on the Carey McWilliam-Upton Sinclair debate in previous issue of magazine.

SA139 Letter to the Editor, *Modern Monthly*, IX (March), 511-512.

Protesting attack on him in previous issue.

SA140 "Upton Sinclair," *New York Times*, 26 April.

Letter to the editor on Alfred Kazin's review of *What God Means to Me*.

SA141 "Roadtown," *New Republic*, LXXXVII (15 July), 297.

Letter to editor on death of Edgar Chambless.

SA142 "Tributes to Gorky," *Soviet Russia Today*, July, p. 8.

Tributes by various writers.

SA143 "Browder Call," *Sunday Worker* [New York], 20 September, p. 7.

Concerning Earl Browder.

SA144 "Election Strategy and Advice," *New Republic*, LXXXVIII (14 October), 282.

Letter to editor on "vote swapping."

SA145 "How They Are Voting," *New Republic*, LXXXVIII (21 October), 304.

Article on why he is voting for Roosevelt.

1936 continued

SA146 "A Prisoner in Poland," *Christian Century*, 9 December, p. 1657.

Letter to editor on imprisonment of Sinclair's Polish translator. Also in *New Republic*, 9 December, p. 177.

SA147 " 'As Deaf as the Post,' " *The Progressive*, I (19 December), 4.

Article castigating *Saturday Evening Post*.

SA148 "A Message to Writers," *The Progressive*, I (26 December), 4.

Article advising young writers.

1937

SA149 "Mr. Sinclair Corrects," *Common Sense*, VI (January), 3.

Letter to editor correcting mistake in November 1936 issue of magazine.

SA150 "How To Stay Out of War," *Forum*, XCVII (April), 253.

Views of various noted figures, Sinclair's on page 253.

SA151 "Upton Sinclair Answers," *Common Sense*, VI (April), 2, 30.

Letter to editor on Rosika Schwimmer.

SA152 "Banning Books," *Boston Traveler*, 1 May.

Letter to editor on Massachusetts' bill to bar Sinclair's books.

SA153 "Both Use Dynamite," *World Wide* [Montreal], 28 August, p. 697.

Extract from article in *The Progressive*.

SA154 "The Settin' Down Job," *Richmond Times-Dispatch*, 10 October, pp. 3, 7.

Article advising young writers.

SA155 "Why I Wrote *The Flivver King*," *United Automobile Worker*, 23 October, p. 3.

SA156 "USSR—A Beacon Light to the World, Upton Sinclair Tells *Russky Golos*," *Russky Golos* [U.S.A.], 7 November.
Letter to the editor of this Russian daily printed in U.S.A.

1938

SA157 "A Plan of Life for the Duke and Duchess of Windsor," *Liberty*, xv (26 February), 11–13.
An article in form of letter to Duke of Windsor.

SA158 "Upton Sinclair Answers Slander Against USSR," *People's World*, 5 March, p. 4.
Letter to Eugene Lyons.

SA159 "A Letter to Eugene Lyons," *New Masses*, XXVI (8 March), 5–6.
Open letter on Soviet Union.

SA160 "They Will Defend Their Freedom," *The Tribune* [London], 10 June, p. 7.
On Soviet Union.

SA161 "Capitalism Plus Murder," *The Labor Union* [Dayton, Ohio], 24 June, p. 4 plus last page.
On Fascism.

SA162 "Whither Civilization?" *Open Forum*, xv (25 June), 1.
Article on current world problems.

SA163 "Defining Liberal," *The Progressive*, II (23 July), 3.
Short article on meaning of "liberal."

1938 continued

SA164 "Upton Sinclair Disagrees," *New Leader* [London], XXI (23 July), 4.
Letter to editor on review of *Terror in Russia.* Reviewer E. L. Tartak replies.

SA165 "This Striving for Peace," *The Progressive,* II (13 August), 3.

SA166 "Upton Sinclair," *New York Times Book Review,* 14 August.
Letter to editor regarding Norah Hoult's review of *Our Lady.*

SA167 "To Some of My Readers," *The Progressive,* II (24 September), 3.

SA168 "Upton Sinclair on Communists," *New York Times,* 27 September.
Letter to editor regarding feature on Sinclair in *New York Times,* 18 September.

SA169 " 'Ham and Eggs' for California," *The Progressive,* II (15 October), 3.

SA170 "Sinclair Books in 39 Countries," *Common Cause* [Australia], 22 October, p. 7.
Letter on his latest activities.

SA171 "To the People of South Africa," *The Voice* [South Africa], 26 October, p. 15.

SA172 "Can We Go That (sic) Way?" *EPIC News,* V (1 December), 3–4.
Article selected from "Your Million Dollars."

SA173 "Your Million Dollars," *New Masses,* XXIX (20 December), 19.
Letter to editor on inflation.

SA174 "Communications," *Free America,* December, p. 17.
Two letters to editor on planned economy.

SA175 "Mental Radio," *Prediction*, December, pp. 1012–1014.
Article answering Robert Blatchford's disbelief.

1939

SA176 *Circular Letter*. Pasadena: Upton Sinclair. 1 p.
Letter to readers regretting unavailability of time to help them.

1940

SA177 "Birthday Greetings," *Nation*, CL (27 January), 112.
Message of congratulations on magazine's 75th anniversary.

SA178 "What Socialism Means to Me," *New York Call*, 4 May, p. 8.
Letter to the editor on Socialism.

SA179 "England's Fighting Strength," *New Republic*, CIII (14 October), 527.
Sinclair sent letter by Phyllis Bottome on England's political situation.

1941

SA180 *Circular Letter*. New York: Upton Sinclair. 1 p.
Announcing publication of *Dragon's Teeth* on January 5 by Viking Press.

SA181 "An Explanatory Note," *The Literary Guide*, March, p. 36.
Letter to the editor explaining his careful research into English accents for his book *World's End*.

SA182 "Cheerful," *Time*, XXXVII (28 April), 6.
Letter to the editor concerning *Time*'s review of *Between Two Worlds*.

SA183 "Waiting for Leadership," *Nation*, CLII (14 June), 707.
Letter to the editor giving text of Sinclair's telegram to President Roosevelt.

1941 continued

SA184 "My Stand in the War," *New Masses*, XL (15 July), 13.

Comments by Lion Feuchtwanger, Upton Sinclair, and Dudley Nichols.

SA185 Two letters to the Editor, *The American Freeman*, no. 2026 (July), p. 4.

First letter offers condolences to editor on death of wife Marcel Haldeman-Julius; Second letter discourses upon events of the time.

SA186 "The Present Great Crisis," *The Publishers' Circular*, CLV (16 August), 83–84.

Article on the times and *World's End* and *Between Two Worlds*.

SA187 "Soviet Anniversary," *Nation*, CLIII (15 November), 496.

Letter to the editor giving text of telegram sent by request to Tass Agency.

SA188 "Supports V-Democracy," *V for Democracy*, I (November), 1.

Message supporting magazine.

SA189 "Sinclair's Answer," *V for Democracy*, I (November), 2.

Reply to speech on isolationism by President of Vassar College.

SA190 "Writer's Declare 'We Have a War to Win,' " *Sunday Worker*, 21 December.

Message from Theodore Dreiser, Upton Sinclair, and Millen Brand.

1942

SA191 "A Puzzled Author," *Saturday Review of Literature*, XXV (7 February), 11.

Letter to editor concerning review of *Dragon's Teeth*.

SA192 Letter to the Editor, *Jewish Spectator*, February, p. 34.

Concerning Jewish "interest" in *Between Two Worlds*.

SA193 "More Moon," *New Republic*, CVI (6 April), 463.
Letter to editor concerning James Thurber's review of Steinbeck's *The Moon Is Down*.

SA194 "U.S.S.R. Locked Up in Hearts of Masses," *Today's PP Booklets*. London: Practical Press, July, p. 7.
Sinclair greets Soviet fellow writers.

SA195 "Upton Sinclair Hits Use of Snobbery," *The American Freeman*, no. 2041 (October), p. 4.
Letter to editor concerning "black tie" and "Red Russia."

1943

SA196 "*Wide Is the Gate*," *New Republic*, CVIII (8 February), 184.
Letter to editor on review of book.

SA197 "From the USSR," *New Masses*, XLVIII (20 July), 18.
Letter to editor on review of *Wide Is the Gate*.

1944

SA198 "My Vote—And Why," *New Masses*, LIII (October), 3-4.
Symposium on presidential election.

1948

SA199 "Mix Well," *Time*, LI (26 January), 4–5.
Letter to editor concerning material in previous issue of *Time*.

SA200 "The Author and His Public," *Books of Today* [London], November, pp. 6–7.

1949

SA201 "Everlasting Sinclair," *Newsweek*, 8 August, p. 2.
Letter to the editor on success of *Lanny Budd*.

1949 continued

SA202 "Sequel to a Sequel," *Saturday Review of Literature*, XXXII (20 August), 25.
Letter to the editor regarding review of *O Shepherd, Speak!*

1953

SA203 "Don't Play Ball With the Reds," *Forward* [Glasgow], 12 December, p. 5.
Letter to the editor.

SA204 *Présence de Zola*. Paris: Fasquelle Editeurs. 246 pp.
Symposium by various writers; Sinclair's contribution on page 29.

1954

SA205 "Slipping Socialism," *New Republic*, CXXX (15 February), 22.
Letter to the editor.

SA206 "Blueprint for a Red World," *World* [Tulsa], 31 March.
Article on modern science.

SA207 "This Was Communist Camouflage," *Forward* [Glasgow], 10 April, p. 5.
Letter to editor on Scott Nearing.

SA208 "When is a Communist?" *Waco News Tribune* [Texas], 19 June.

SA209 "Eisenhower's Liberalism," *New Republic*, CXXXI (13 September), 23.
Letter to the editor.

1955

SA210 "Today's Dr. Faustus," *Trenton Evening Times*, 16 February, p. 20.
Article on state of world.

SA211 "To My Friends: The People of Japan," *Japan News* [Tokyo], 16 July, p. 4.

SA212 "A Resort to Rice Diet," *The Malabar Herald*, 3 September, p. 7.

1956

SA213 "*The Cup of Fury*," *New Republic*, CXXXV (15 October), 31.

Letter to editor on success of book.

SA214 Letter to Editor, *Time*, LXVIII (10 December), 12.

Letter to the editor on Psi Epsilon Fraternity disgrace.

1958

SA215 "Reflections at Eighty," *New Leader* [London], XLI (8 September), 16–18.

Sinclair looks at the U.S.A. and the world scene.

1962

SA216 "Upton Sinclair, Homer Croy and Robert Graves Dissent," *Mark Twain Journal*, XI (Summer), 17. Ernest Hemingway Memorial Number.

"I am afraid that anything I would say about poor Hemingway would not please his readers. He was one more of those pitiful victims of 'John Barleycorn'; and if you want to know what I think about that read *The Cup of Fury*."

1964

SA217 "A Comment by Upton Sinclair." In *Walter P. Reuther on First Things First*. Santa Barbara: The Center for the Study of Democratic Institutions, March, p. 11.

An occasional paper in which Sinclair expresses amazement at the advanced technology used in topping the eugenia trees round his home.

1964 continued

SA218 "The Class War," *Saturday Review*, XLVII, (29 August), 63.

Reprint of letter to editor first published in *Saturday Review* 16 July 1927.

SA219 "The Chaplin Story—Gags to Riches," *Los Angeles Times*, 11 October.

Review of Charlie Chaplin's autobiography.

SA220 Foreword to *Tongue Speaking*, by Morton T. Kelsey. New York: Doubleday & Co., pp. v–vi.

1968

SA221 "Once a Nation's Conscience, Upton Sinclair Looks Back," *The Sunday Oregonian*, 15 September, p. 11F.

Sinclair's health at this time would have prevented him from actually writing this, although he has the by-line.

1969

SA222 W. Storrs Lee. *California: A Literary Chronicle.* New York: Funk & Wagnalls. 537 pp.

A chronicle by various writers. Sinclair's contribution on pages 472–476 entitled "This Land of Hope"—reprint of Chapter 2 of *Oil!*.

Supplement to Section C: Upton Sinclair's Books and Pamphlets in Translation and Foreign Editions

English

1971

They Call Me Carpenter (1922)

SC1 *They Call Me Carpenter*, Bath: Cedric Chivers, 1971. 225 pp.

Supplement to Section F: Books and Articles about Upton Sinclair

1906

SF1 Raymond. "President 'Calls' *Jungle* Author," *Chicago Daily Tribune*, 10 April.

On President Theodore Roosevelt's decision to send investigating team to look into Sinclair's allegations about the Chicago meatpackers.

SF2 A. M. Simons. "Packingtown, *The Jungle*, und seine Kritiker," *Neue Zeit* [Stuttgart], II (1906), 453–460.

1911

SF3 Walter Lippmann. "Upton Sinclair's Dilemma," *The International*, IV (December), 7–8.

Article on *Love's Pilgrimage*.

1913

SF4 Gerald Gould. "Homer and Mr. Sinclair," *The New Statesman*, I (24 May), 209–210.

A reply to Sinclair's article "On Re-Reading Homer" in *The New Statesman*, 10 May.

1916

SF5 "Upton Sinclair Pays Tribute to London," *San Francisco Chronicle*, 24 November, p. 3.

Quoting Sinclair on Jack London's death.

1918

SF6 Frank Harris. "Upton Sinclair As Critic," *Pearson's Magazine*, XXXVIII (February), 381.

1920

SF7 William Marion Reedy. "His Last Manuscript," *Reedy's Mirror*, 5 August, pp. 603–604.

This MS is entitled "Sinclair, the Jungler"; a facsimile of Reedy's holograph beginning of the article preceeds the printed article.

1921

SF8 H. L. Mencken. *Prejudices, First Series*. New York: Alfred Knopf, pp. 145–146.

1925

SF9 William Lyons Phelps. "As I Like It," *Scribner's Magazine*, LXXVII (May), 546.

On Sinclair's attack on Yale.

1927

SF10 F. Lauriston Bullard. "Book-Banning Issue Burning in Boston," *New York Times*, 3 July.

On Boston's penchant for censoring books, including Sinclair's *Oil*!.

1928

SF11 F. Lauriston Bullard. "Boston Comments on Novelist's Luck," *New York Times*, 5 February.

On the Rumford Press's decision not to print *The Bookman*, in which installments of Sinclair's novel had been appearing.

SF12 S. A. de Witt. "The Chatter Box," *New Leader* [London], VII (24 November), 5.

A weekly column which contains a 13 verse poem entitled "Lines for Upton Sinclair" by de Witt, written to mark Sinclair's 50th birthday.

1929

SF13 "Boston Book Censors Lose in Legislature," *New York Herald Tribune*, 21 March, p. 2.

On revision of Massachusetts' censorship laws, partly resulting from the arrest of Sinclair for selling novel *Boston* in the streets.

1933

SF14 "Upton Sinclair, Another ex-Socialist," *The World Tomorrow*, 12 October, p. 559.

Editorial on Sinclair's intention to run for Governor of California as Democrat.

1934

SF14 "Upton Sinclair Opens Campaign," *The Christian Century*, III (January), 33.

On Sinclair's speech in Berkeley outlining his EPIC program.

SF16 Clifford Cashman. "Upton Sinclair, California's New Dealer," *Plain Talk Magazine*, X (March), 22–23, 40.

SF17 George P. West. "Democrats Gain Lead in California," *New York Times*, 22 April.

On registration of Party affiliation and Sinclair's success in the gubernatorial campaign to date.

SF18 Kenneth Stewart. "Upton Sinclair and His *EPIC* Plan for California," *Literary Digest*, CXVIII (25 August), 10.

SF19 Robert Ordway Foote. "The Radical vs. Conservative Issue in California," *Literary Digest*, CXVIII (8 September), 7–8.

SF20 George P. West. "Sinclair Modifies Some of His Plans," *New York Times*, 16 September.

SF21 "Charm," *Time*, XXIV (17 September), 1.

Part of magazine's National Affairs feature concerning Sinclair's visit with President Franklin D. Roosevelt at Hyde Park.

1934 continued

SF22 Sherwin C. Badger. "Uptonia: California's Millenium," *Barron's*, 1 October, pp. 3,10.

SF23 Walter Davenport. "Sinclair Gets the Glory Vote," *Collier's*, XCIV (27 October), 12–13, 32, 34, 36.

SF24 "The EPIC Plan of Upton Sinclair," *Nation*, CXXXIX (31 October), 495.
An editorial on the California gubernatorial election.

SF25 Carey McWilliams. "Sinclair Wanes," *New Republic*, LXXX (7 November), 356.

SF26 "The Week," *New Republic*, LXXX (7 November), 349–350.
An editorial about the California election.

SF27 "Sinclair, La Follette, and Cutting," *Nation*, CXXXIX (7 November), 522.
An editorial on the Wisconsin, New Mexico, and California gubernatorial elections.

SF28 W. B. "The Great Game of American Politics—Sinclair, Long, Bilbo and the New Deal," *The China Weekly Review*, III (November), 320–321.

SF29 "Merriam Tops Sinclair in Final Poll Report," *Literary Digest*, CXVIII (November), 5, 43.
Feature on opinion poll four days before election day.

1935

SF30 Richard S. Ames. "The Screen Enters Politics," *Harper's Monthly Magazine*, CLXX (March), 473–482.
On the motion picture industry's part in influencing political opinion in California during the 1934 gubernatorial election.

1936

SF31 Lillian Symes. "After EPIC in California," *Nation*, CXLII (22 April), 509–511.

On the continuation of the EPIC movement.

1938

SF32 Editors of *International Literature*. "To our dear friend, Upton Sinclair," *International Literature*, no. 9 (September), p. 63.

A letter congratulating Sinclair on his 60th birthday.

1939

SF33 David Sinclair. "An Open Letter to Upton Sinclair From His Socialist Son," New York *Call*, 16 December.

1943

SF34 "Recipients of 1943 Pulitzer Prizes . . . ," *New York Times*, 4 May.

On Sinclair's award for *Dragon's Teeth*.

SF35 Florence Wagner. "Our Cover Boy," *Rob Wagner's Script*, XXIX (29 May), 10-11.

SF36 "Upton Sinclair Threatens to Sue WPB If It Refuses More Paper for a Book," *New York Times*, 8 August.

On War Production Board refusal to allow paper for book that criticises U.S. Government's handling of World War II.

1947

SF37 Anna Mary Wells. "Mr. Sinclair's Fallacy," *Saturday Review of Literature*, XXX (26 April), 19.

A letter to the editor about Sinclair's choice of Isaiah for "I Wish I'd Written That" in *Saturday Review*, 11 January.

1948

SF38 S. Gorley Putt. "World Without End," *The Wind and the Rain*, Winter, pp. 105–117.

1949

SF39 P. Pavlenko. "Upton Sinclair—Careerist and Slanderer," *Literaturnaya Gazeta*, 20 April.
Reprinted in English in *Current Digest of Soviet Press*, 24 May.

1953

SF40 Enriqueta Lopez Lira. *Colegio de Mexico, Estudios Historicos Americanos*; *Homenje a Silvio Zavala*, pp. 685-717.

1956

SF41 David Herreshoff. "Upton Sinclair's *The Jungle*," *The American Socialist*, III (November), 16–19.

1958

SF42 Roy Ringer. "Upton Sinclair, 80, Looks Back on EPIC Crusades," *Los Angeles Evening Mirror News*, 18 September, pp. 1, 8.

1960

SF43 Elizabeth Coulsen. "City Backs Sinclair Privacy," *Los Angeles Examiner*, 18 September.
News story on eve of Sinclair's 82nd birthday.

SF44 Harry W. Flannery. "Upton Sinclair Tapes Available to Teachers," *American Teacher Magazine*, XLV (October), 16–17.
Article on availability of tape recordings of "The Sinclair Story."

1961

SF45 "Educate on Labor's Struggle with 'The Upton Sinclair Story,'" *AFL-CIO Education News and Views*, VI (January/February), 18–19.

An article about the tape recordings of "The Upton Sinclair Story," and a new edition of *The Jungle* published by the New American Library.

SF46 John Drury. "The Book That Blew Up the Stockyards," *The Butcher Workman*, May/June, pp. 11–13, 32.

An article on *The Jungle*.

1962

SF47 Elinor Hopper Bishop. "World Figure Lives Peacefully in Monrovia Foothill Setting," *Daily News-Post* [Monrovia, California], 12 May.

SF48 Joseph Wershba. "An Old-Time Muckraker Still Puts His Trust in the People," *New York Post*, 7 May, p. 44.

SF49 Wesley Marx. "Upton Sinclair: Rebel in Retirement," *Los Angeles Times*, 3 June, pp. 41–44.

1963

SF50 Al Heaner. "Upton Sinclair, Still Seeks Justice," *U.A.W. Solidarity*, VI (March), 7.

SF51 Marilyn Anker. "Upton Sinclair, The Gentleman Rebel," *Dial* [Milwaukee-Downer College Magazine], I (18 October).

1964

SF52 Peter Cutchek. "Conversation across the Ocean," *Ogonok*, no. 19 (May), pp. 20–21.

In Russian.

1964 continued

SF53 George Reasons. "War Begun on Poverty Years Ago," *Los Angeles Times*, 1 July.

On Sinclair's life-long struggle to get better conditions for the poor.

SF54 Gladwin Hill. "Upton Sinclair, 85, Recalls EPIC and Salutes Antipoverty Drive," *New York Times*, 1 July.

On Sinclair's reaction to President Johnson's poverty program.

SF55 Bob Barger. "Raymond L. Haight and the Commonwealth Progressive Campaign of 1934," *The California Historical Society Quarterly*, XLIII (September), 219–230.

An article concerning one of Sinclair's opponents in the 1934 Californian gubernatorial election.

1965

SF56 Elmont Waite. "The Radical Who's Had His Say," *San Francisco Chronicle*, 19 January, p. 7.

On Sinclair's decision to finally give up his writing.

1966

SF57 Boris Yaro. "Civil Libertarian Sinclair Honored," *Los Angeles Times*, 21 March.

On the American Civil Liberties Union's tribute to Sinclair.

SF58 Edward Lahart. "Upton Sinclair, Still an Unabashed Reformer and Optimist," *Frontier*, 17 August, pp. 13–14.

SF59 William L. O'Neill, Ed. *Echoes of Revolt: The Masses 1911 to 1917*. Chicago: Quadrangle Books, 1966, pp. 94, 255–257.

1967

SF60 Richard L. Coe. "Upton Sinclair Rides Again," *The Washington Post*, 26 July, p. C5.

SF61 N. Brian Eastman. "Teachers, To the Rear," *Changing Education*, II (Fall), 12–18.

SF62 Max Frankel. "Johnson Welcomes Upton Sinclair, 89, at Meat Bill Signing," *New York Times*, 16 December.

On Sinclair's presence at Meat Inspection Bill signing. This story also carried by most important newspapers across the U.S.A.

1968

SF63 "Prolific and Enduring," *New York Times*, 21 September.

On celebration of Sinclair's 90th birthday.

SF64 Roy Haines. "Upton Sinclair, 90, Noted Author, Dies," *Los Angeles Times*, 26 November, pp. 1, 22.

On Sinclair's death. This story carried by nearly all important newspapers throughout the world.

SF65 Gerald Johnson. "Upton Sinclair: Not to be Dismissed," *Baltimore Sunday Sun*, 1 December, p. K1.

1969

SF66 Boris Alexandrov. "In Memory of Upton Sinclair," *Soviet Literature*, IV (April), 182–184.

SF67 Judson A. Grenier. "Upton Sinclair: A Remembrance," *The California Historical Society Quarterly*, XLVIII (June), 165–169.

SF68 Edward Allatt. "Collecting Upton Sinclair in England," *American Book Collector*, XX (October), 23–24.

1970

SF69 Justin G. Turner. "Conversation with Upton Sinclair," *American Book Collector*, XXI (Summer), 7–10.

SF70 Lawrence Clark Powell. "California Classics Reread: *Oil!*" *Westways*, LXII (September), 14–17, 58–59.

SF71 Peter A. Soderbergh. "Upton Sinclair and Hollywood," *Midwest Quarterly*, XI (Winter), 173–191.

A good detailed account of Hollywood's treatment of Sinclair.

1970 continued

SF72 Will and Ariel Durant. *Interpretations of Life*. New York: Simon and Schuster, pp. 43–48.

SF73 Jackson K. Putnam. *Old-Age Politics in California*. Stanford, Calif.: Stanford University Press, pp. 32–48.

1971

SF74 Charles L. P. Silet and Sharon Sperry Silet. "Charmian London to Upton Sinclair: Selected Letters," *Jack London Newsletter*, IV (January/April), 25–46.

Carefully edited letters with annotation and an introduction.

Appendix

A Chronological Listing of Upton Sinclair's Major Books

Springtime and Harvest (1901, reissued as *King Midas*, 1901)
The Journal of Arthur Stirling (1903)
Prince Hagen (1903; as play, 1910)
Manassas: A Novel of the War (1904; revised as *Theirs Be the Guilt*, 1959)
The Jungle (1906)
A Captain of Industry (1906)
The Industrial Republic (1907)
The Overman (1907)
The Metropolis (1908)
The Moneychangers (1908)
Good Health And How We Won It (1909; with Michael Williams)
Samuel the Seeker (1910)
The Fasting Cure (1911)
Love's Pilgrimage (1911)
Plays of Protest (1912)
Sylvia (1913)
Damaged Goods (1913)
Sylvia's Marriage (1914)
The Cry for Justice (1915)
King Coal (1917)
The Profits of Religion (1918)

Jimmie Higgins (1919)
The Brass Check (1920)
100%: The Story of a Patriot (1920)
The Book of Life, vol. I (1921)
The Book of Life, vol. II (1922)
They Call Me Carpenter (1922)
The Goose-Step (1923)
Hell: A Verse Drama and Photoplay (1923)
The Goslings (1924)
The Millennium (1924)
Singing Jailbirds (1924)
Mammonart (1925)
Bill Porter: A Drama of O. Henry in Prison (1925)
The Spokesman's Secretary (1926)
Letters to Judd (1926)
Oil! (1927)
Money Writes! (1927)
Boston (1928; abridged as *August 22nd*, 1965)
Mountain City (1930)
Mental Radio (1930)
Roman Holiday (1931)
The Wet Parade (1931)
American Outpost (1932)
Upton Sinclair Presents William Fox (1933)
The Way Out (1933)
I, Governor of California, and How I Ended Poverty (1933)
The EPIC Plan for California (1934)
Upton Sinclair Anthology (1934; rev. ed. 1947)
I, Candidate for Governor, and How I Got Licked (1935)
We, People of America: And How We Ended Poverty (1935)
Depression Island (1935)
What God Means to Me (1936)
Co-op (1936)

The Gnomobile (1936)
The Flivver King (1937)
No Parasan! (1937)
Little Steel (1938)
Our Lady (1938)
Terror in Russia (1938; with Eugene Lyons)
Expect No Peace (1939)
Marie Antoinette (1939)
Telling the World (1939; England only)
World's End (1940)
Between Two Worlds (1941)
Dragon's Teeth (1942)
Wide Is the Gate (1943)
Presidential Agent (1944)
Dragon Harvest (1945)
A World to Win (1946)
Presidential Mission (1947)
A Giant's Strength (1948)
One Clear Call (1948)
O Shepherd, Speak! (1949)
Another Pamela (1950)
The Enemy Had It Too (1950)
A Personal Jesus (1952; as *The Secret Life of Jesus*, 1962)
The Return of Lanny Budd (1953)
What Didymus Did (1954, England; as *It Happened to Didymus*, 1958, U.S.A.)
The Cup of Fury (1956)
Theirs Be the Guilt (1959; revision of *Manassas*, 1904)
My Lifetime in Letters (1960)
Affectionately, Eve (1961)
The Autobiography of Upton Sinclair (1962)
The Secret Life of Jesus (1962; reissue of *A Personal Jesus*, 1952)
August 22nd (1965; see *Boston*, 1928)

An Alphabetical Listing of Upton Sinclair's Major Books

Affectionately, Eve (1961)
American Outpost (1932)
Another Pamela (1950)
August 22nd (1965; abridgement of *Boston*, 1928)
The Autobiography of Upton Sinclair (1962)
Between Two Worlds (1941)
Bill Porter: A Drama of O. Henry in Prison (1925)
The Book of Life, vol. I (1921)
The Book of Life, vol. II (1922)
Boston (1928; see *August 22nd*)
The Brass Check (1920)
A Captain of Industry (1906)
Co-op (1936)
The Cry for Justice (1915)
The Cup of Fury (1956)
Damaged Goods (1913)
Depression Island (1935)
Dragon Harvest (1945)
Dragon's Teeth (1942)
The Enemy Had It Too (1950)
The EPIC Plan for California (1934)
Expect No Peace (1939)
The Fasting Cure (1911)
The Flivver King (1937)
A Giant's Strength (1948)

The Gnomobile (1936)
Good Health And How We Won It (1909; with Michael Williams)
The Goose-Step (1923)
The Goslings (1924)
Hell: A Verse Drama and Photoplay (1923)
I, Candidate for Governor, and How I Got Licked (1935)
I, Governor of California, and How I Ended Poverty (1933)
The Industrial Republic (1907)
It Happened to Didymus (1958; *What Didymus Did*, 1954, *England*)
Jimmie Higgins (1919)
The Journal of Arthur Stirling (1903)
The Jungle (1906)
King Coal (1917)
King Midas (1901; reissue of *Springtime and Harvest*, 1901)
Letters to Judd (1926)
Little Steel (1938)
Love's Pilgrimage (1911)
Mammonart (1925)
Manassas: A Novel of the War (1904; revised as *Theirs Be The Guilt*, 1959)
Marie Antoinette (1939)
Mental Radio (1930)
The Metropolis (1908)
The Millennium (1924)
The Moneychangers (1908)
Money Writes! (1927)
Mountain City (1930)
My Lifetime in Letters (1960)
No Pasaran! (1937)
Oil! (1927)
One Clear Call (1948)

100%: The Story of a Patriot (1920)
O Shepherd, Speak! (1949)
Our Lady (1938)
The Overman (1907)
A Personal Jesus (1952; reissued as *The Secret Life of Jesus*, 1962)
Plays of Protest (1912)
Presidential Agent (1944)
Presidential Mission (1947)
Prince Hagen (1903, novel; 1910, play)
The Profits of Religion (1918)
The Return of Lanny Budd (1953)
Roman Holiday (1931)
Samuel the Seeker (1910)
The Secret Life of Jesus (1962; reissue of *A Personal Jesus*, 1952)
Singing Jailbirds (1924)
The Spokesman's Secretary (1926)
Springtime and Harvest (1901; reissued as *King Midas*, 1901)
Sylvia (1913)
Sylvia's Marriage (1914)
Telling the World (1939; England only)
Terror in Russia (1938; with Eugene Lyons)
Theirs Be the Guilt (1959; revision of *Manassas*, 1904)
They Call Me Carpenter (1922)
Upton Sinclair Anthology (1934; rev. ed. 1947)
Upton Sinclair Presents William Fox (1933)
The Way Out (1933)
We, People of America: And How We Ended Poverty (1935)
The Wet Parade (1931)
What God Means to Me (1936)
Wide Is the Gate (1943)
A World to Win (1946)
World's End (1940)

Index to Proper Names